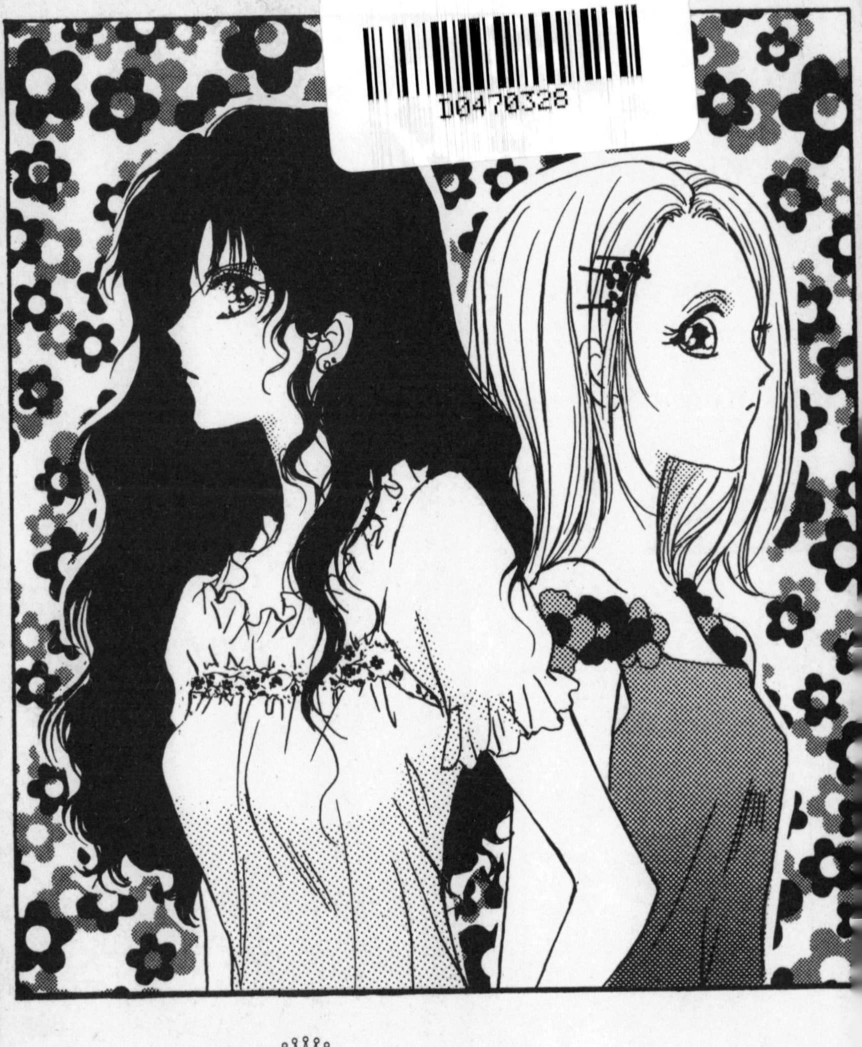

KING OF CARDS

Volume 6

By Makoto Tateno

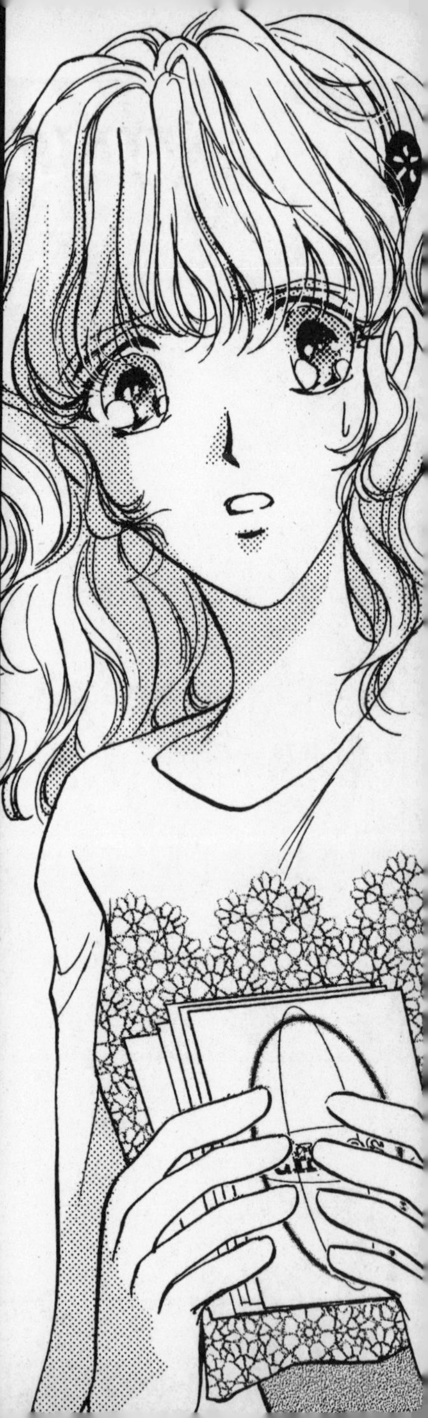

CONTENTS

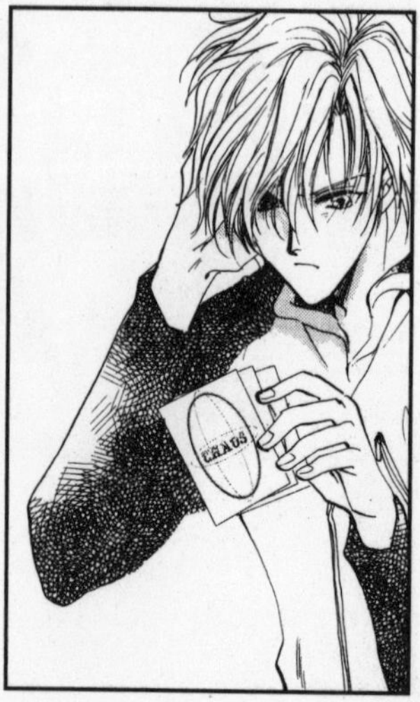

KING OF CARDS 19

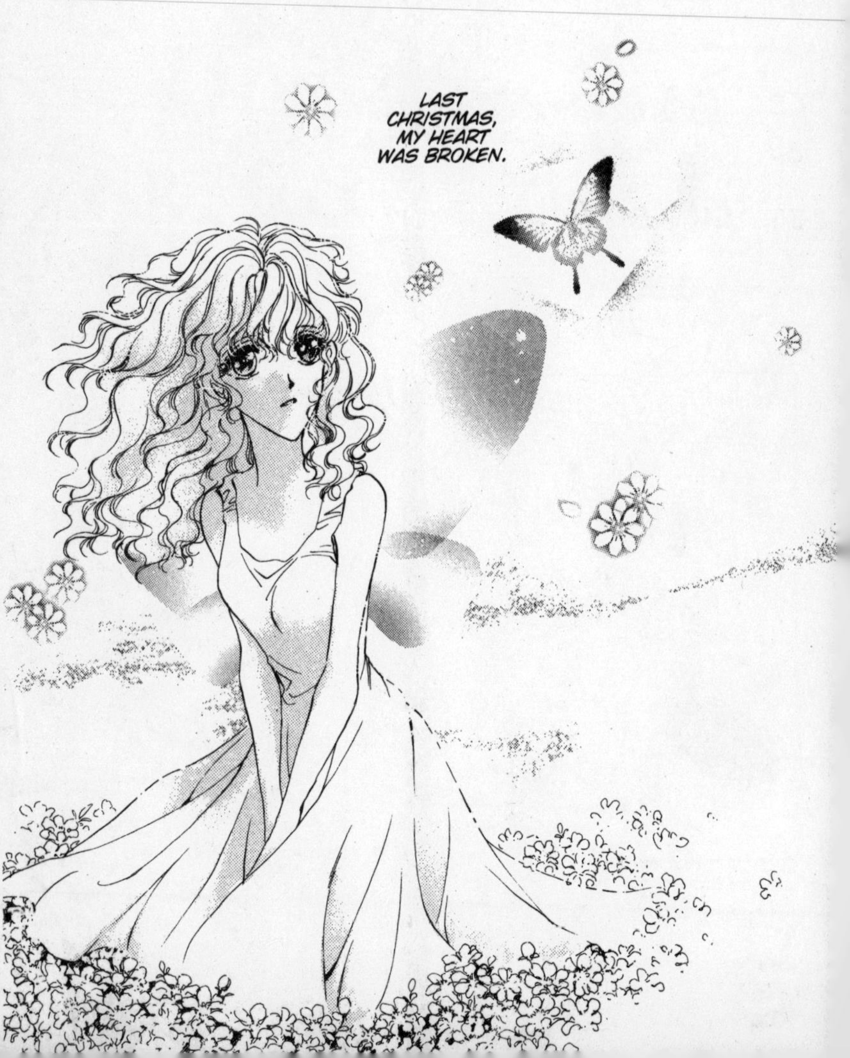
LAST CHRISTMAS, MY HEART WAS BROKEN.

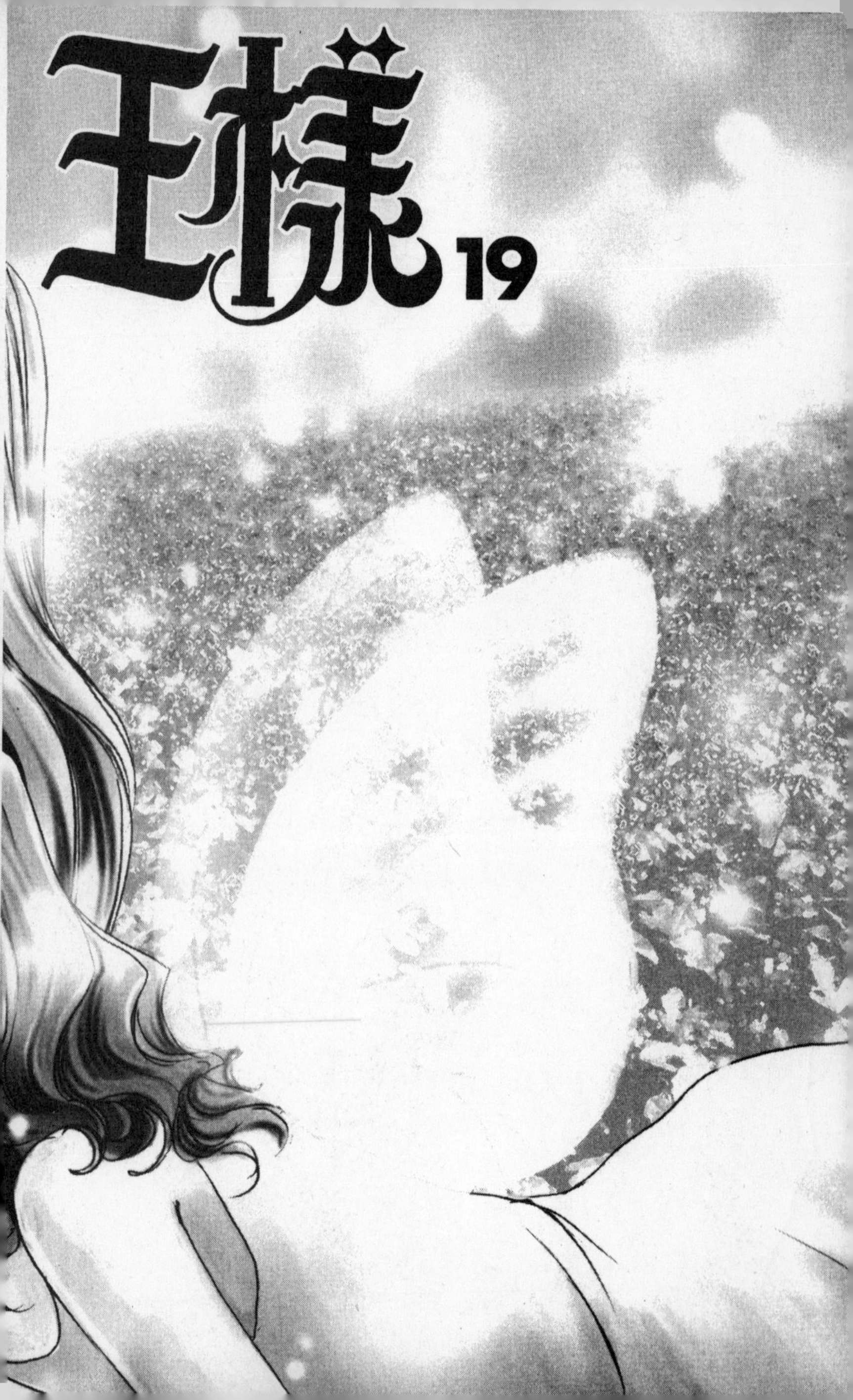
王様
19

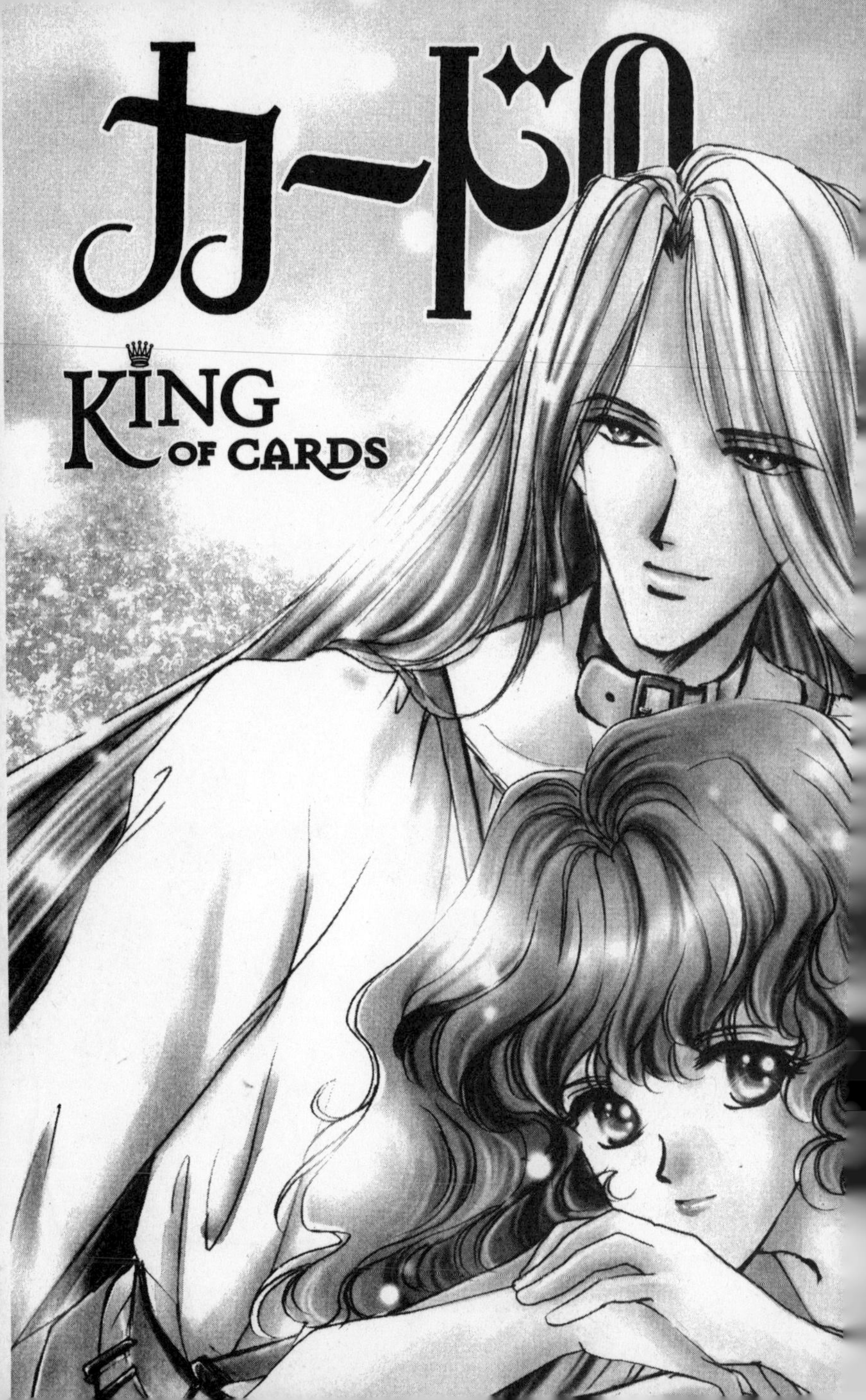
カード
KING
OF CARDS

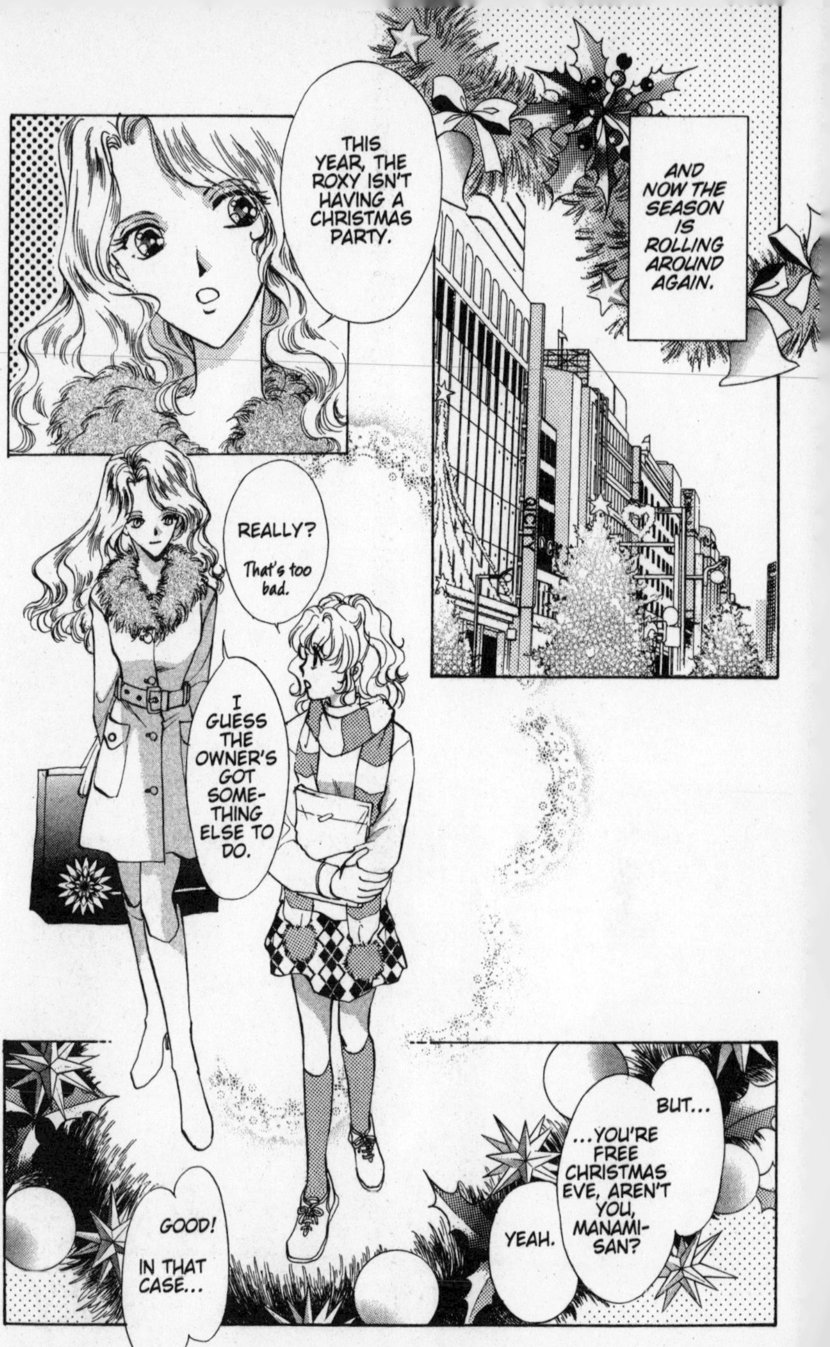
AND NOW THE SEASON IS ROLLING AROUND AGAIN.
THIS YEAR, THE ROXY ISN'T HAVING A CHRISTMAS PARTY.
REALLY?
That's too bad.
I GUESS THE OWNER'S GOT SOME-THING ELSE TO DO.
BUT...
...YOU'RE FREE CHRISTMAS EVE, AREN'T YOU, MANAMI-SAN?
YEAH.
GOOD!
IN THAT CASE...

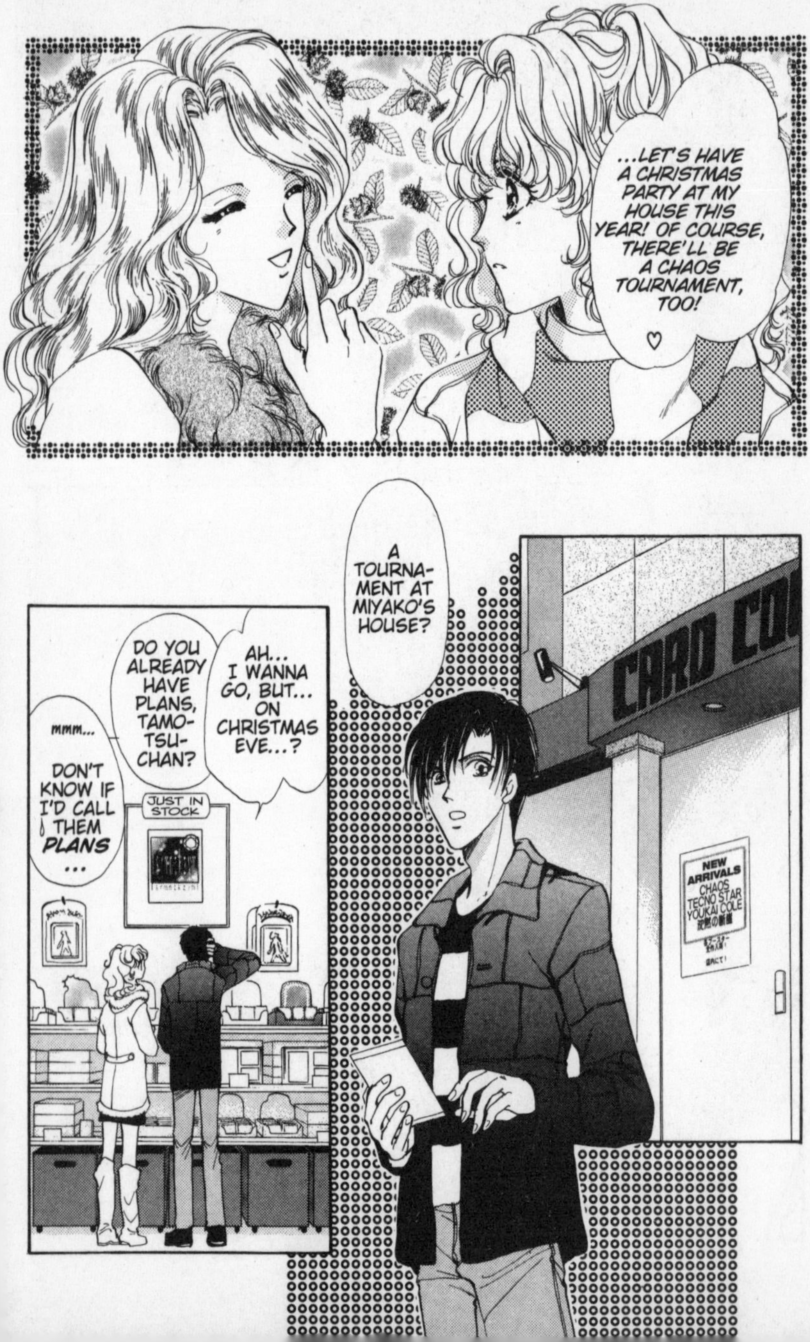
...LET'S HAVE A CHRISTMAS PARTY AT MY HOUSE THIS YEAR! OF COURSE, THERE'LL BE A CHAOS TOURNAMENT, TOO! ♡
A TOURNAMENT AT MIYAKO'S HOUSE?
NEW ARRIVALS CHAOS TECNO STAR YOUKAI COLE
AH... I WANNA GO, BUT... ON CHRISTMAS EVE...?
DO YOU ALREADY HAVE PLANS, TAMOTSU-CHAN?
mmm...
DON'T KNOW IF I'D CALL THEM *PLANS*...
JUST IN STOCK

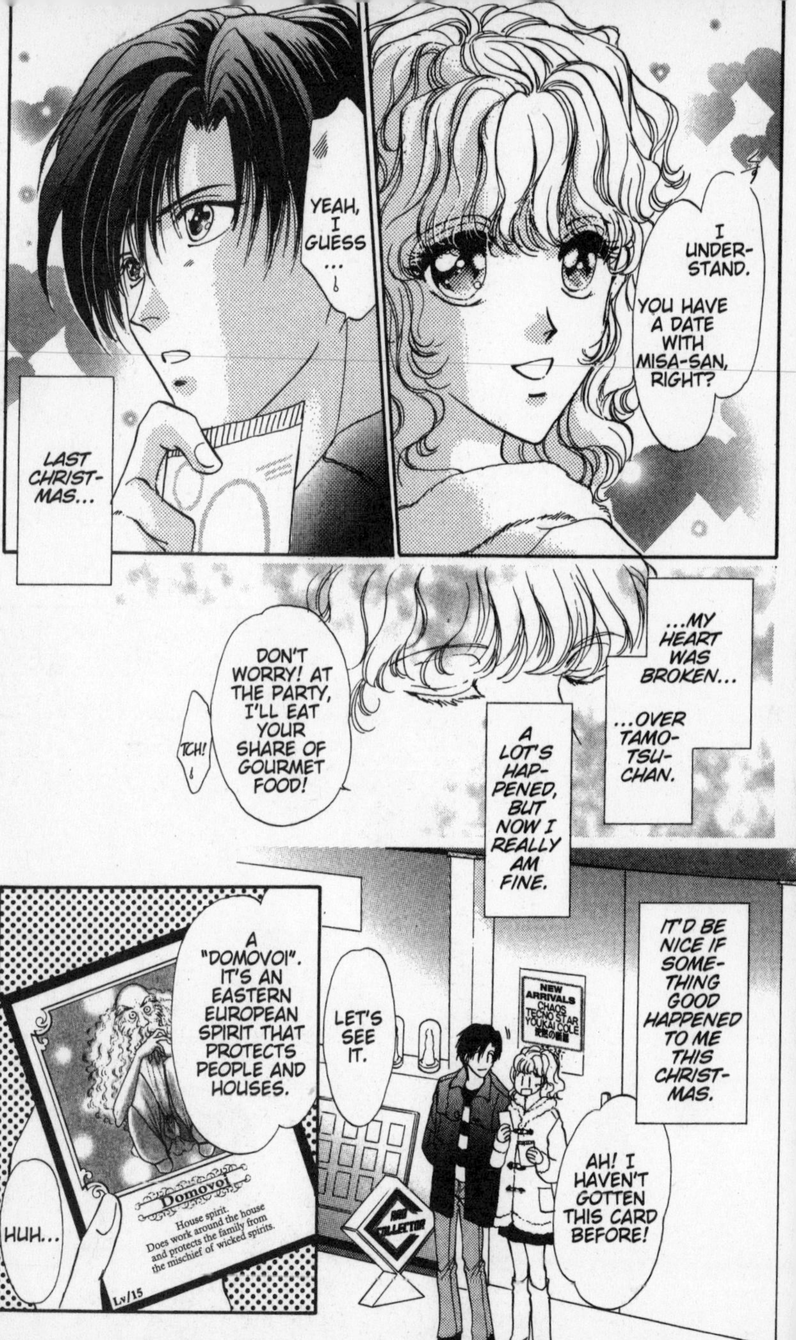
I UNDERSTAND.
YOU HAVE A DATE WITH MISA-SAN, RIGHT?
YEAH, I GUESS ...
LAST CHRISTMAS...
...MY HEART WAS BROKEN...
...OVER TAMOTSU-CHAN.
A LOT'S HAPPENED, BUT NOW I REALLY AM FINE.
DON'T WORRY! AT THE PARTY, I'LL EAT YOUR SHARE OF GOURMET FOOD!
TCH!
IT'D BE NICE IF SOMETHING GOOD HAPPENED TO ME THIS CHRISTMAS.
NEW ARRIVALS
CHAOS
TECNO STAR
YOUKAI COLE
AH! I HAVEN'T GOTTEN THIS CARD BEFORE!
LET'S SEE IT.
A "DOMOVOI". IT'S AN EASTERN EUROPEAN SPIRIT THAT PROTECTS PEOPLE AND HOUSES.
HUH...
Domovoi
House spirit.
Does work around the house and protects the family from the mischief of wicked spirits.
Lv/15

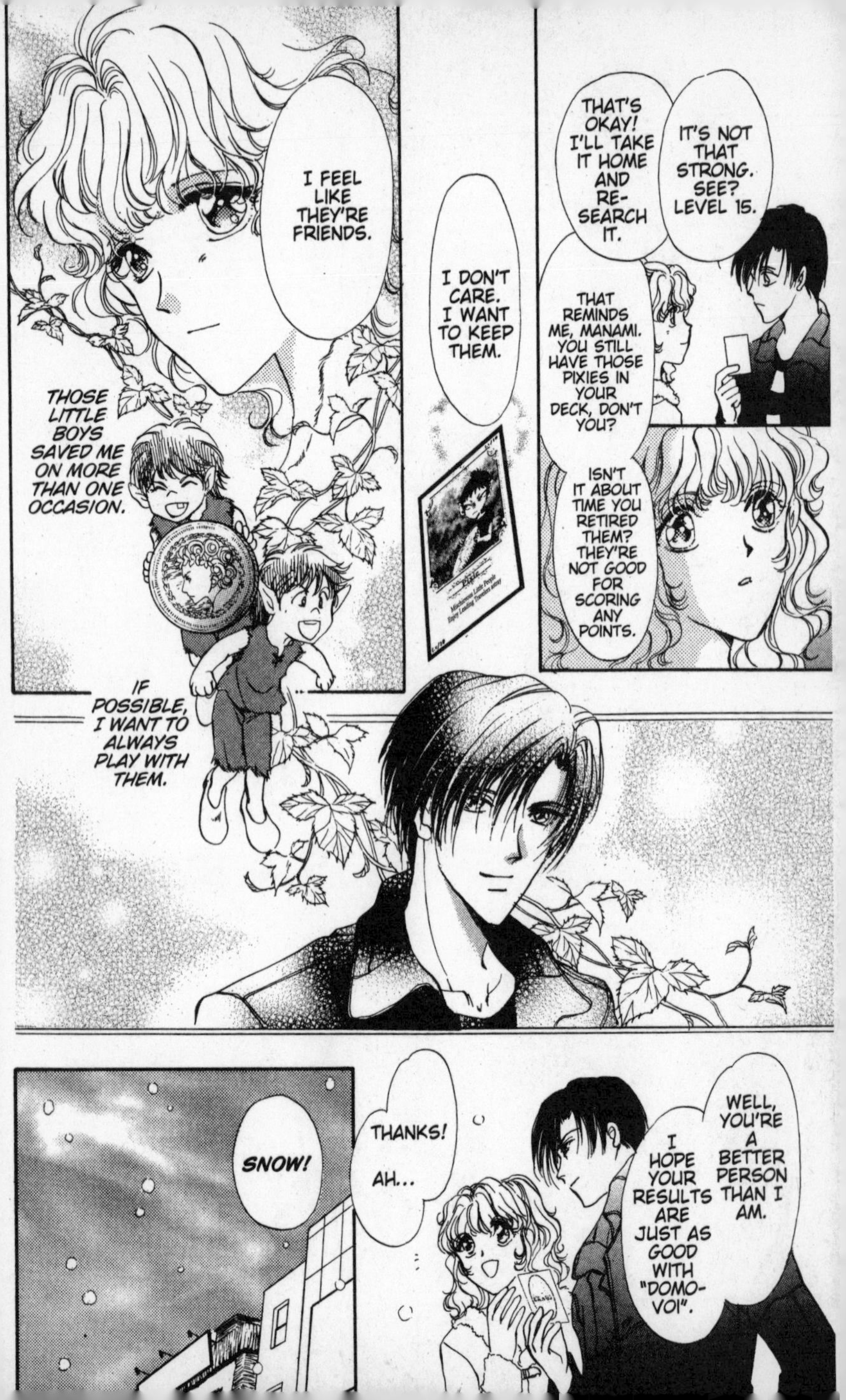
IT'S NOT THAT STRONG. SEE? LEVEL 15.
THAT'S OKAY! I'LL TAKE IT HOME AND RE-SEARCH IT.
THAT REMINDS ME, MANAMI. YOU STILL HAVE THOSE PIXIES IN YOUR DECK, DON'T YOU?
ISN'T IT ABOUT TIME YOU RETIRED THEM? THEY'RE NOT GOOD FOR SCORING ANY POINTS.
I DON'T CARE. I WANT TO KEEP THEM.
I FEEL LIKE THEY'RE FRIENDS.
THOSE LITTLE BOYS SAVED ME ON MORE THAN ONE OCCASION.
IF POSSIBLE, I WANT TO ALWAYS PLAY WITH THEM.
WELL, YOU'RE A BETTER PERSON THAN I AM.
I HOPE YOUR RESULTS ARE JUST AS GOOD WITH "DOMO-VOI".
THANKS!
AH...
SNOW!

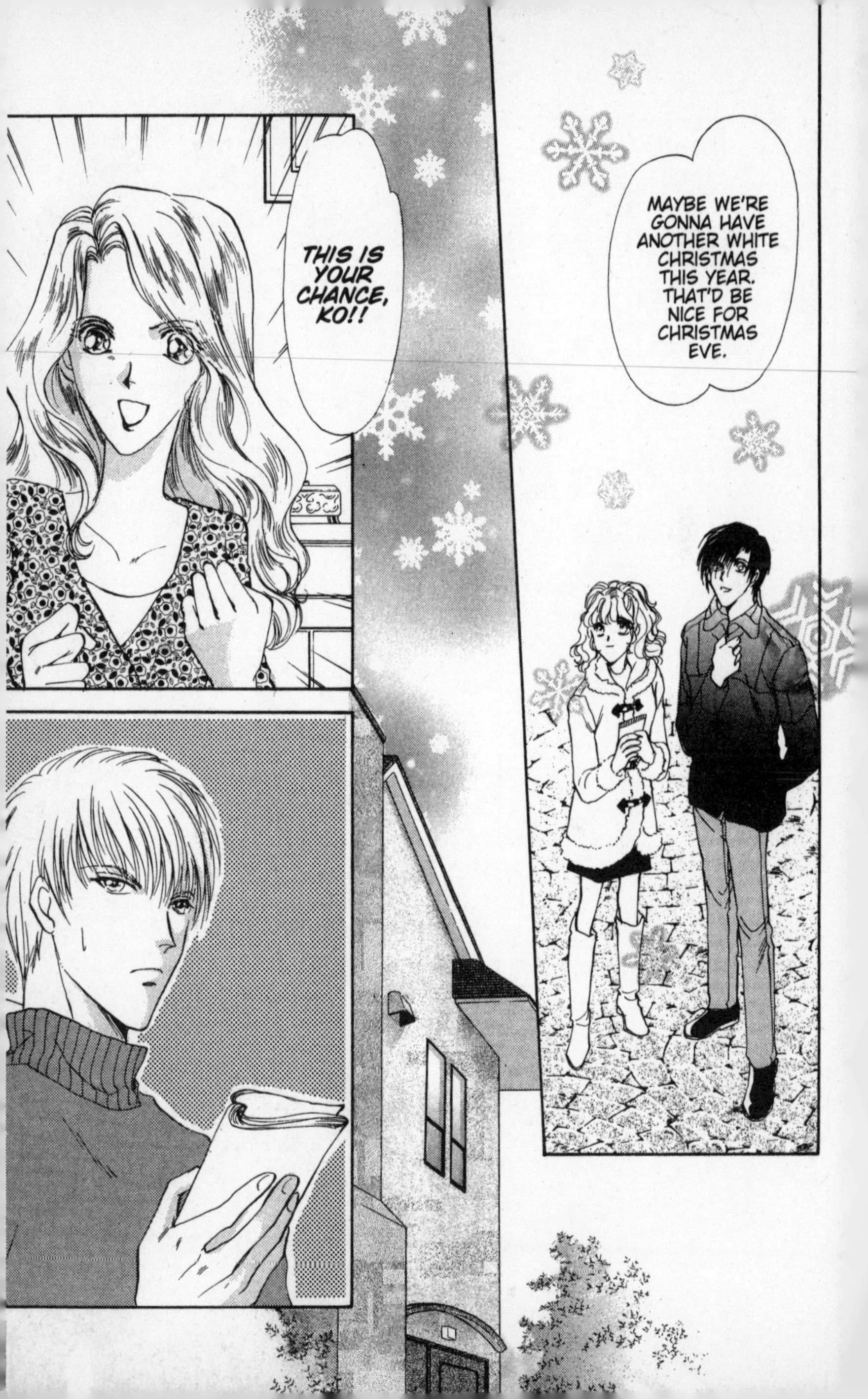
MAYBE WE'RE GONNA HAVE ANOTHER WHITE CHRISTMAS THIS YEAR. THAT'D BE NICE FOR CHRISTMAS EVE.
THIS IS YOUR CHANCE, KO!!

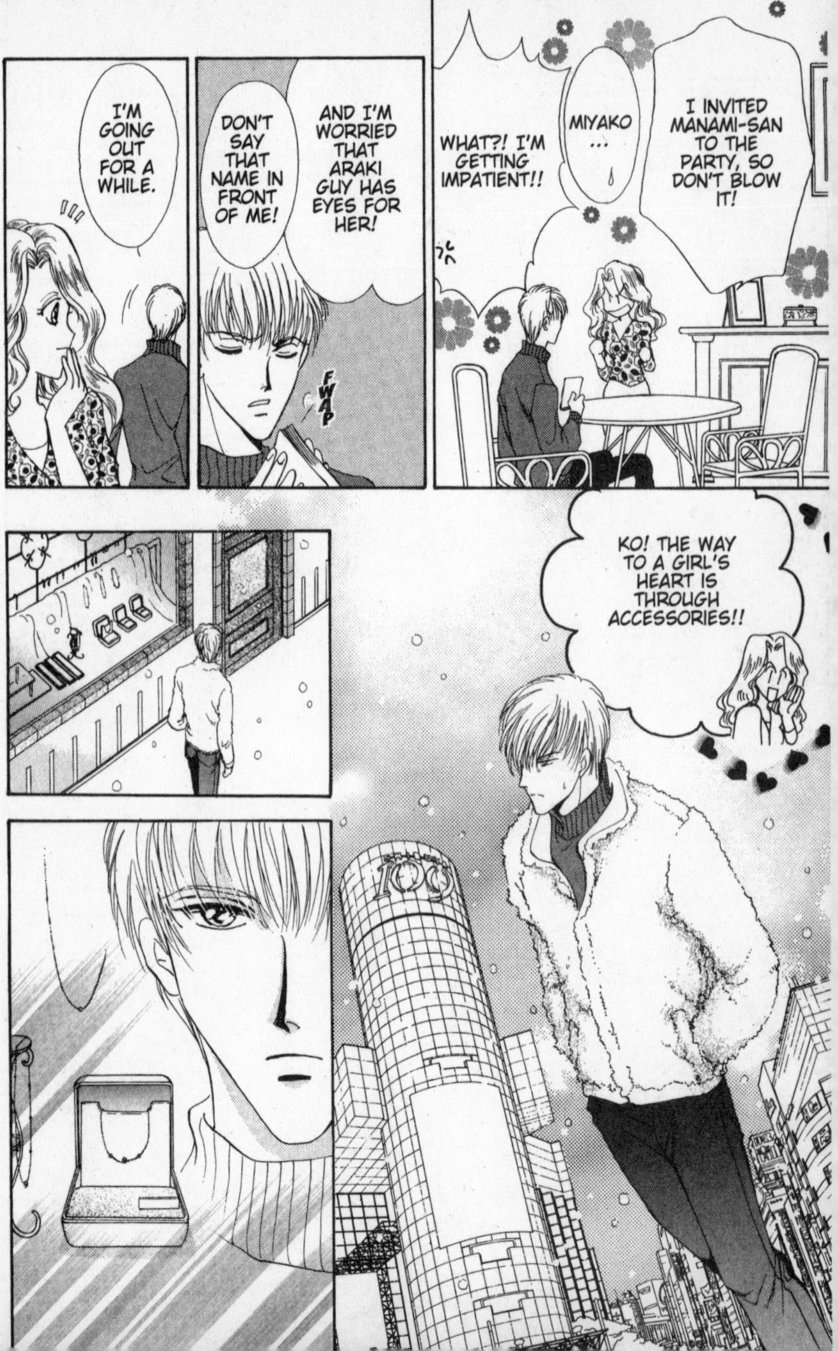
I INVITED MANAMI-SAN TO THE PARTY, SO DON'T BLOW IT!
MIYAKO ...
WHAT?! I'M GETTING IMPATIENT!!
AND I'M WORRIED THAT ARAKI GUY HAS EYES FOR HER!
DON'T SAY THAT NAME IN FRONT OF ME!
FWAP
I'M GOING OUT FOR A WHILE.
KO! THE WAY TO A GIRL'S HEART IS THROUGH ACCESSORIES!!

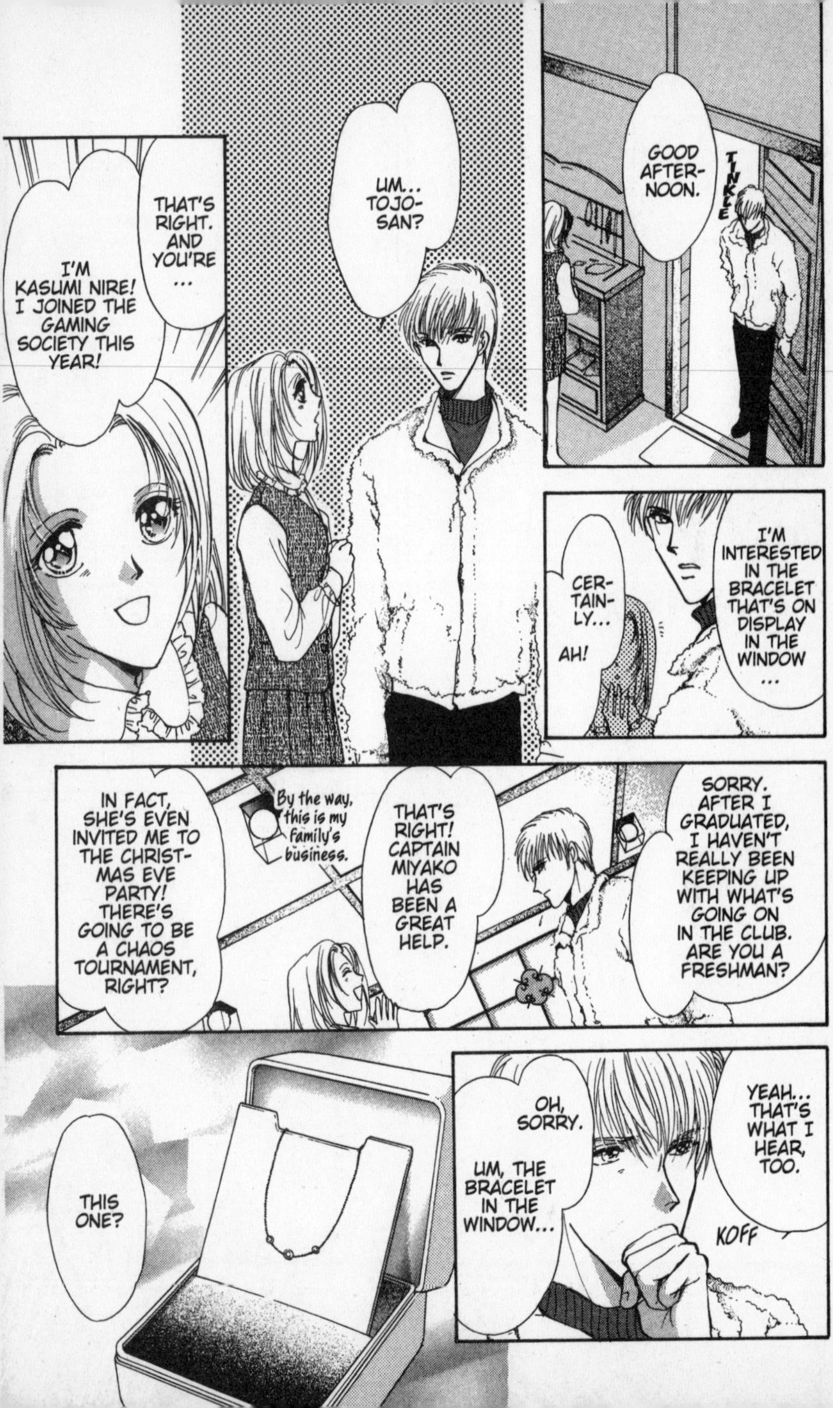
GOOD AFTER-NOON.
TINKLE
I'M INTERESTED IN THE BRACELET THAT'S ON DISPLAY IN THE WINDOW...
CER-TAIN-LY...
AH!
UM... TOJO-SAN?
THAT'S RIGHT. AND YOU'RE...
I'M KASUMI NIRE! I JOINED THE GAMING SOCIETY THIS YEAR!
SORRY. AFTER I GRADUATED, I HAVEN'T REALLY BEEN KEEPING UP WITH WHAT'S GOING ON IN THE CLUB. ARE YOU A FRESHMAN?
THAT'S RIGHT! CAPTAIN MIYAKO HAS BEEN A GREAT HELP.
By the way, this is my family's business.
IN FACT, SHE'S EVEN INVITED ME TO THE CHRISTMAS EVE PARTY! THERE'S GOING TO BE A CHAOS TOURNAMENT, RIGHT?
YEAH... THAT'S WHAT I HEAR, TOO.
KOFF
OH, SORRY.
UM, THE BRACELET IN THE WINDOW...
THIS ONE?

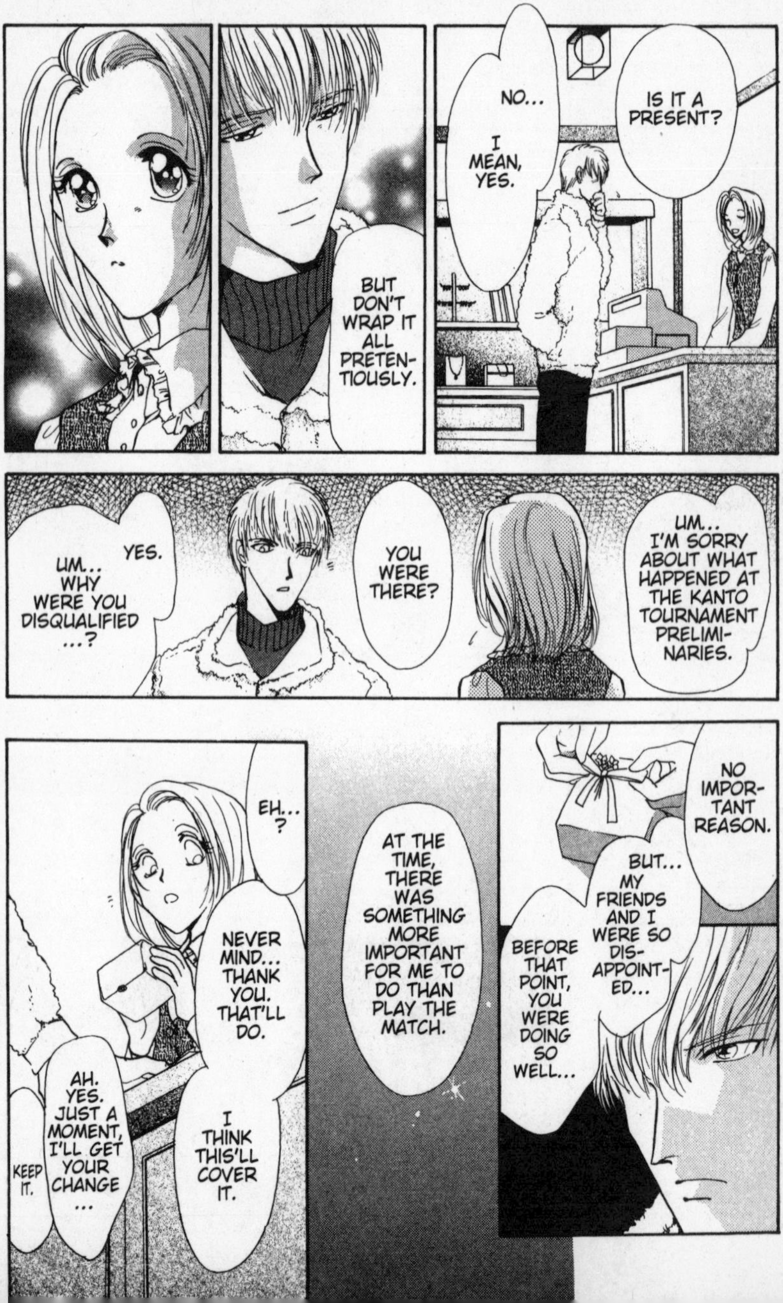
IS IT A PRESENT?
NO...
I MEAN, YES.
BUT DON'T WRAP IT ALL PRETEN-TIOUSLY.
UM... I'M SORRY ABOUT WHAT HAPPENED AT THE KANTO TOURNAMENT PRELIMI-NARIES.
YOU WERE THERE?
YES.
UM... WHY WERE YOU DISQUALIFIED...?
NO IMPOR-TANT REASON.
BUT... MY FRIENDS AND I WERE SO DIS-APPOINT-ED...
BEFORE THAT POINT, YOU WERE DOING SO WELL...
AT THE TIME, THERE WAS SOMETHING MORE IMPORTANT FOR ME TO DO THAN PLAY THE MATCH.
EH...?
NEVER MIND... THANK YOU. THAT'LL DO.
I THINK THIS'LL COVER IT.
AH. YES. JUST A MOMENT, I'LL GET YOUR CHANGE...
KEEP IT.

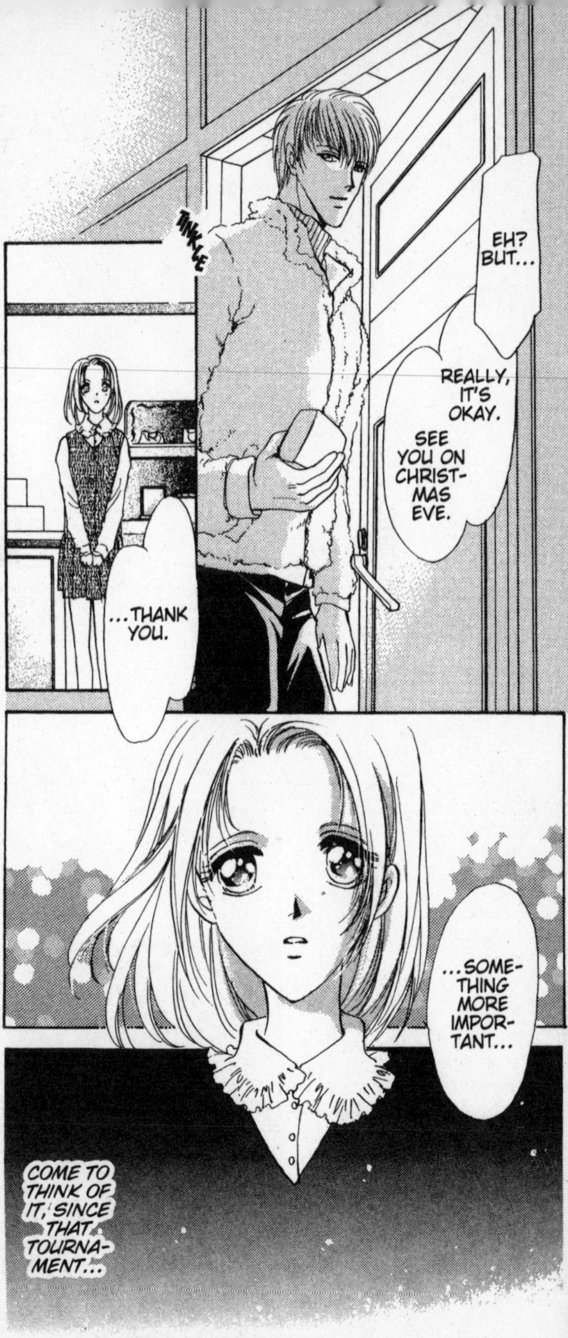
EH? BUT...
TINKLE
REALLY, IT'S OKAY.
SEE YOU ON CHRIST-MAS EVE.
...THANK YOU.
...SOME-THING MORE IMPOR-TANT...
COME TO THINK OF IT, SINCE THAT TOURNA-MENT...

HELLO. TATENO HERE, WITH "KING OF CARDS" VOLUME 6!!

BOY, IT'S COME AROUND FAST... THANKS TO ALL OF YOU!! WHILE I WAS FIRST WORKING ON THE STORIES IN THIS VOLUME, "HANA TO YUME"* WENT FROM A MONTHLY MAGAZINE TO A BIMONTHLY PUBLICATION AND AS A RESULT, IT'S NOW TWICE AS THICK!! IT CAN STAND UP ON A TABLE!!

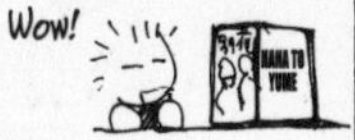
Wow!
HANA TO YUME

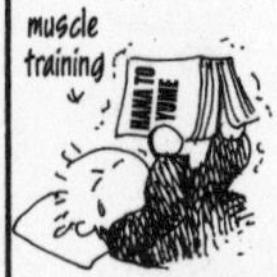
muscle training
HANA TO YUME

I PLAN TO KEEP GOING WITH "KING OF CARDS" IN THE PAGES OF "HANA TO YUME", THE MAGAZINE THAT STRENGTHENS YOUR ARM MUSCLES IF YOU READ IT IN BED! AND ALONG WITH THE NEW FORMAT IN THE MAGAZINE, IT FEELS LIKE WE'VE ENTERED A NEW CHAPTER IN THE STORY. WE'VE GOT NEW FEMALE CHARACTERS AND I'VE GOT A LOT OF IDEAS, BUT FOR NOW, I'LL JUST BE HAPPY IF YOU ENJOY THIS VOLUME! ♥

SO GO AHEAD!!

*HANA TO YUME IS A JAPANESE PUBLICATION WHERE KING OF CARDS WAS ORIGINALLY SERIALIZED.

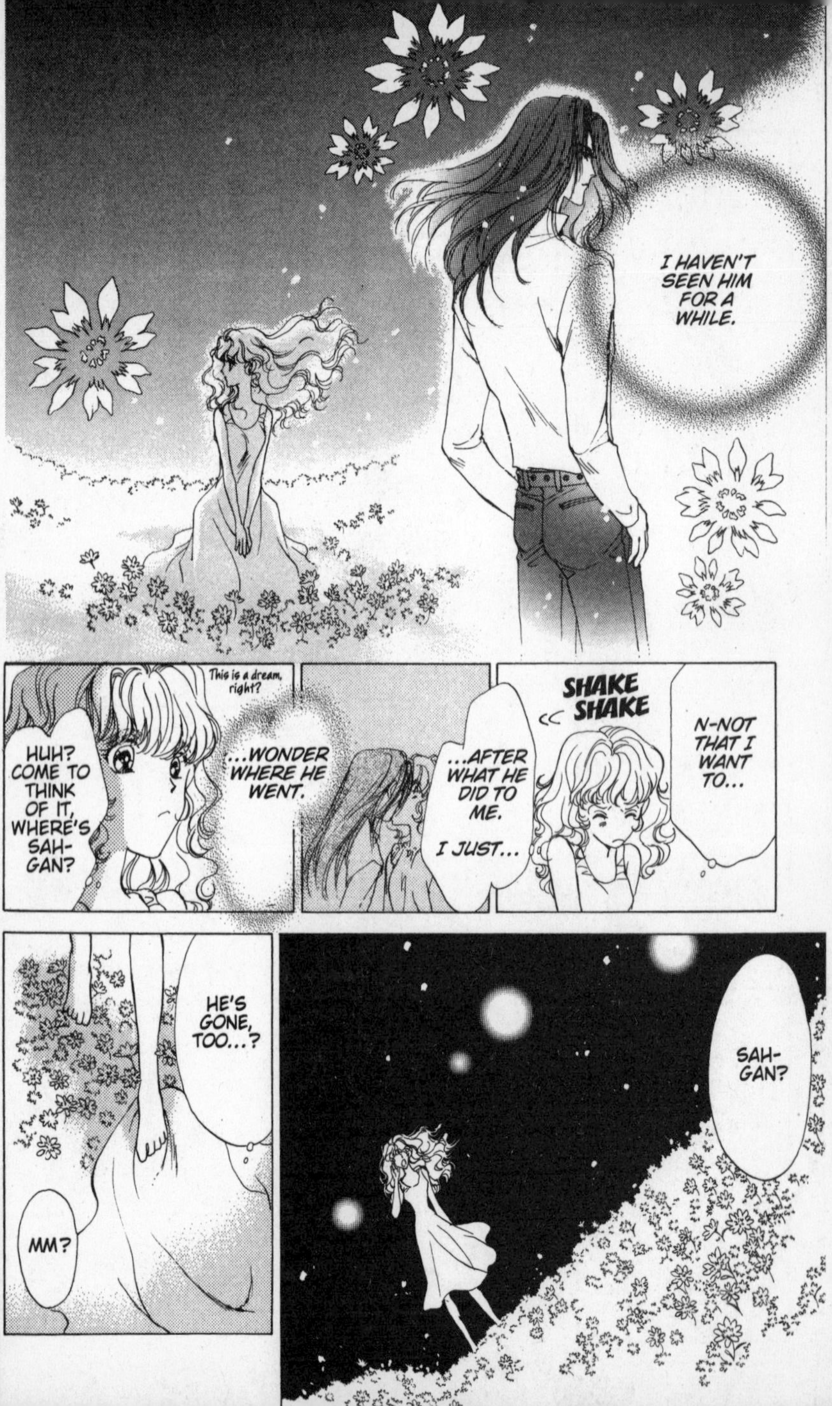
I HAVEN'T SEEN HIM FOR A WHILE.
N-NOT THAT I WANT TO...
SHAKE SHAKE
...AFTER WHAT HE DID TO ME.
I JUST...
This is a dream, right?
...WONDER WHERE HE WENT.
HUH? COME TO THINK OF IT, WHERE'S SAH-GAN?
SAH-GAN?
HE'S GONE, TOO...?
MM?

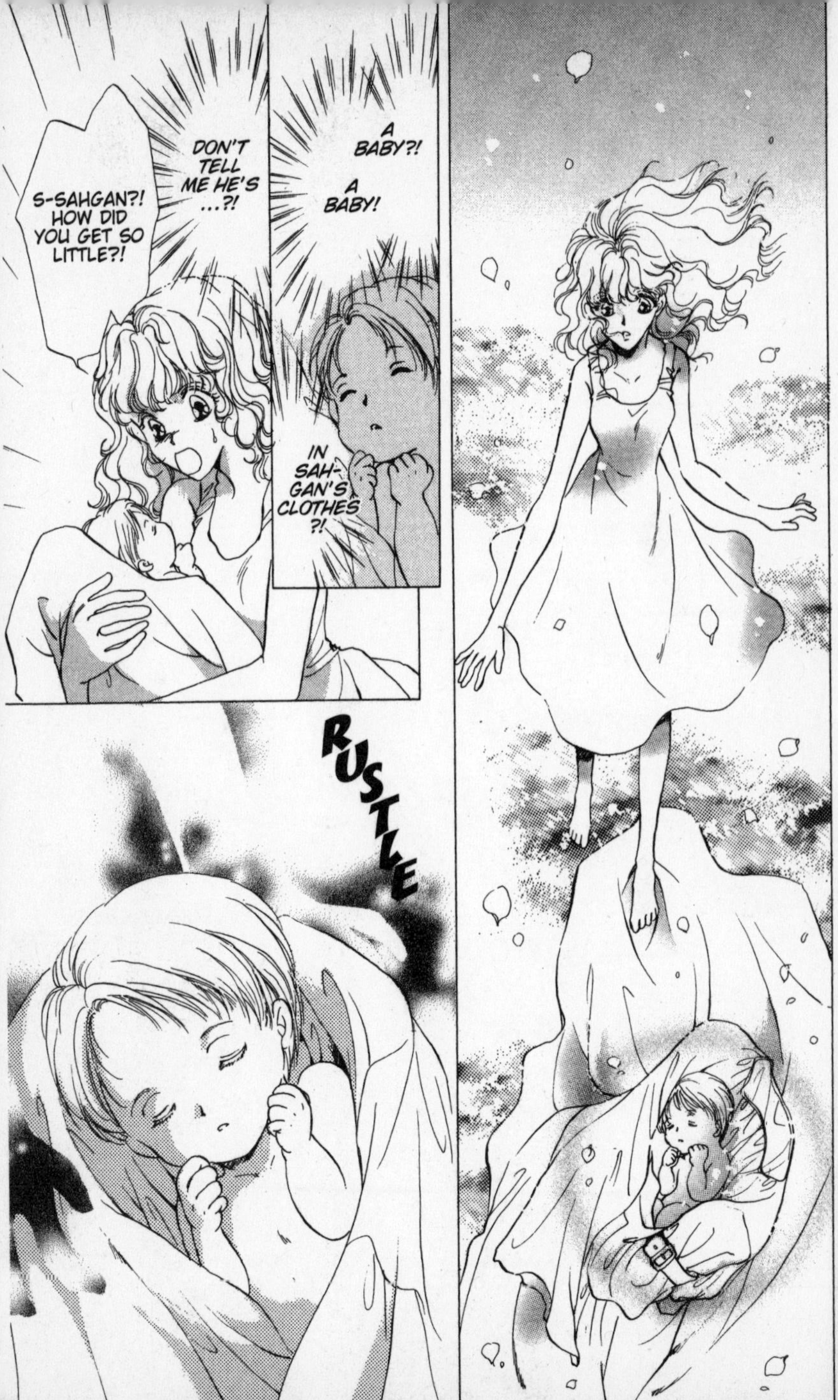
A BABY?!
A BABY!
IN SAH-GAN'S CLOTHES ?!
DON'T TELL ME HE'S ...?!
S-SAHGAN?! HOW DID YOU GET SO LITTLE?!
RUSTLE

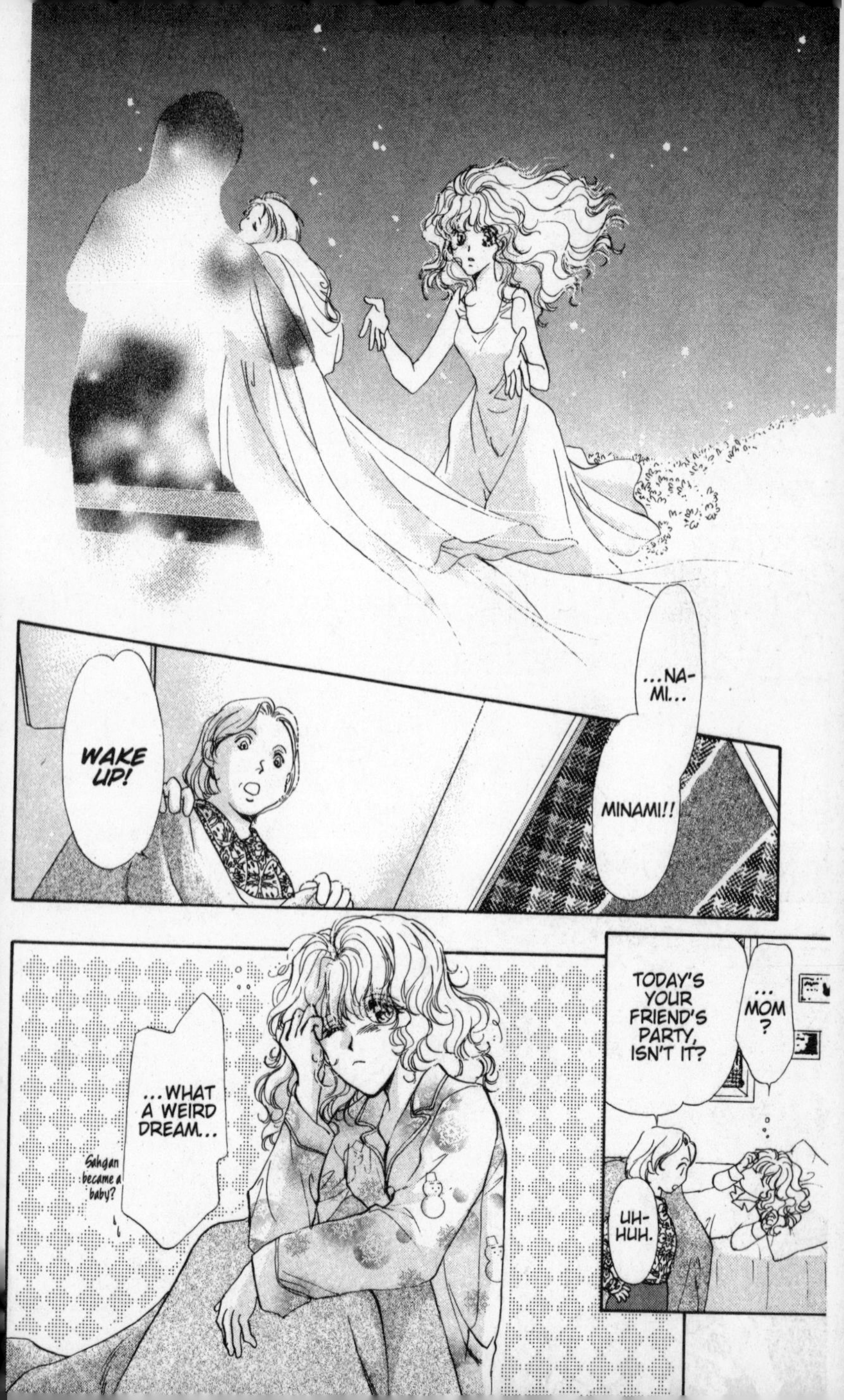
...NA-MI...
MINAMI!!
WAKE UP!
...MOM?
TODAY'S YOUR FRIEND'S PARTY, ISN'T IT?
UH-HUH.
...WHAT A WEIRD DREAM...
Sahgan became a baby?

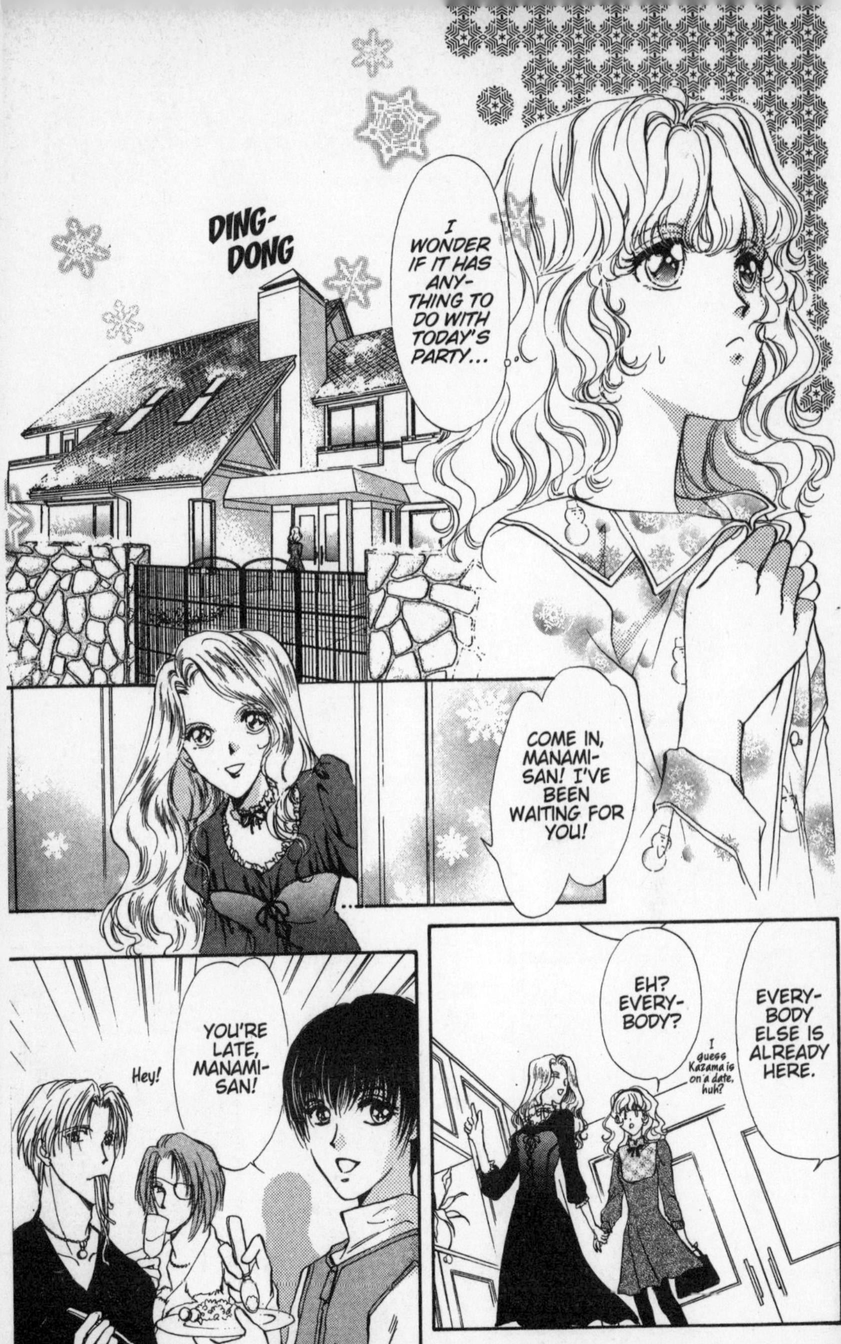
I WONDER IF IT HAS ANY-THING TO DO WITH TODAY'S PARTY...
DING-DONG
COME IN, MANAMI-SAN! I'VE BEEN WAITING FOR YOU!
EVERY-BODY ELSE IS ALREADY HERE.
EH? EVERY-BODY?
I guess Kazama is on a date, huh?
YOU'RE LATE, MANAMI-SAN!
Hey!

UWAAA! SO MANY PEOPLE!

THERE ARE QUITE A FEW MEMBERS IN MY SCHOOL'S GAMING SOCIETY. BUT YOU KNOW SOME OF THESE FACES, RIGHT?

Ah! Minami-san!

I THOUGHT AS LONG AS WE'RE HAVING A CHAOS TOURNAMENT, THE MORE THE MERRIER.

WAIT RIGHT HERE. I'LL GET YOU SOMETHING TO DRINK.

FOO

IS CHAMPAGNE ALL RIGHT?

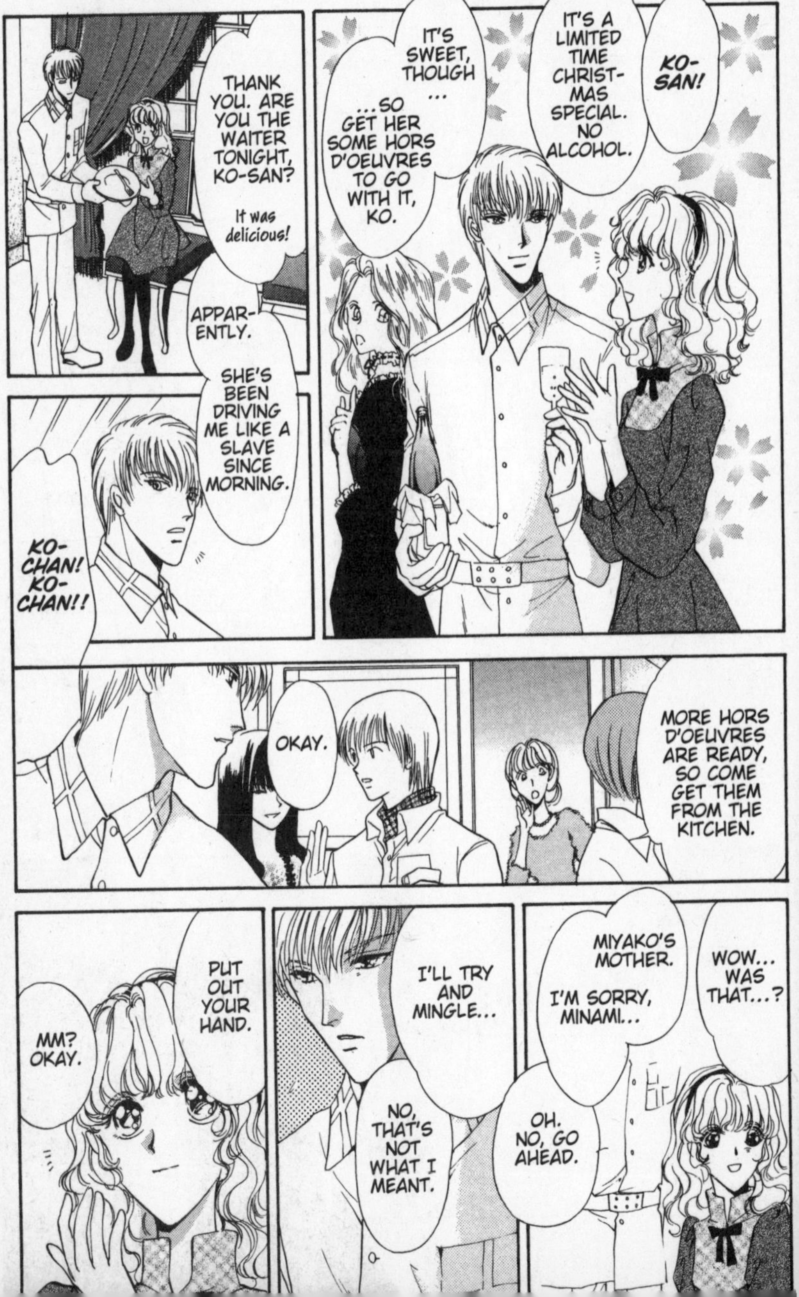
KO-SAN!
IT'S A LIMITED TIME CHRIST-MAS SPECIAL. NO ALCOHOL.
IT'S SWEET, THOUGH ...
...SO GET HER SOME HORS D'OEUVRES TO GO WITH IT, KO.
THANK YOU. ARE YOU THE WAITER TONIGHT, KO-SAN?
It was delicious!
APPAR-ENTLY.
SHE'S BEEN DRIVING ME LIKE A SLAVE SINCE MORNING.
KO-CHAN! KO-CHAN!!
MORE HORS D'OEUVRES ARE READY, SO COME GET THEM FROM THE KITCHEN.
OKAY.
WOW... WAS THAT...?
MIYAKO'S MOTHER.
I'M SORRY, MINAMI...
OH. NO, GO AHEAD.
I'LL TRY AND MINGLE...
NO, THAT'S NOT WHAT I MEANT.
PUT OUT YOUR HAND.
MM? OKAY.

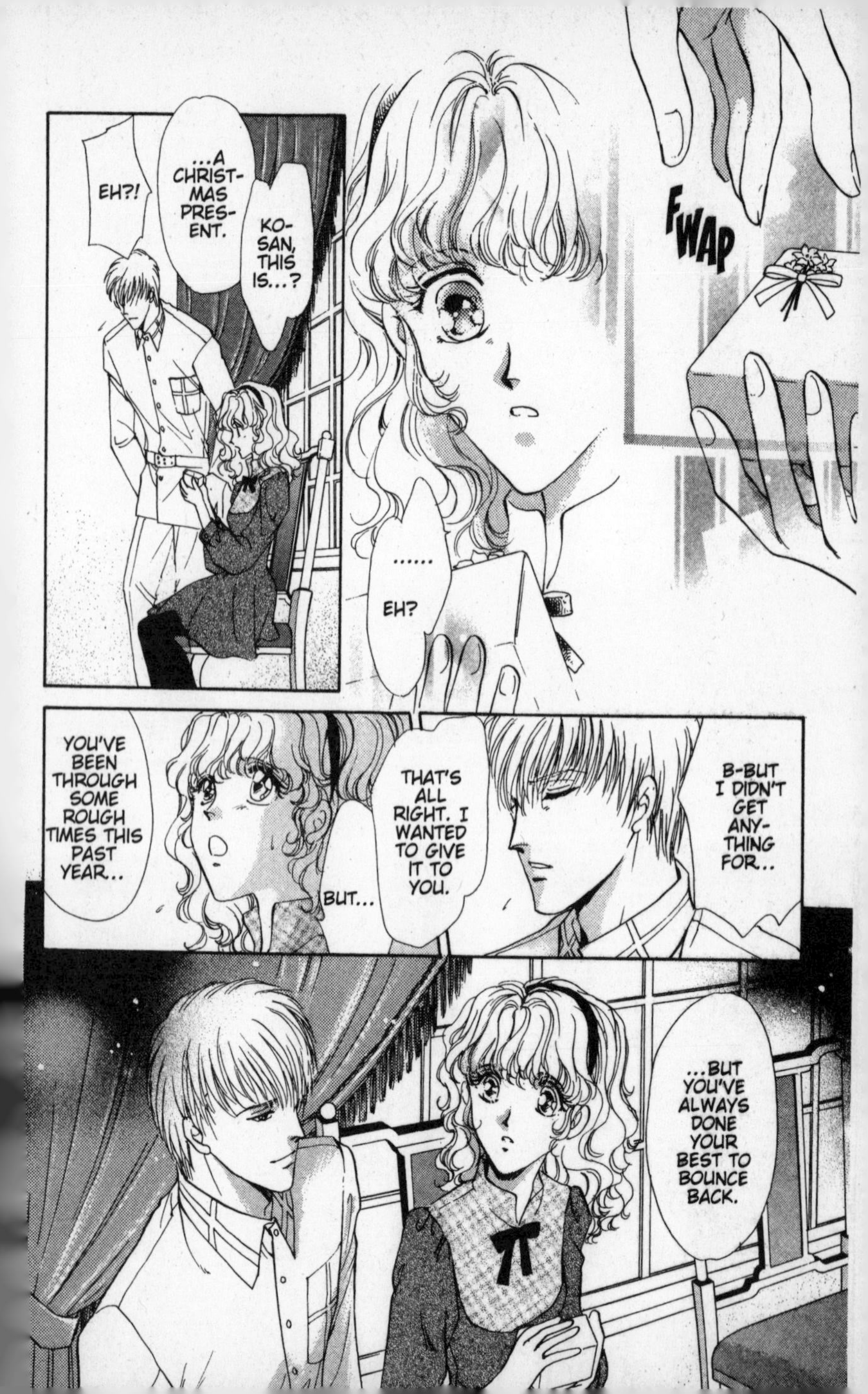
FWAP
...... EH?
KO-SAN, THIS IS...?
...A CHRISTMAS PRESENT.
EH?!
B-BUT I DIDN'T GET ANYTHING FOR...
THAT'S ALL RIGHT. I WANTED TO GIVE IT TO YOU.
BUT...
YOU'VE BEEN THROUGH SOME ROUGH TIMES THIS PAST YEAR...
...BUT YOU'VE ALWAYS DONE YOUR BEST TO BOUNCE BACK.

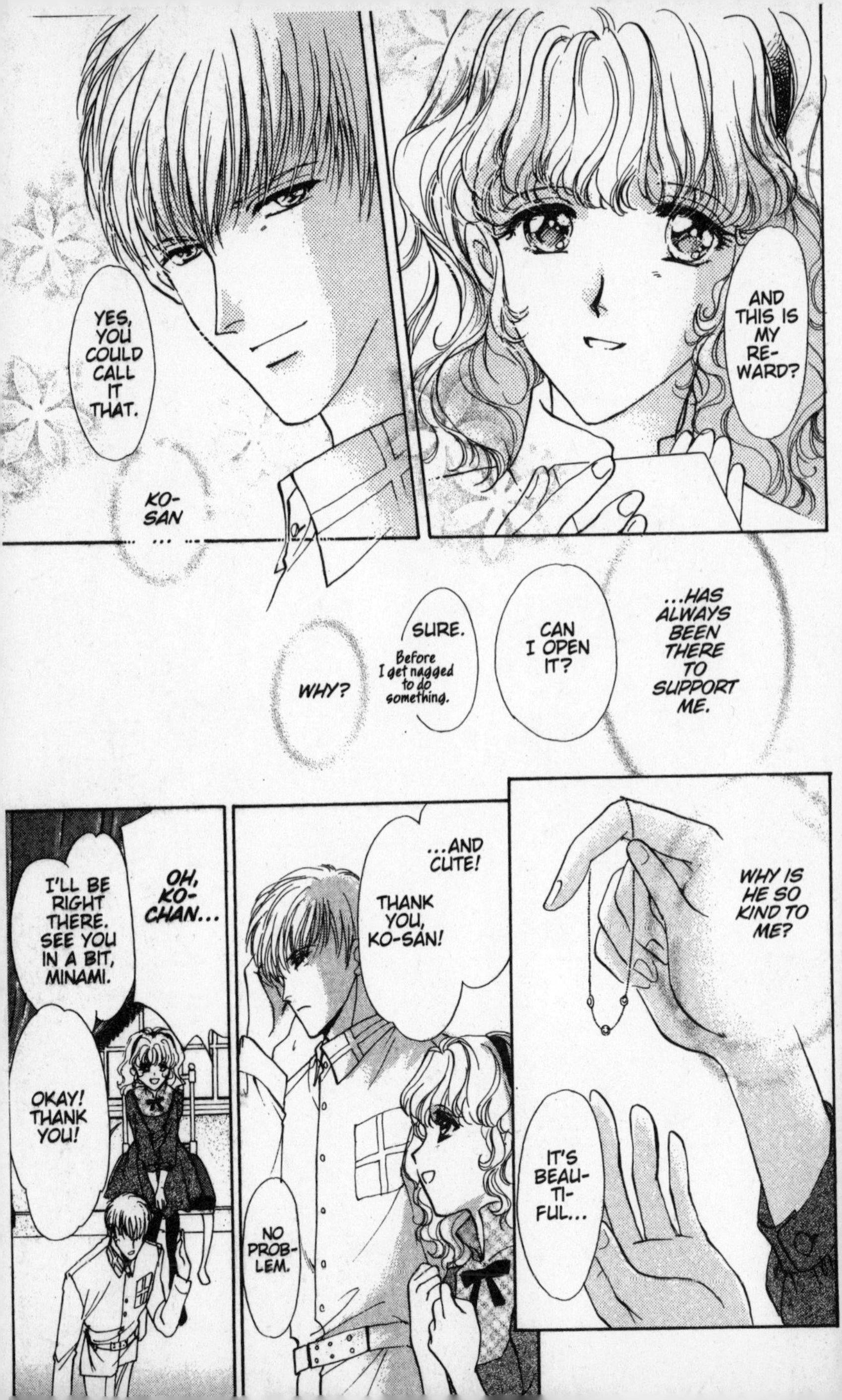
AND THIS IS MY RE-WARD?
YES, YOU COULD CALL IT THAT.
KO-SAN
... ...
...HAS ALWAYS BEEN THERE TO SUPPORT ME.
CAN I OPEN IT?
SURE.
Before I get nagged to do something.
WHY?
WHY IS HE SO KIND TO ME?
IT'S BEAU-TI-FUL...
...AND CUTE!
THANK YOU, KO-SAN!
NO PROB-LEM.
OH, KO-CHAN...
I'LL BE RIGHT THERE. SEE YOU IN A BIT, MINAMI.
OKAY! THANK YOU!

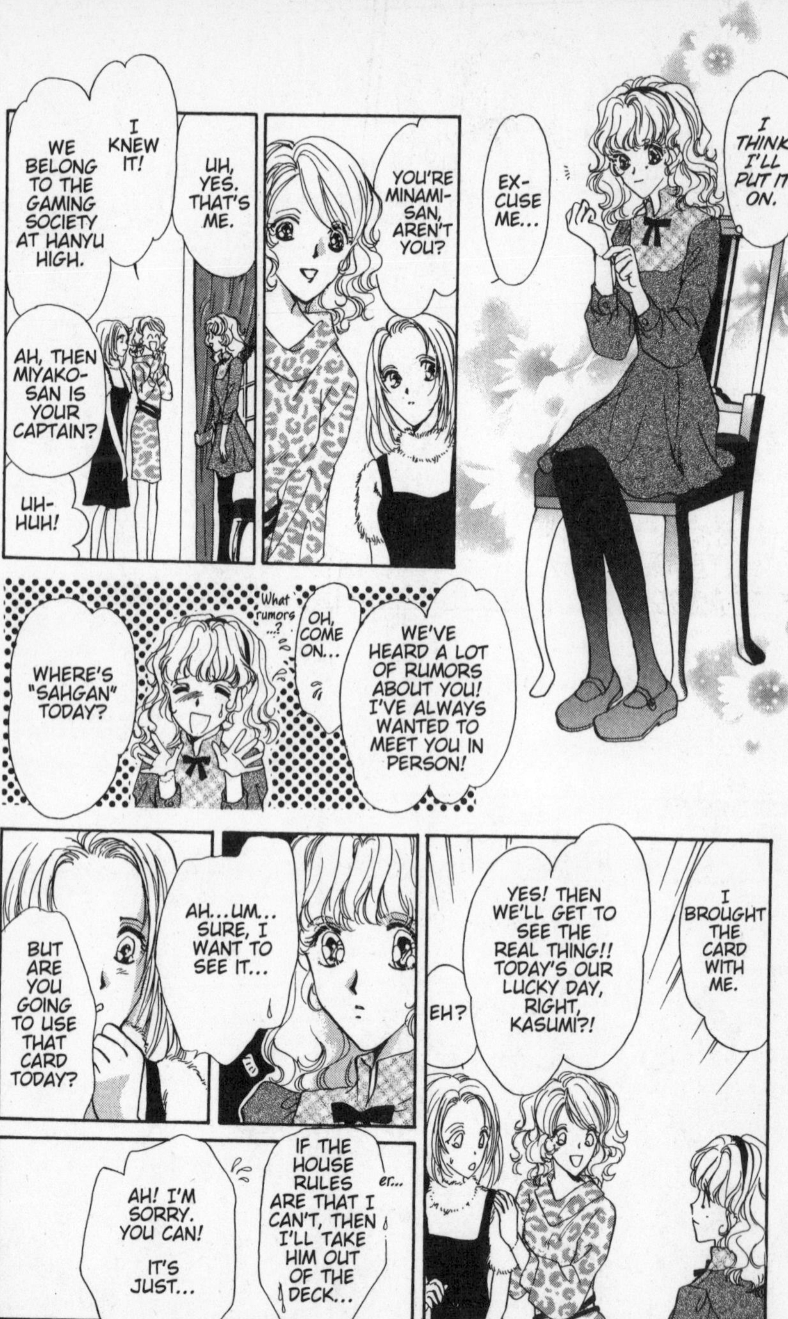
I THINK I'LL PUT IT ON.
EX-CUSE ME...
YOU'RE MINAMI-SAN, AREN'T YOU?
UH, YES. THAT'S ME.
I KNEW IT!
WE BELONG TO THE GAMING SOCIETY AT HANYU HIGH.
AH, THEN MIYAKO-SAN IS YOUR CAPTAIN?
UH-HUH!
WE'VE HEARD A LOT OF RUMORS ABOUT YOU! I'VE ALWAYS WANTED TO MEET YOU IN PERSON!
OH, COME ON...
What rumors ...?
WHERE'S "SAHGAN" TODAY?
I BROUGHT THE CARD WITH ME.
YES! THEN WE'LL GET TO SEE THE REAL THING!! TODAY'S OUR LUCKY DAY, RIGHT, KASUMI?!
EH?
AH...UM... SURE, I WANT TO SEE IT...
BUT ARE YOU GOING TO USE THAT CARD TODAY?
IF THE HOUSE RULES ARE THAT I CAN'T, THEN I'LL TAKE HIM OUT OF THE DECK...
er...
AH! I'M SORRY. YOU CAN!
IT'S JUST...

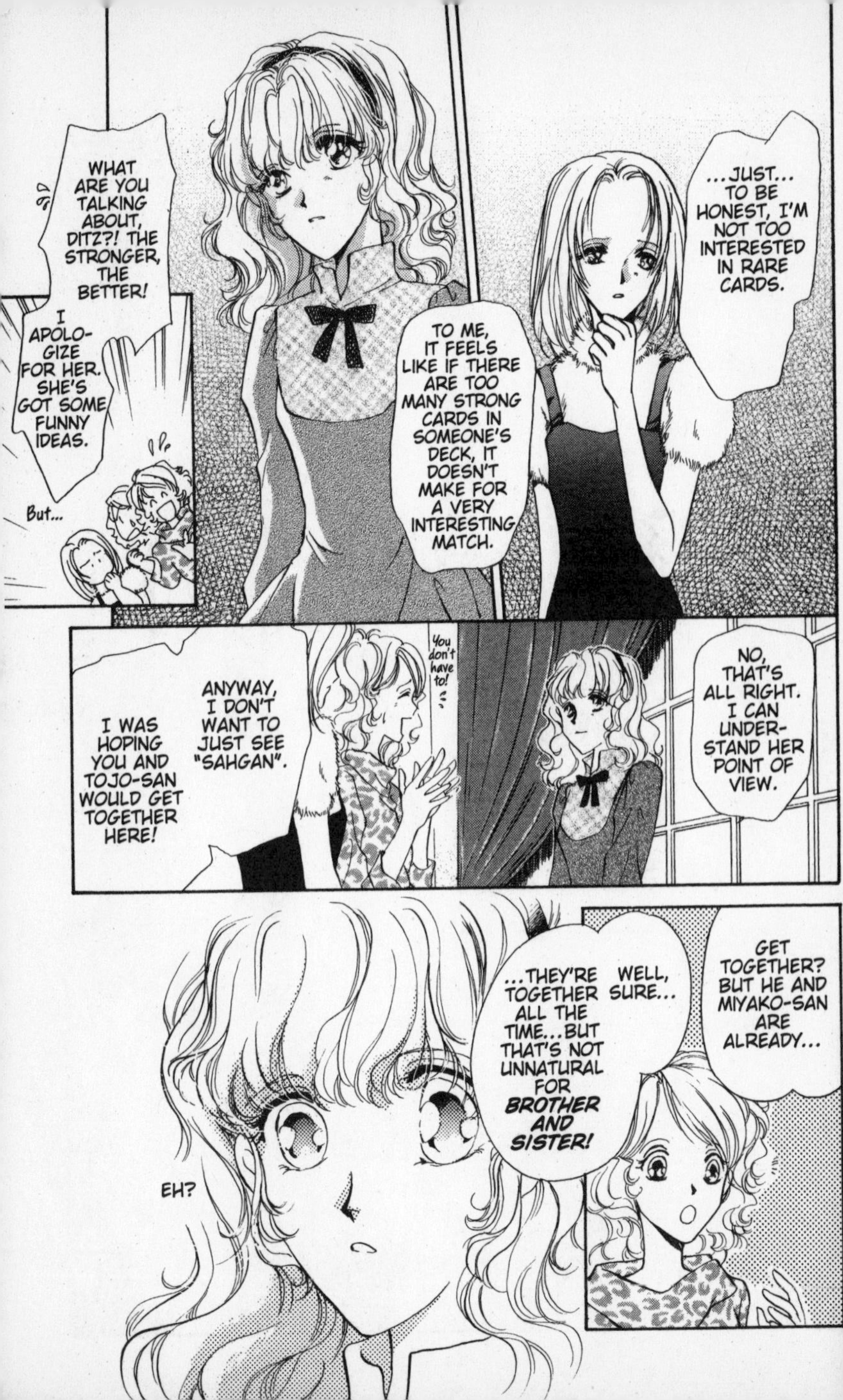
...JUST... TO BE HONEST, I'M NOT TOO INTERESTED IN RARE CARDS.
TO ME, IT FEELS LIKE IF THERE ARE TOO MANY STRONG CARDS IN SOMEONE'S DECK, IT DOESN'T MAKE FOR A VERY INTERESTING MATCH.
WHAT ARE YOU TALKING ABOUT, DITZ?! THE STRONGER, THE BETTER!
I APOLOGIZE FOR HER. SHE'S GOT SOME FUNNY IDEAS.
But...
NO, THAT'S ALL RIGHT. I CAN UNDERSTAND HER POINT OF VIEW.
You don't have to!
ANYWAY, I DON'T WANT TO JUST SEE "SAHGAN".
I WAS HOPING YOU AND TOJO-SAN WOULD GET TOGETHER HERE!
GET TOGETHER? BUT HE AND MIYAKO-SAN ARE ALREADY...
WELL, SURE...
...THEY'RE TOGETHER ALL THE TIME...BUT THAT'S NOT UNNATURAL FOR **BROTHER AND SISTER!**
EH?

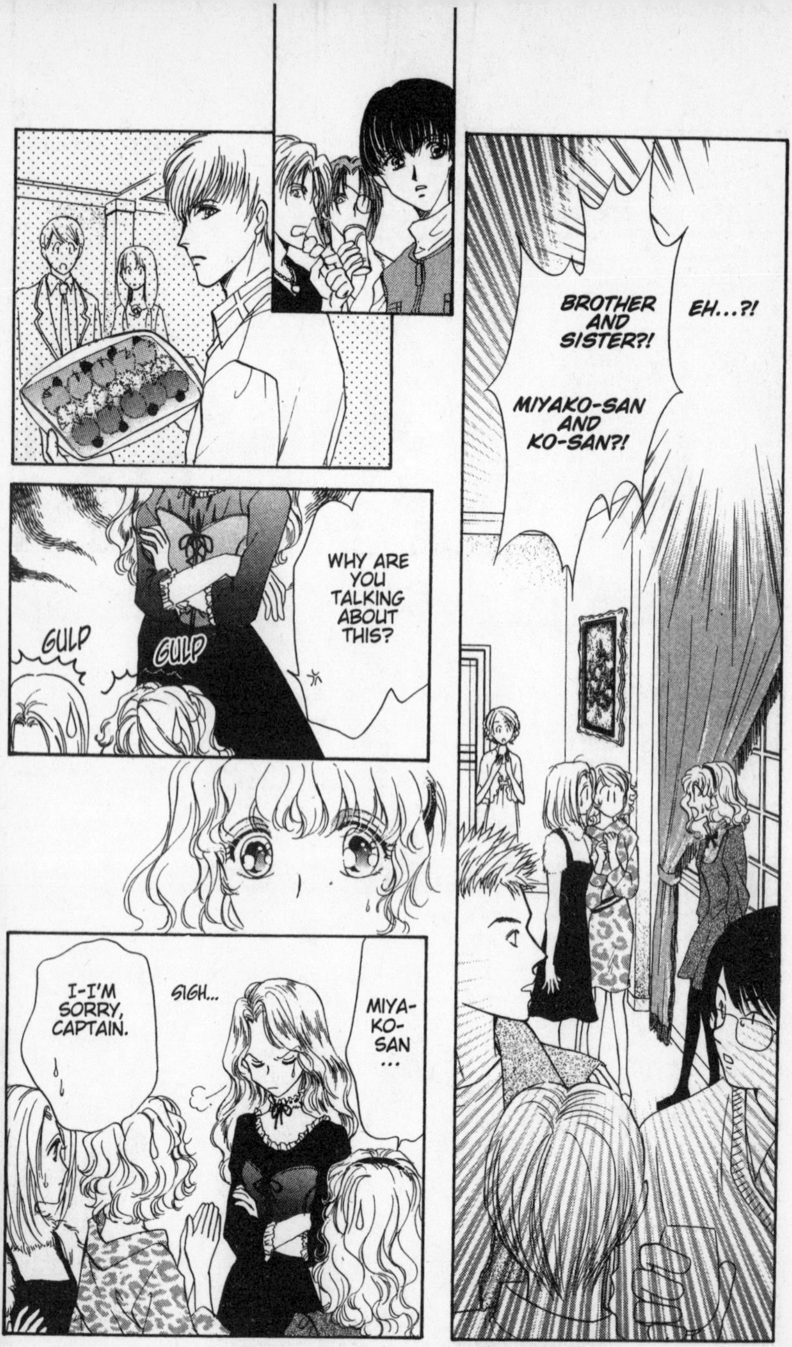
EH...?!
BROTHER AND SISTER?!
MIYAKO-SAN AND KO-SAN?!
WHY ARE YOU TALKING ABOUT THIS?
GULP
GULP
MIYA-KO-SAN ...
SIGH...
I-I'M SORRY, CAPTAIN.

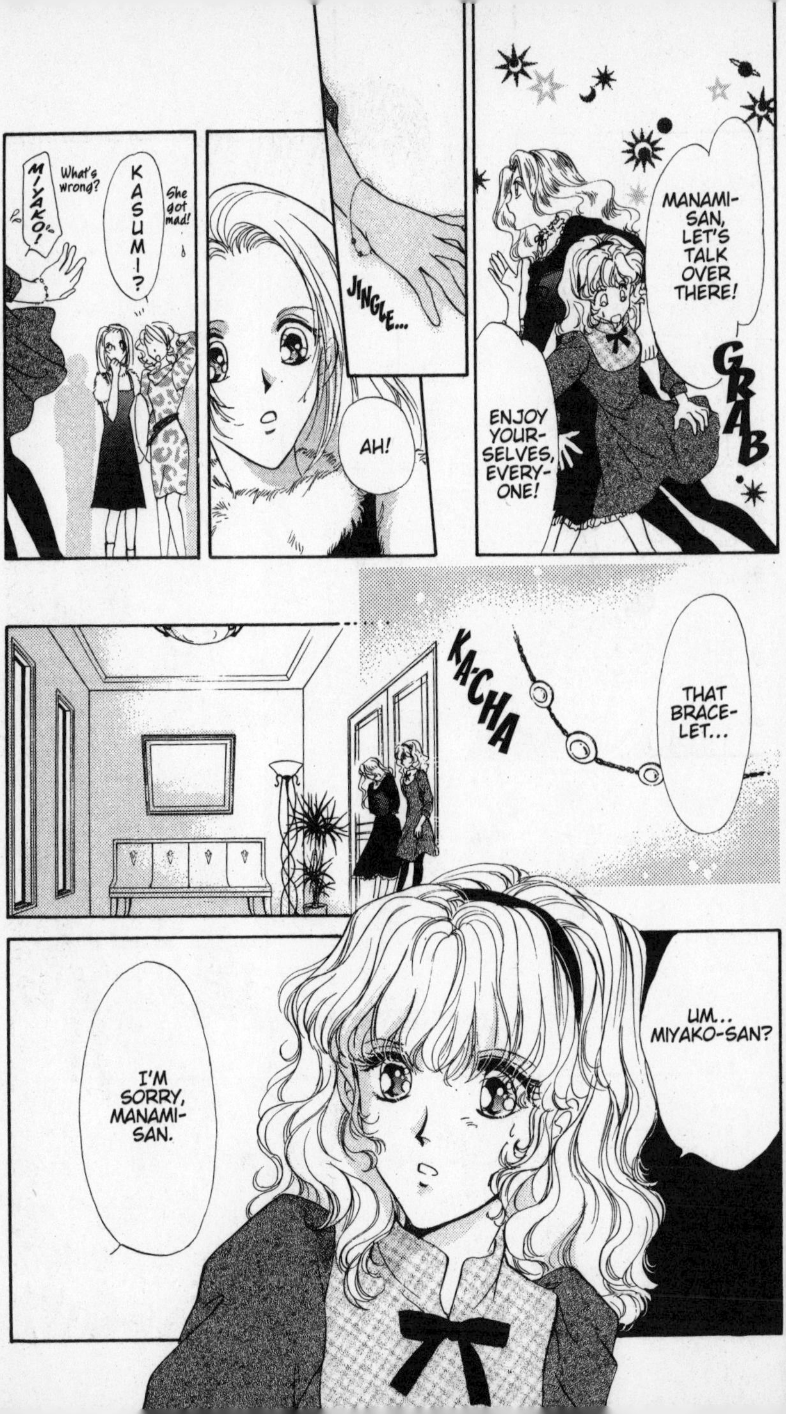
MANAMI-SAN, LET'S TALK OVER THERE!
GRAB
ENJOY YOURSELVES, EVERYONE!
JINGLE...
AH!
She got mad!
KASUMI-?
What's wrong?
MIYAKO!
THAT BRACELET...
KA-CHA
UM.. MIYAKO-SAN?
I'M SORRY, MANAMI-SAN.

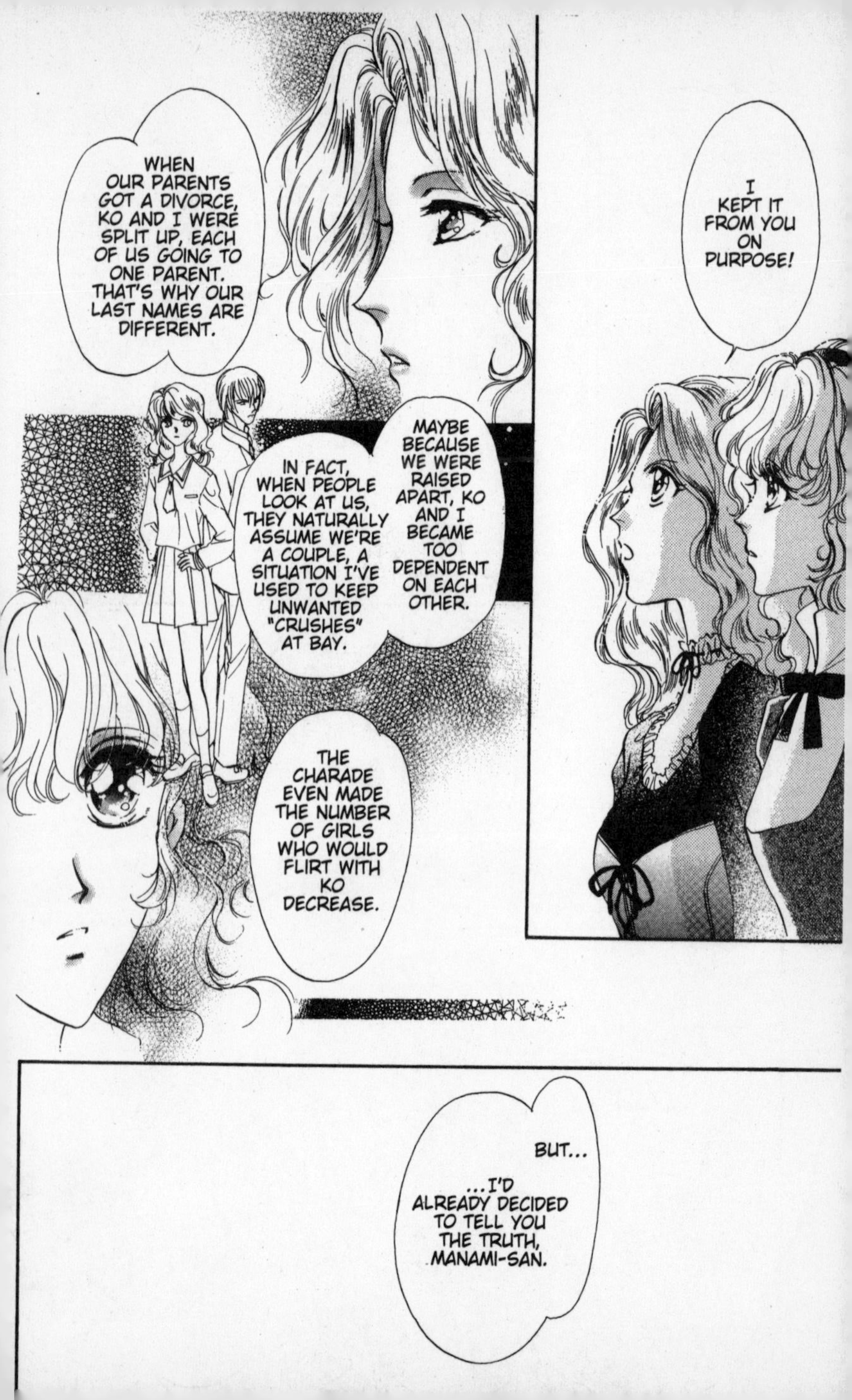
I KEPT IT FROM YOU ON PURPOSE!
WHEN OUR PARENTS GOT A DIVORCE, KO AND I WERE SPLIT UP, EACH OF US GOING TO ONE PARENT. THAT'S WHY OUR LAST NAMES ARE DIFFERENT.
MAYBE BECAUSE WE WERE RAISED APART, KO AND I BECAME TOO DEPENDENT ON EACH OTHER.
IN FACT, WHEN PEOPLE LOOK AT US, THEY NATURALLY ASSUME WE'RE A COUPLE, A SITUATION I'VE USED TO KEEP UNWANTED "CRUSHES" AT BAY.
THE CHARADE EVEN MADE THE NUMBER OF GIRLS WHO WOULD FLIRT WITH KO DECREASE.
BUT...
...I'D ALREADY DECIDED TO TELL YOU THE TRUTH, MANAMI-SAN.

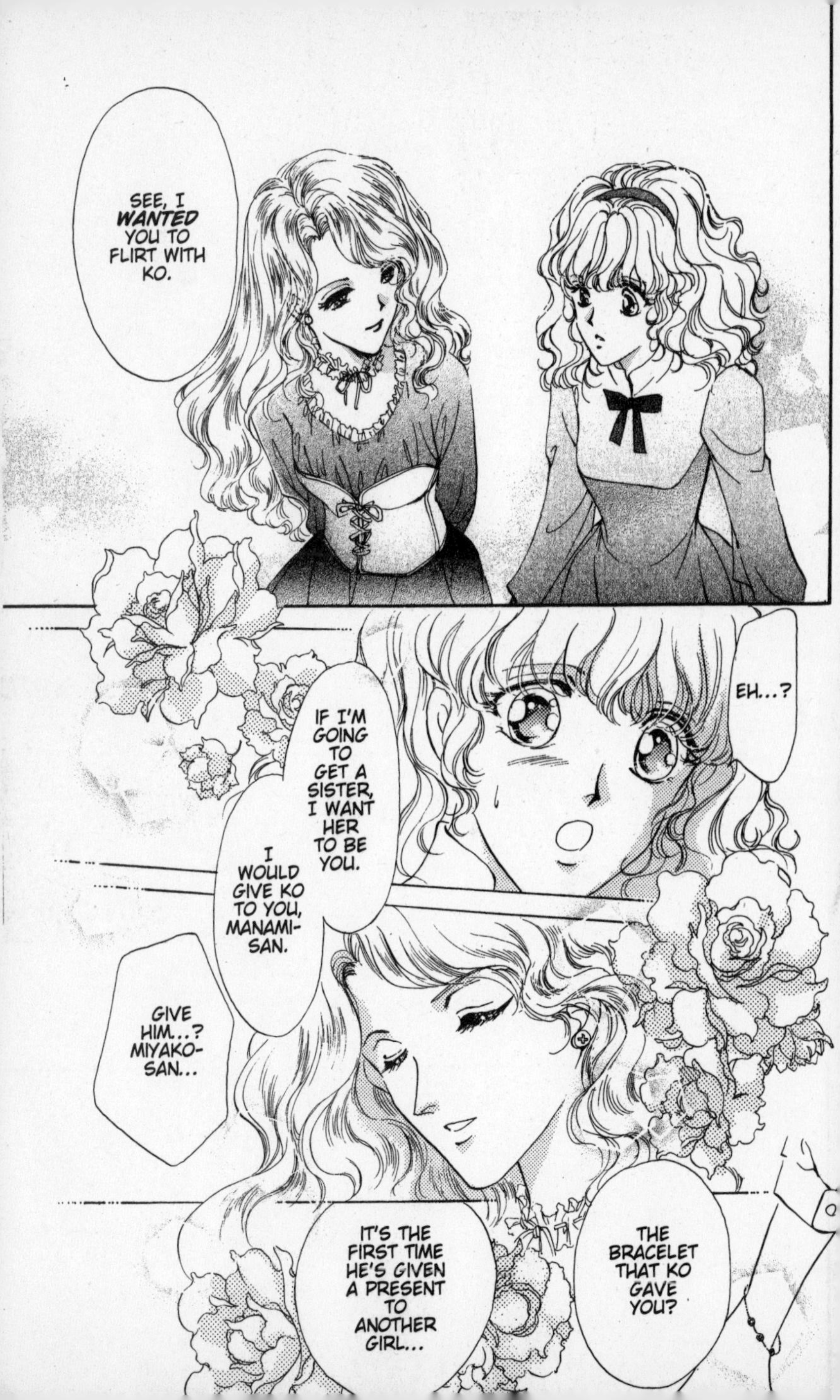

SEE, I *WANTED* YOU TO FLIRT WITH KO.
EH...?
IF I'M GOING TO GET A SISTER, I WANT HER TO BE YOU.
I WOULD GIVE KO TO YOU, MANAMI-SAN.
GIVE HIM...? MIYAKO-SAN...
THE BRACELET THAT KO GAVE YOU?
IT'S THE FIRST TIME HE'S GIVEN A PRESENT TO ANOTHER GIRL...

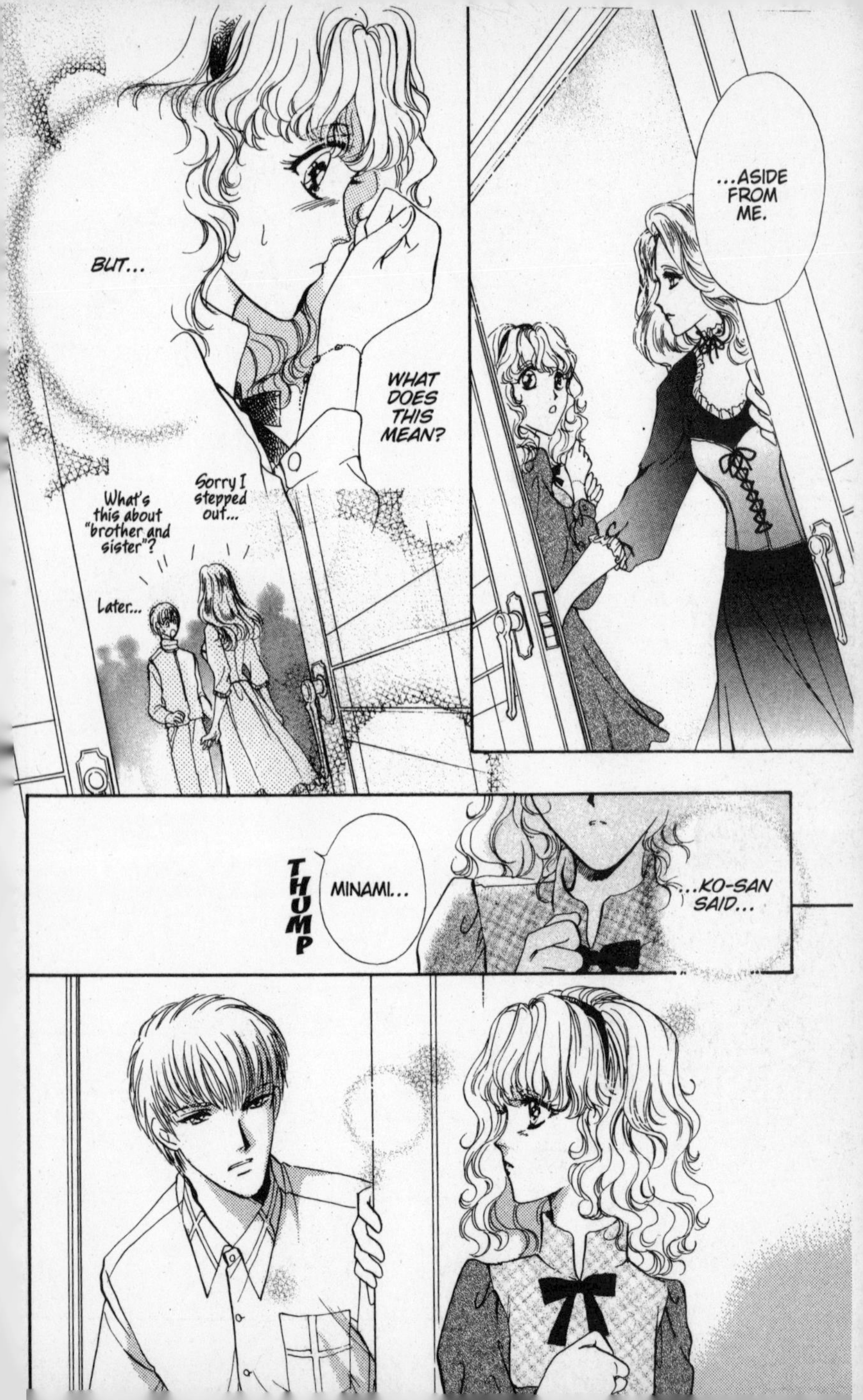
...ASIDE FROM ME.
BUT...
WHAT DOES THIS MEAN?
Sorry I stepped out...
What's this about "brother and sister"?
Later...
...KO-SAN SAID...
MINAMI...
THUMP

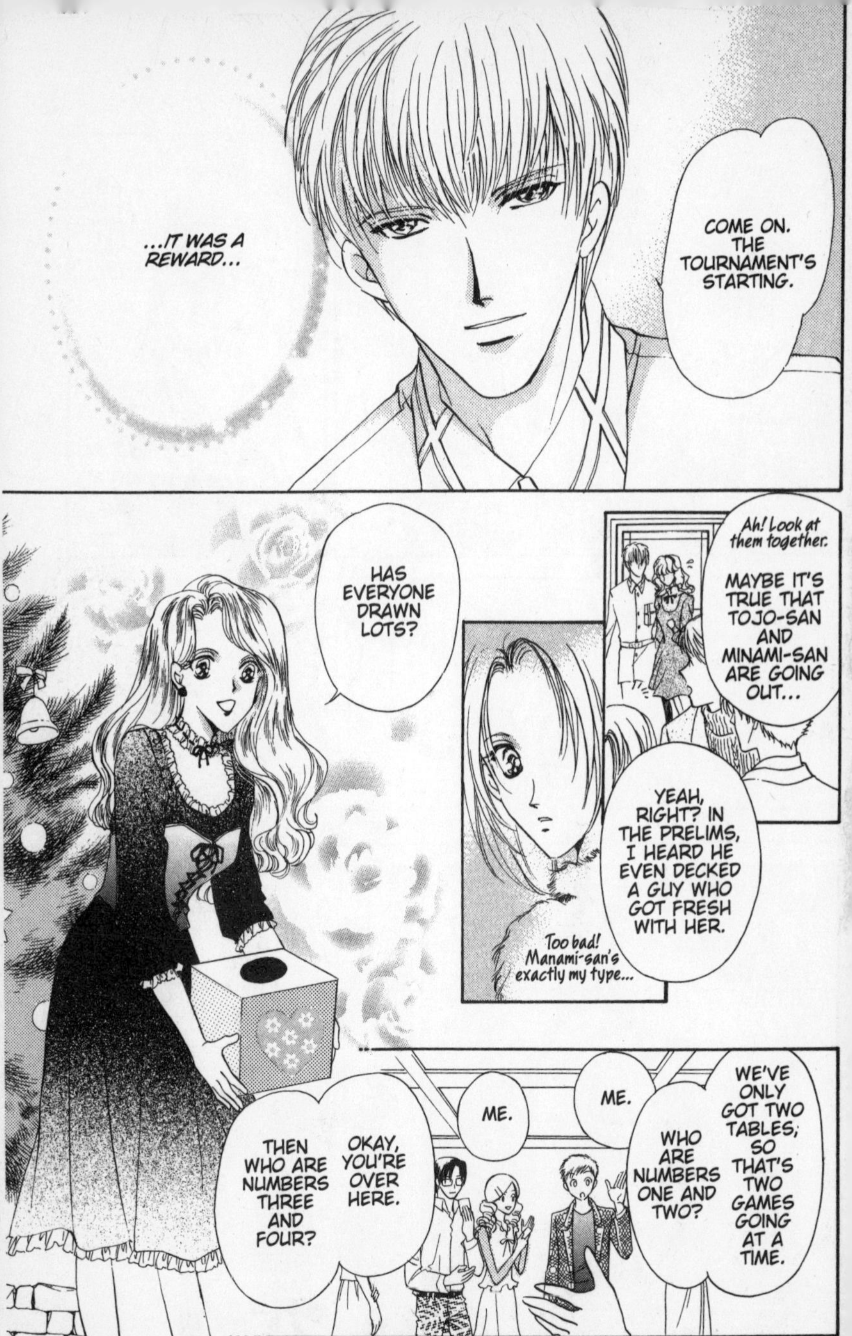

COME ON. THE TOURNAMENT'S STARTING.
...IT WAS A REWARD...
Ah! Look at them together.
MAYBE IT'S TRUE THAT TOJO-SAN AND MINAMI-SAN ARE GOING OUT...
YEAH, RIGHT? IN THE PRELIMS, I HEARD HE EVEN DECKED A GUY WHO GOT FRESH WITH HER.
Too bad! Manami-san's exactly my type...
WE'VE ONLY GOT TWO TABLES; SO THAT'S TWO GAMES GOING AT A TIME.
WHO ARE NUMBERS ONE AND TWO?
ME.
ME.
OKAY, YOU'RE OVER HERE.
THEN WHO ARE NUMBERS THREE AND FOUR?
HAS EVERYONE DRAWN LOTS?

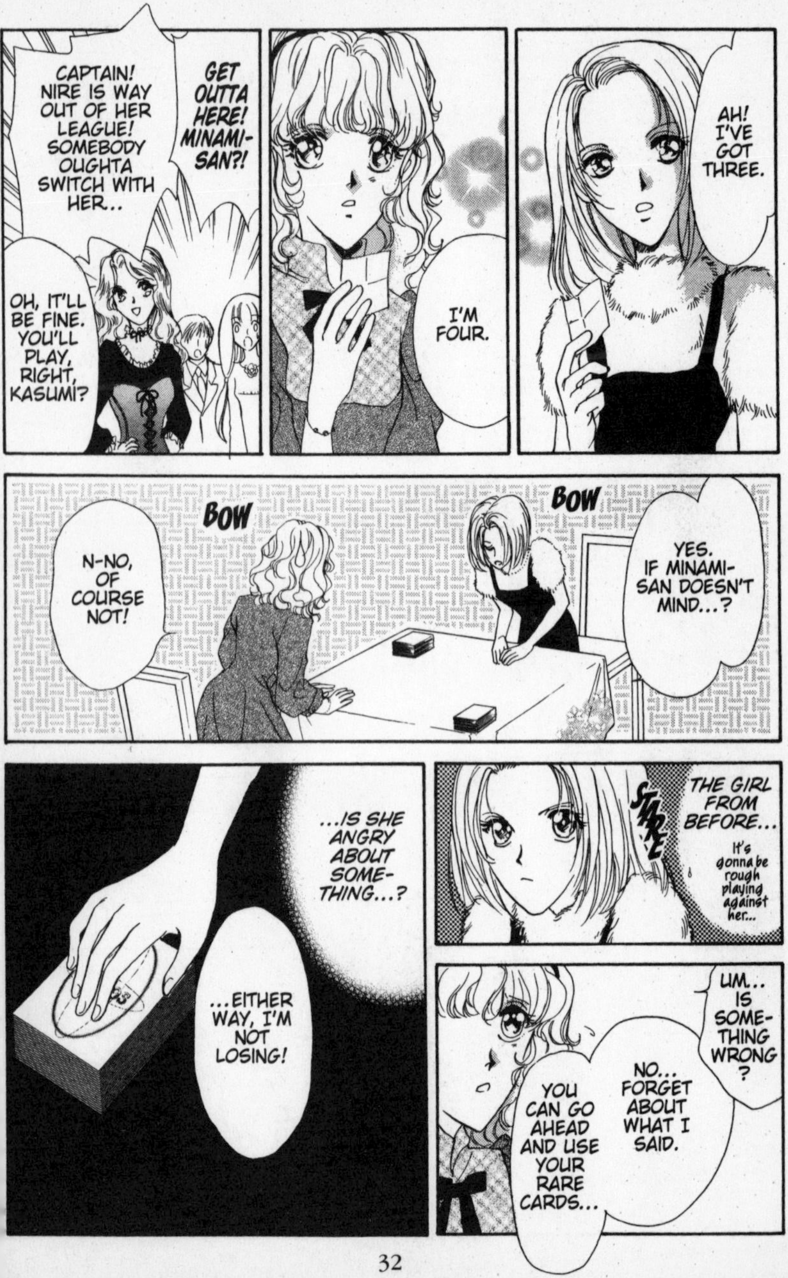
AH! I'VE GOT THREE.
I'M FOUR.
GET OUTTA HERE! MINAMI-SAN?!
CAPTAIN! NIRE IS WAY OUT OF HER LEAGUE! SOMEBODY OUGHTA SWITCH WITH HER...
OH, IT'LL BE FINE. YOU'LL PLAY, RIGHT, KASUMI?
YES. IF MINAMI-SAN DOESN'T MIND...?
BOW
BOW
N-NO, OF COURSE NOT!
THE GIRL FROM BEFORE...
It's gonna be rough playing against her...
STARE
UM... IS SOMETHING WRONG?
NO... FORGET ABOUT WHAT I SAID.
YOU CAN GO AHEAD AND USE YOUR RARE CARDS...
...IS SHE ANGRY ABOUT SOMETHING...?
...EITHER WAY, I'M NOT LOSING!

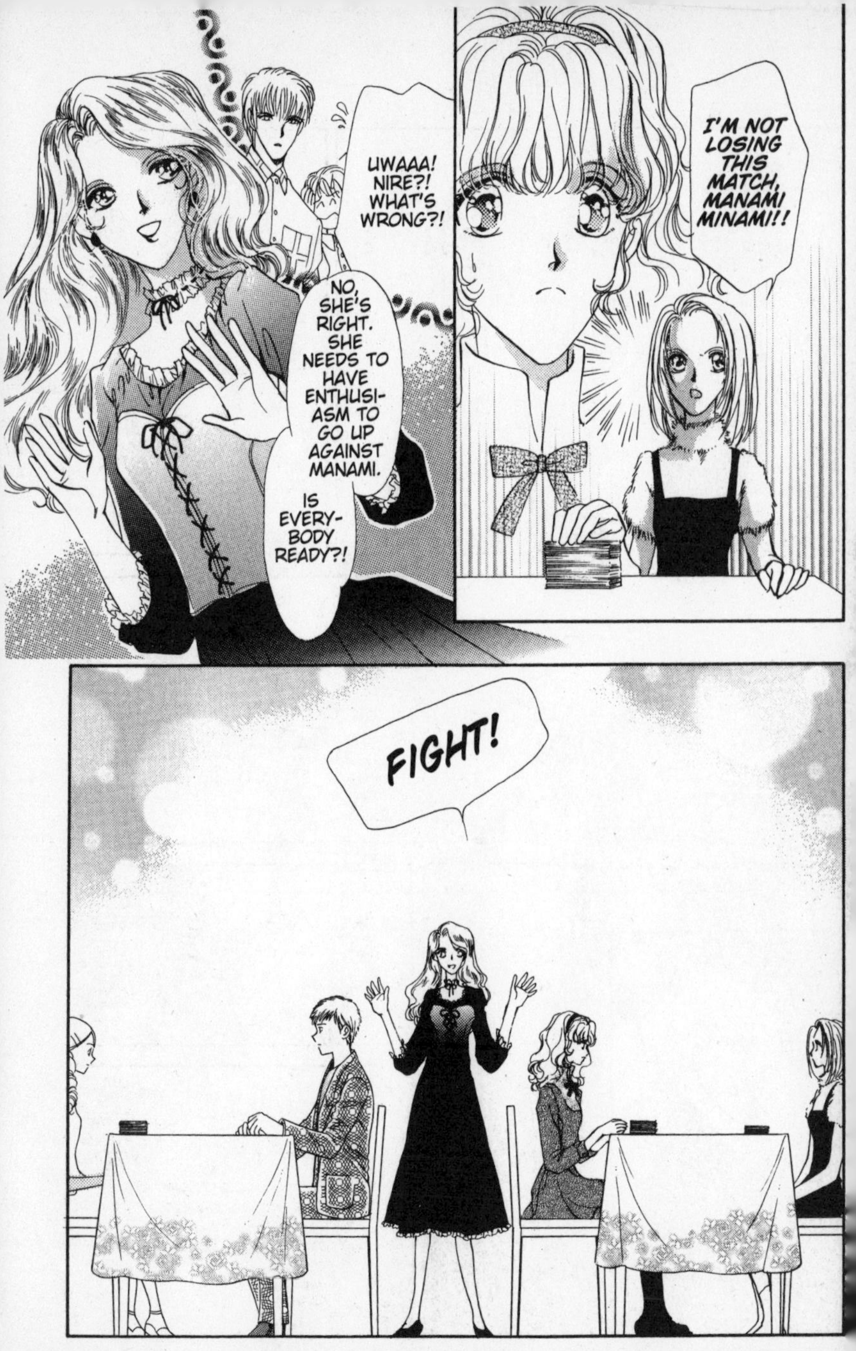
I'M NOT LOSING THIS MATCH, MANAMI MINAMI!!
UWAAA! NIRE?! WHAT'S WRONG?!
NO, SHE'S RIGHT. SHE NEEDS TO HAVE ENTHUSI-ASM TO GO UP AGAINST MANAMI.
IS EVERY-BODY READY?!
FIGHT!

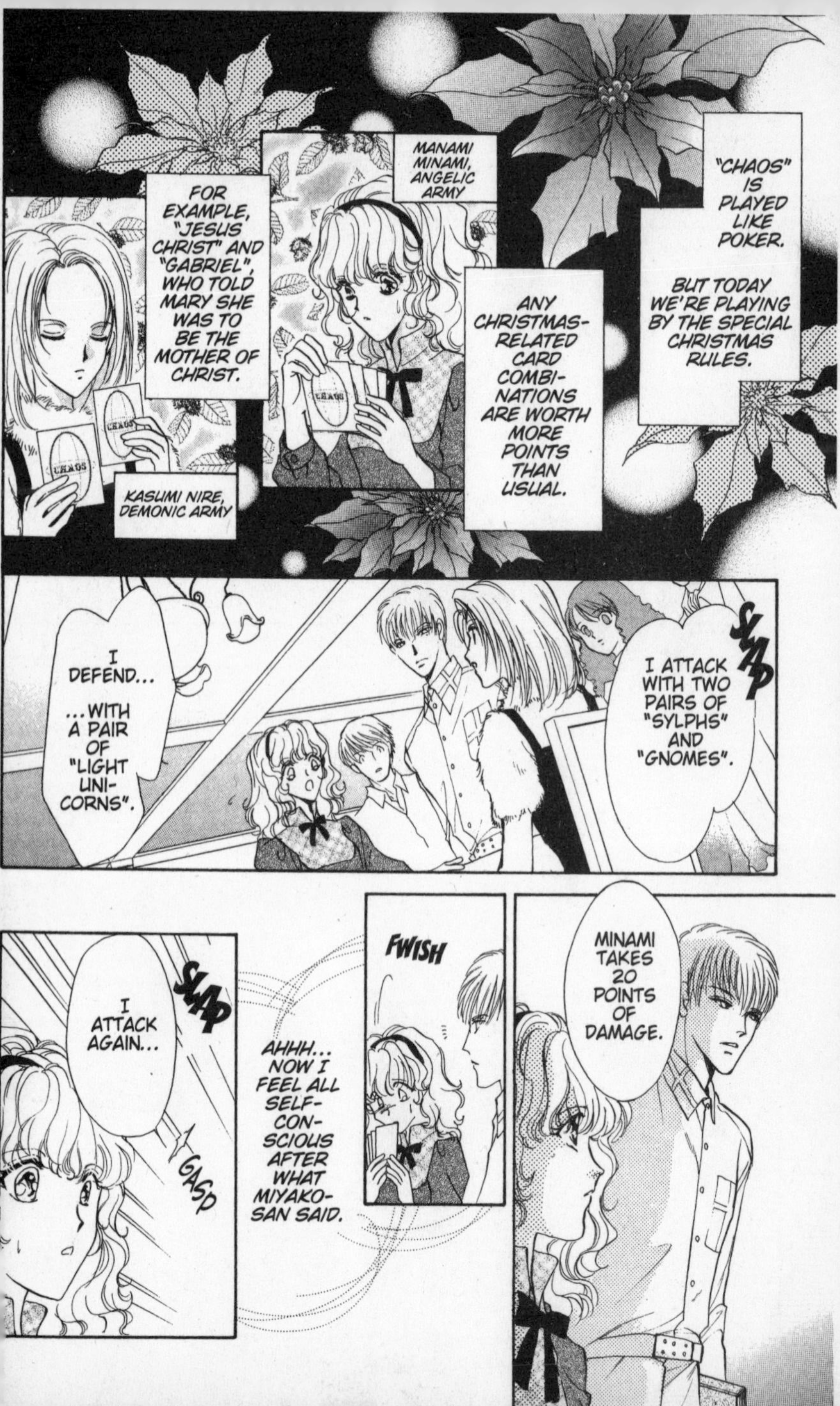
"CHAOS" IS PLAYED LIKE POKER.
BUT TODAY WE'RE PLAYING BY THE SPECIAL CHRISTMAS RULES.
ANY CHRISTMAS-RELATED CARD COMBINATIONS ARE WORTH MORE POINTS THAN USUAL.
MANAMI MINAMI, ANGELIC ARMY
FOR EXAMPLE, "JESUS CHRIST" AND "GABRIEL", WHO TOLD MARY SHE WAS TO BE THE MOTHER OF CHRIST.
KASUMI NIRE, DEMONIC ARMY
SLAP
I ATTACK WITH TWO PAIRS OF "SYLPHS" AND "GNOMES".
I DEFEND...
...WITH A PAIR OF "LIGHT UNICORNS".
MINAMI TAKES 20 POINTS OF DAMAGE.
FWISH
AHHH... NOW I FEEL ALL SELF-CONSCIOUS AFTER WHAT MIYAKO-SAN SAID.
SLAP
I ATTACK AGAIN...
GASP

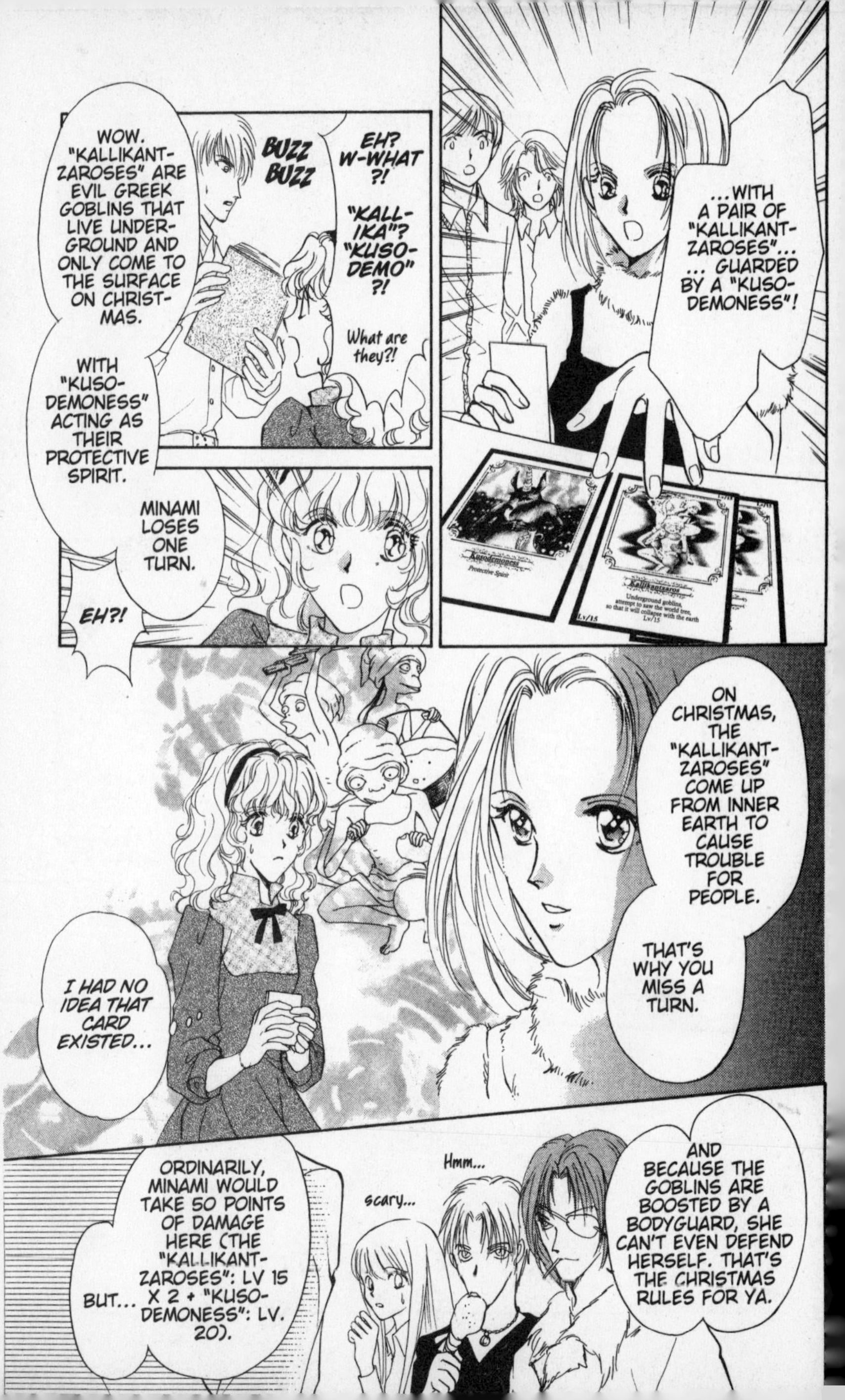
...WITH A PAIR OF "KALLIKANTZAROSES"... ... GUARDED BY A "KUSO-DEMONESS"!
Kusodemoness
Protective Spirit
Kallikantzaros
Underground goblins, attempt to saw the world tree, so that it will collapse with the earth
Lv/15
Lv/15
EH? W-WHAT ?!
"KALLI-KA"? "KUSO-DEMO" ?!
What are they?!
BUZZ BUZZ
WOW. "KALLIKANTZAROSES" ARE EVIL GREEK GOBLINS THAT LIVE UNDERGROUND AND ONLY COME TO THE SURFACE ON CHRISTMAS.
WITH "KUSO-DEMONESS" ACTING AS THEIR PROTECTIVE SPIRIT.
MINAMI LOSES ONE TURN.
EH?!
ON CHRISTMAS, THE "KALLIKANTZAROSES" COME UP FROM INNER EARTH TO CAUSE TROUBLE FOR PEOPLE.
THAT'S WHY YOU MISS A TURN.
I HAD NO IDEA THAT CARD EXISTED...
AND BECAUSE THE GOBLINS ARE BOOSTED BY A BODYGUARD, SHE CAN'T EVEN DEFEND HERSELF. THAT'S THE CHRISTMAS RULES FOR YA.
Hmm...
scary...
ORDINARILY, MINAMI WOULD TAKE 50 POINTS OF DAMAGE HERE (THE "KALLIKANTZAROSES": LV 15 X 2 + "KUSO-DEMONESS": LV. 20).
BUT...

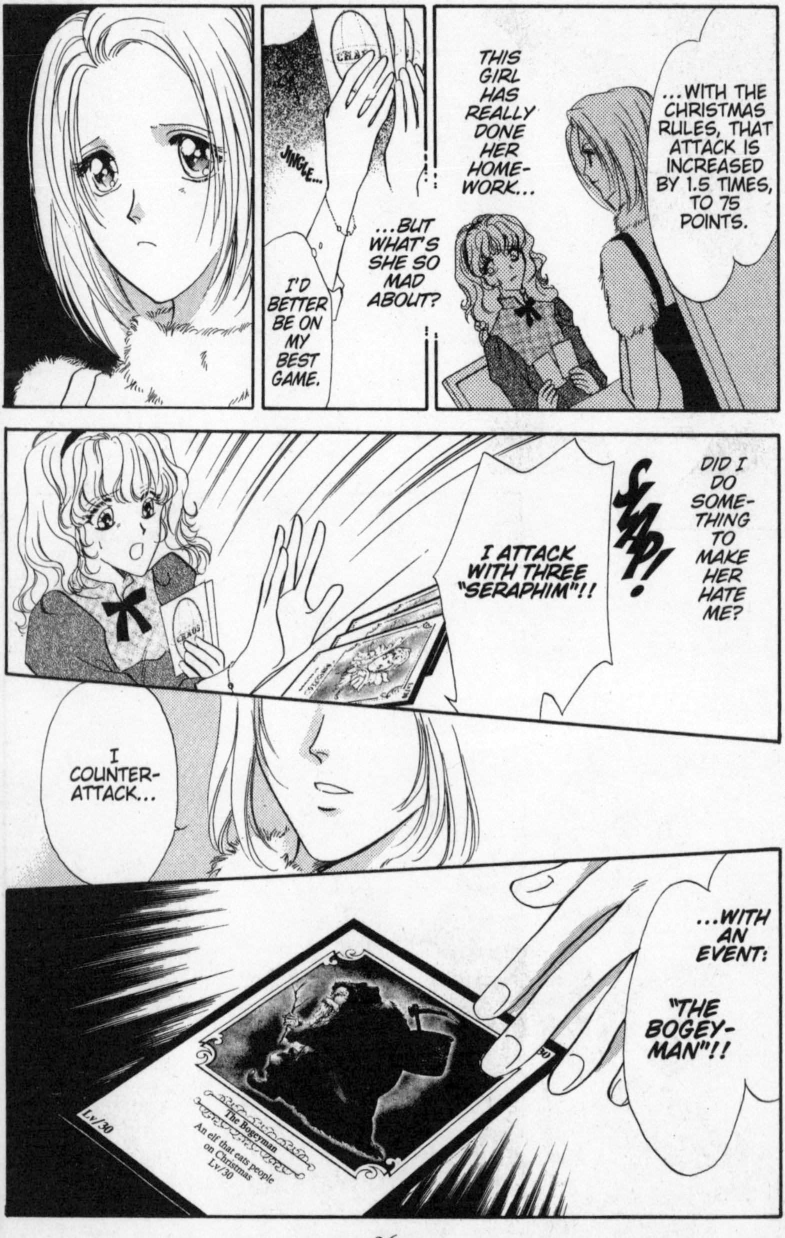
...WITH THE CHRISTMAS RULES, THAT ATTACK IS INCREASED BY 1.5 TIMES, TO 75 POINTS.
THIS GIRL HAS REALLY DONE HER HOMEWORK...
...BUT WHAT'S SHE SO MAD ABOUT?
I'D BETTER BE ON MY BEST GAME.
JINGLE...
CHAOS
DID I DO SOMETHING TO MAKE HER HATE ME?
SLAP!
I ATTACK WITH THREE "SERAPHIM"!!
CHAOS
I COUNTER-ATTACK...
...WITH AN EVENT:
"THE BOGEYMAN"!!
The Bogeyman
An elf that eats people on Christmas
Lv/30
Lv/30

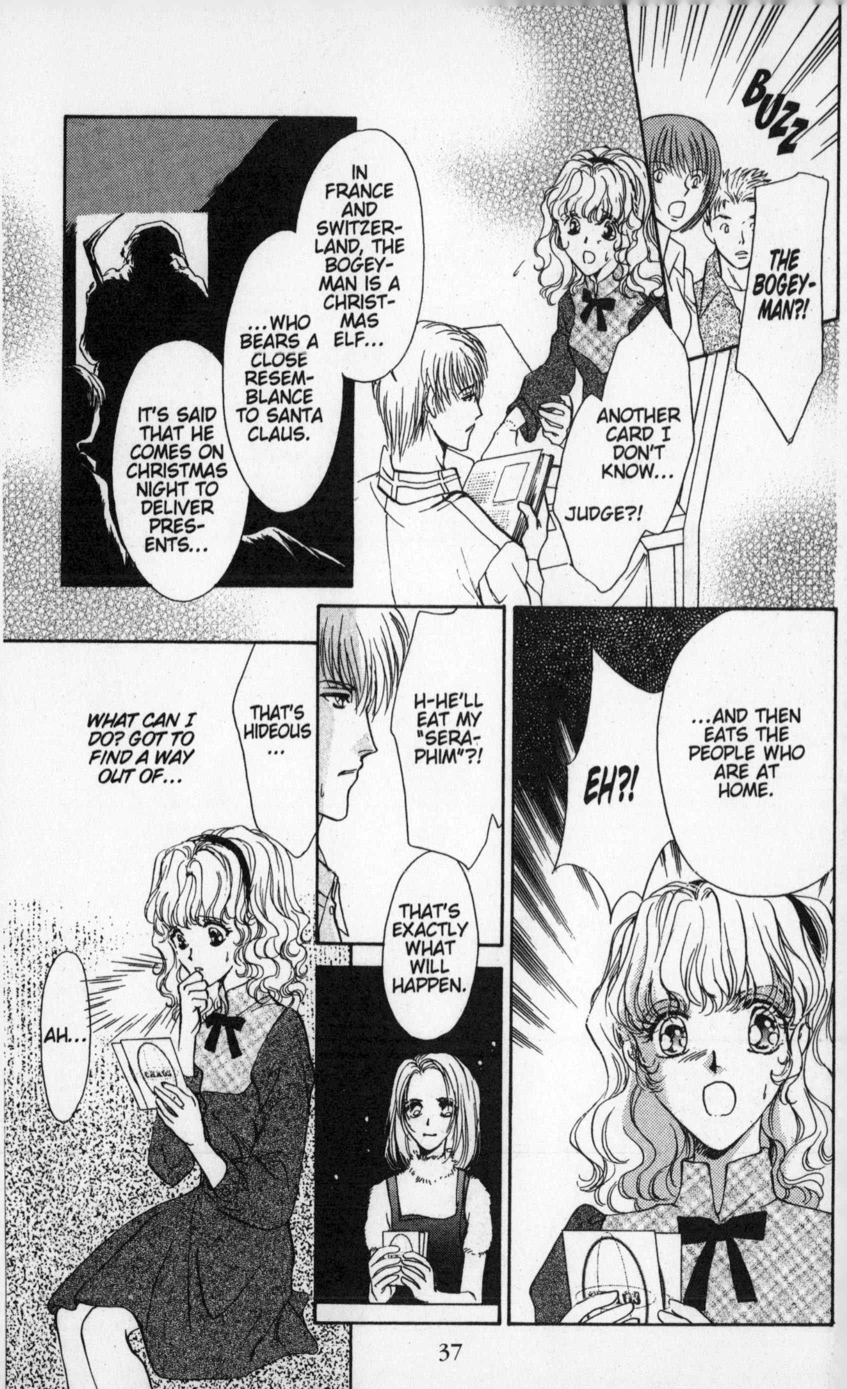
BUZZ
THE BOGEY-MAN?!
ANOTHER CARD I DON'T KNOW...
JUDGE?!
IN FRANCE AND SWITZER-LAND, THE BOGEY-MAN IS A CHRIST-MAS ELF...
...WHO BEARS A CLOSE RESEM-BLANCE TO SANTA CLAUS.
IT'S SAID THAT HE COMES ON CHRISTMAS NIGHT TO DELIVER PRES-ENTS...
...AND THEN EATS THE PEOPLE WHO ARE AT HOME.
EH?!
H-HE'LL EAT MY "SERA-PHIM"?!
THAT'S EXACTLY WHAT WILL HAPPEN.
THAT'S HIDEOUS...
WHAT CAN I DO? GOT TO FIND A WAY OUT OF...
AH...

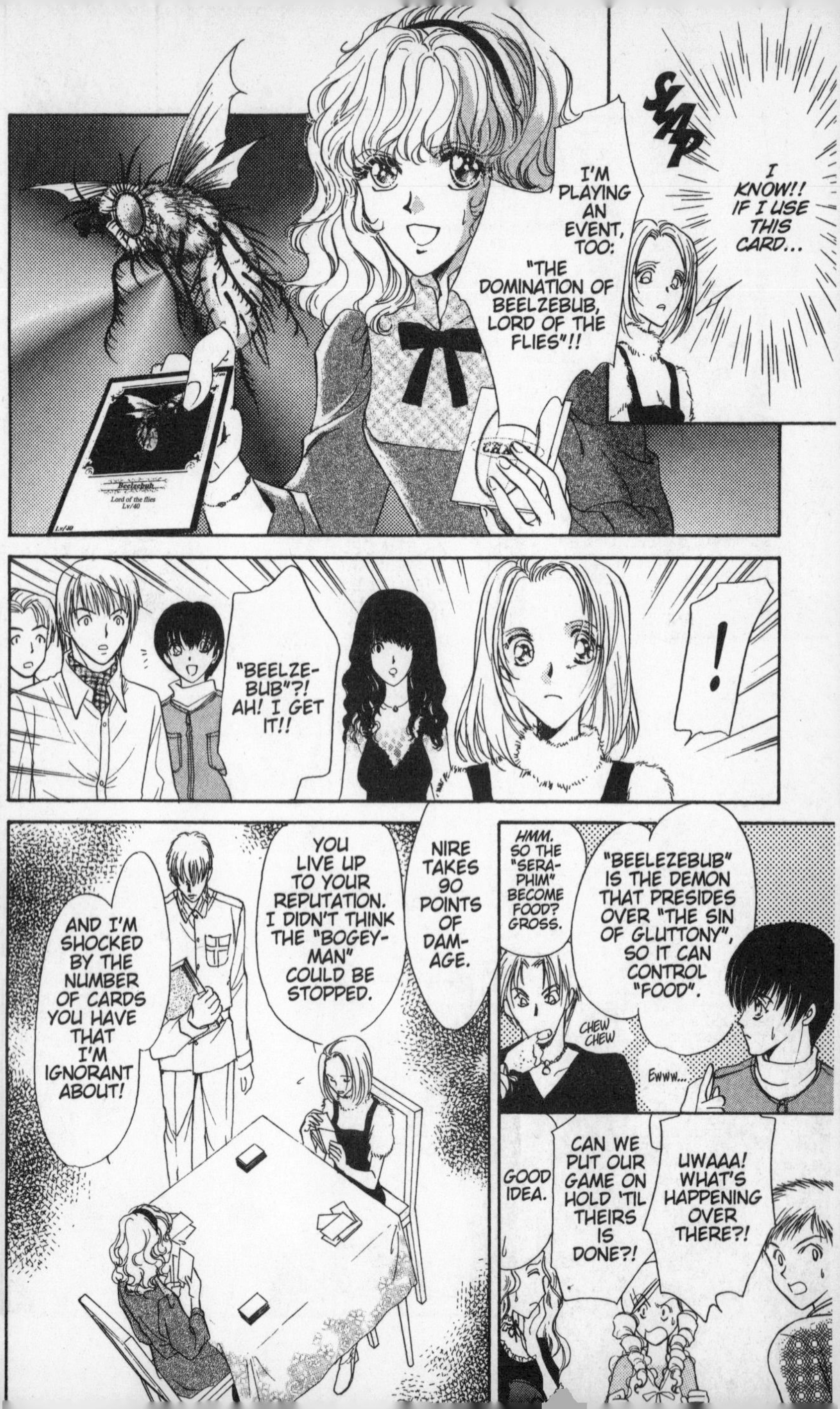
SLAP
I KNOW!! IF I USE THIS CARD...
I'M PLAYING AN EVENT, TOO:
"THE DOMINATION OF BEELZEBUB, LORD OF THE FLIES"!!
Beelzebub
Lord of the flies
Lv/40
!
"BEELZE-BUB"?! AH! I GET IT!!
"BEELEZEBUB" IS THE DEMON THAT PRESIDES OVER "THE SIN OF GLUTTONY", SO IT CAN CONTROL "FOOD".
HMM. SO THE "SERA-PHIM" BECOME FOOD? GROSS.
CHEW CHEW
Ewww...
UWAAA! WHAT'S HAPPENING OVER THERE?!
CAN WE PUT OUR GAME ON HOLD 'TIL THEIRS IS DONE?!
GOOD IDEA.
NIRE TAKES 90 POINTS OF DAM-AGE.
YOU LIVE UP TO YOUR REPUTATION. I DIDN'T THINK THE "BOGEY-MAN" COULD BE STOPPED.
AND I'M SHOCKED BY THE NUMBER OF CARDS YOU HAVE THAT I'M IGNORANT ABOUT!

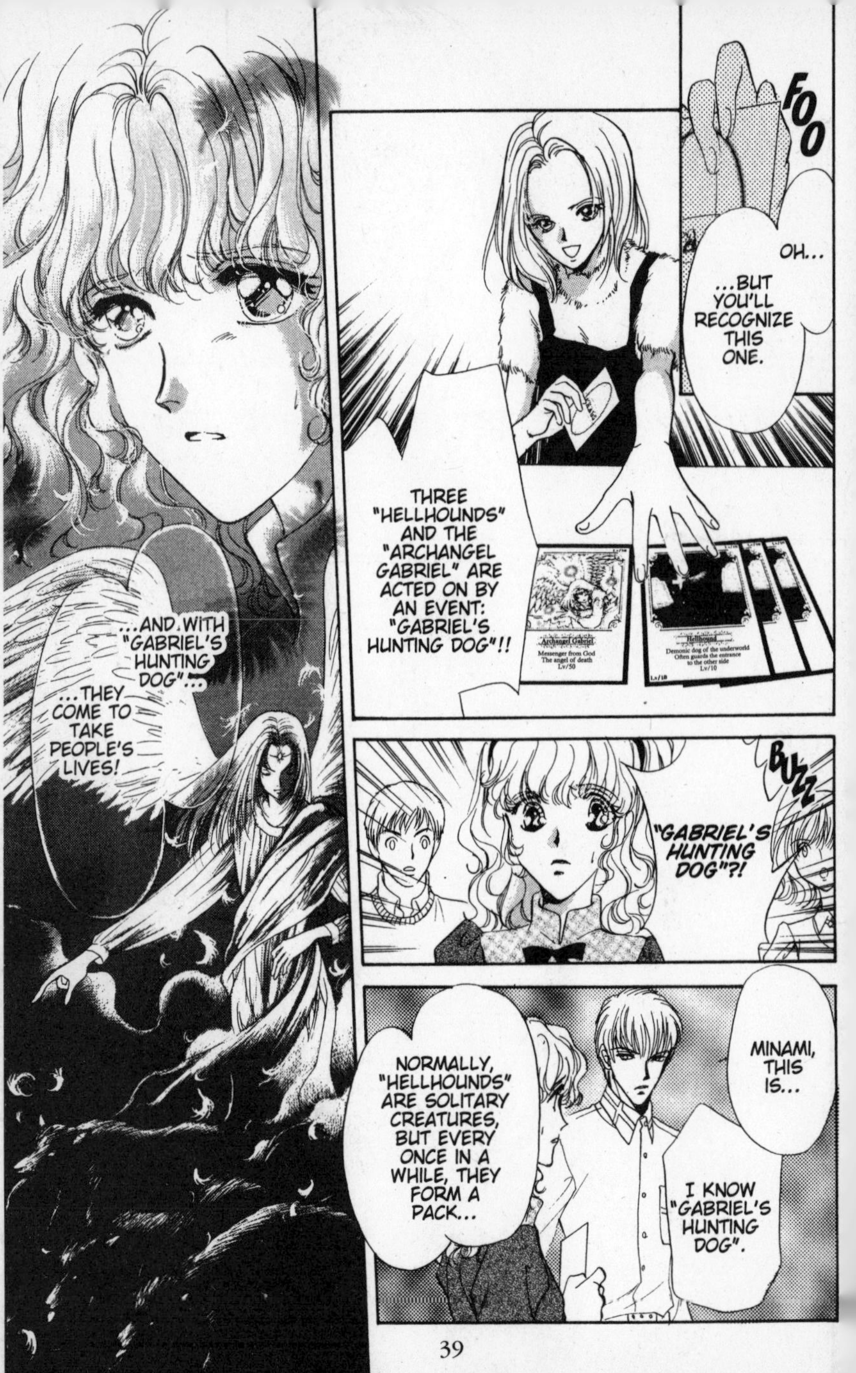
FOO
OH...
...BUT YOU'LL RECOGNIZE THIS ONE.
THREE "HELLHOUNDS" AND THE "ARCHANGEL GABRIEL" ARE ACTED ON BY AN EVENT: "GABRIEL'S HUNTING DOG"!!
Archangel Gabriel
Messenger from God
The angel of death
Lv/50
Hellhound
Demonic dog of the underworld
Often guards the entrance to the other side
Lv/10
BUZZ
"GABRIEL'S HUNTING DOG"?!
MINAMI, THIS IS...
I KNOW "GABRIEL'S HUNTING DOG".
NORMALLY, "HELLHOUNDS" ARE SOLITARY CREATURES, BUT EVERY ONCE IN A WHILE, THEY FORM A PACK...
...AND WITH "GABRIEL'S HUNTING DOG"...
...THEY COME TO TAKE PEOPLE'S LIVES!

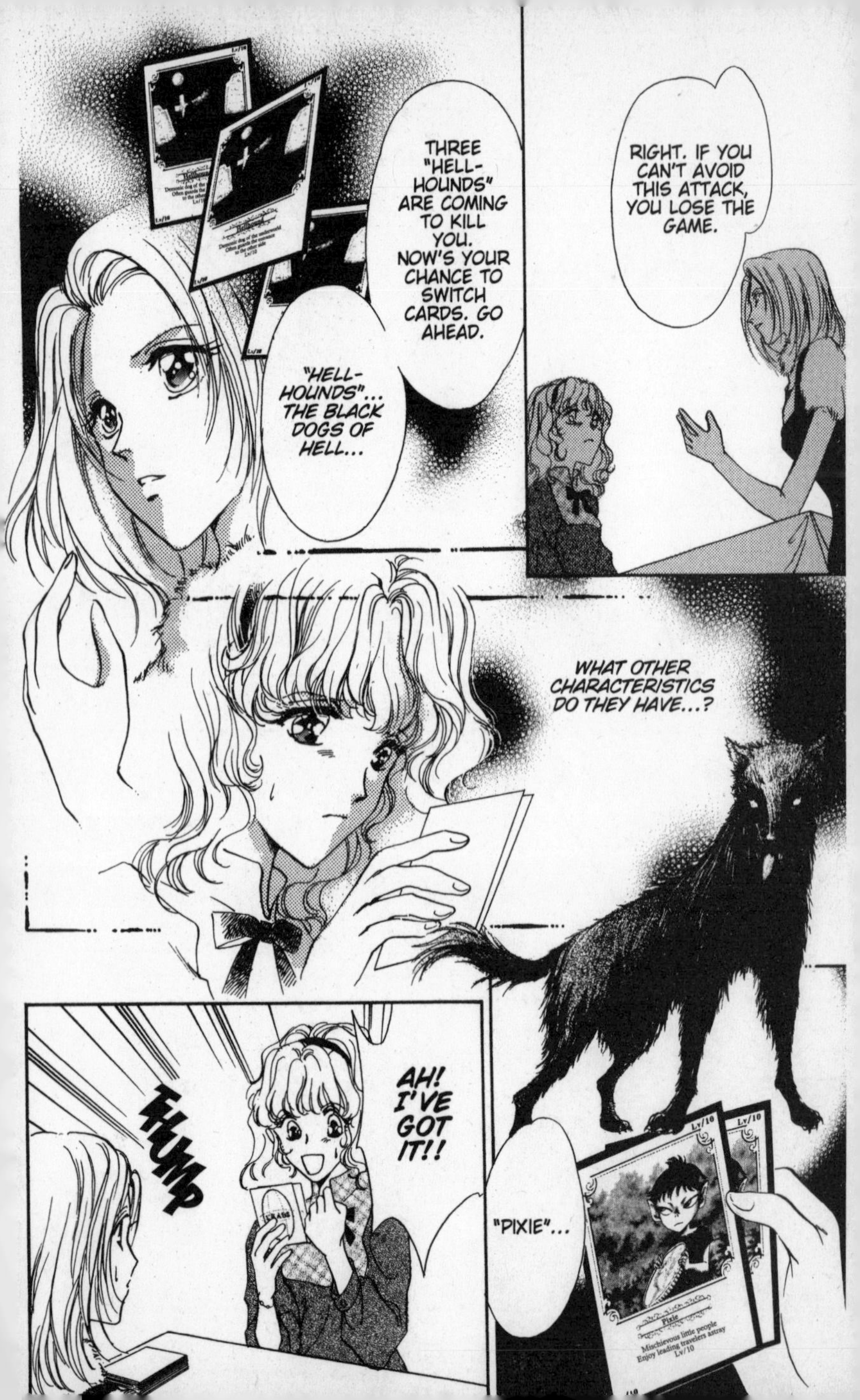
RIGHT. IF YOU CAN'T AVOID THIS ATTACK, YOU LOSE THE GAME.
THREE "HELL-HOUNDS" ARE COMING TO KILL YOU. NOW'S YOUR CHANCE TO SWITCH CARDS. GO AHEAD.
"HELL-HOUNDS"... THE BLACK DOGS OF HELL...
WHAT OTHER CHARACTERISTICS DO THEY HAVE...?
Lv/10
Pixie
Mischievous little people
Enjoy leading travelers astray
Lv/10
"PIXIE"...
AH! I'VE GOT IT!!
THUMP

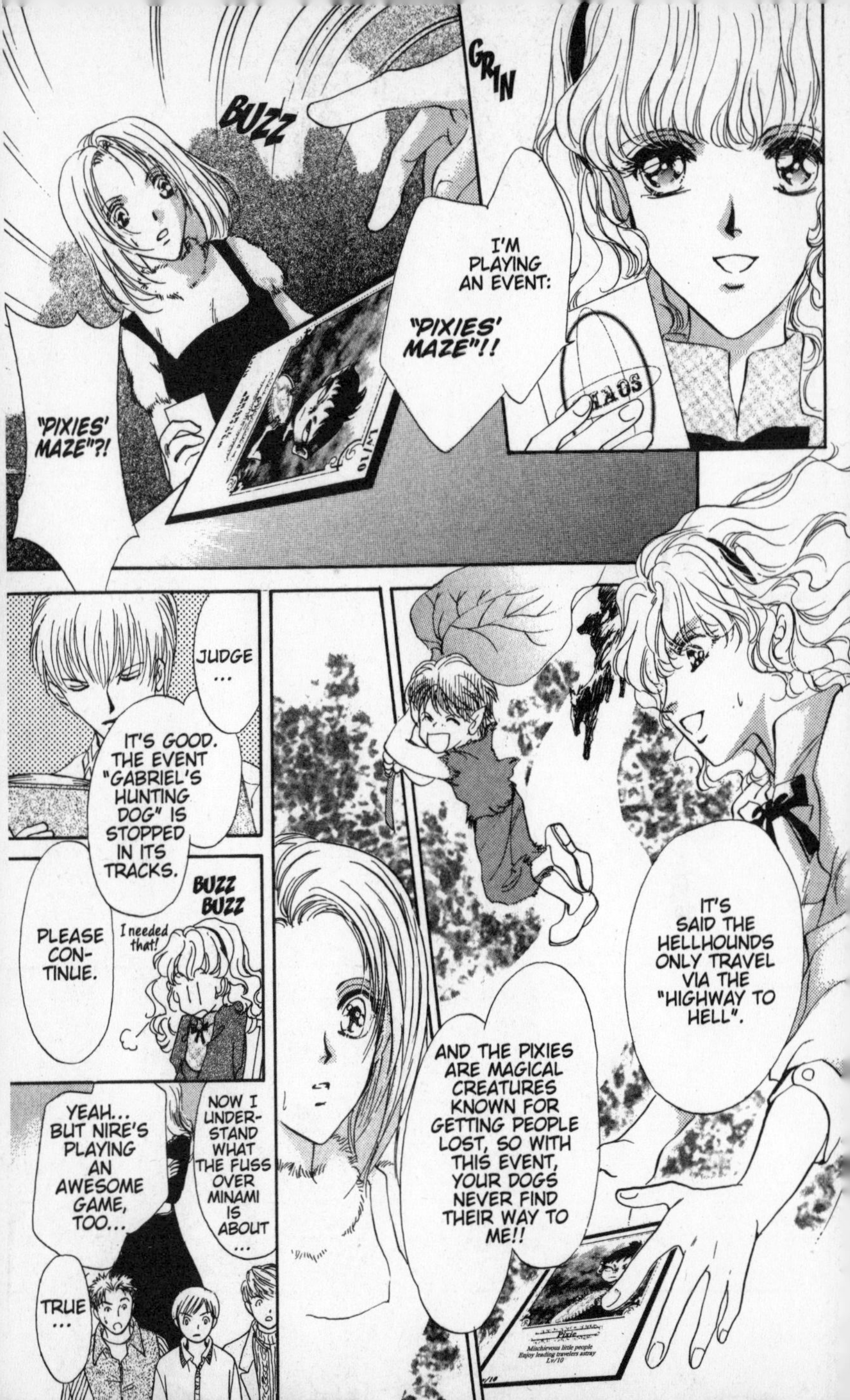
GRIN
I'M PLAYING AN EVENT:
"PIXIES' MAZE"!!
BUZZ
"PIXIES' MAZE"?!
IT'S SAID THE HELLHOUNDS ONLY TRAVEL VIA THE "HIGHWAY TO HELL".
AND THE PIXIES ARE MAGICAL CREATURES KNOWN FOR GETTING PEOPLE LOST, SO WITH THIS EVENT, YOUR DOGS NEVER FIND THEIR WAY TO ME!!
Pixie
Mischievous little people
Enjoy leading travelers astray
Lv/10
JUDGE ...
IT'S GOOD. THE EVENT "GABRIEL'S HUNTING DOG" IS STOPPED IN ITS TRACKS.
BUZZ BUZZ
I needed that!
PLEASE CON-TINUE.
NOW I UNDER-STAND WHAT THE FUSS OVER MINAMI IS ABOUT ...
YEAH... BUT NIRE'S PLAYING AN AWESOME GAME, TOO...
TRUE ...

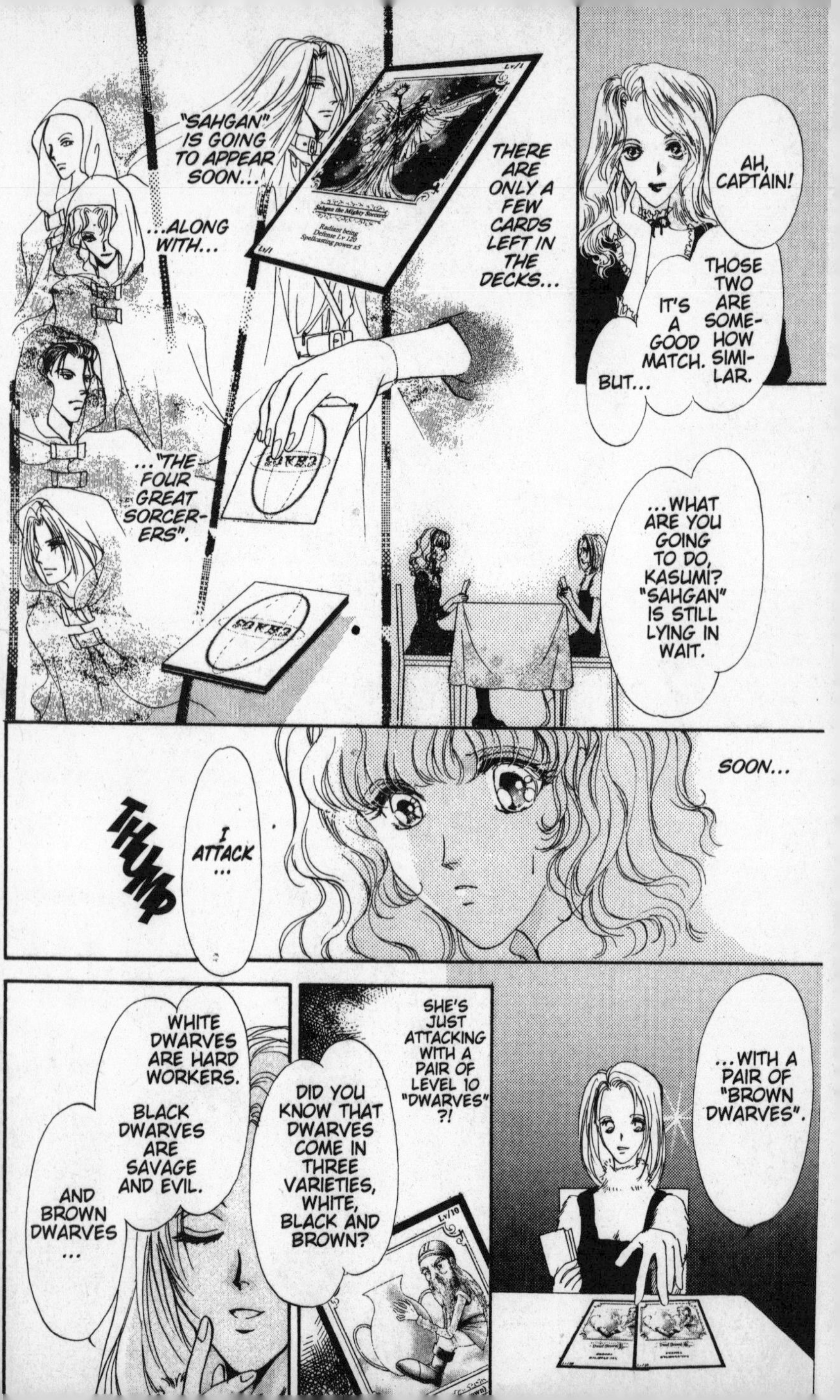
AH, CAPTAIN!
THOSE TWO ARE SOMEHOW SIMILAR.
IT'S A GOOD MATCH. BUT...
...WHAT ARE YOU GOING TO DO, KASUMI? "SAHGAN" IS STILL LYING IN WAIT.
THERE ARE ONLY A FEW CARDS LEFT IN THE DECKS...
Sahgan the Mighty Sorcerer
Radiant being
Defense Lv 120
Spellcasting power x5
"SAHGAN" IS GOING TO APPEAR SOON...
...ALONG WITH...
..."THE FOUR GREAT SORCERERS".
SOON...
I ATTACK...
THUMP
...WITH A PAIR OF "BROWN DWARVES".
SHE'S JUST ATTACKING WITH A PAIR OF LEVEL 10 "DWARVES"?!
DID YOU KNOW THAT DWARVES COME IN THREE VARIETIES, WHITE, BLACK AND BROWN?
WHITE DWARVES ARE HARD WORKERS.
BLACK DWARVES ARE SAVAGE AND EVIL.
AND BROWN DWARVES...

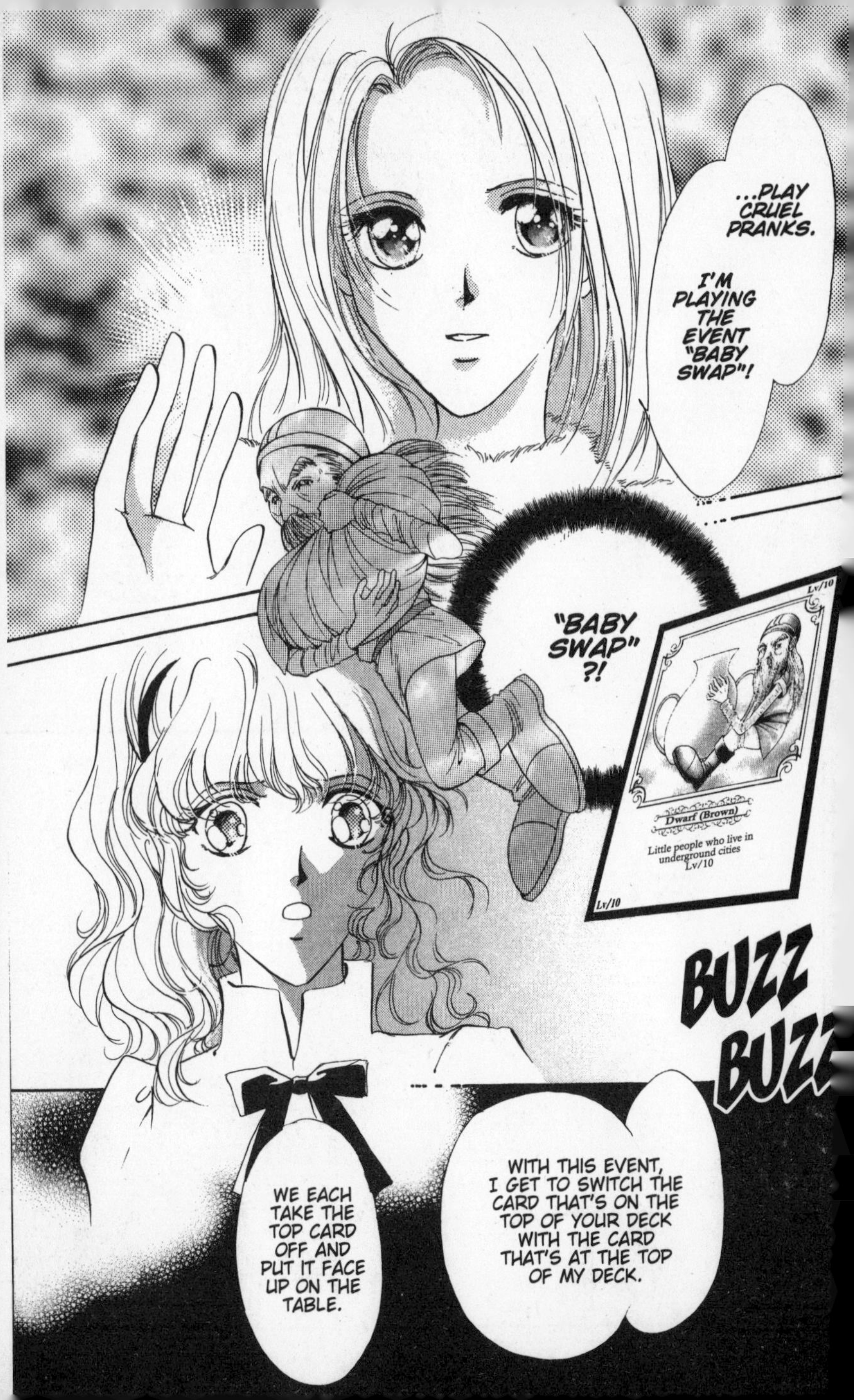
...PLAY CRUEL PRANKS.
I'M PLAYING THE EVENT "BABY SWAP"!
"BABY SWAP" ?!
Lv/10
Dwarf (Brown)
Little people who live in underground cities
Lv/10
Lv/10
BUZZ
BUZZ
WITH THIS EVENT, I GET TO SWITCH THE CARD THAT'S ON THE TOP OF YOUR DECK WITH THE CARD THAT'S AT THE TOP OF MY DECK.
WE EACH TAKE THE TOP CARD OFF AND PUT IT FACE UP ON THE TABLE.

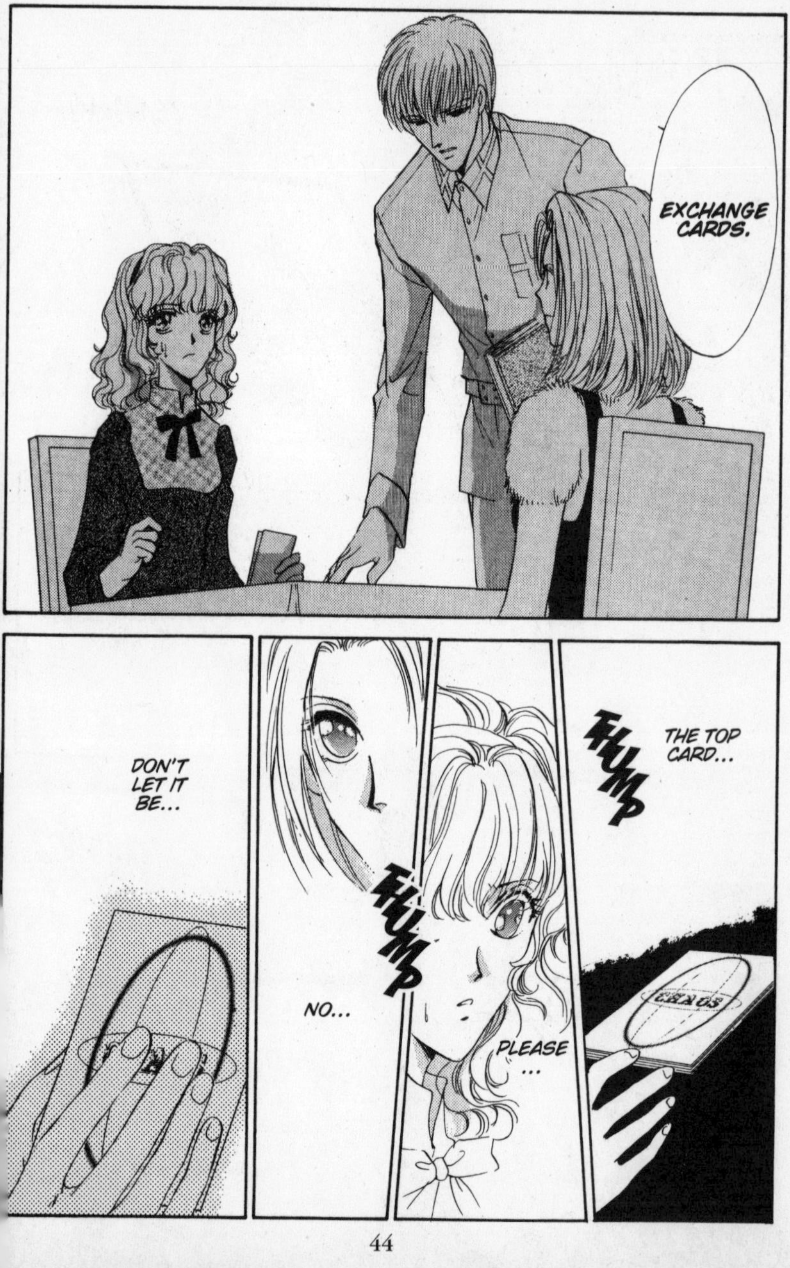
EXCHANGE CARDS.
THUMP
THE TOP CARD...
PLEASE ...
THUMP
NO...
DON'T LET IT BE...

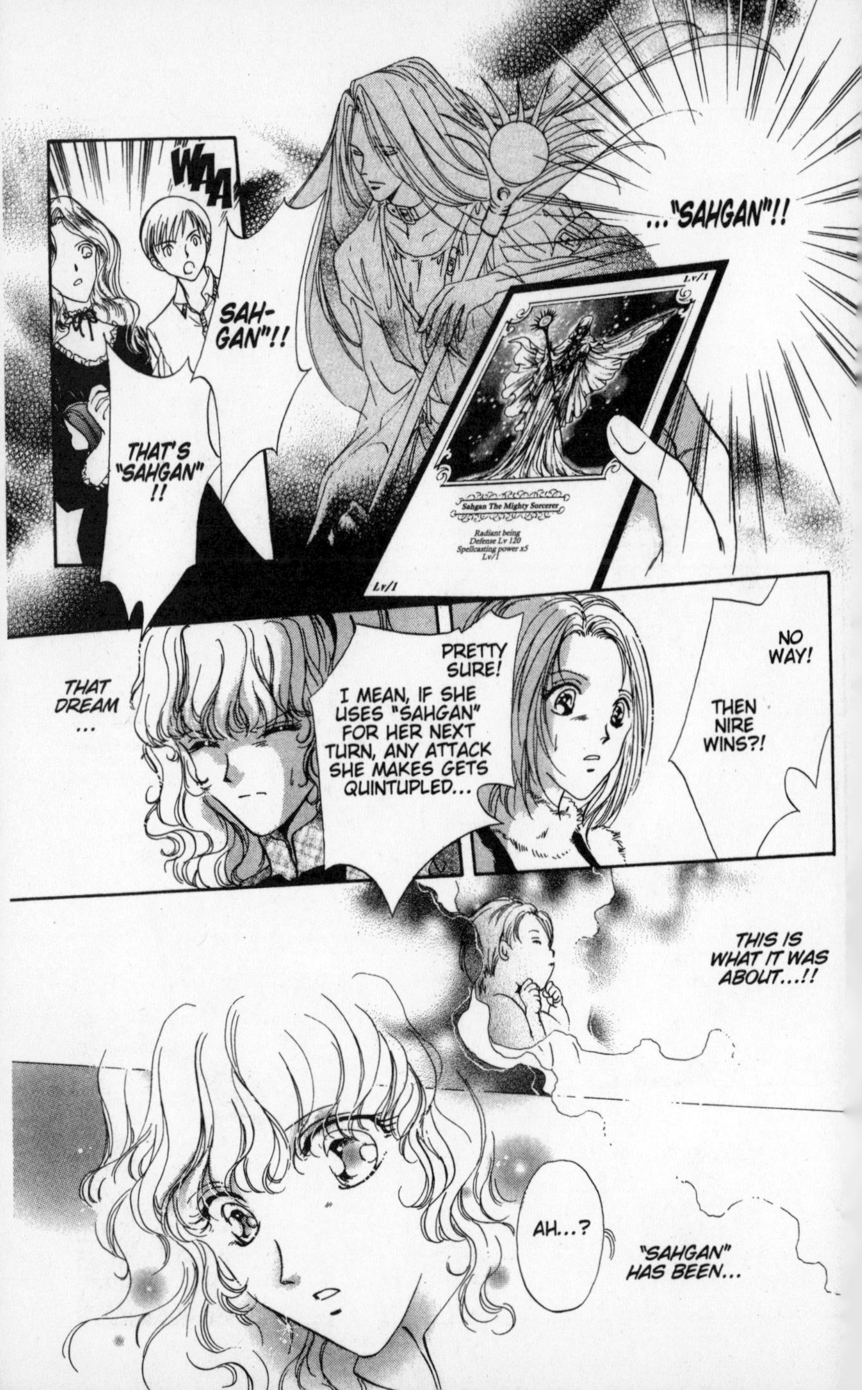
..."SAHGAN"!!
Lv/1
Sahgan The Mighty Sorcerer
Radiant being
Defense Lv 120
Spellcasting power x5
Lv/1
Lv/1
WAA
SAH-GAN"!!
THAT'S "SAHGAN" !!
NO WAY!
THEN NIRE WINS?!
PRETTY SURE!
I MEAN, IF SHE USES "SAHGAN" FOR HER NEXT TURN, ANY ATTACK SHE MAKES GETS QUINTUPLED...
THAT DREAM ...
THIS IS WHAT IT WAS ABOUT...!!
"SAHGAN" HAS BEEN...
AH...?

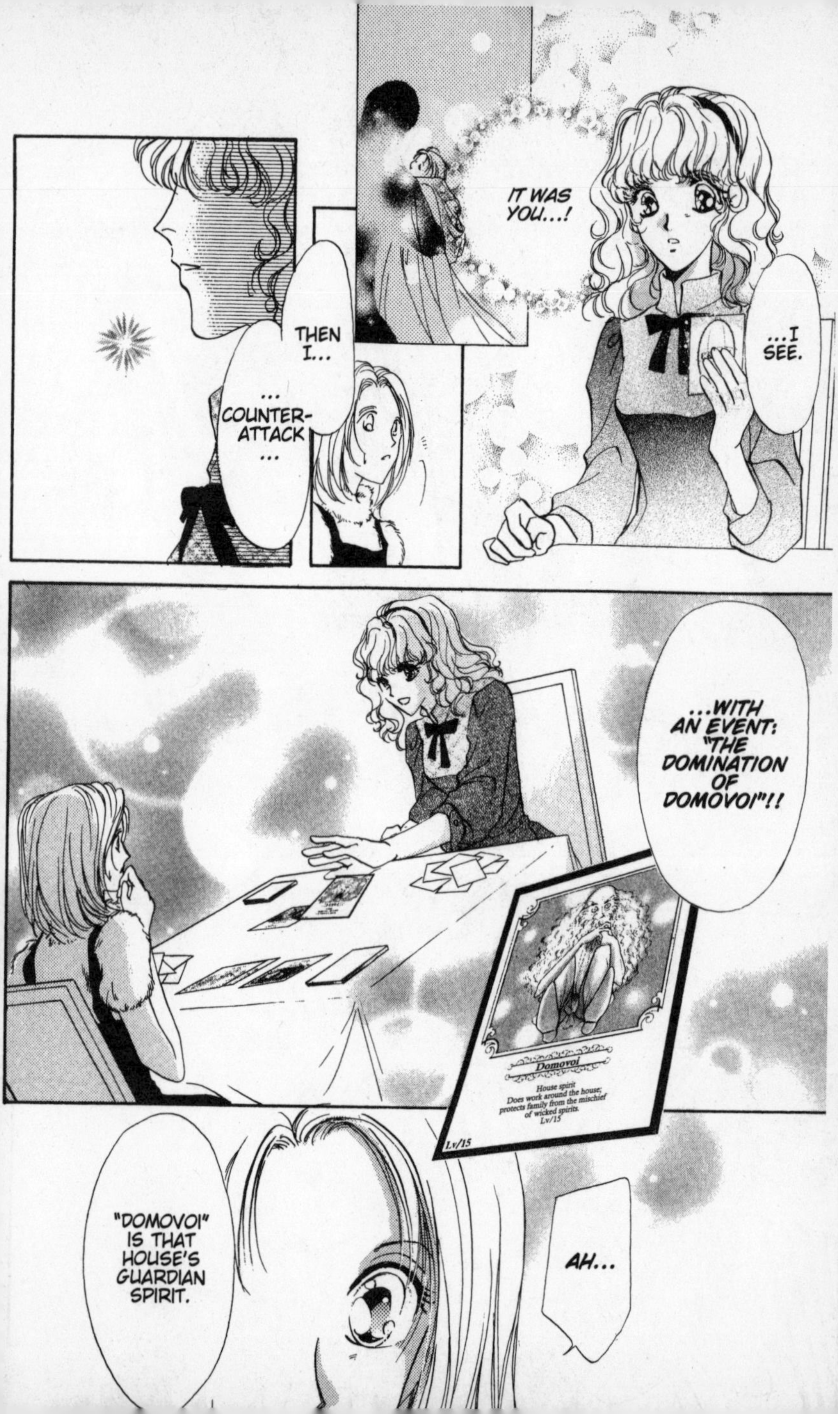
...I SEE.
IT WAS YOU...!
THEN I...
... COUNTER-ATTACK ...
...WITH AN EVENT: "THE DOMINATION OF DOMOVOI"!!
Domovoi
House spirit
Does work around the house; protects family from the mischief of wicked spirits.
Lv/15
Lv/15
AH...
"DOMOVOI" IS THAT HOUSE'S GUARDIAN SPIRIT.

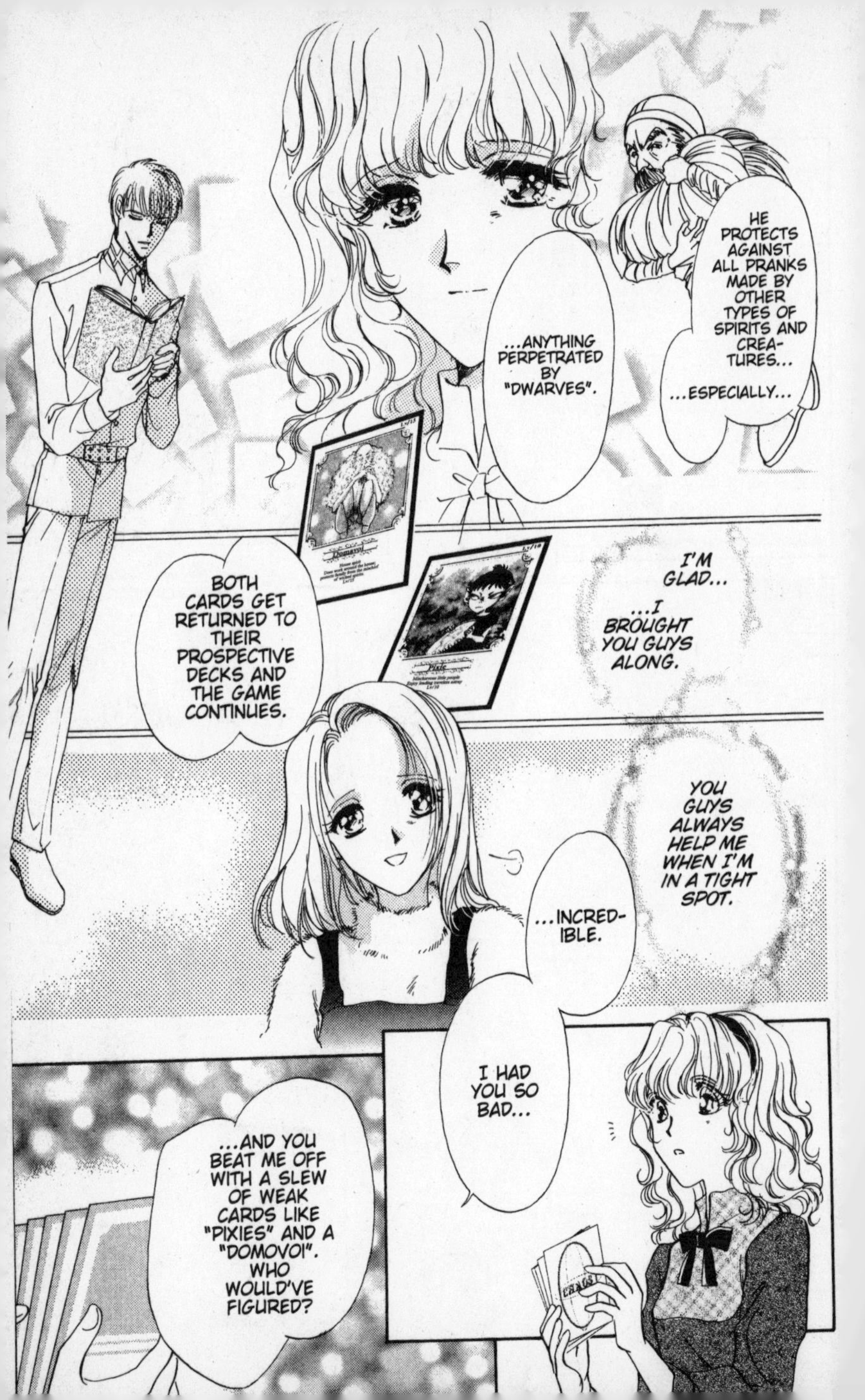
HE PROTECTS AGAINST ALL PRANKS MADE BY OTHER TYPES OF SPIRITS AND CREA-TURES...
...ESPECIALLY...
...ANYTHING PERPETRATED BY "DWARVES".
I'M GLAD...
...I BROUGHT YOU GUYS ALONG.
BOTH CARDS GET RETURNED TO THEIR PROSPECTIVE DECKS AND THE GAME CONTINUES.
YOU GUYS ALWAYS HELP ME WHEN I'M IN A TIGHT SPOT.
...INCRED-IBLE.
I HAD YOU SO BAD...
...AND YOU BEAT ME OFF WITH A SLEW OF WEAK CARDS LIKE "PIXIES" AND A "DOMOVOI". WHO WOULD'VE FIGURED?

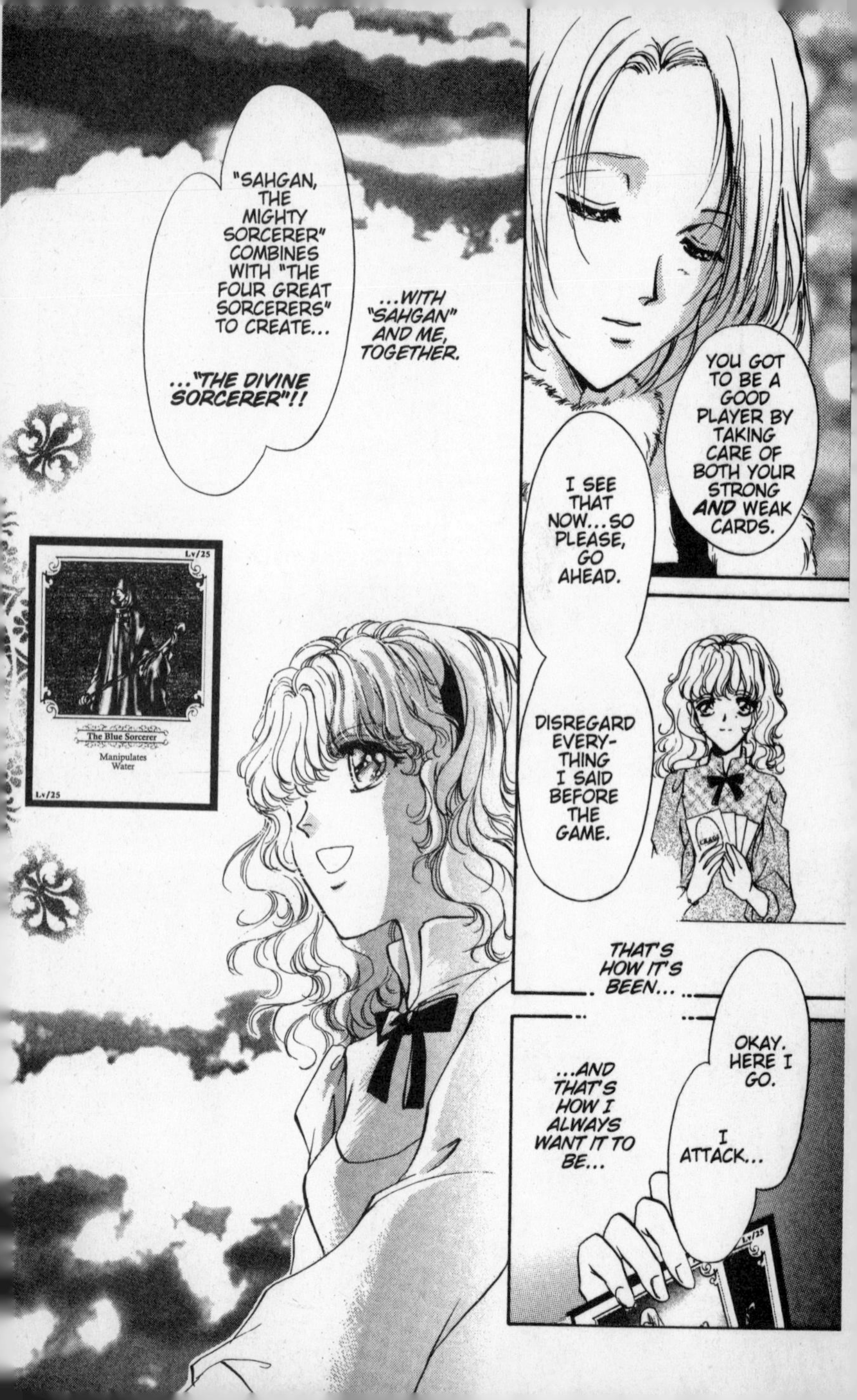
YOU GOT TO BE A GOOD PLAYER BY TAKING CARE OF BOTH YOUR STRONG *AND* WEAK CARDS.
I SEE THAT NOW... SO PLEASE, GO AHEAD.
DISREGARD EVERYTHING I SAID BEFORE THE GAME.
THAT'S HOW IT'S BEEN...
OKAY. HERE I GO.
I ATTACK...
...AND THAT'S HOW I ALWAYS WANT IT TO BE...
"SAHGAN, THE MIGHTY SORCERER" COMBINES WITH "THE FOUR GREAT SORCERERS" TO CREATE...
..."THE DIVINE SORCERER"!!
...WITH "SAHGAN" AND ME, TOGETHER.
Lv/25
The Blue Sorcerer
Manipulates Water
Lv/25

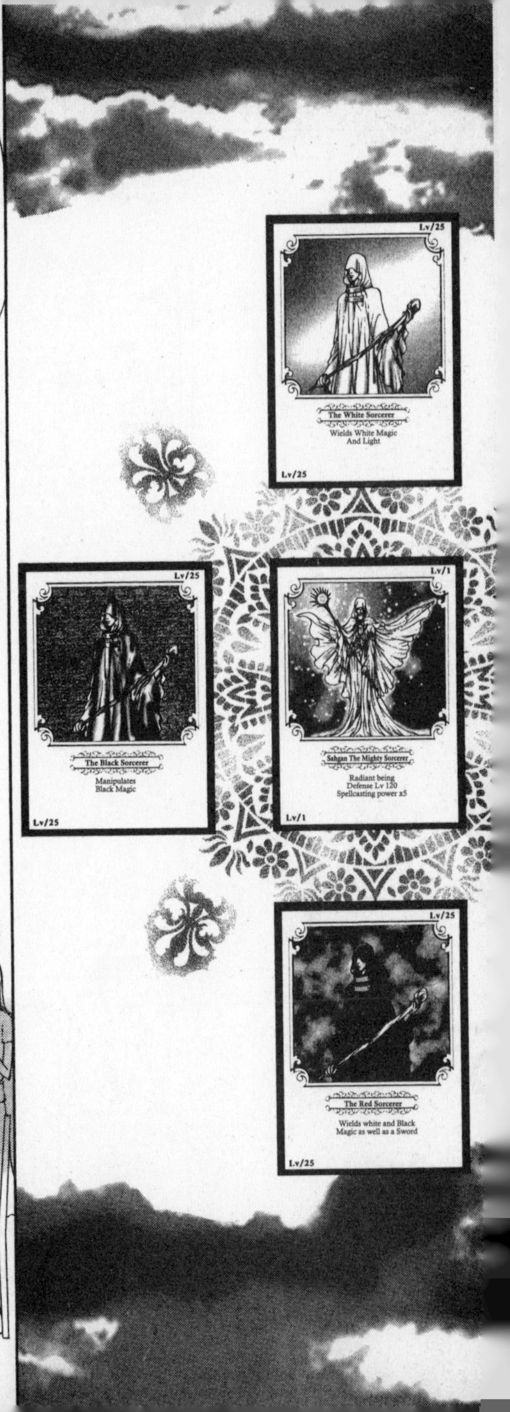
Lv/25
The White Sorcerer
Wields White Magic And Light
Lv/25
Lv/1
Sahgan The Mighty Sorcerer
Radiant being Defense Lv 120 Spellcasting power x5
Lv/1
Lv/25
The Black Sorcerer
Manipulates Black Magic
Lv/25
Lv/25
The Red Sorcerer
Wields white and Black Magic as well as a Sword
Lv/25

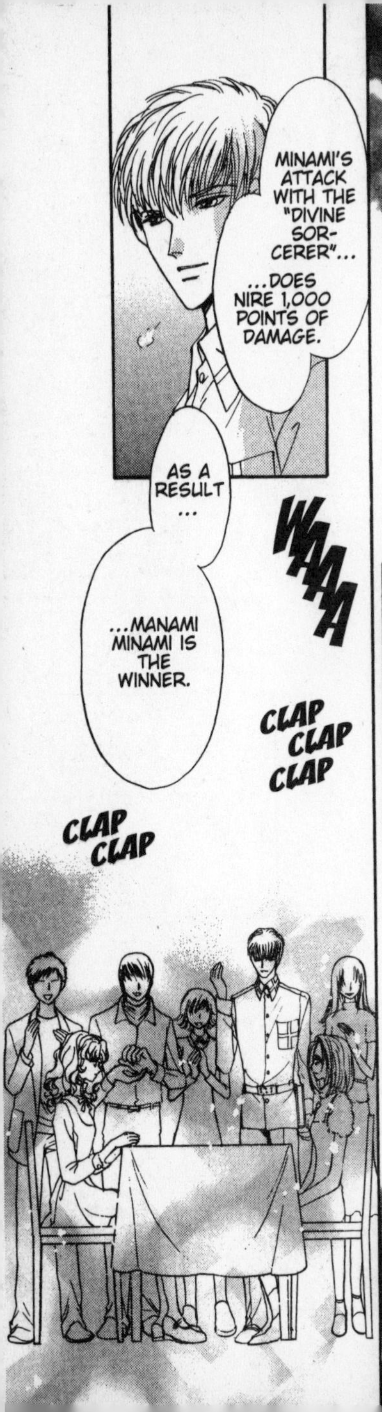
MINAMI'S ATTACK WITH THE "DIVINE SORCERER"...
...DOES NIRE 1,000 POINTS OF DAMAGE.
AS A RESULT...
...MANAMI MINAMI IS THE WINNER.
WAAAA
CLAP CLAP CLAP
CLAP CLAP

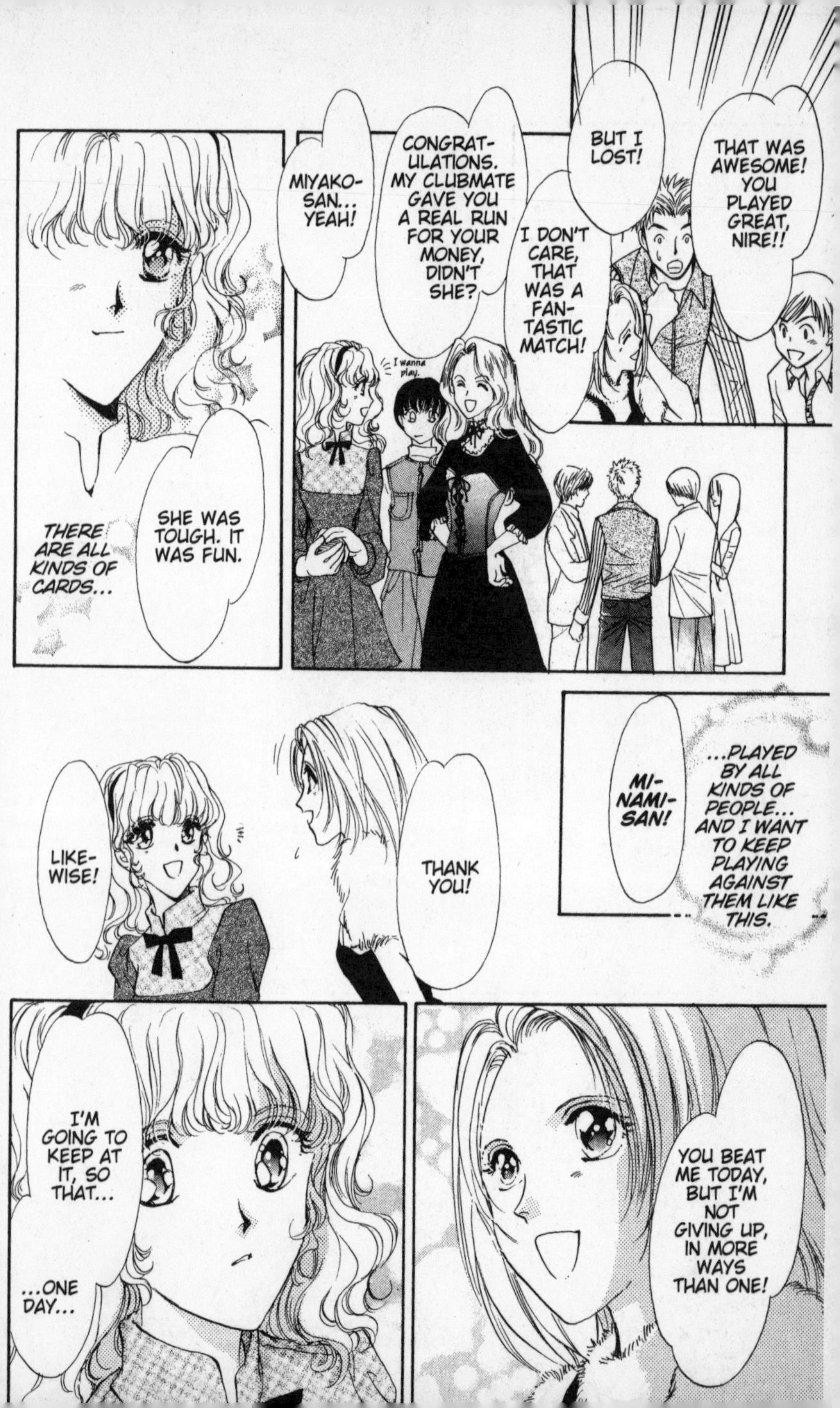
THAT WAS AWESOME! YOU PLAYED GREAT, NIRE!!
BUT I LOST!
I DON'T CARE, THAT WAS A FANTASTIC MATCH!
CONGRATULATIONS. MY CLUBMATE GAVE YOU A REAL RUN FOR YOUR MONEY, DIDN'T SHE?
MIYAKO-SAN... YEAH!
I wanna play.
SHE WAS TOUGH. IT WAS FUN.
THERE ARE ALL KINDS OF CARDS...
MI-NAMI-SAN!
...PLAYED BY ALL KINDS OF PEOPLE... AND I WANT TO KEEP PLAYING AGAINST THEM LIKE THIS.
THANK YOU!
LIKE-WISE!
YOU BEAT ME TODAY, BUT I'M NOT GIVING UP, IN MORE WAYS THAN ONE!
I'M GOING TO KEEP AT IT, SO THAT...
...ONE DAY...

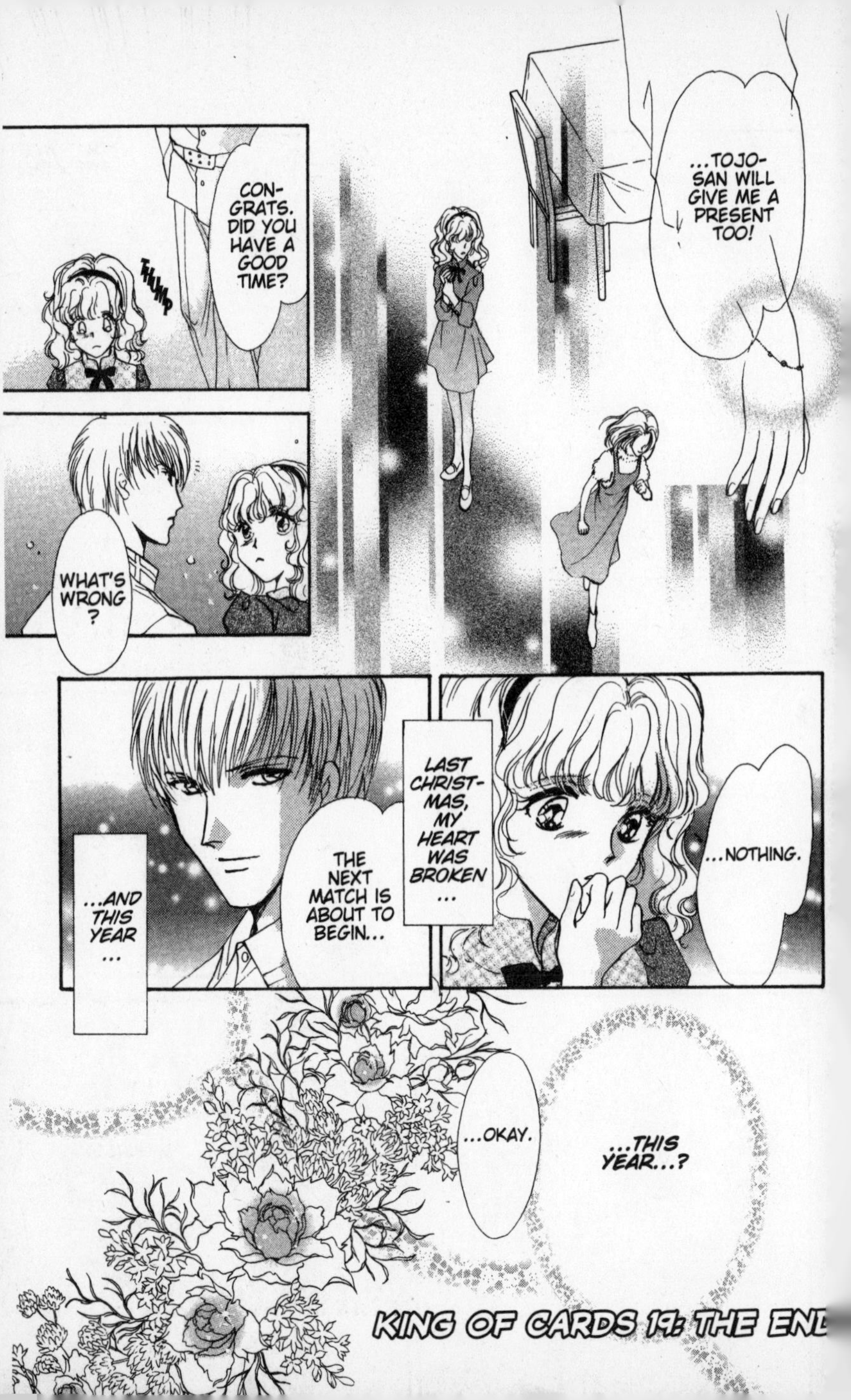
...TOJO-SAN WILL GIVE ME A PRESENT TOO!
CON-GRATS. DID YOU HAVE A GOOD TIME?
THUMP
WHAT'S WRONG?
...NOTHING.
LAST CHRIST-MAS, MY HEART WAS BROKEN...
THE NEXT MATCH IS ABOUT TO BEGIN...
...AND THIS YEAR...
...THIS YEAR...?
...OKAY.
KING OF CARDS 19: THE END

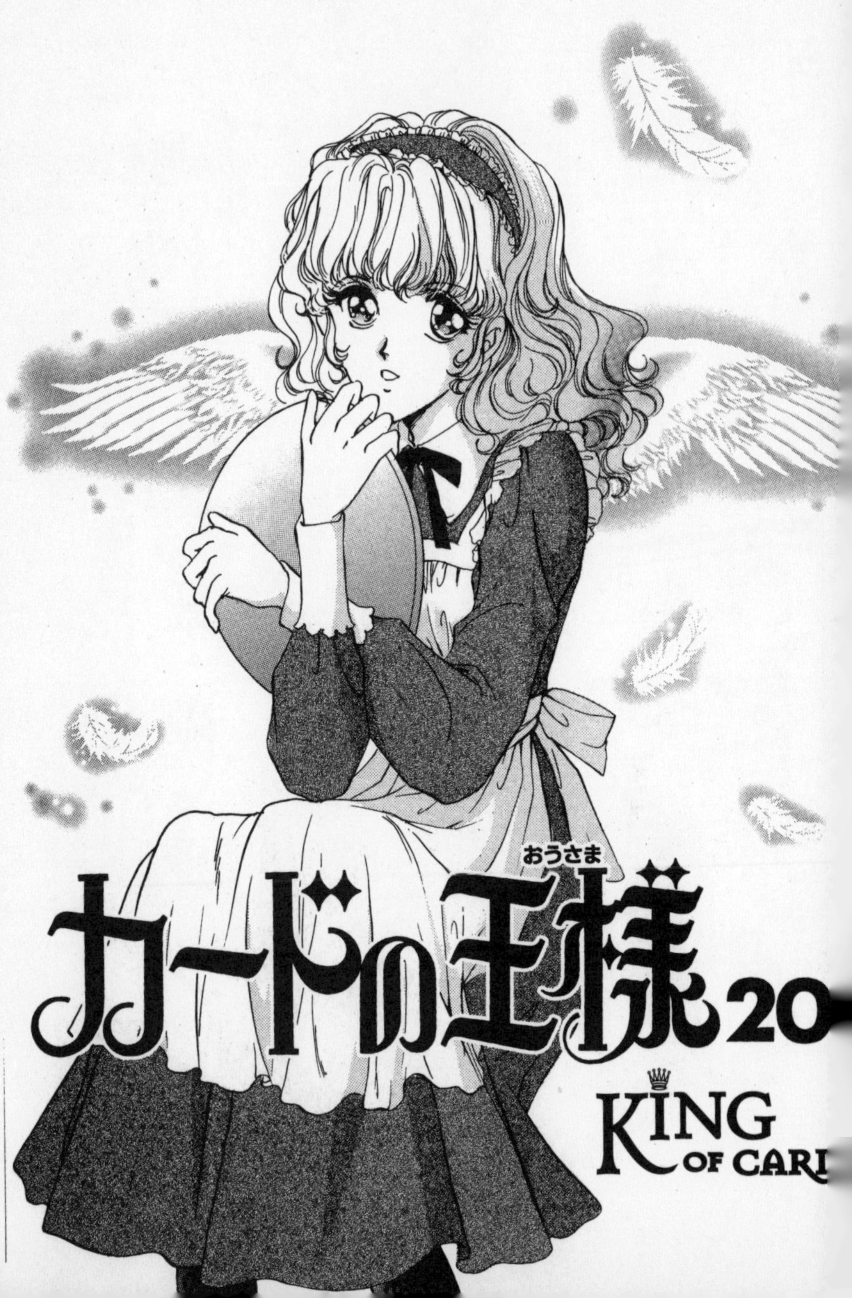
カードの王様(おうさま)20
KING
OF CAR

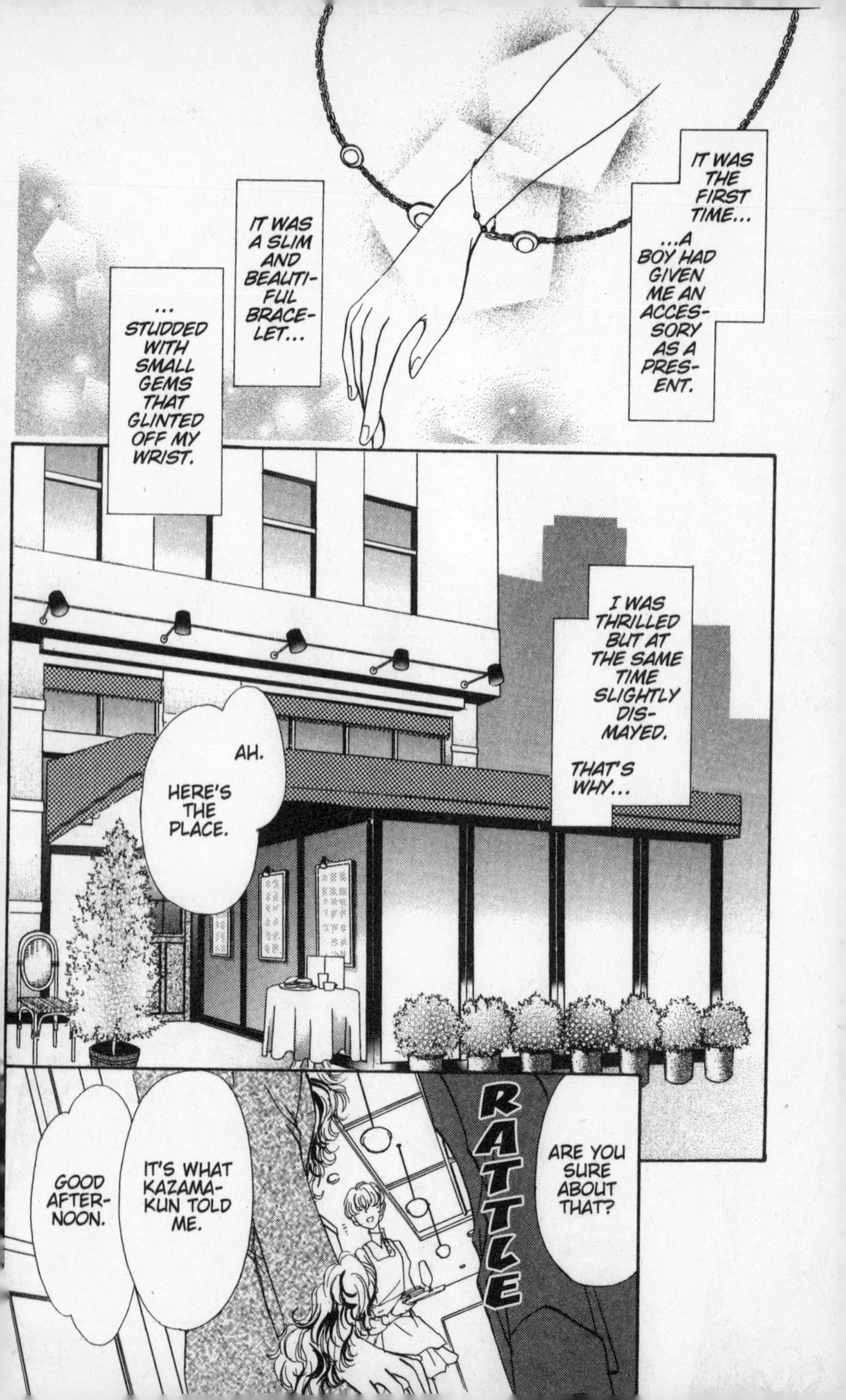
IT WAS THE FIRST TIME...
...A BOY HAD GIVEN ME AN ACCESSORY AS A PRESENT.
IT WAS A SLIM AND BEAUTIFUL BRACELET...
...STUDDED WITH SMALL GEMS THAT GLINTED OFF MY WRIST.
I WAS THRILLED BUT AT THE SAME TIME SLIGHTLY DISMAYED.
THAT'S WHY...
AH.
HERE'S THE PLACE.
ARE YOU SURE ABOUT THAT?
RATTLE
IT'S WHAT KAZAMA-KUN TOLD ME.
GOOD AFTERNOON.

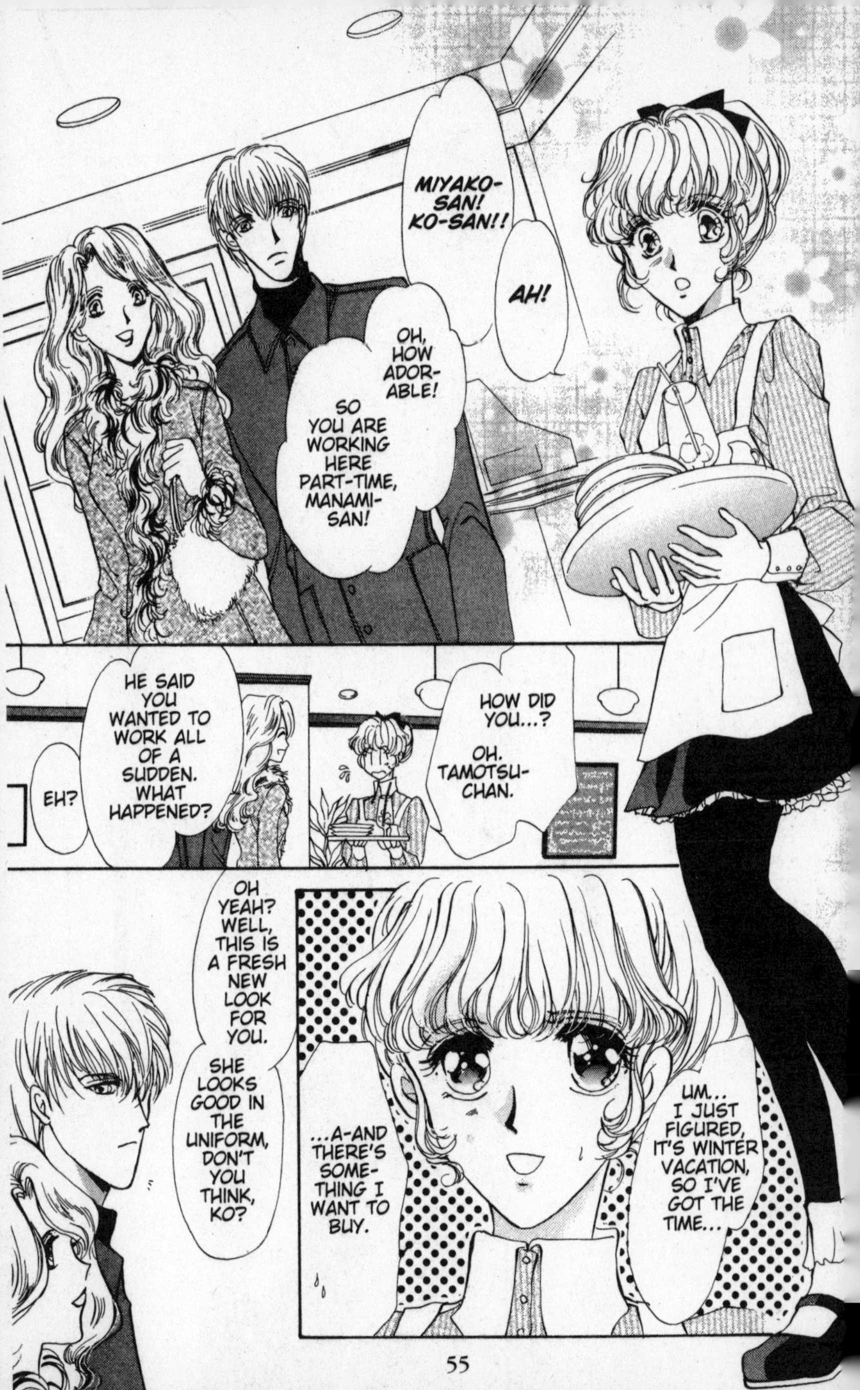

MIYAKO-SAN! KO-SAN!!
AH!
OH, HOW ADORABLE!
SO YOU ARE WORKING HERE PART-TIME, MANAMI-SAN!
HOW DID YOU...?
OH. TAMOTSU-CHAN.
HE SAID YOU WANTED TO WORK ALL OF A SUDDEN. WHAT HAPPENED?
EH?
UM... I JUST FIGURED, IT'S WINTER VACATION, SO I'VE GOT THE TIME...
...A-AND THERE'S SOME-THING I WANT TO BUY.
OH YEAH? WELL, THIS IS A FRESH NEW LOOK FOR YOU.
SHE LOOKS GOOD IN THE UNIFORM, DON'T YOU THINK, KO?

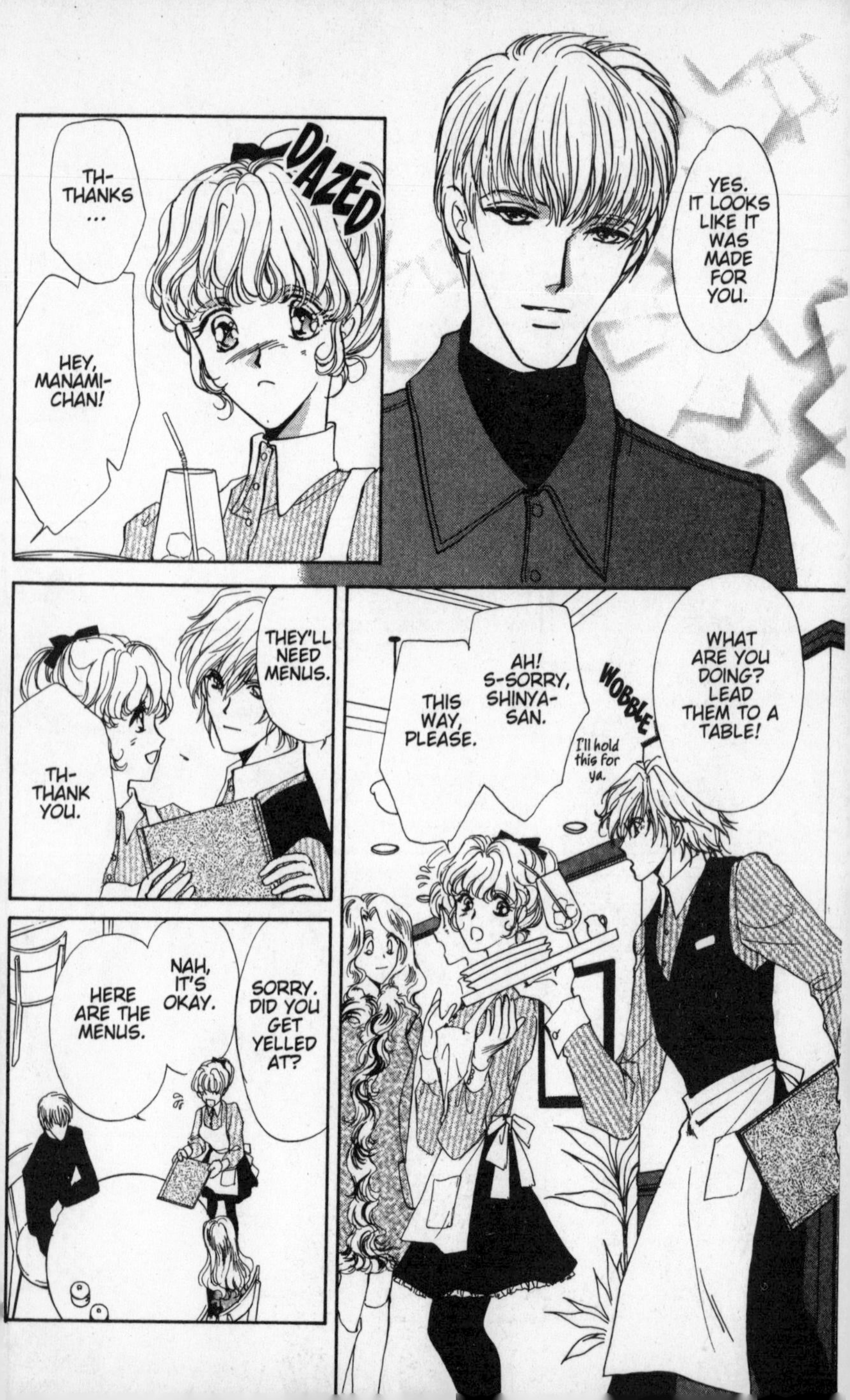
YES. IT LOOKS LIKE IT WAS MADE FOR YOU.
DAZED
TH-THANKS ...
HEY, MANAMI-CHAN!
WHAT ARE YOU DOING? LEAD THEM TO A TABLE!
WOBBLE
I'll hold this for ya.
AH! S-SORRY, SHINYA-SAN.
THIS WAY, PLEASE.
THEY'LL NEED MENUS.
TH-THANK YOU.
SORRY. DID YOU GET YELLED AT?
NAH, IT'S OKAY.
HERE ARE THE MENUS.

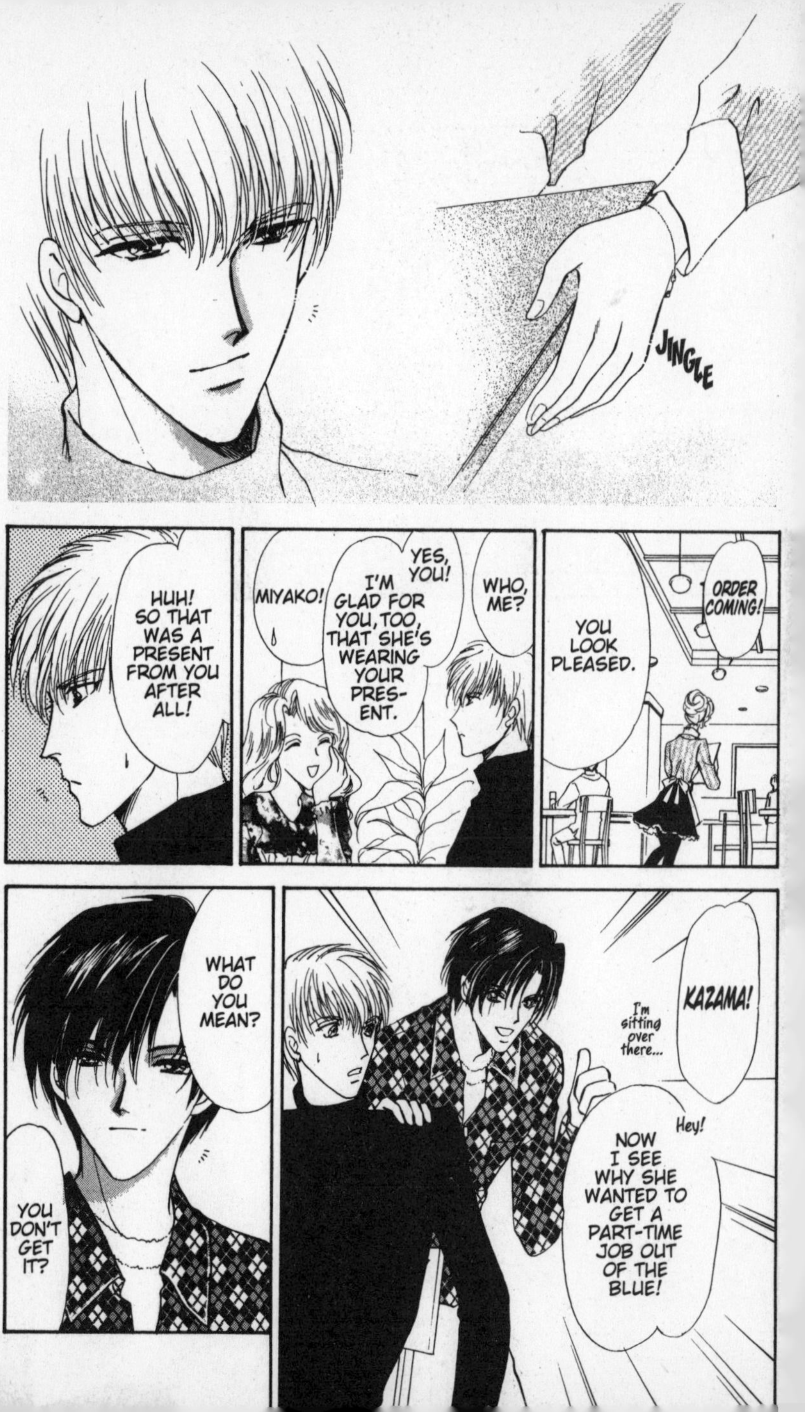
JINGLE
ORDER COMING!
YOU LOOK PLEASED.
WHO, ME?
YES, YOU!
I'M GLAD FOR YOU, TOO, THAT SHE'S WEARING YOUR PRES-ENT.
MIYAKO!
HUH! SO THAT WAS A PRESENT FROM YOU AFTER ALL!
KAZAMA!
I'm sitting over there...
Hey!
NOW I SEE WHY SHE WANTED TO GET A PART-TIME JOB OUT OF THE BLUE!
WHAT DO YOU MEAN?
YOU DON'T GET IT?

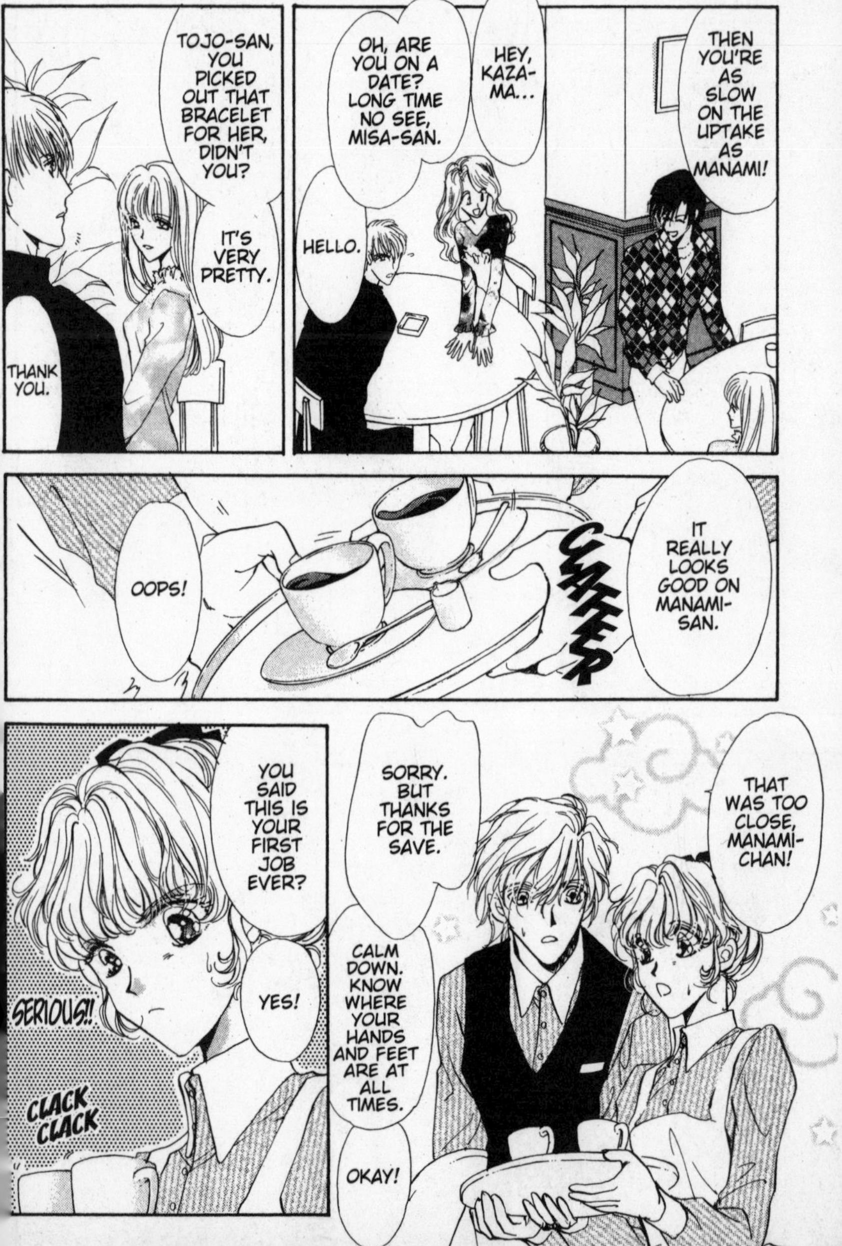
THEN YOU'RE AS SLOW ON THE UPTAKE AS MANAMI!
HEY, KAZAMA-MA...
OH, ARE YOU ON A DATE? LONG TIME NO SEE, MISA-SAN.
HELLO.
TOJO-SAN, YOU PICKED OUT THAT BRACELET FOR HER, DIDN'T YOU?
IT'S VERY PRETTY.
THANK YOU.
IT REALLY LOOKS GOOD ON MANAMI-SAN.
CLATTER
OOPS!
THAT WAS TOO CLOSE, MANAMI-CHAN!
SORRY. BUT THANKS FOR THE SAVE.
CALM DOWN. KNOW WHERE YOUR HANDS AND FEET ARE AT ALL TIMES.
OKAY!
YOU SAID THIS IS YOUR FIRST JOB EVER?
YES!
SERIOUS!!
CLACK CLACK

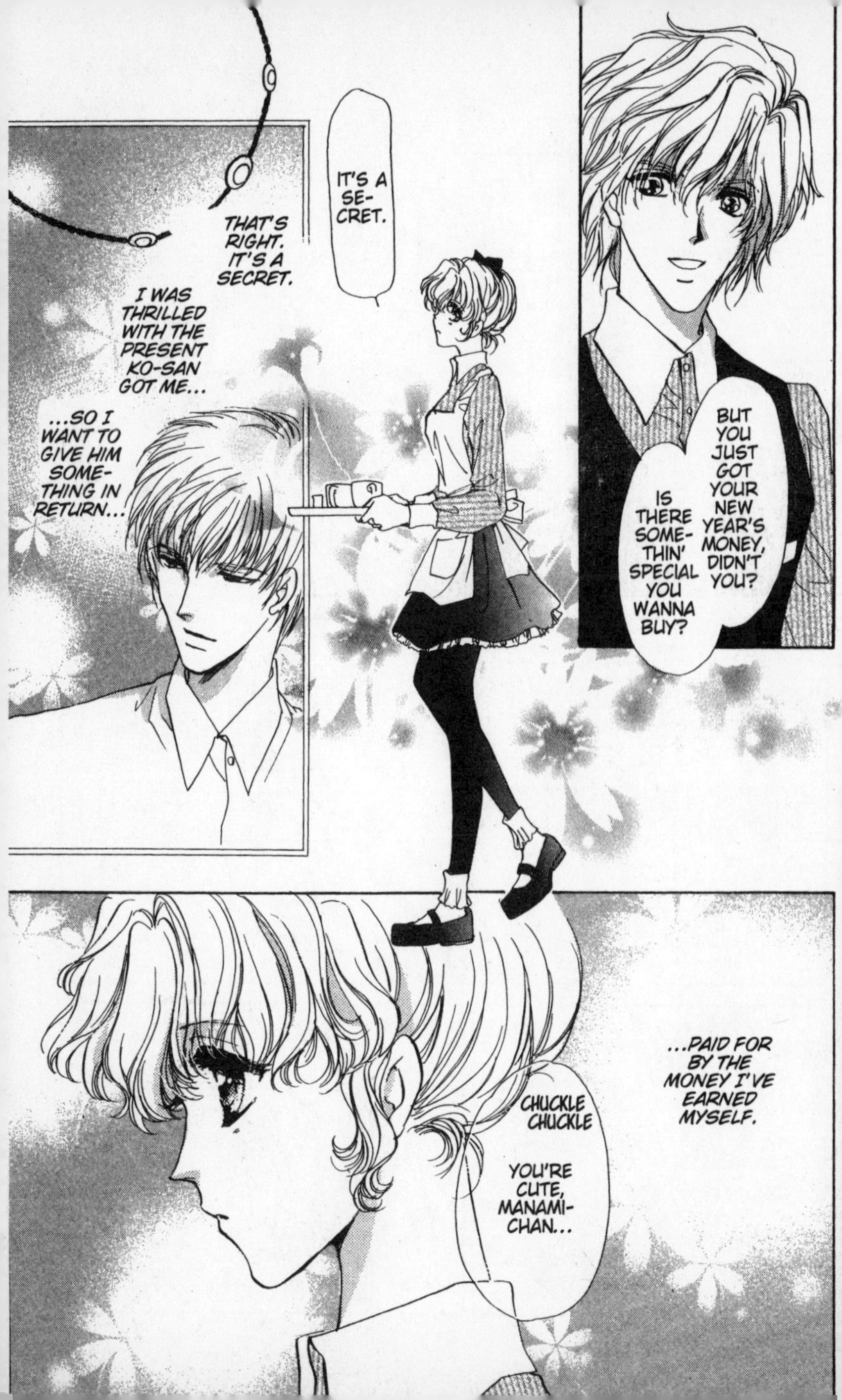
BUT YOU JUST GOT YOUR NEW YEAR'S MONEY, DIDN'T YOU?
IS THERE SOME-THIN' SPECIAL YOU WANNA BUY?
IT'S A SE-CRET.
THAT'S RIGHT. IT'S A SECRET.
I WAS THRILLED WITH THE PRESENT KO-SAN GOT ME...
...SO I WANT TO GIVE HIM SOME-THING IN RETURN...
...PAID FOR BY THE MONEY I'VE EARNED MYSELF.
CHUCKLE CHUCKLE
YOU'RE CUTE, MANAMI-CHAN...

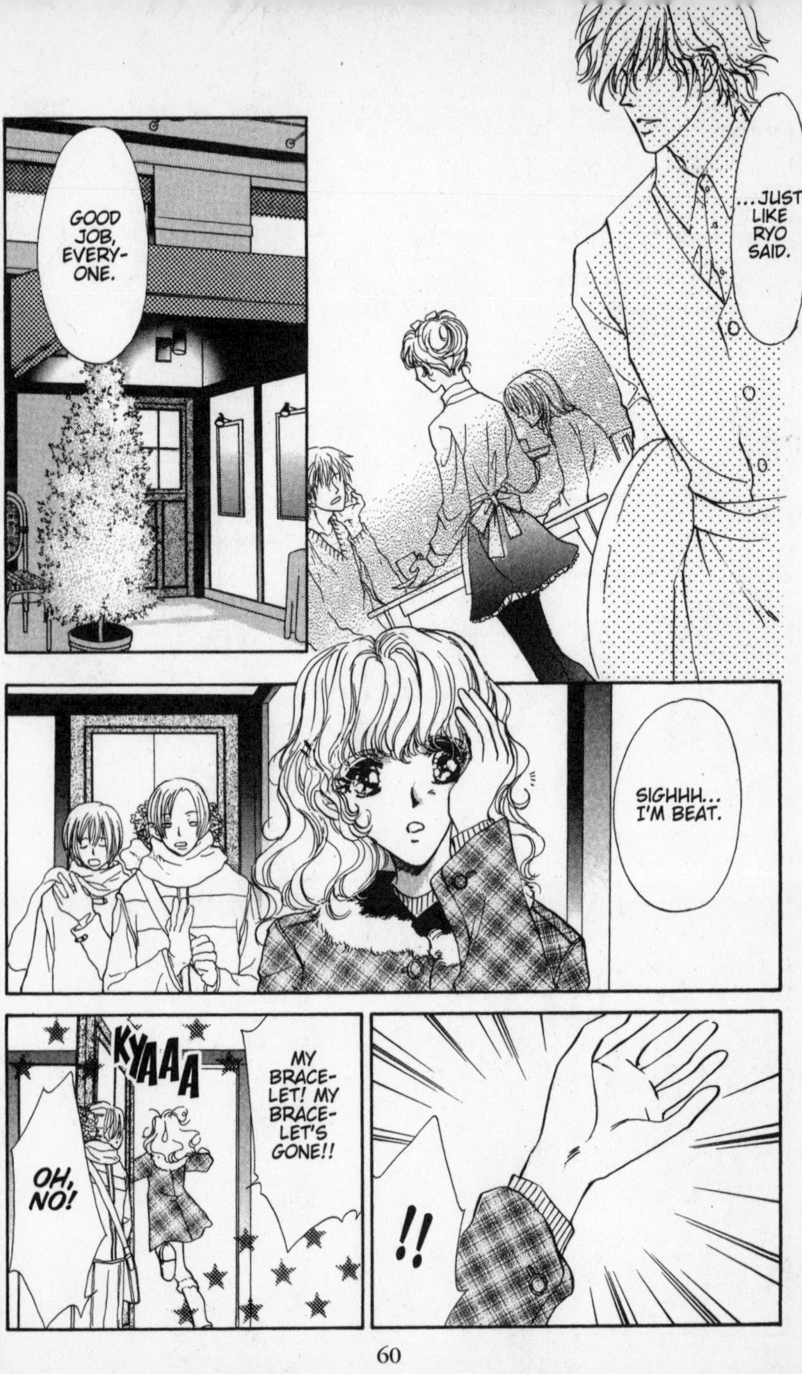
...JUST LIKE RYO SAID.
GOOD JOB, EVERY-ONE.
SIGHHH... I'M BEAT.
!!
MY BRACE-LET! MY BRACE-LET'S GONE!!
KYAAA
OH, NO!

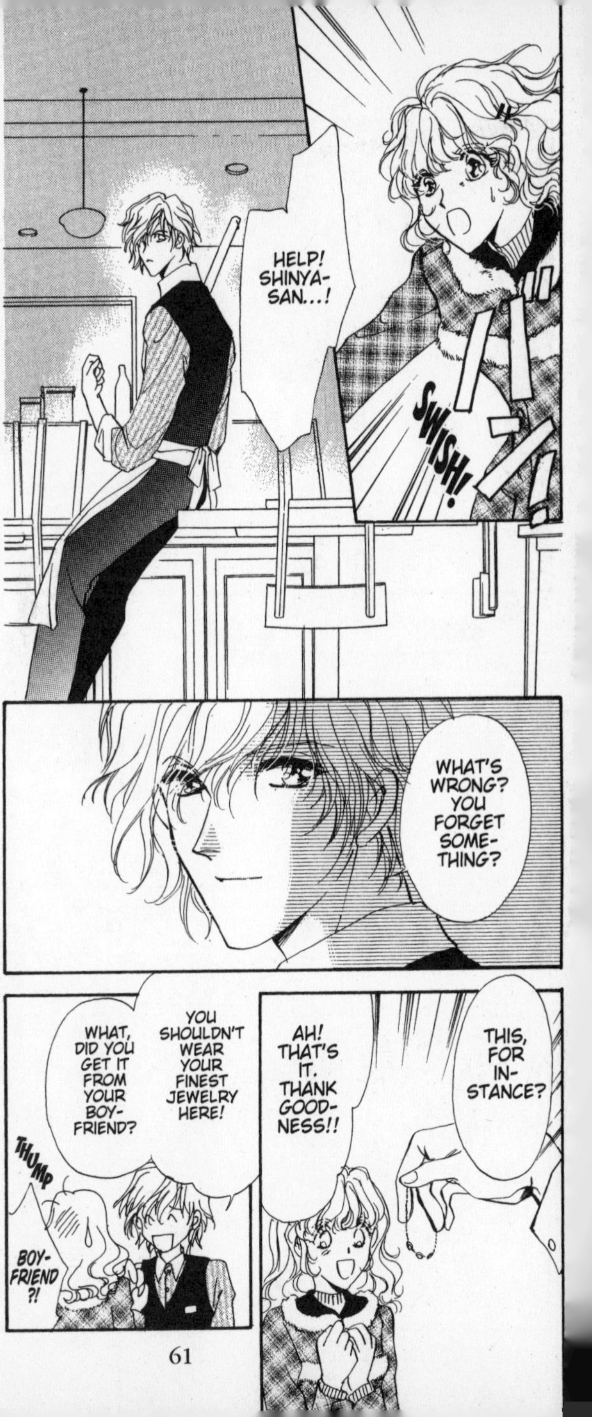
HELP! SHINYA-SAN...!
SWISH!
WHAT'S WRONG? YOU FORGET SOME-THING?
THIS, FOR IN-STANCE?
AH! THAT'S IT. THANK GOOD-NESS!!
YOU SHOULDN'T WEAR YOUR FINEST JEWELRY HERE!
WHAT, DID YOU GET IT FROM YOUR BOY-FRIEND?
THUMP
BOY-FRIEND?!

NEIGHBORHOOD REPORT

LAST TIME AROUND, I RELATED THE STORY OF MY NEIGHBORS AND HOW THE POLICE CAME TO THEIR DOOR IN THE MIDDLE OF THE NIGHT, BUT I'VE COME TO REALIZE THAT THERE ARE A LOT OF FIGHTS IN MY AREA, SPECIFICALLY ON MY STREET.

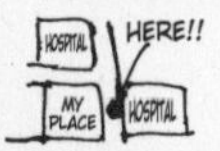
HOSPITAL
HERE!!
MY PLACE
HOSPITAL

THE STREET RUNNING BY MY BUILDING IS VERY NARROW BUT A LOT OF CARS USE THE STREET. MAYBE THAT'S THE REASON FOR THE HIGH NUMBER OF COLLISIONS AND RESULTANT ARGUMENTS BETWEEN DRIVERS/PASSENGERS. ALSO, THERE'S A BENCH IN FRONT OF ONE OF THE HOSPITALS. MAYBE BECAUSE OF THAT, COUPLES SIT DOWN AND SQUABBLE OR OLD DRUNK GUYS FIGHT ON THE WAY HOME FROM EATING SUSHI. IT'S COMMON FOR ME TO HEAR ANGRY SHOUTING IN THE MIDDLE OF THE NIGHT. THAT, AND CHILDREN'S LAUGHTER. ONCE THE LAUGHTER WAS SO HIGH-PITCHED THAT I THOUGHT IT WAS COMING FROM SOME KIND OF GHOST, BUT WHEN I LOOKED OUTSIDE, I SAW THAT IT WAS JUST A KID, RUNNING AND PLAYING IN THE STREET... ***I WAS SCARED!!***

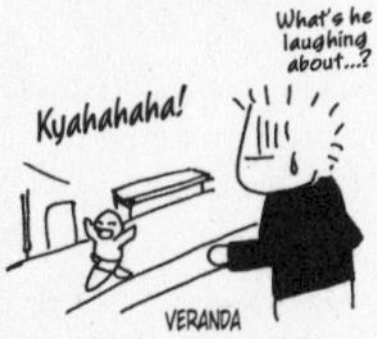
What's he laughing about...?
Kyahahaha!
VERANDA

WHAT WAS HE LAUGHING ABOUT WHILE RUNNING ALONE?! WHAT WAS FUNNY ABOUT IT?!? CERTAINLY, I HAVE MEMORIES OF LAUGHING WHILE RUNNING AS A KID, EVEN THOUGH I DON'T REMEMBER WHAT WAS FUNNY AT THE TIME. BUT ANYWAY, WHOSE KID WAS HE? IT WAS AFTER MIDNIGHT! WAS HE REALLY A GHOST? THOSE ARE THE QUESTIONS I ASKED MYSELF WITH A SHIVER THAT NIGHT.

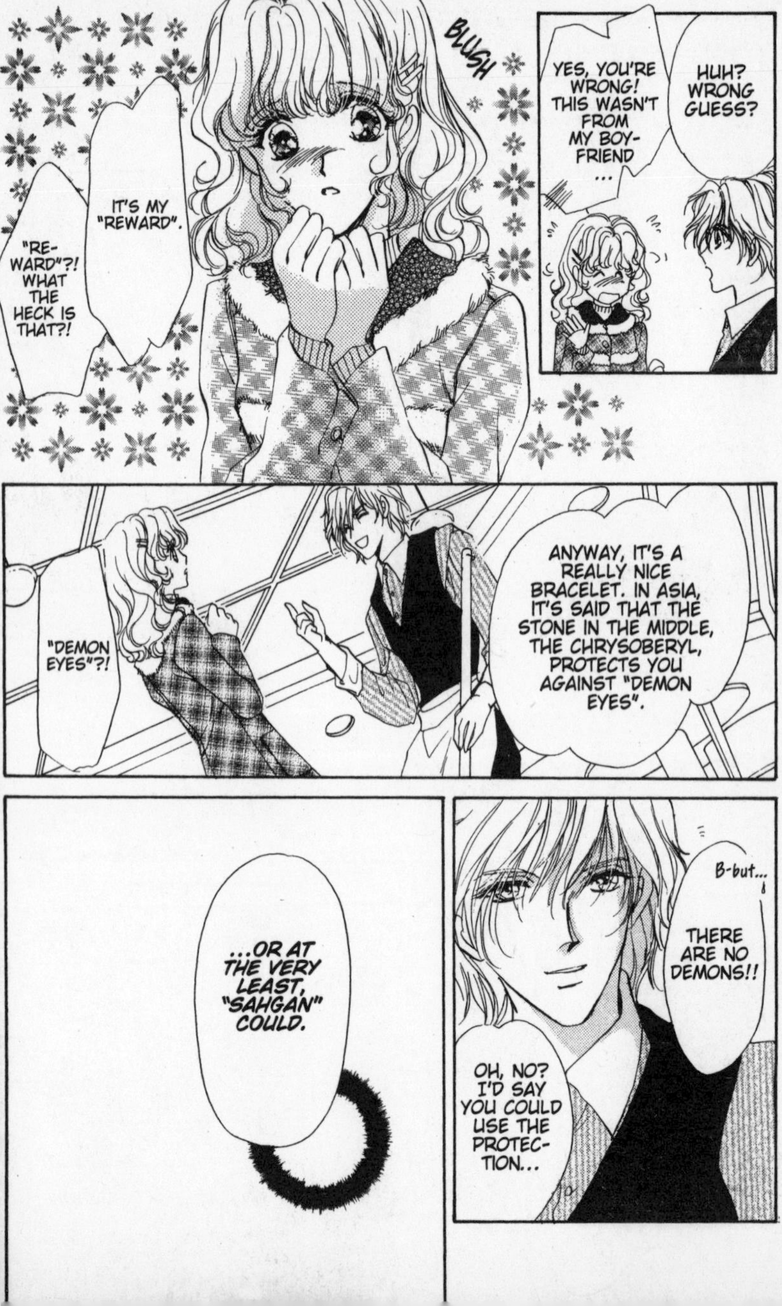
HUH? WRONG GUESS?
YES, YOU'RE WRONG! THIS WASN'T FROM MY BOY-FRIEND ...
BLUSH
IT'S MY "REWARD".
"RE-WARD"?! WHAT THE HECK IS THAT?!
ANYWAY, IT'S A REALLY NICE BRACELET. IN ASIA, IT'S SAID THAT THE STONE IN THE MIDDLE, THE CHRYSOBERYL, PROTECTS YOU AGAINST "DEMON EYES".
"DEMON EYES"?!
B-but...
THERE ARE NO DEMONS!!
OH, NO? I'D SAY YOU COULD USE THE PROTEC-TION...
...OR AT THE VERY LEAST, "SAHGAN" COULD.

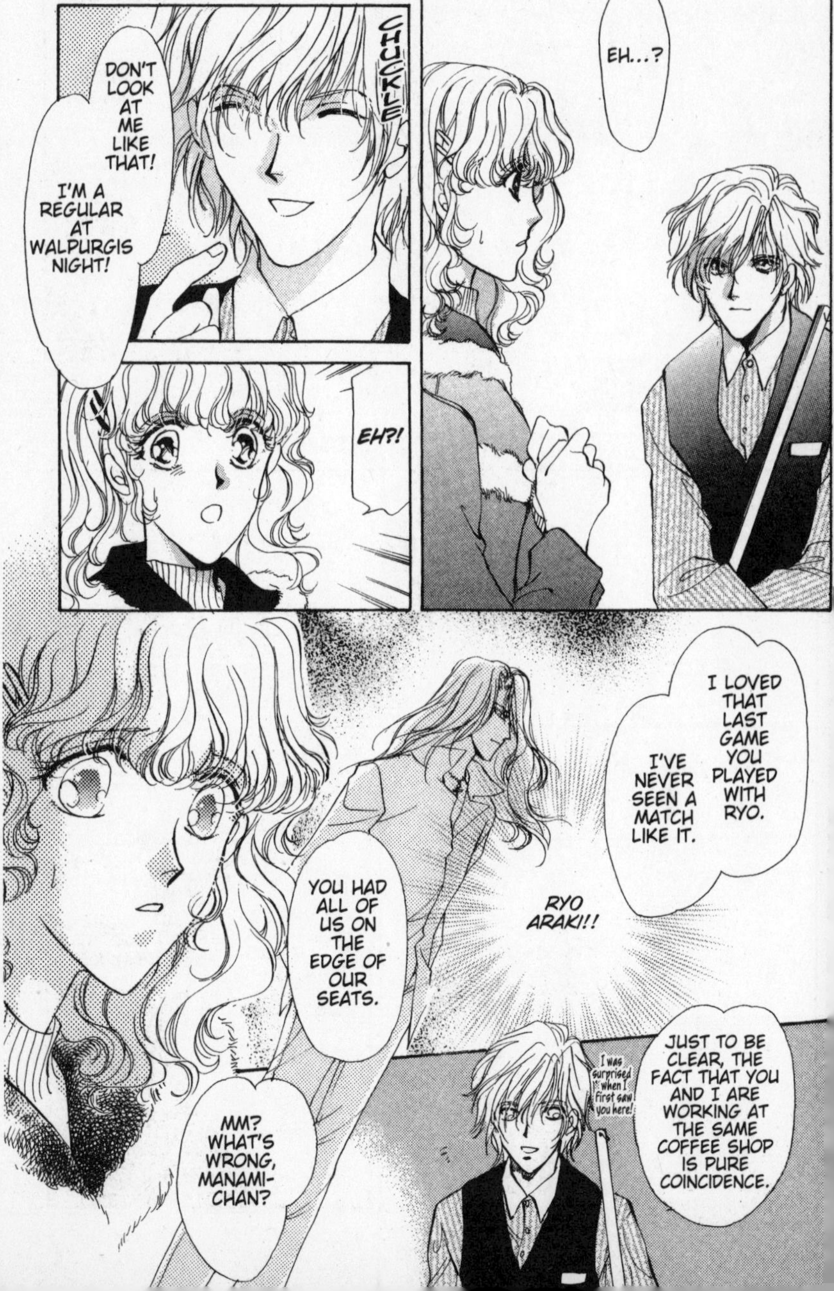
EH...?
DON'T LOOK AT ME LIKE THAT!
I'M A REGULAR AT WALPURGIS NIGHT!
CHUCKLE
EH?!
I LOVED THAT LAST GAME YOU PLAYED WITH RYO.
I'VE NEVER SEEN A MATCH LIKE IT.
RYO ARAKI!!
YOU HAD ALL OF US ON THE EDGE OF OUR SEATS.
JUST TO BE CLEAR, THE FACT THAT YOU AND I ARE WORKING AT THE SAME COFFEE SHOP IS PURE COINCIDENCE.
I was surprised when I first saw you here!
MM? WHAT'S WRONG, MANAMI-CHAN?

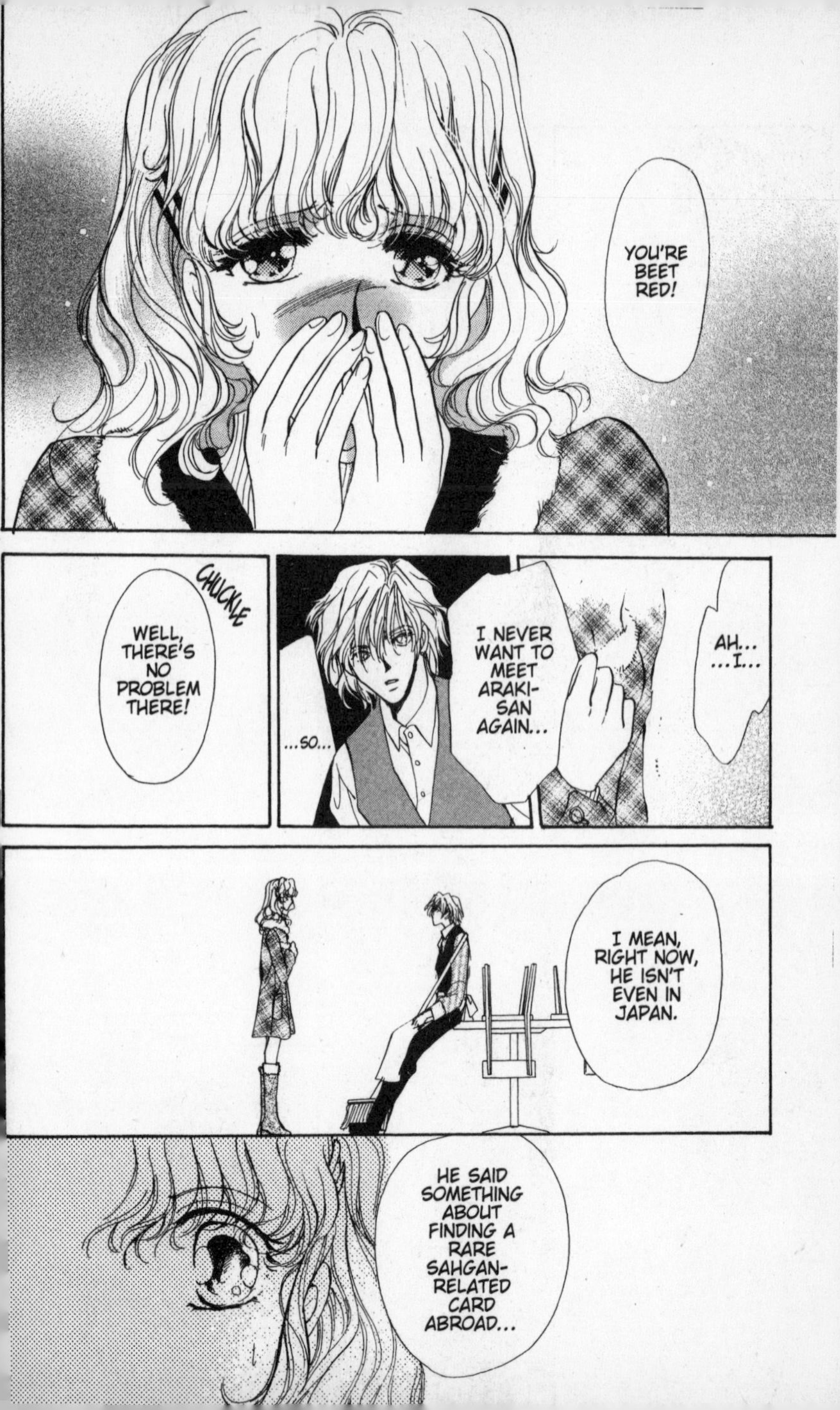
YOU'RE BEET RED!
AH... ...I...
I NEVER WANT TO MEET ARAKI-SAN AGAIN...
...SO...
CHUCKLE
WELL, THERE'S NO PROBLEM THERE!
I MEAN, RIGHT NOW, HE ISN'T EVEN IN JAPAN.
HE SAID SOMETHING ABOUT FINDING A RARE SAHGAN-RELATED CARD ABROAD...

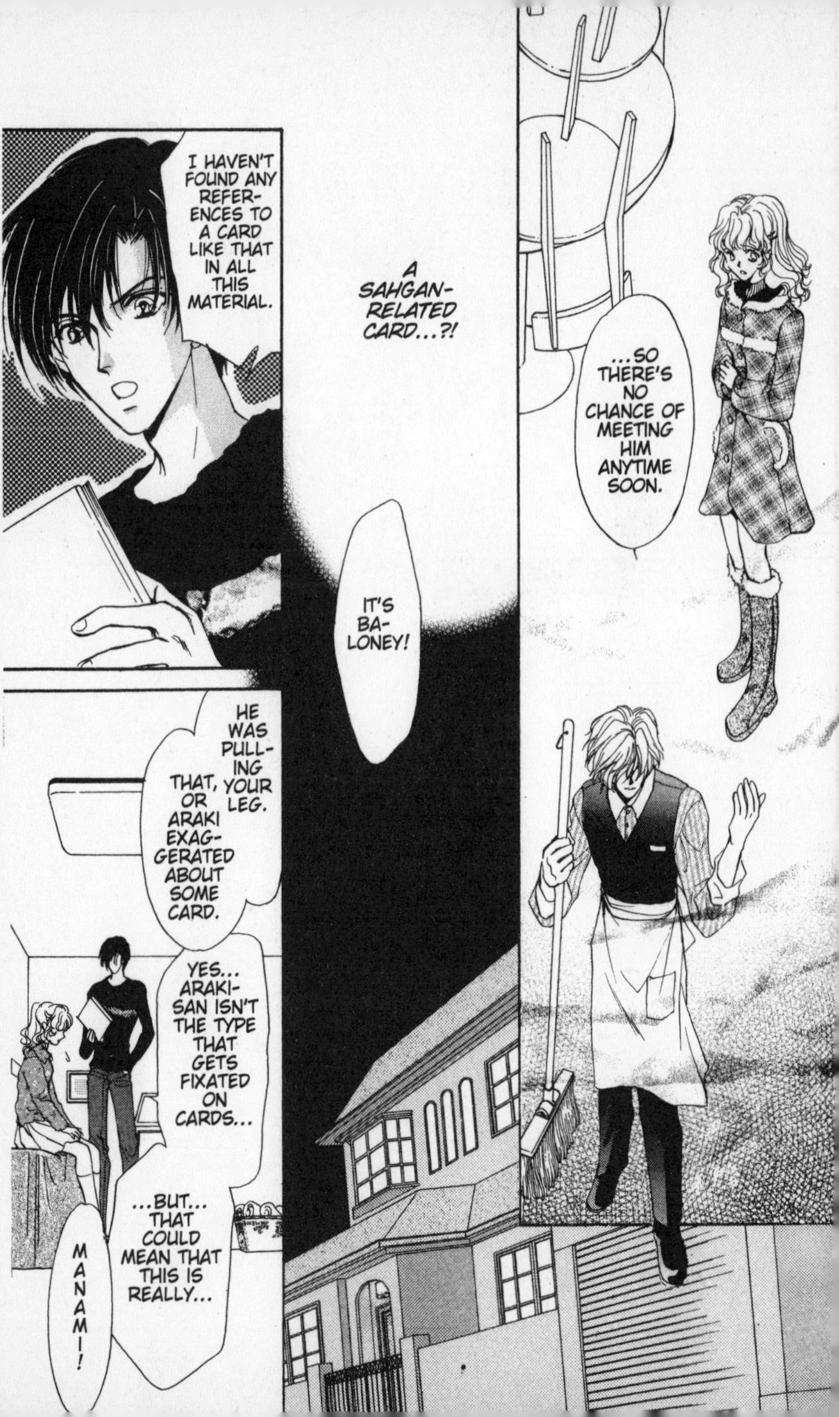
...SO THERE'S NO CHANCE OF MEETING HIM ANYTIME SOON.
A SAHGAN-RELATED CARD...?!
I HAVEN'T FOUND ANY REFERENCES TO A CARD LIKE THAT IN ALL THIS MATERIAL.
IT'S BALONEY!
HE WAS PULLING YOUR LEG.
THAT, OR ARAKI EXAGGERATED ABOUT SOME CARD.
YES... ARAKI-SAN ISN'T THE TYPE THAT GETS FIXATED ON CARDS...
...BUT... THAT COULD MEAN THAT THIS IS REALLY...
MANAMI!

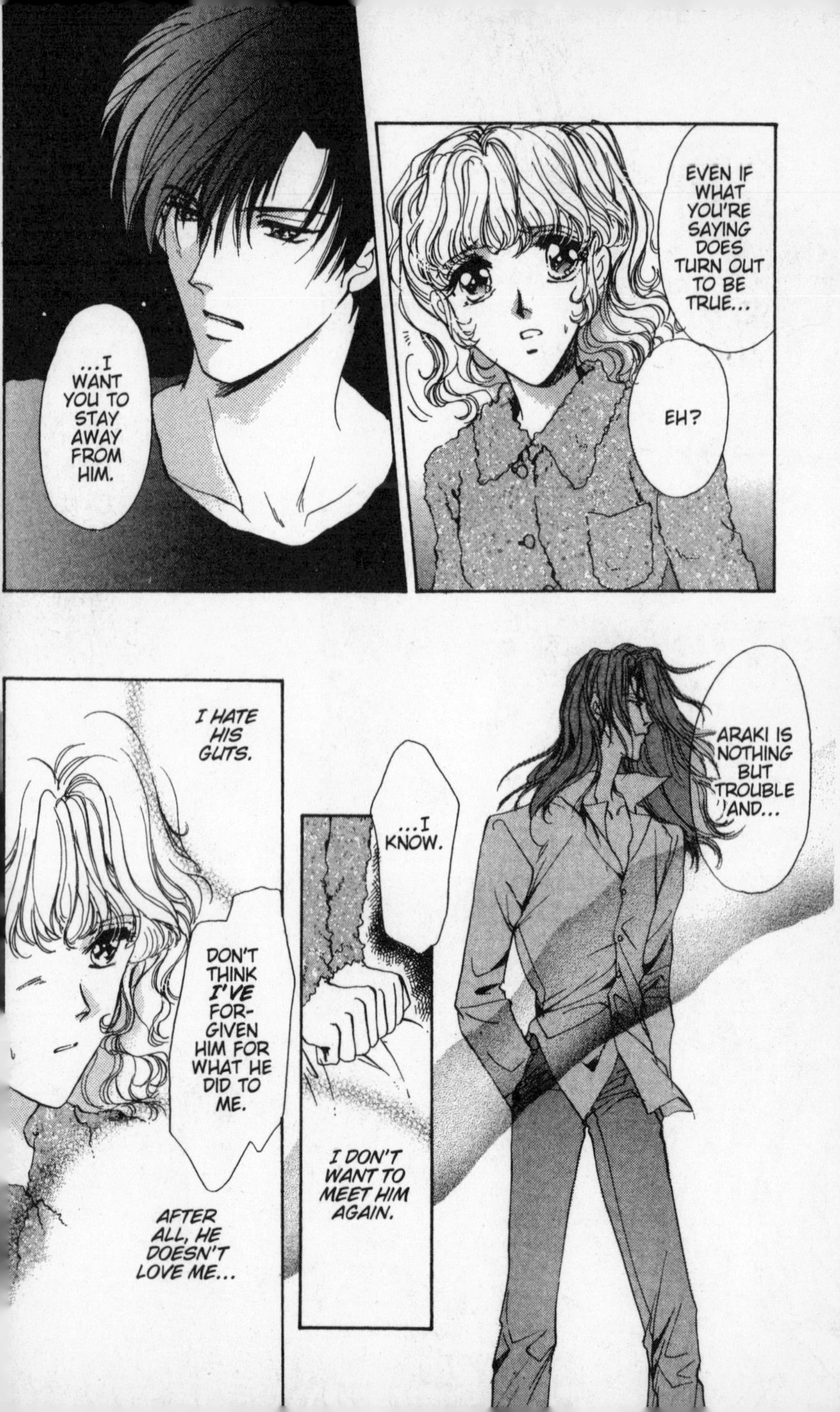
EVEN IF WHAT YOU'RE SAYING DOES TURN OUT TO BE TRUE...
EH?
...I WANT YOU TO STAY AWAY FROM HIM.
ARAKI IS NOTHING BUT TROUBLE AND...
...I KNOW.
I DON'T WANT TO MEET HIM AGAIN.
I HATE HIS GUTS.
DON'T THINK *I'VE* FORGIVEN HIM FOR WHAT HE DID TO ME.
AFTER ALL, HE DOESN'T LOVE ME...

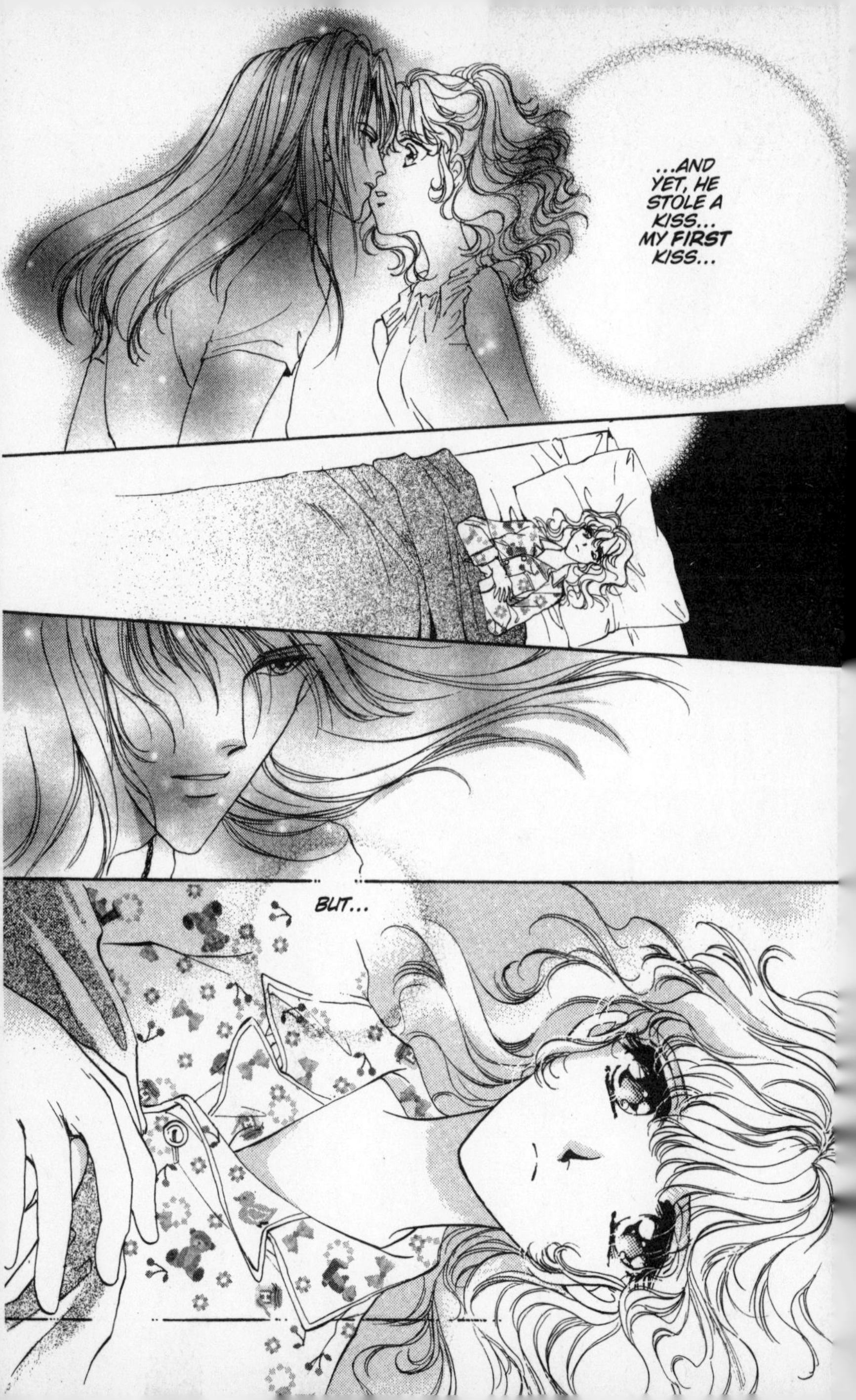
...AND YET, HE STOLE A KISS... MY FIRST KISS...
BUT...

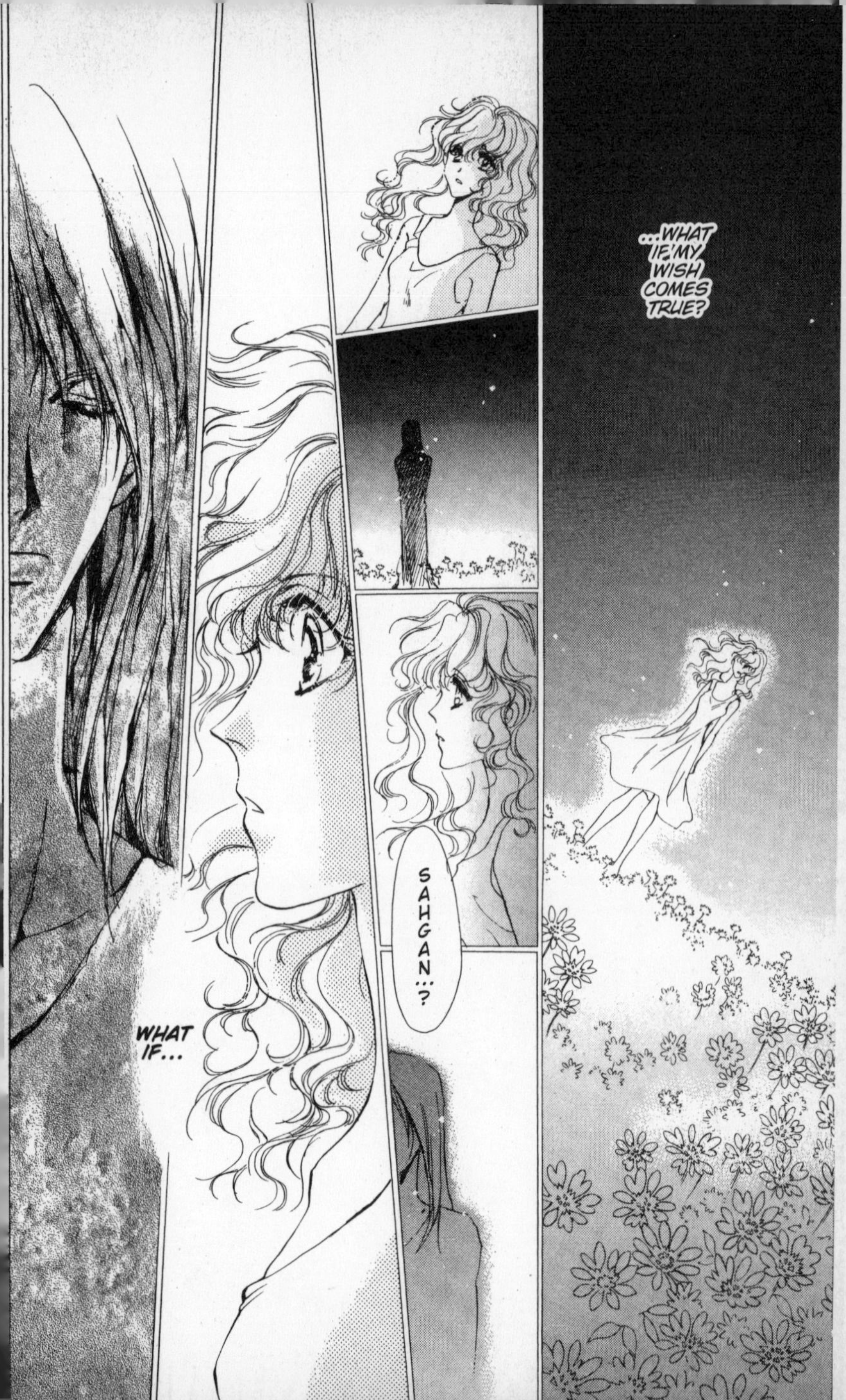
...WHAT IF MY WISH COMES TRUE?
SAHGAN...?
WHAT IF...

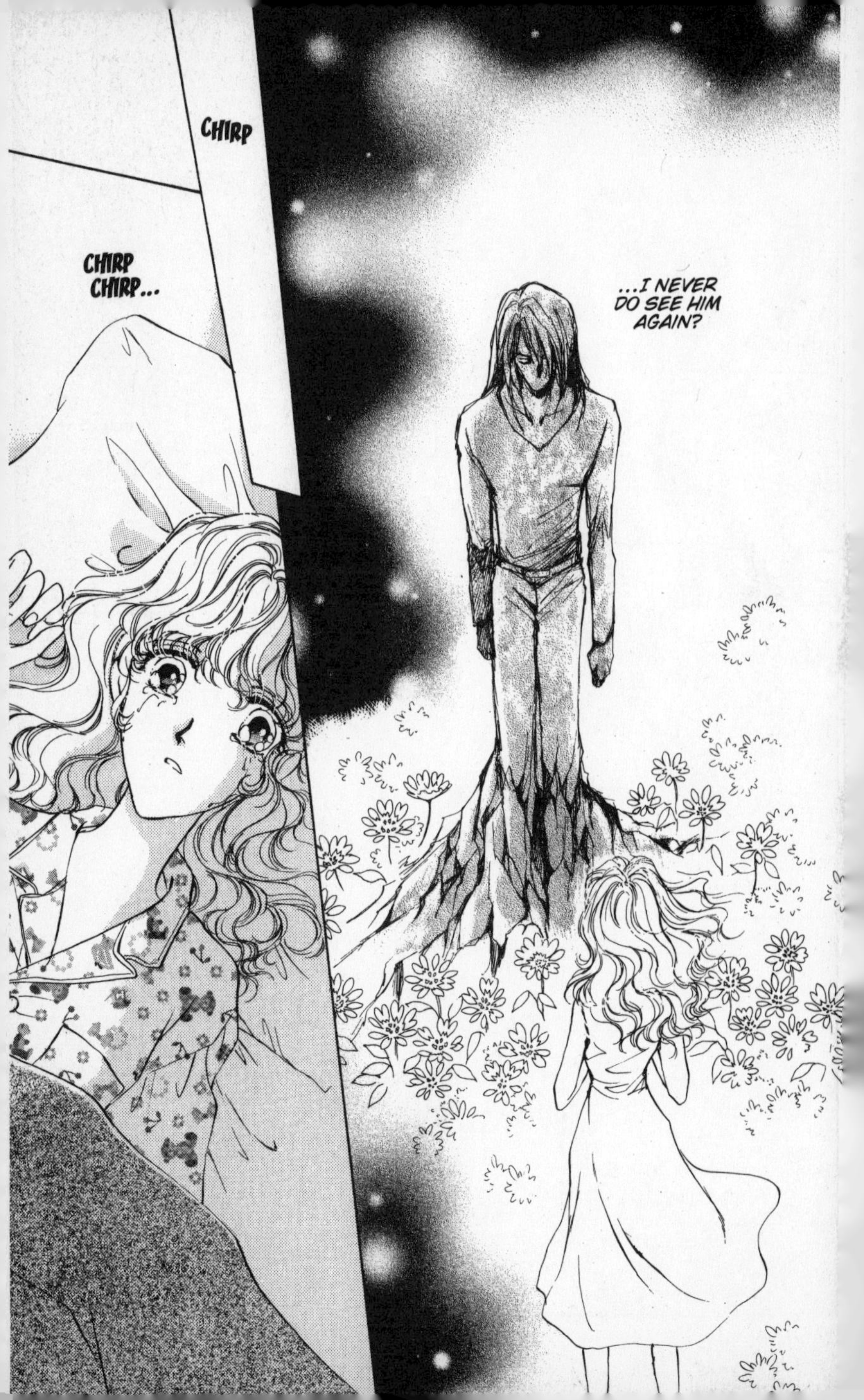
...I NEVER DO SEE HIM AGAIN?
CHIRP
CHIRP CHIRP...

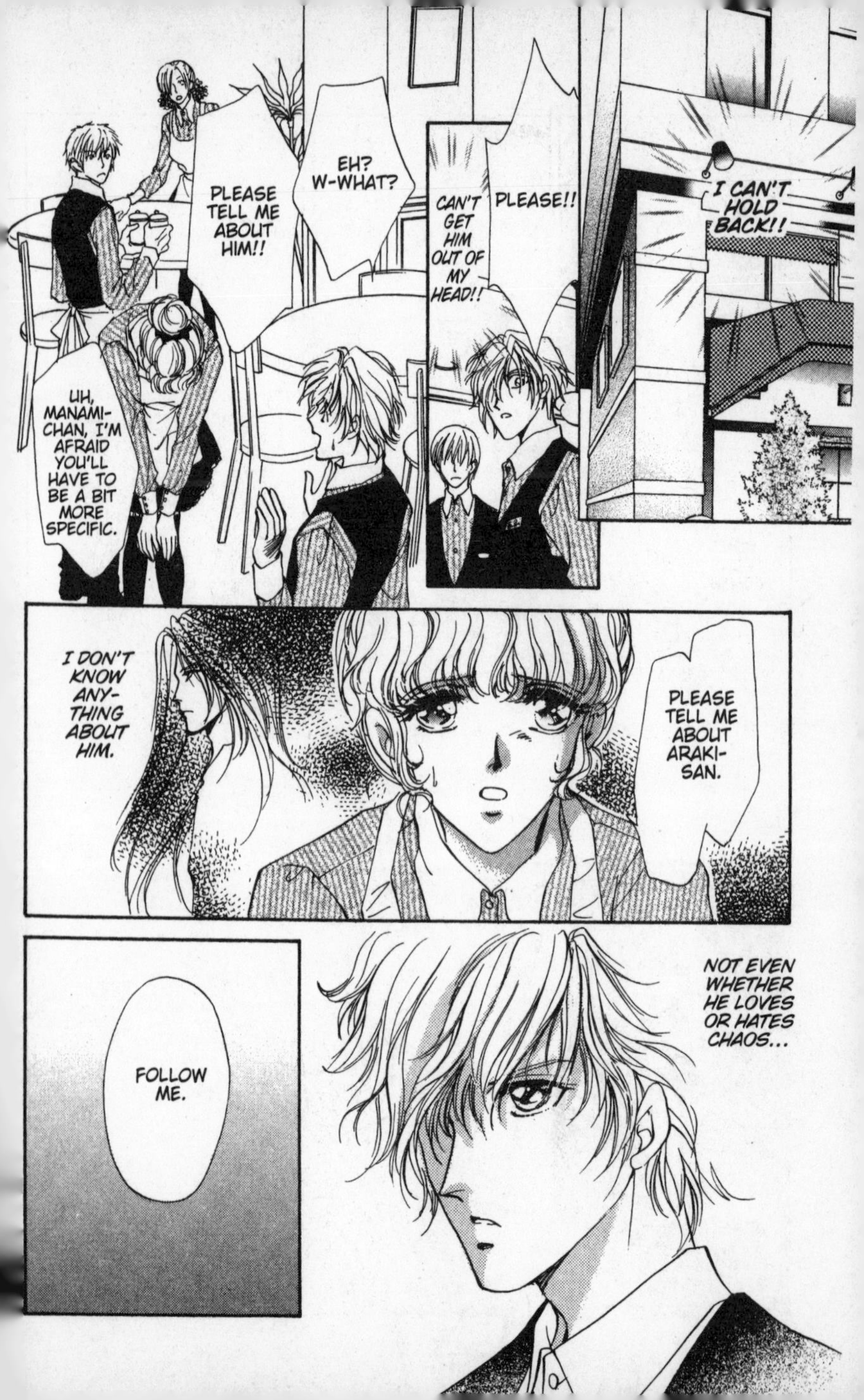
I CAN'T HOLD BACK!!
PLEASE!!
CAN'T GET HIM OUT OF MY HEAD!!
EH? W-WHAT?
PLEASE TELL ME ABOUT HIM!!
UH, MANAMI-CHAN, I'M AFRAID YOU'LL HAVE TO BE A BIT MORE SPECIFIC.
PLEASE TELL ME ABOUT ARAKI-SAN.
I DON'T KNOW ANY-THING ABOUT HIM.
NOT EVEN WHETHER HE LOVES OR HATES CHAOS...
FOLLOW ME.

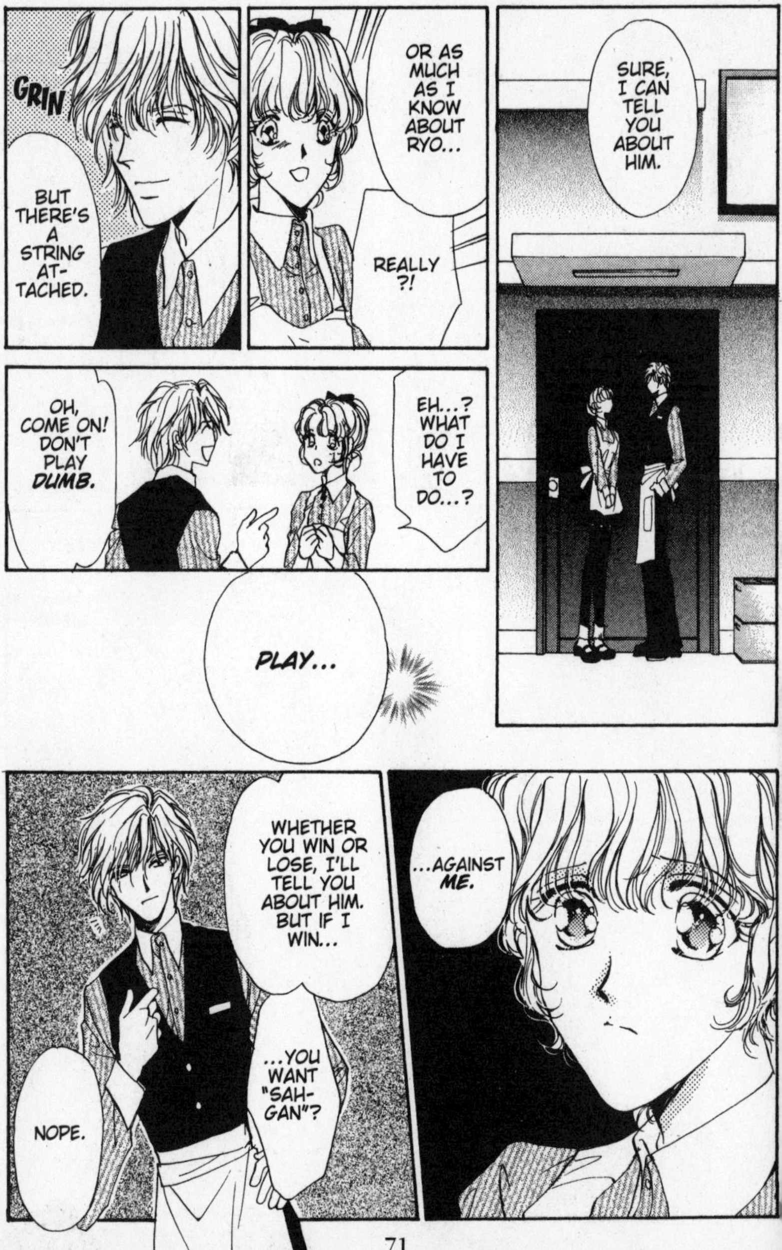
SURE, I CAN TELL YOU ABOUT HIM.
OR AS MUCH AS I KNOW ABOUT RYO...
REALLY?!
GRIN
BUT THERE'S A STRING AT-TACHED.
EH...? WHAT DO I HAVE TO DO...?
OH, COME ON! DON'T PLAY *DUMB.*
PLAY...
...AGAINST *ME.*
WHETHER YOU WIN OR LOSE, I'LL TELL YOU ABOUT HIM. BUT IF I WIN...
...YOU WANT "SAH-GAN"?
NOPE.

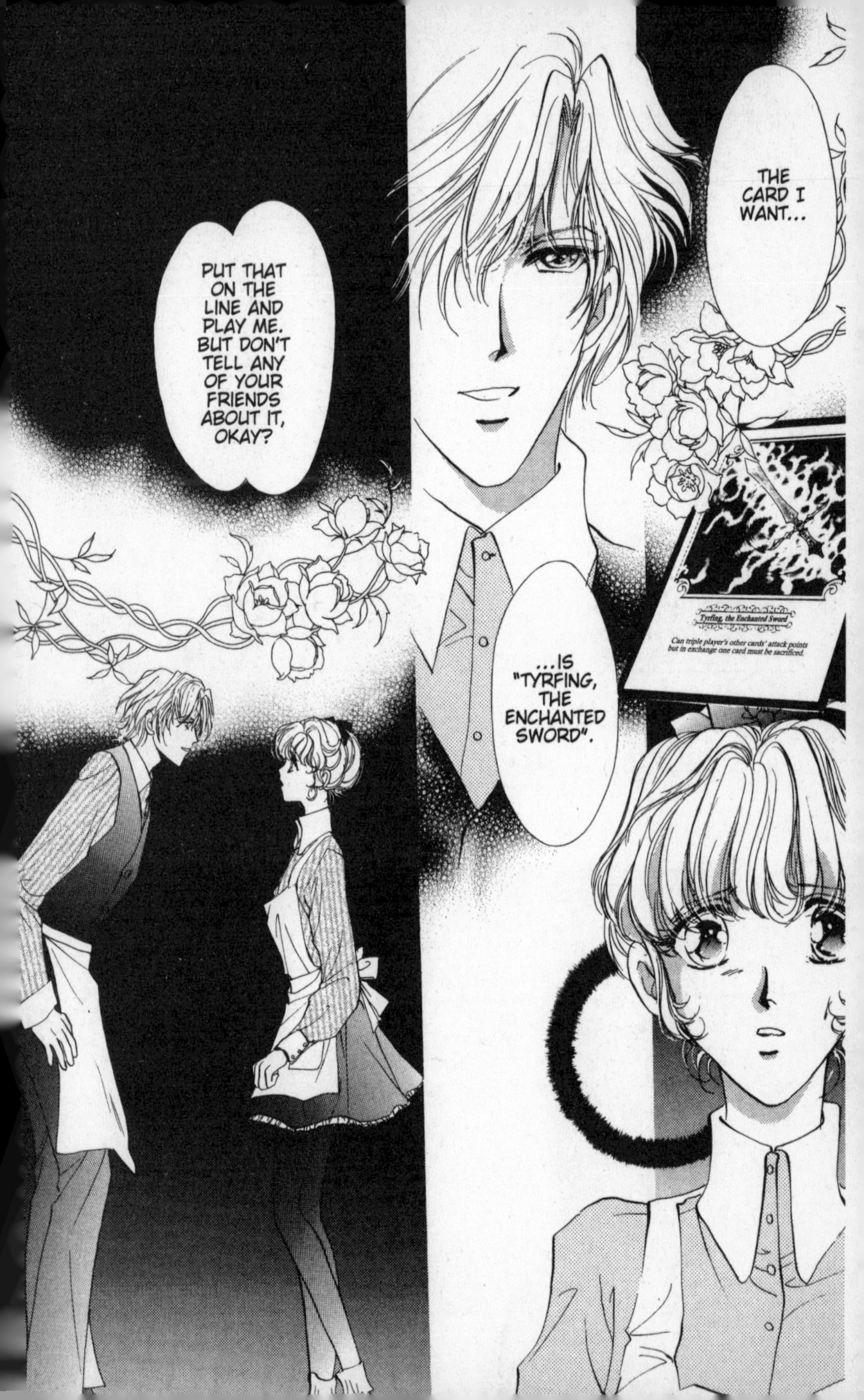
THE CARD I WANT...
Tyrfing, the Enchanted Sword
Can triple player's other cards' attack points but in exchange one card must be sacrificed.
...IS "TYRFING, THE ENCHANTED SWORD".
PUT THAT ON THE LINE AND PLAY ME. BUT DON'T TELL ANY OF YOUR FRIENDS ABOUT IT, OKAY?

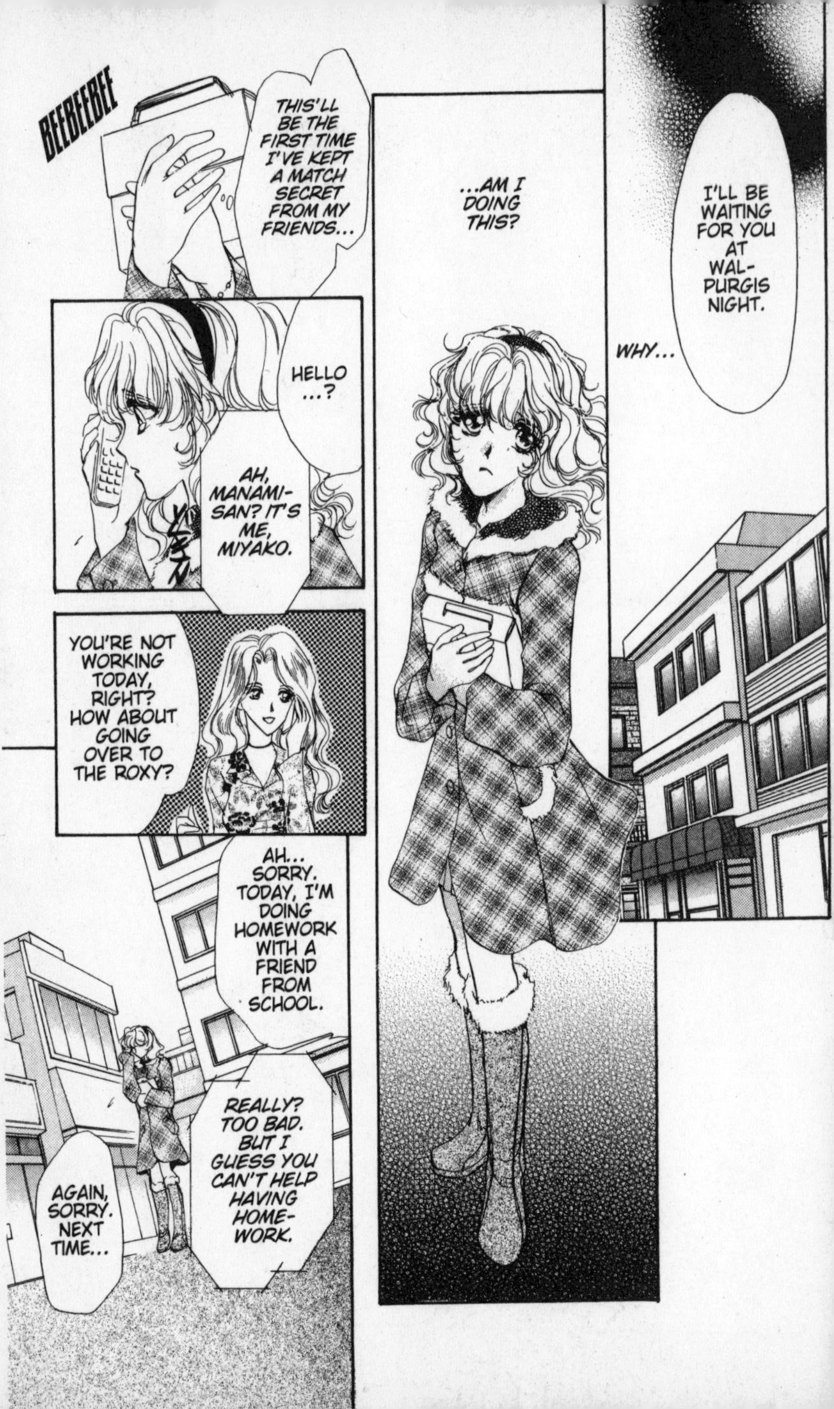
I'LL BE WAITING FOR YOU AT WAL-PURGIS NIGHT.
WHY...
...AM I DOING THIS?
BEEBEEBEE
THIS'LL BE THE FIRST TIME I'VE KEPT A MATCH SECRET FROM MY FRIENDS...
HELLO ...?
AH, MANAMI-SAN? IT'S ME, MIYAKO.
YOU'RE NOT WORKING TODAY, RIGHT? HOW ABOUT GOING OVER TO THE ROXY?
AH... SORRY. TODAY, I'M DOING HOMEWORK WITH A FRIEND FROM SCHOOL.
REALLY? TOO BAD. BUT I GUESS YOU CAN'T HELP HAVING HOME-WORK.
AGAIN, SORRY. NEXT TIME...

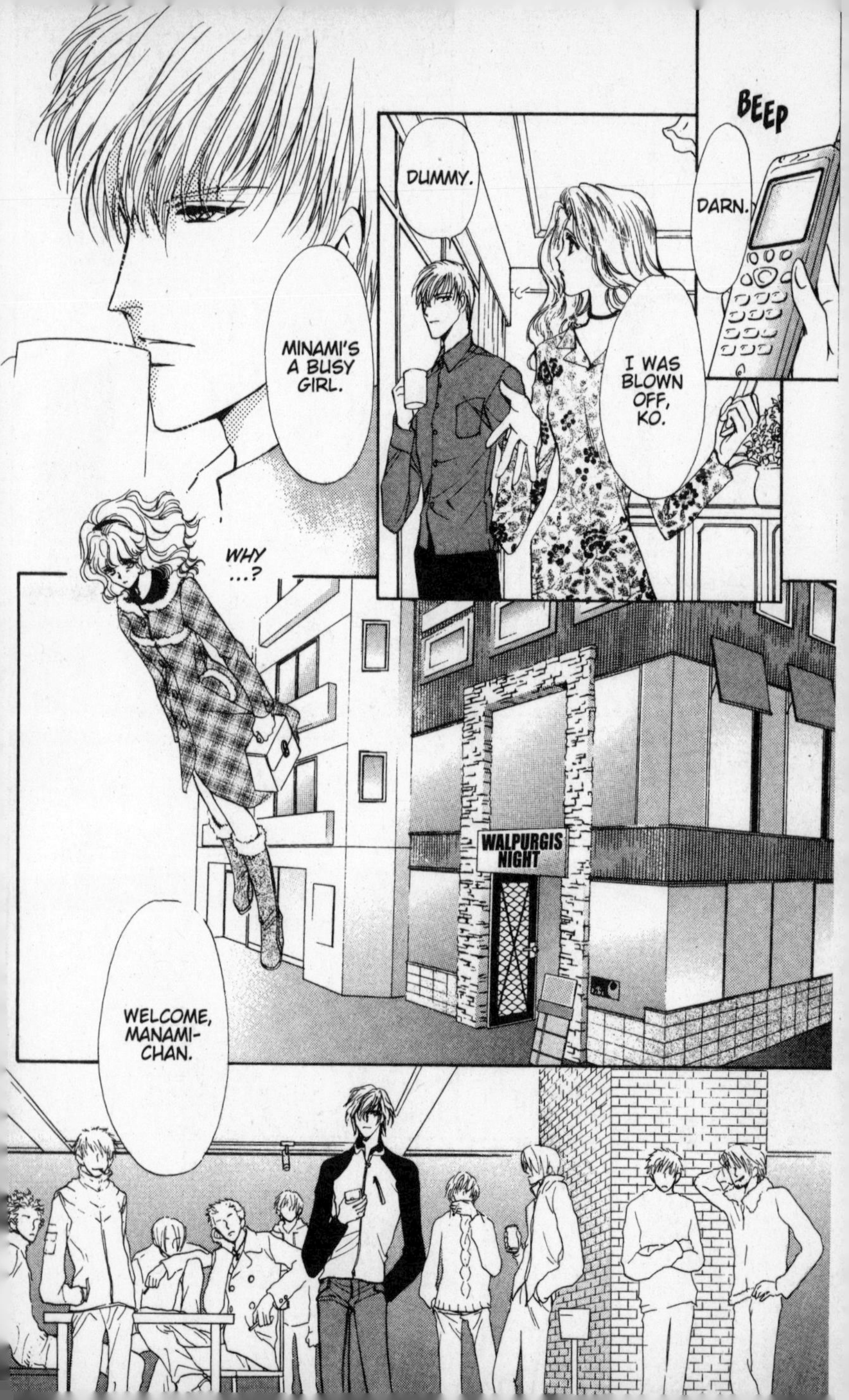
BEEP
DARN.
I WAS BLOWN OFF, KO.
DUMMY.
MINAMI'S A BUSY GIRL.
WHY ...?
WALPURGIS NIGHT
WELCOME, MANAMI-CHAN.

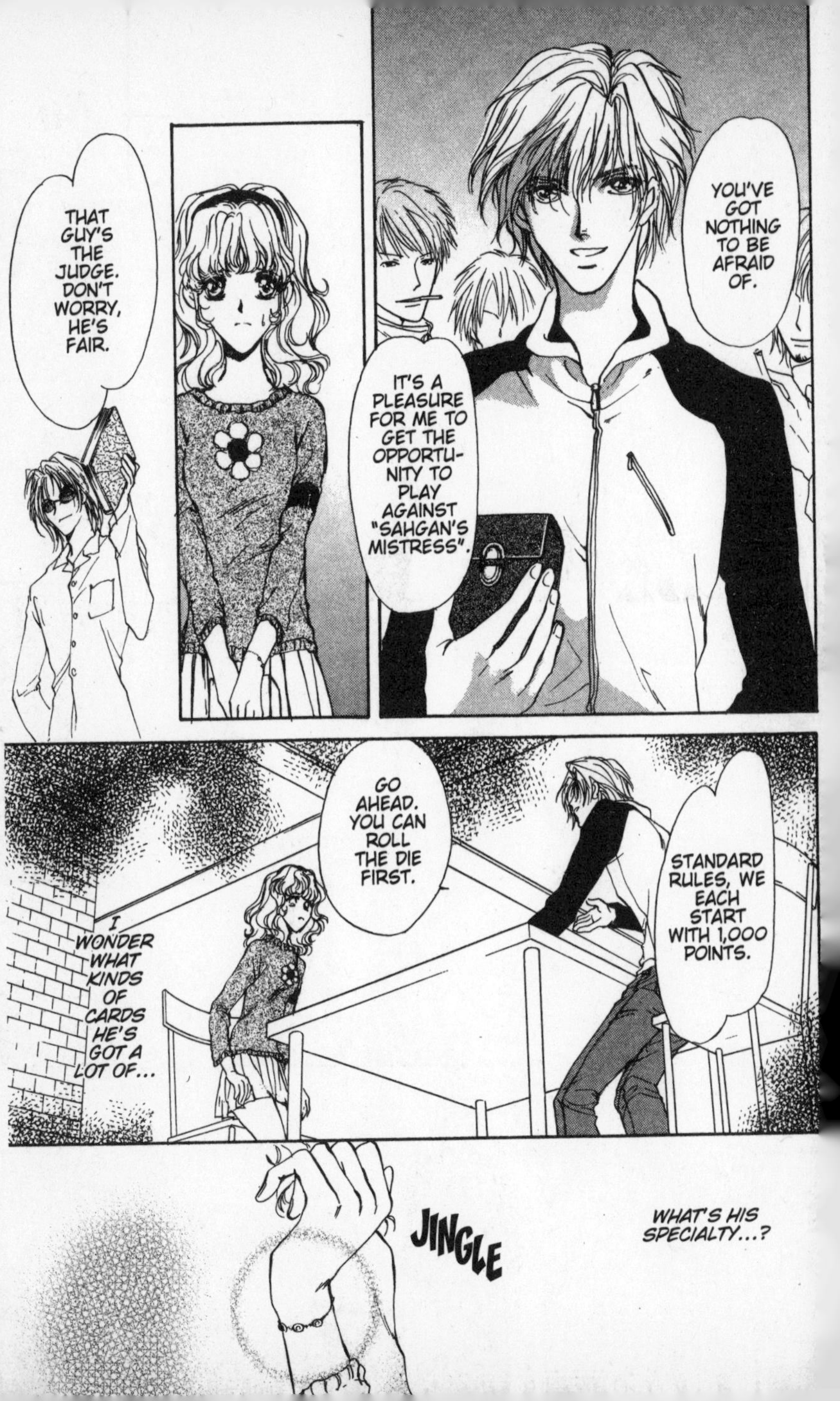
YOU'VE GOT NOTHING TO BE AFRAID OF.
IT'S A PLEASURE FOR ME TO GET THE OPPORTUNITY TO PLAY AGAINST "SAHGAN'S MISTRESS".
THAT GUY'S THE JUDGE. DON'T WORRY, HE'S FAIR.
STANDARD RULES, WE EACH START WITH 1,000 POINTS.
GO AHEAD. YOU CAN ROLL THE DIE FIRST.
I WONDER WHAT KINDS OF CARDS HE'S GOT A LOT OF...
WHAT'S HIS SPECIALTY...?
JINGLE

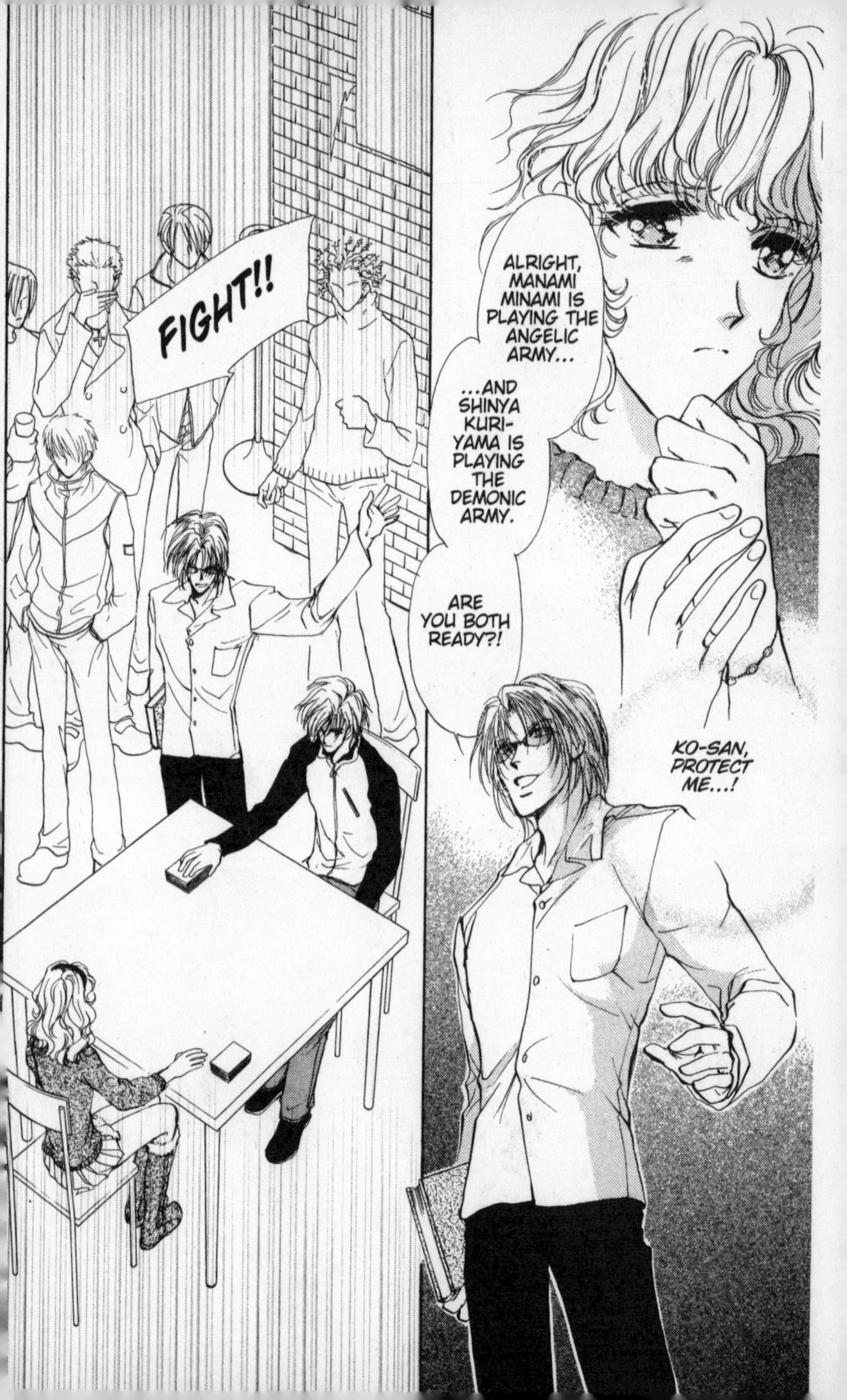
ALRIGHT, MANAMI MINAMI IS PLAYING THE ANGELIC ARMY...
...AND SHINYA KURI-YAMA IS PLAYING THE DEMONIC ARMY.
ARE YOU BOTH READY?!
KO-SAN, PROTECT ME...!
FIGHT!!

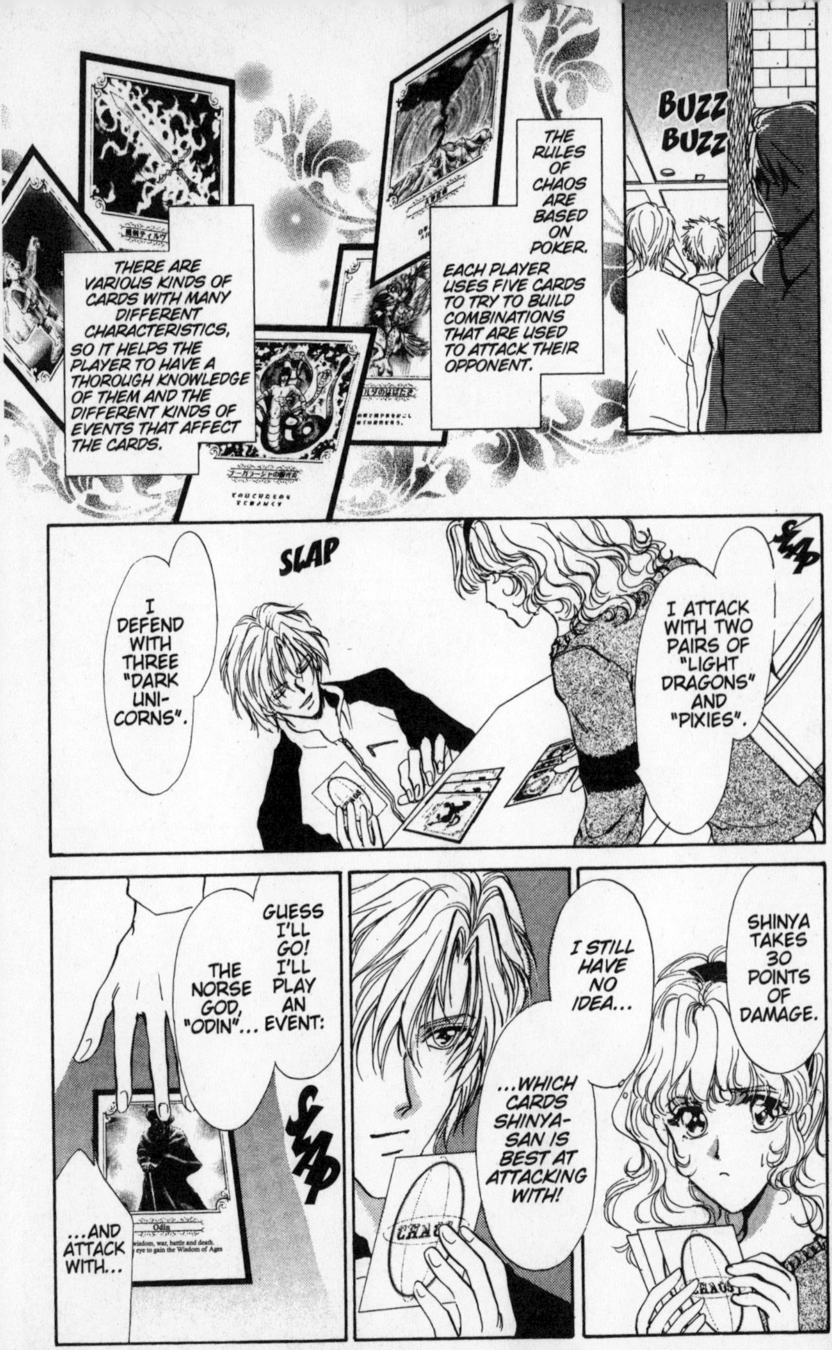
BUZZ BUZZ
THE RULES OF CHAOS ARE BASED ON POKER.
EACH PLAYER USES FIVE CARDS TO TRY TO BUILD COMBINATIONS THAT ARE USED TO ATTACK THEIR OPPONENT.
THERE ARE VARIOUS KINDS OF CARDS WITH MANY DIFFERENT CHARACTERISTICS, SO IT HELPS THE PLAYER TO HAVE A THOROUGH KNOWLEDGE OF THEM AND THE DIFFERENT KINDS OF EVENTS THAT AFFECT THE CARDS.
SLAP
I ATTACK WITH TWO PAIRS OF "LIGHT DRAGONS" AND "PIXIES".
SLAP
I DEFEND WITH THREE "DARK UNI-CORNS".
SHINYA TAKES 30 POINTS OF DAMAGE.
I STILL HAVE NO IDEA...
...WHICH CARDS SHINYA-SAN IS BEST AT ATTACKING WITH!
GUESS I'LL GO! I'LL PLAY AN EVENT:
THE NORSE GOD, "ODIN"...
SLAP
...AND ATTACK WITH...
Odin

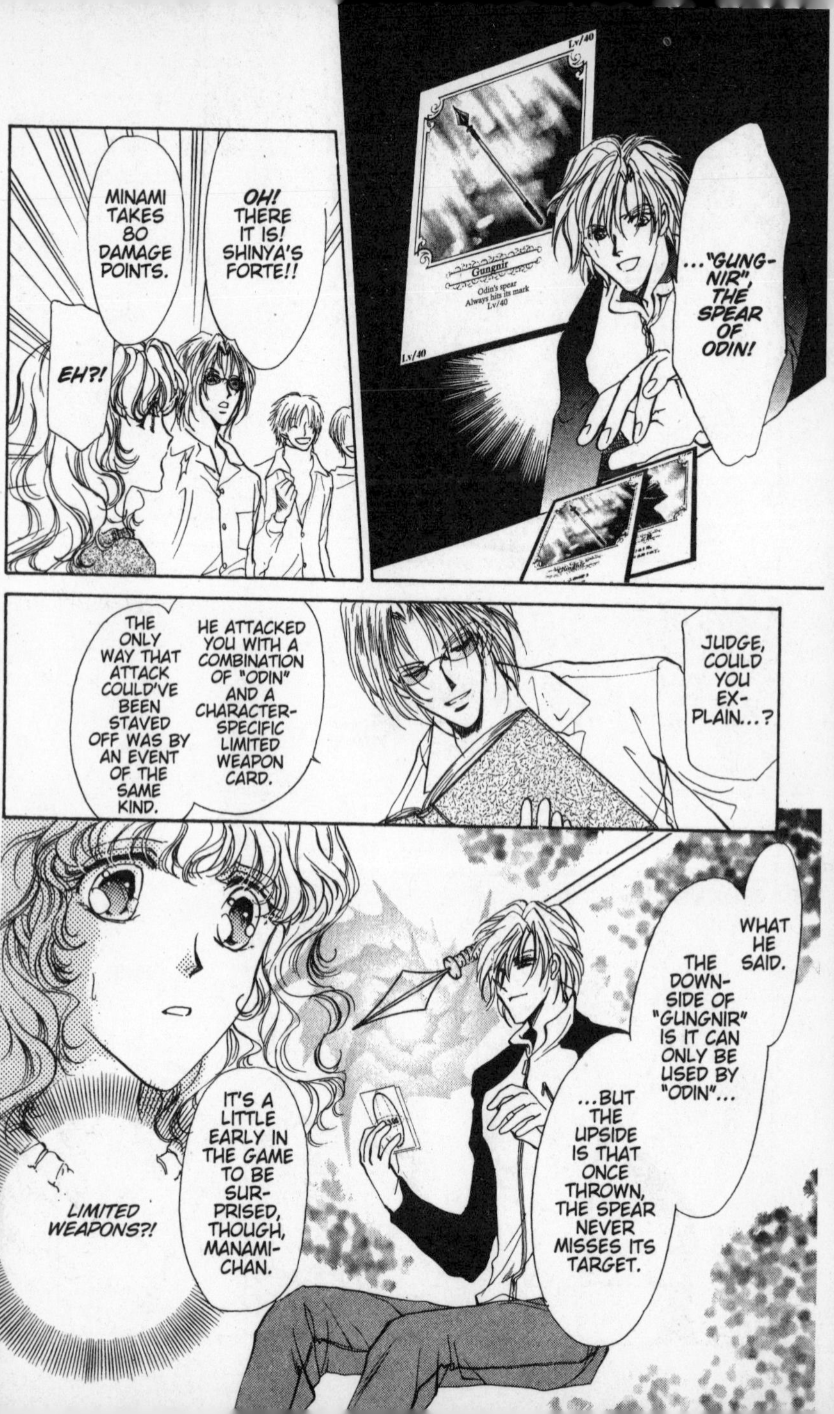
Lv/40
Gungnir
Odin's spear
Always hits its mark
Lv/40
Lv/40
..."GUNGNIR", THE SPEAR OF ODIN!
OH! THERE IT IS! SHINYA'S FORTE!!
MINAMI TAKES 80 DAMAGE POINTS.
EH?!
JUDGE, COULD YOU EX-PLAIN...?
HE ATTACKED YOU WITH A COMBINATION OF "ODIN" AND A CHARACTER-SPECIFIC LIMITED WEAPON CARD.
THE ONLY WAY THAT ATTACK COULD'VE BEEN STAVED OFF WAS BY AN EVENT OF THE SAME KIND.
WHAT HE SAID.
THE DOWN-SIDE OF "GUNGNIR" IS IT CAN ONLY BE USED BY "ODIN"...
...BUT THE UPSIDE IS THAT ONCE THROWN, THE SPEAR NEVER MISSES ITS TARGET.
IT'S A LITTLE EARLY IN THE GAME TO BE SUR-PRISED, THOUGH, MANAMI-CHAN.
LIMITED WEAPONS?!

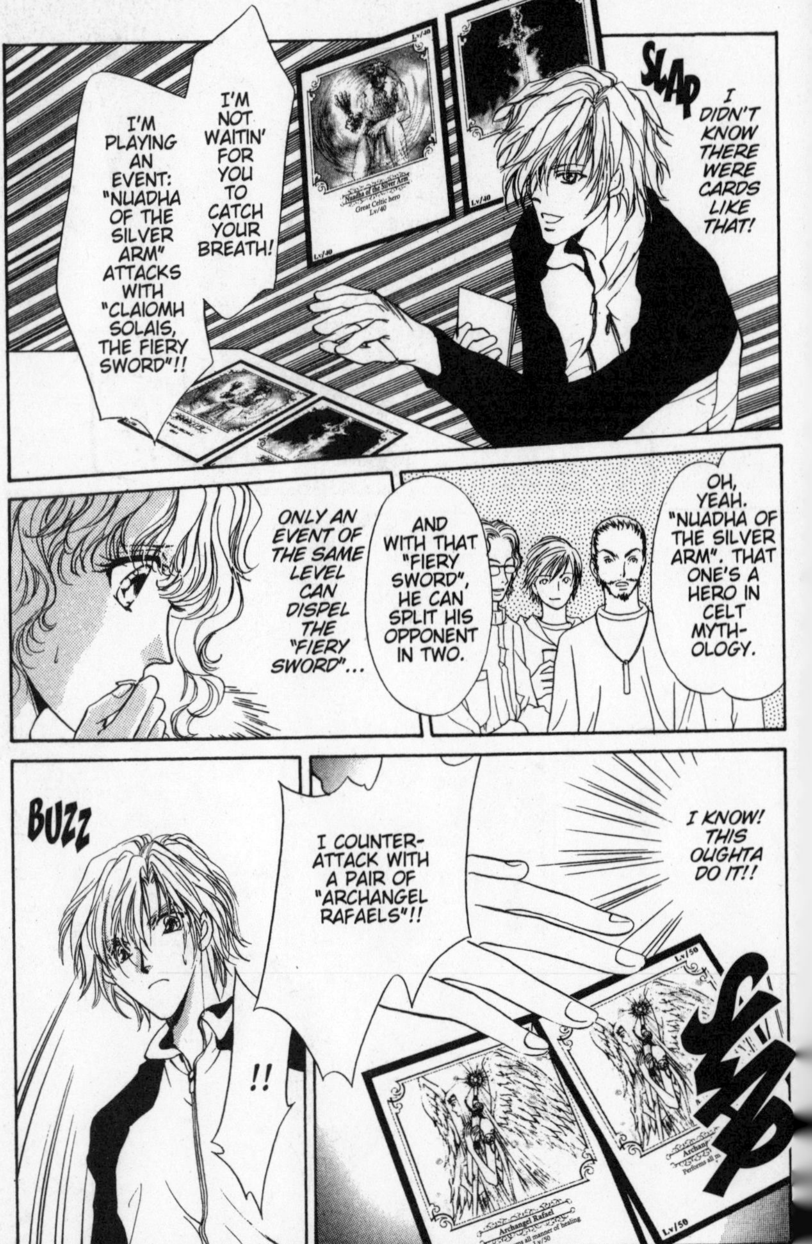
SLAP
I DIDN'T KNOW THERE WERE CARDS LIKE THAT!
Nuadha of the Silver Arm
Great Celtic hero
Lv/40
I'M NOT WAITIN' FOR YOU TO CATCH YOUR BREATH!
I'M PLAYING AN EVENT: "NUADHA OF THE SILVER ARM" ATTACKS WITH "CLAIOMH SOLAIS, THE FIERY SWORD"!!
OH, YEAH. "NUADHA OF THE SILVER ARM". THAT ONE'S A HERO IN CELT MYTH-OLOGY.
AND WITH THAT "FIERY SWORD", HE CAN SPLIT HIS OPPONENT IN TWO.
ONLY AN EVENT OF THE SAME LEVEL CAN DISPEL THE "FIERY SWORD"...
I KNOW! THIS OUGHTA DO IT!!
I COUNTER-ATTACK WITH A PAIR OF "ARCHANGEL RAFAELS"!!
SLAP
Archangel Rafael
Lv/50
BUZZ
!!

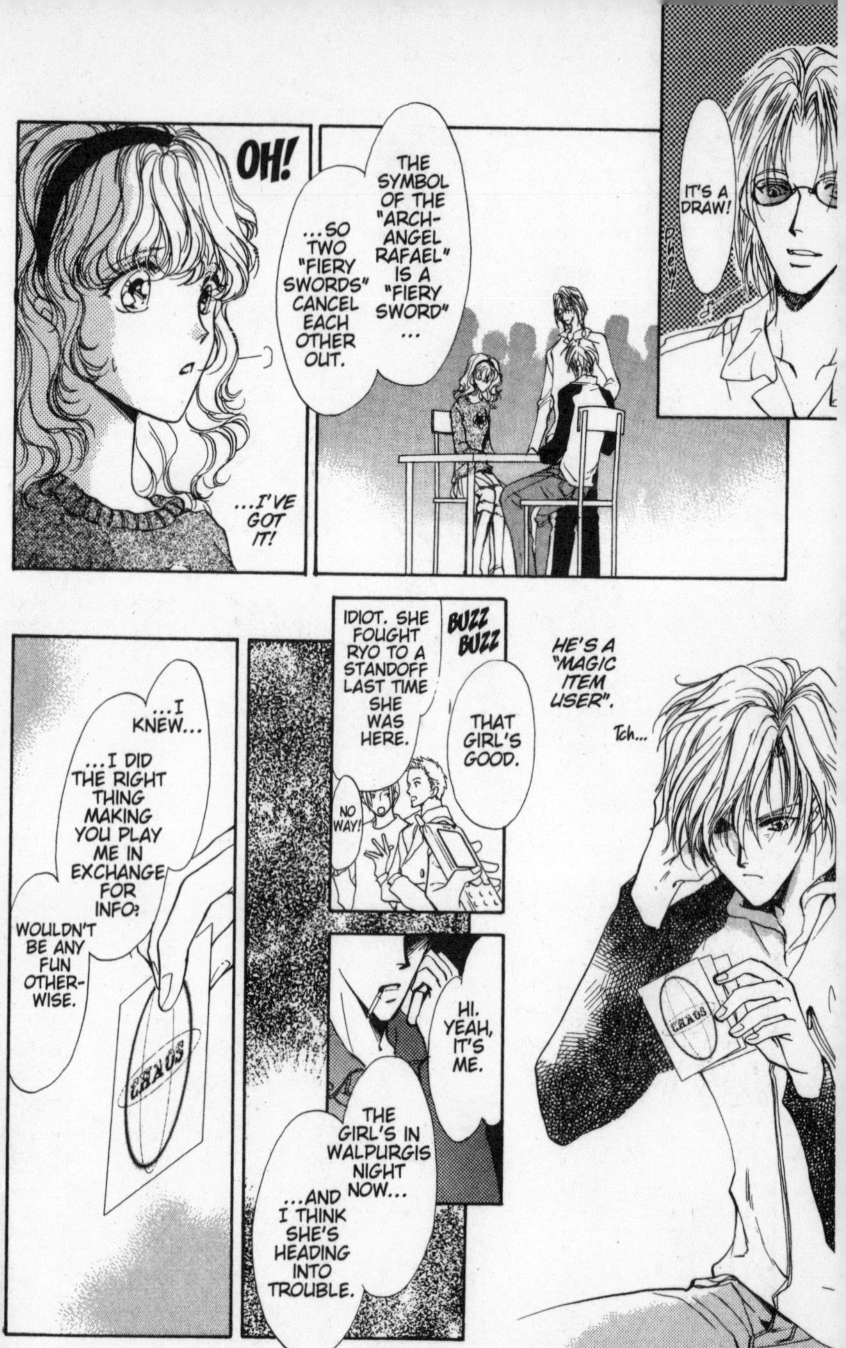
IT'S A DRAW!
Phew!
THE SYMBOL OF THE "ARCH-ANGEL RAFAEL" IS A "FIERY SWORD"...
...SO TWO "FIERY SWORDS" CANCEL EACH OTHER OUT.
OH!
...I'VE GOT IT!
HE'S A "MAGIC ITEM USER".
Tch...
BUZZ BUZZ
THAT GIRL'S GOOD.
IDIOT. SHE FOUGHT RYO TO A STANDOFF LAST TIME SHE WAS HERE.
NO WAY!
HI. YEAH, IT'S ME.
THE GIRL'S IN WALPURGIS NIGHT NOW...
...AND I THINK SHE'S HEADING INTO TROUBLE.
...I KNEW...
...I DID THE RIGHT THING MAKING YOU PLAY ME IN EXCHANGE FOR INFO?
WOULDN'T BE ANY FUN OTHER-WISE.
CHAOS

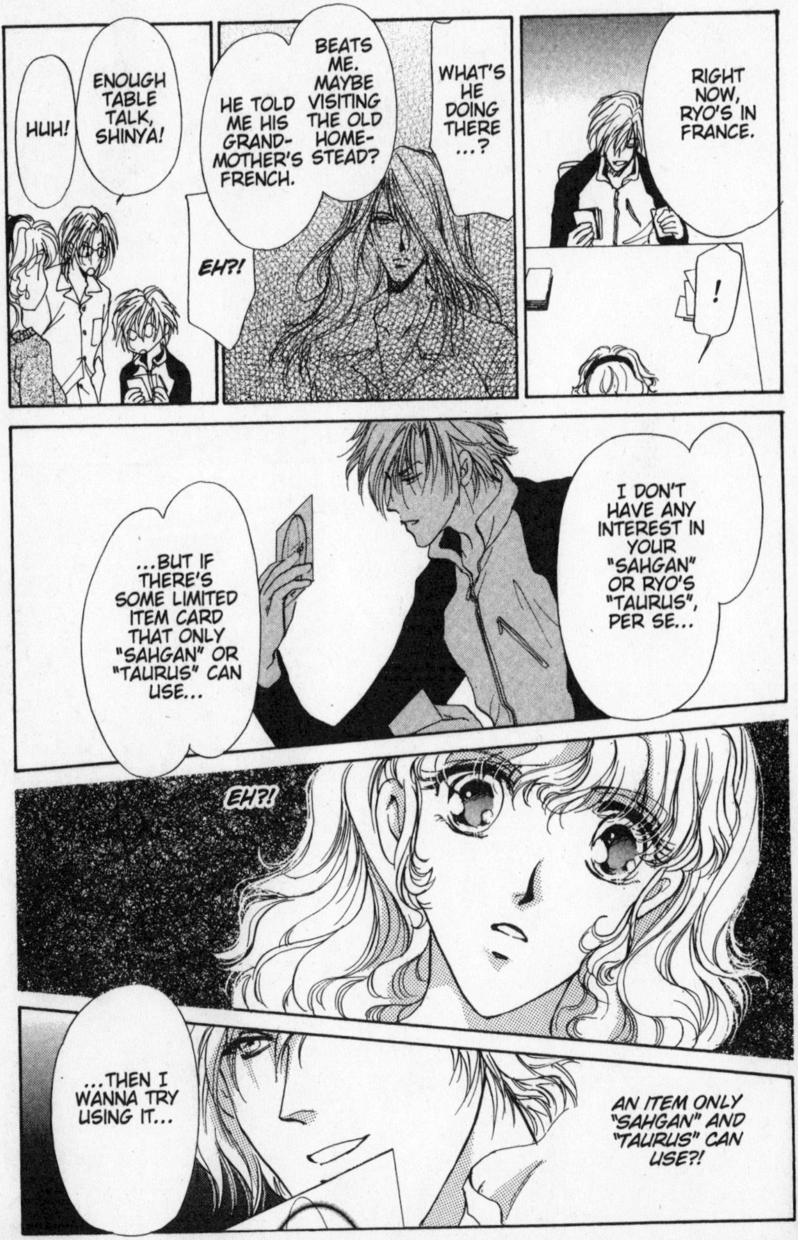
RIGHT NOW, RYO'S IN FRANCE.
!
WHAT'S HE DOING THERE ...?
BEATS ME. MAYBE VISITING THE OLD HOMESTEAD?
HE TOLD ME HIS GRANDMOTHER'S FRENCH.
EH?!
ENOUGH TABLE TALK, SHINYA!
HUH!
I DON'T HAVE ANY INTEREST IN YOUR "SAHGAN" OR RYO'S "TAURUS", PER SE...
...BUT IF THERE'S SOME LIMITED ITEM CARD THAT ONLY "SAHGAN" OR "TAURUS" CAN USE...
EH?!
AN ITEM ONLY "SAHGAN" AND "TAURUS" CAN USE?!
...THEN I WANNA TRY USING IT...

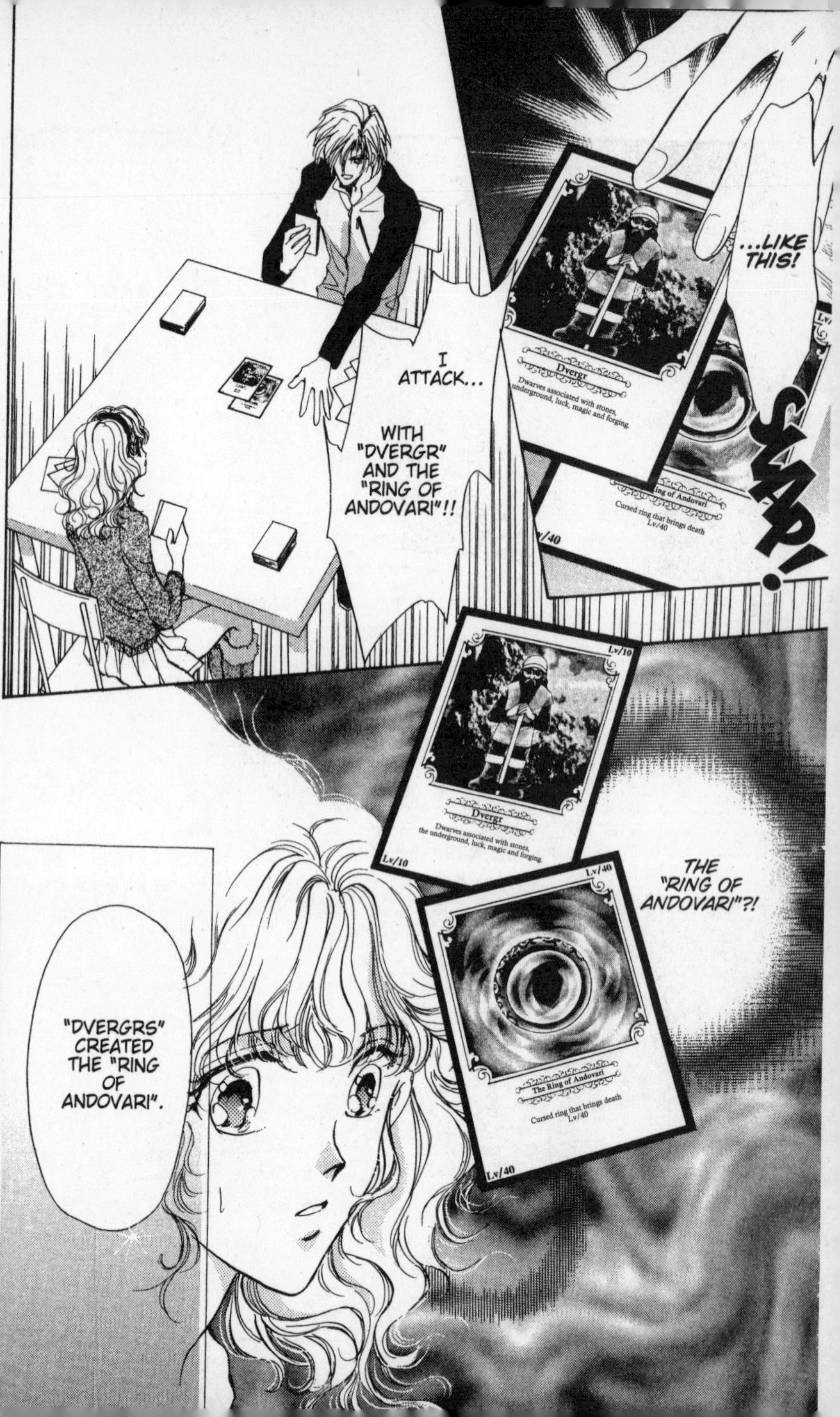
I ATTACK...
WITH "DVERGR" AND THE "RING OF ANDOVARI"!!
...LIKE THIS!
SLAP!
Dvergr
Dwarves associated with stones, underground, luck, magic and forging.
Cursed ring that brings death
THE "RING OF ANDOVARI"?!
Lv/10
Dvergr
Dwarves associated with stones, the underground, luck, magic and forging.
Lv/10
Lv/40
The Ring of Andovari
Cursed ring that brings death
Lv/40
Lv/40
"DVERGRS" CREATED THE "RING OF ANDOVARI".

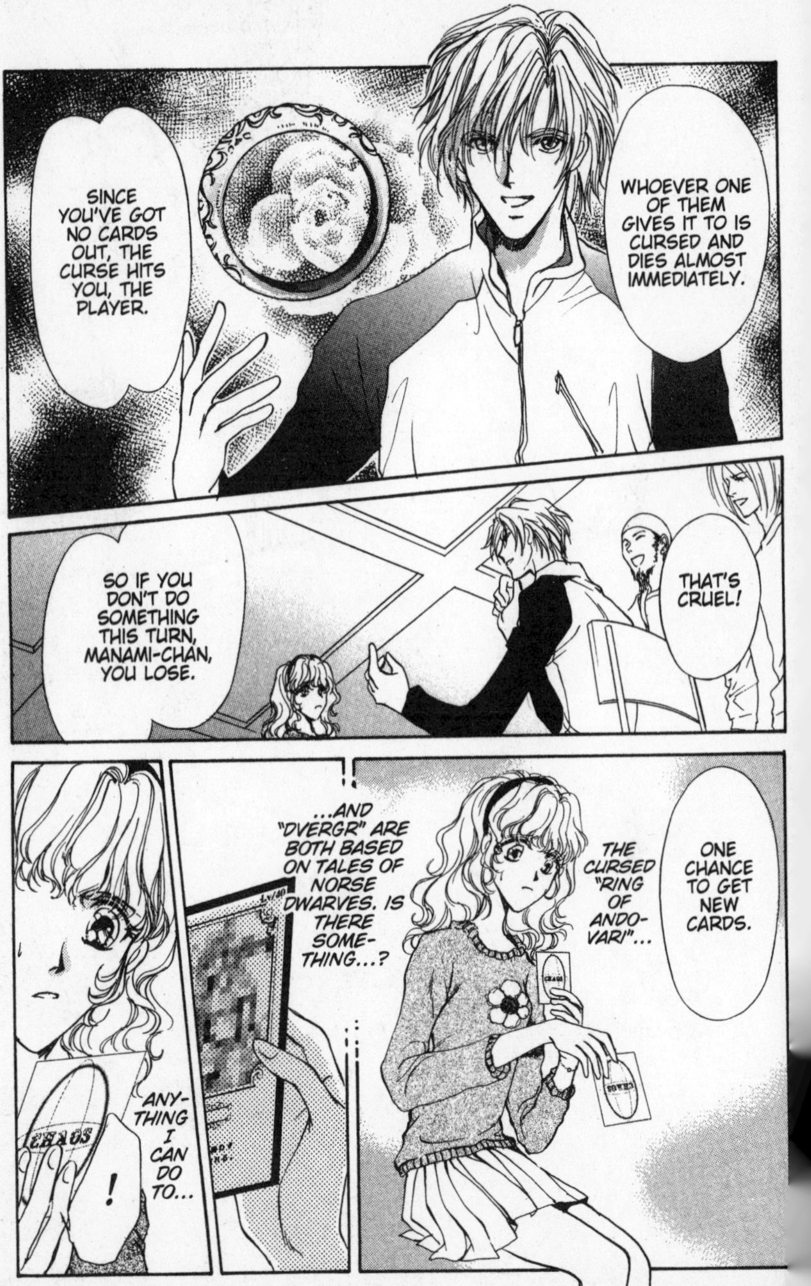
WHOEVER ONE OF THEM GIVES IT TO IS CURSED AND DIES ALMOST IMMEDIATELY.
SINCE YOU'VE GOT NO CARDS OUT, THE CURSE HITS YOU, THE PLAYER.
THAT'S CRUEL!
SO IF YOU DON'T DO SOMETHING THIS TURN, MANAMI-CHAN, YOU LOSE.
ONE CHANCE TO GET NEW CARDS.
THE CURSED "RING OF ANDO-VARI"...
...AND "DVERGR" ARE BOTH BASED ON TALES OF NORSE DWARVES. IS THERE SOME-THING...?
ANY-THING I CAN DO TO...
!

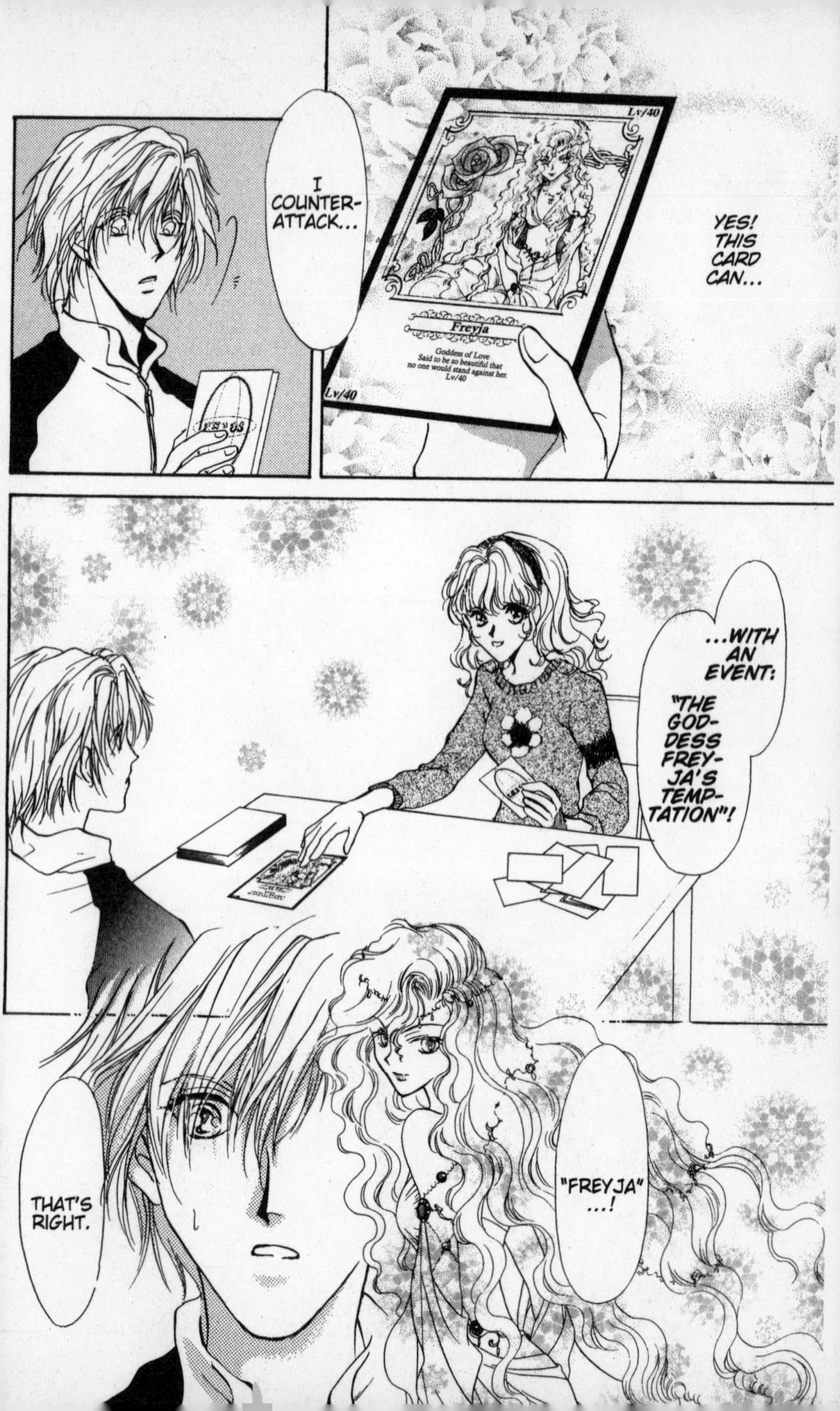

YES! THIS CARD CAN...
I COUNTER-ATTACK...
Lv/40
Freyja
Goddess of Love Said to be so beautiful that no one would stand against her. Lv/40
Lv/40
...WITH AN EVENT: "THE GOD-DESS FREY-JA'S TEMP-TATION"!
"FREYJA" ...!
THAT'S RIGHT.

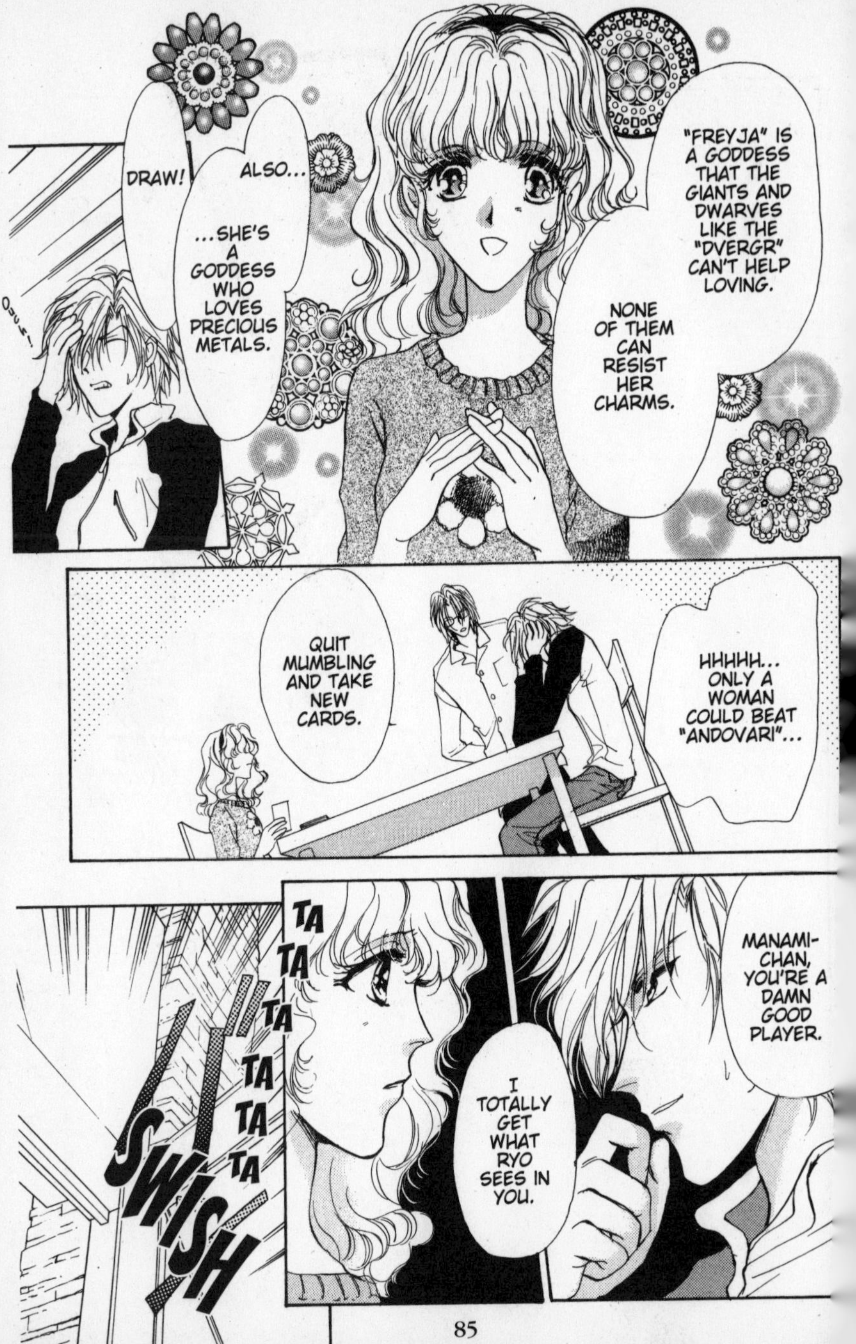
"FREYJA" IS A GODDESS THAT THE GIANTS AND DWARVES LIKE THE "DVERGR" CAN'T HELP LOVING.
NONE OF THEM CAN RESIST HER CHARMS.
ALSO...
...SHE'S A GODDESS WHO LOVES PRECIOUS METALS.
DRAW!
HHHHH... ONLY A WOMAN COULD BEAT "ANDOVARI"...
QUIT MUMBLING AND TAKE NEW CARDS.
MANAMI-CHAN, YOU'RE A DAMN GOOD PLAYER.
I TOTALLY GET WHAT RYO SEES IN YOU.
TA TA TA TA TA TA TA
SWISH

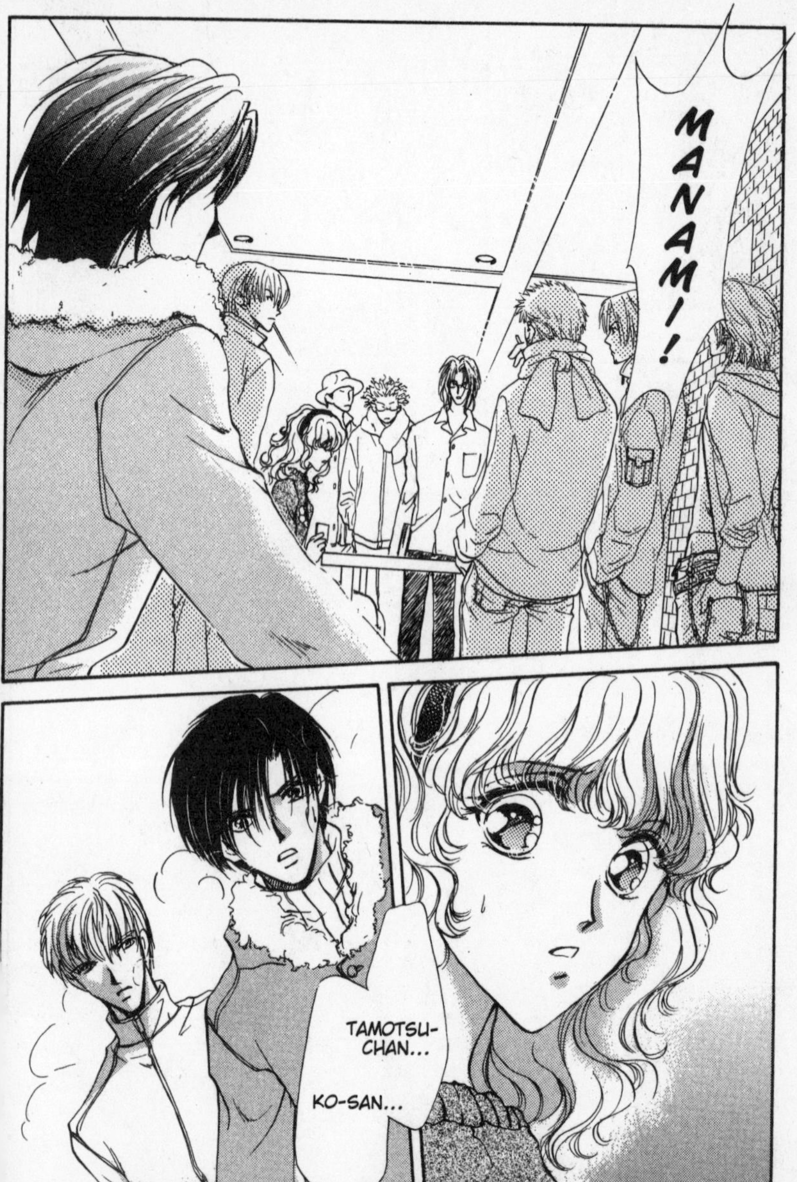
MANAMI!
TAMOTSU-CHAN...
KO-SAN...

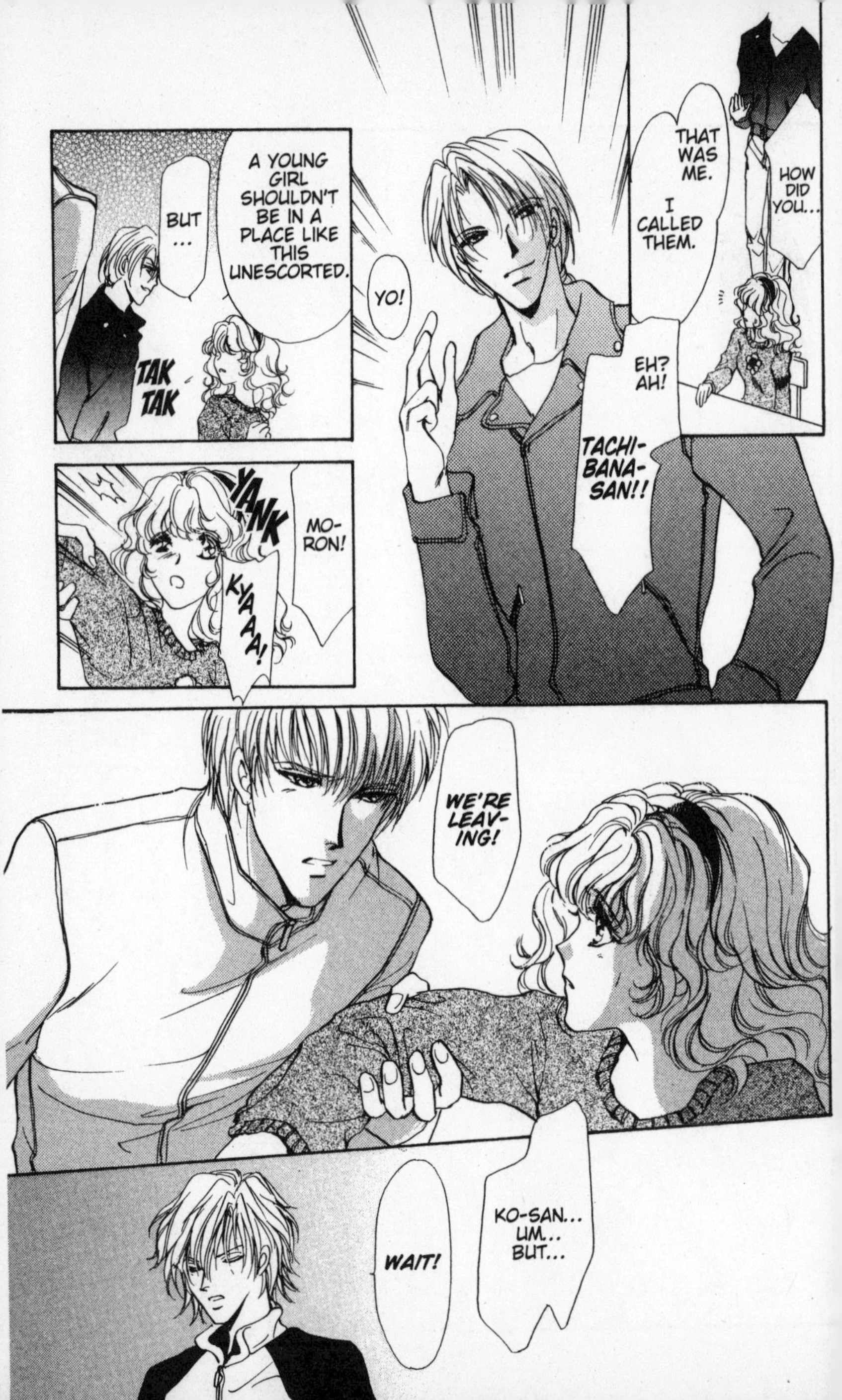
HOW DID YOU...
THAT WAS ME. I CALLED THEM.
EH? AH!
TACHIBANA-SAN!!
YO!
A YOUNG GIRL SHOULDN'T BE IN A PLACE LIKE THIS UNESCORTED.
BUT...
TAK TAK
MO-RON!
YANK
KYAAAA!
WE'RE LEAVING!
KO-SAN... UM... BUT...
WAIT!

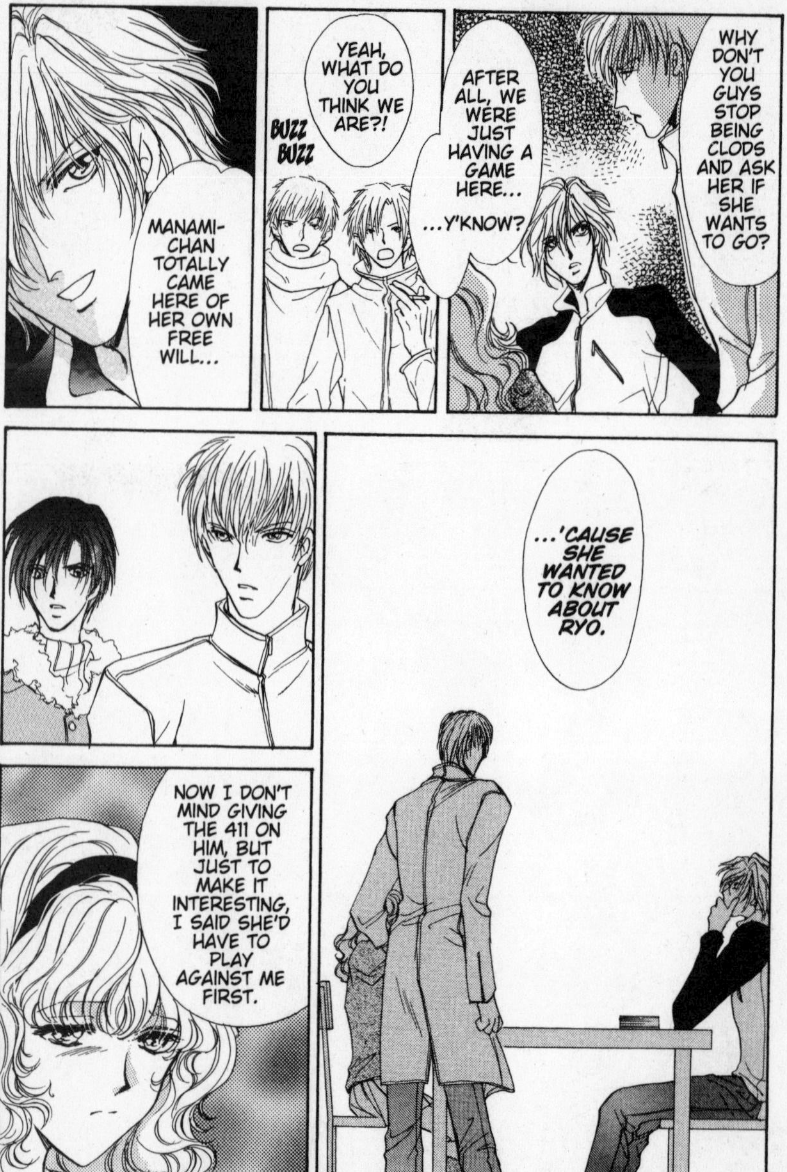
WHY DON'T YOU GUYS STOP BEING CLODS AND ASK HER IF SHE WANTS TO GO?
AFTER ALL, WE WERE JUST HAVING A GAME HERE...
...Y'KNOW?
YEAH, WHAT DO YOU THINK WE ARE?!
BUZZ BUZZ
MANAMI-CHAN TOTALLY CAME HERE OF HER OWN FREE WILL...
...'CAUSE SHE WANTED TO KNOW ABOUT RYO.
NOW I DON'T MIND GIVING THE 411 ON HIM, BUT JUST TO MAKE IT INTERESTING, I SAID SHE'D HAVE TO PLAY AGAINST ME FIRST.

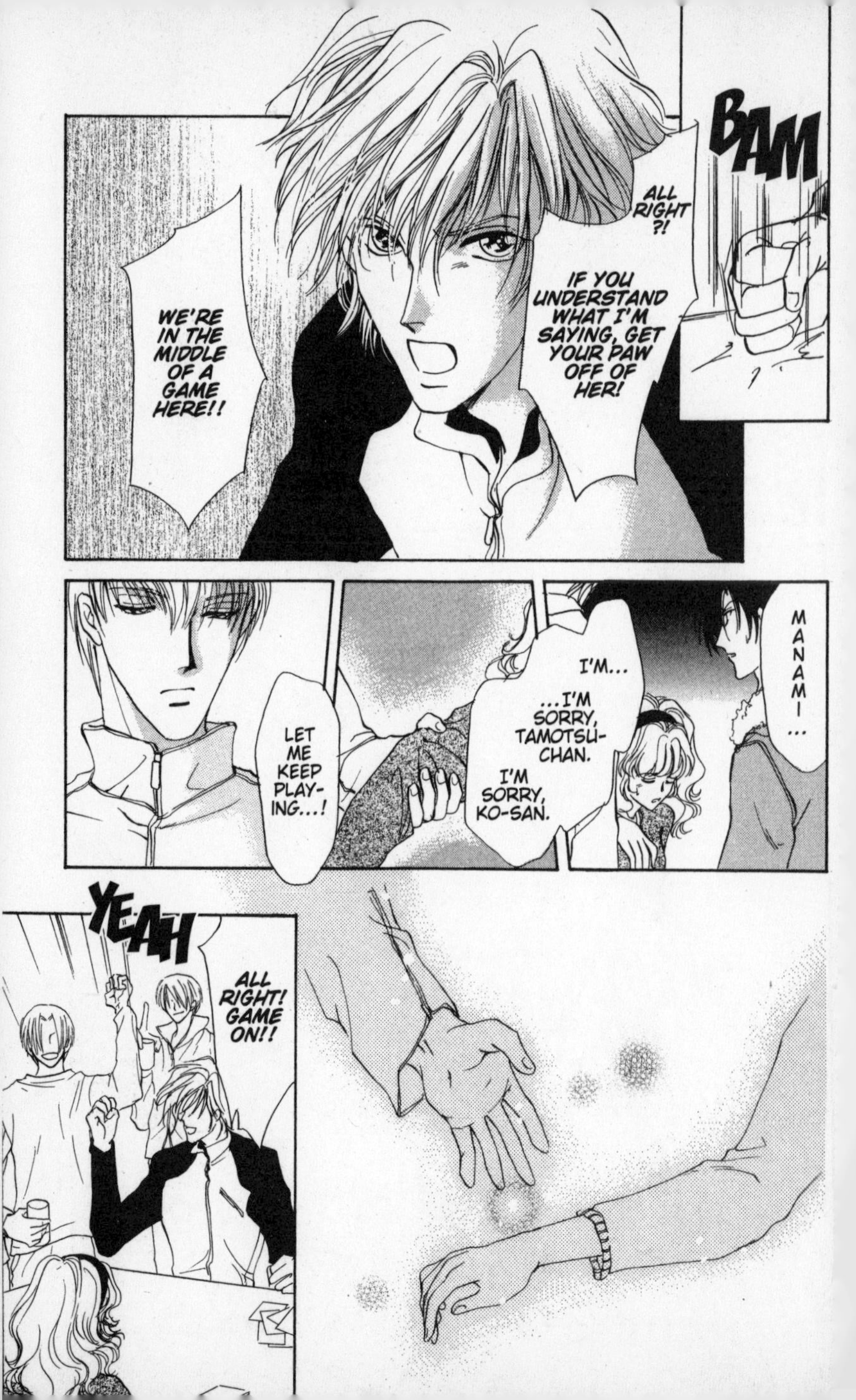
BAM
ALL RIGHT ?!
IF YOU UNDERSTAND WHAT I'M SAYING, GET YOUR PAW OFF OF HER!
WE'RE IN THE MIDDLE OF A GAME HERE!!
MANAMI...
I'M...
...I'M SORRY, TAMOTSU-CHAN.
I'M SORRY, KO-SAN.
LET ME KEEP PLAYING...!
YEAH
ALL RIGHT! GAME ON!!

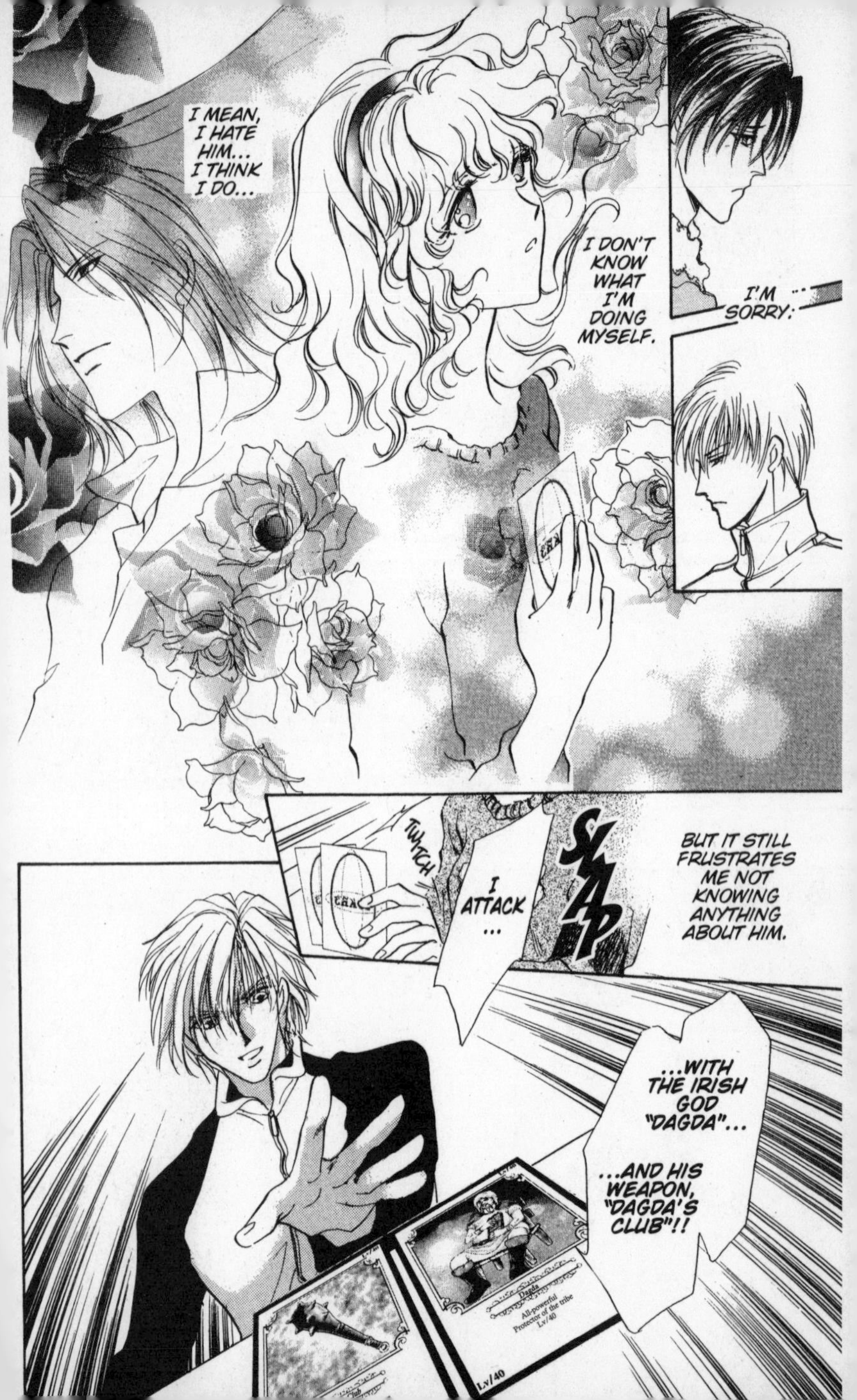
I'M SORRY...
I MEAN, I HATE HIM... I THINK I DO...
I DON'T KNOW WHAT I'M DOING MYSELF.
BUT IT STILL FRUSTRATES ME NOT KNOWING ANYTHING ABOUT HIM.
SLAP
TWITCH
I ATTACK...
...WITH THE IRISH GOD "DAGDA"...
...AND HIS WEAPON, "DAGDA'S CLUB"!!
Dagda
All-powerful
Protector of the tribe
Lv/40
Lv/40

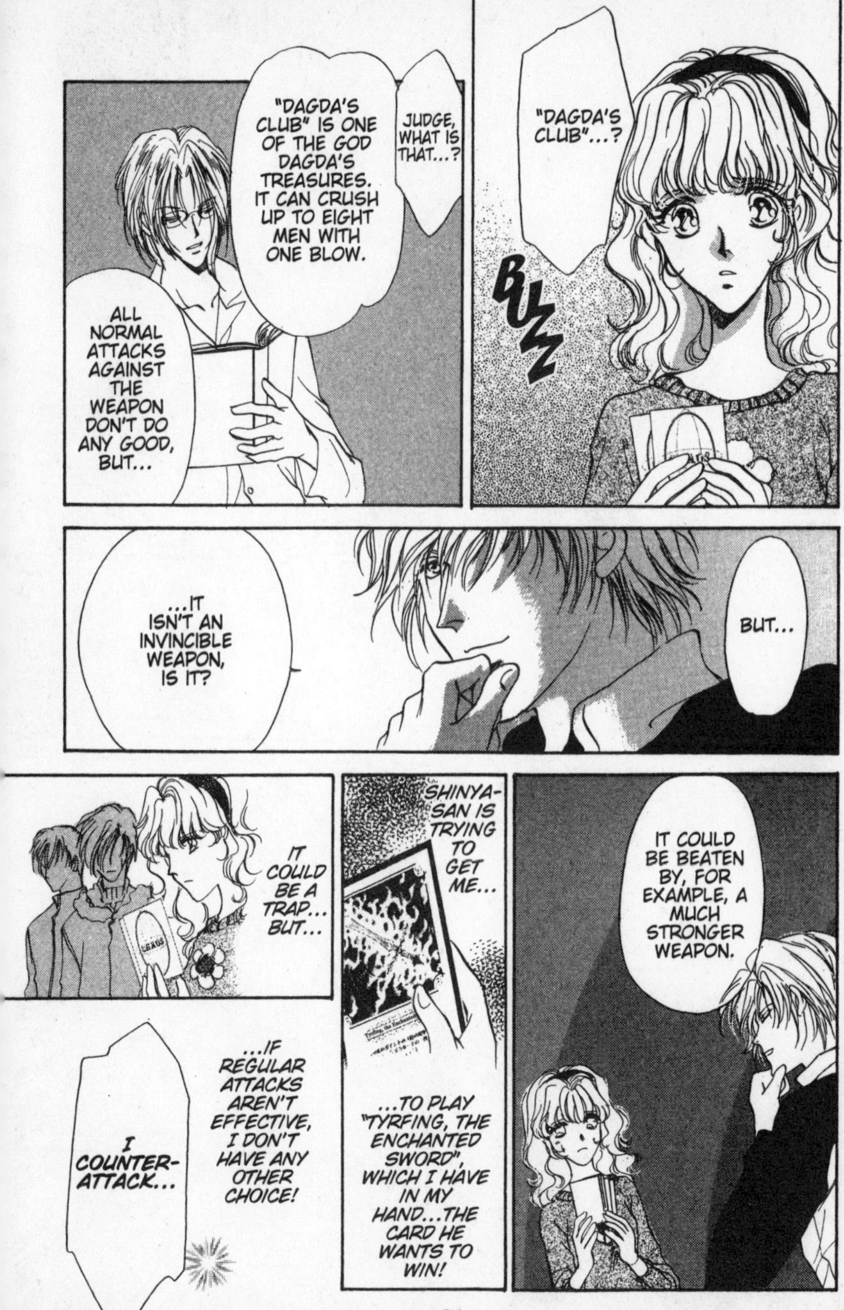

"DAGDA'S CLUB"...?
BZZZ
JUDGE, WHAT IS THAT...?
"DAGDA'S CLUB" IS ONE OF THE GOD DAGDA'S TREASURES. IT CAN CRUSH UP TO EIGHT MEN WITH ONE BLOW.
ALL NORMAL ATTACKS AGAINST THE WEAPON DON'T DO ANY GOOD, BUT...
BUT...
...IT ISN'T AN INVINCIBLE WEAPON, IS IT?
IT COULD BE BEATEN BY, FOR EXAMPLE, A MUCH STRONGER WEAPON.
SHINYA-SAN IS TRYING TO GET ME...
...TO PLAY "TYRFING, THE ENCHANTED SWORD", WHICH I HAVE IN MY HAND...THE CARD HE WANTS TO WIN!
IT COULD BE A TRAP... BUT...
...IF REGULAR ATTACKS AREN'T EFFECTIVE, I DON'T HAVE ANY OTHER CHOICE!
I COUNTER-ATTACK...

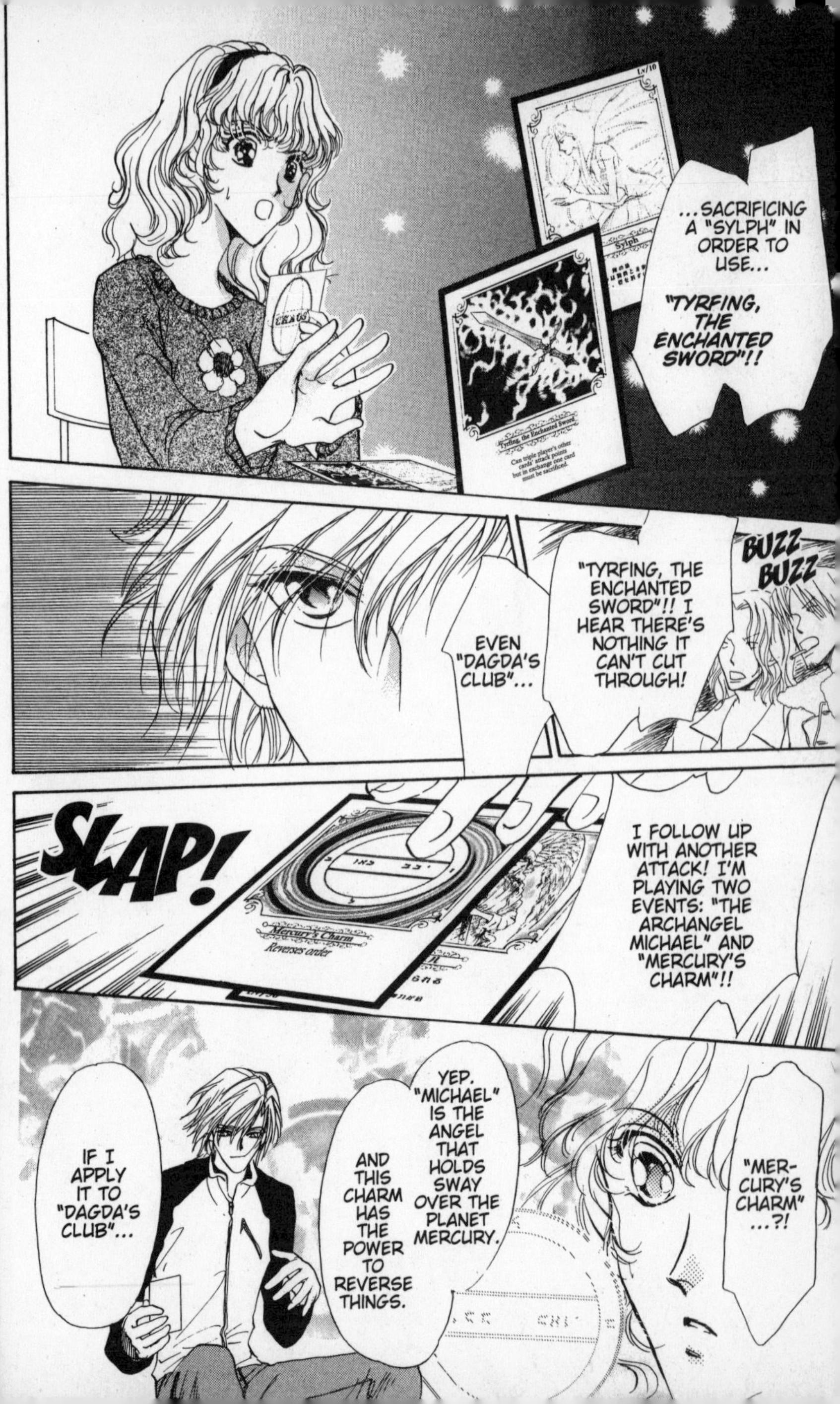
...SACRIFICING A "SYLPH" IN ORDER TO USE... "TYRFING, THE ENCHANTED SWORD"!!
Ln/10
Sylph
Tyrfing, the Enchanted Sword
Can triple player's other cards' attack points but in exchange one card must be sacrificed.
BUZZ BUZZ
"TYRFING, THE ENCHANTED SWORD"!! I HEAR THERE'S NOTHING IT CAN'T CUT THROUGH!
EVEN "DAGDA'S CLUB"...
I FOLLOW UP WITH ANOTHER ATTACK! I'M PLAYING TWO EVENTS: "THE ARCHANGEL MICHAEL" AND "MERCURY'S CHARM"!!
SLAP!
Mercury's Charm
Reverses order
"MER-CURY'S CHARM"...?!
YEP. "MICHAEL" IS THE ANGEL THAT HOLDS SWAY OVER THE PLANET MERCURY.
AND THIS CHARM HAS THE POWER TO REVERSE THINGS.
IF I APPLY IT TO "DAGDA'S CLUB"...

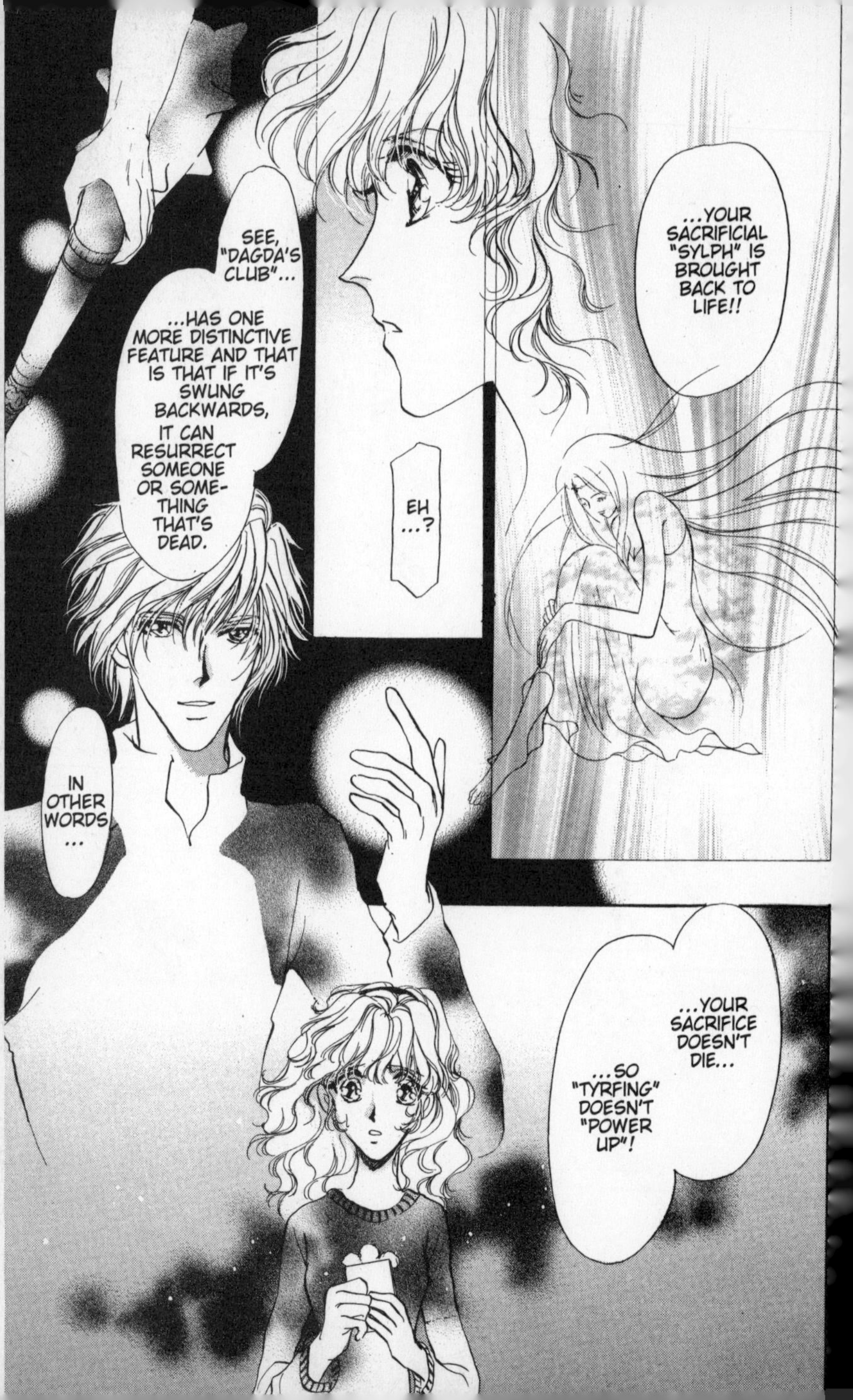
SEE, "DAGDA'S CLUB"...
...HAS ONE MORE DISTINCTIVE FEATURE AND THAT IS THAT IF IT'S SWUNG BACKWARDS, IT CAN RESURRECT SOMEONE OR SOME-THING THAT'S DEAD.
EH ...?
IN OTHER WORDS ...
...YOUR SACRIFICIAL "SYLPH" IS BROUGHT BACK TO LIFE!!
...YOUR SACRIFICE DOESN'T DIE...
...SO "TYRFING" DOESN'T "POWER UP"!

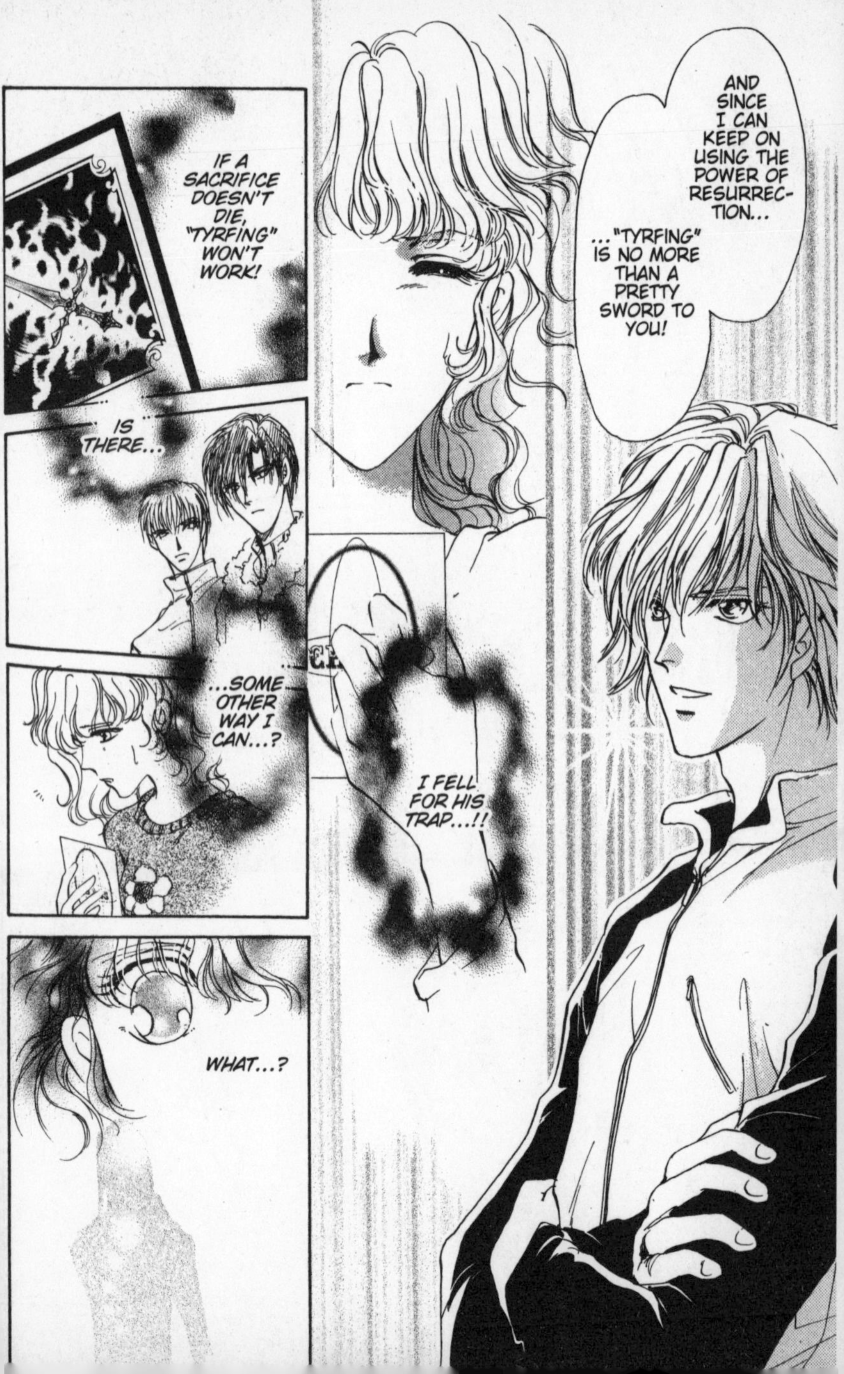
AND SINCE I CAN KEEP ON USING THE POWER OF RESURREC-TION...
..."TYRFING" IS NO MORE THAN A PRETTY SWORD TO YOU!
I FELL FOR HIS TRAP...!!
IF A SACRIFICE DOESN'T DIE, "TYRFING" WON'T WORK!
...IS THERE...
...SOME OTHER WAY I CAN...?
WHAT...?

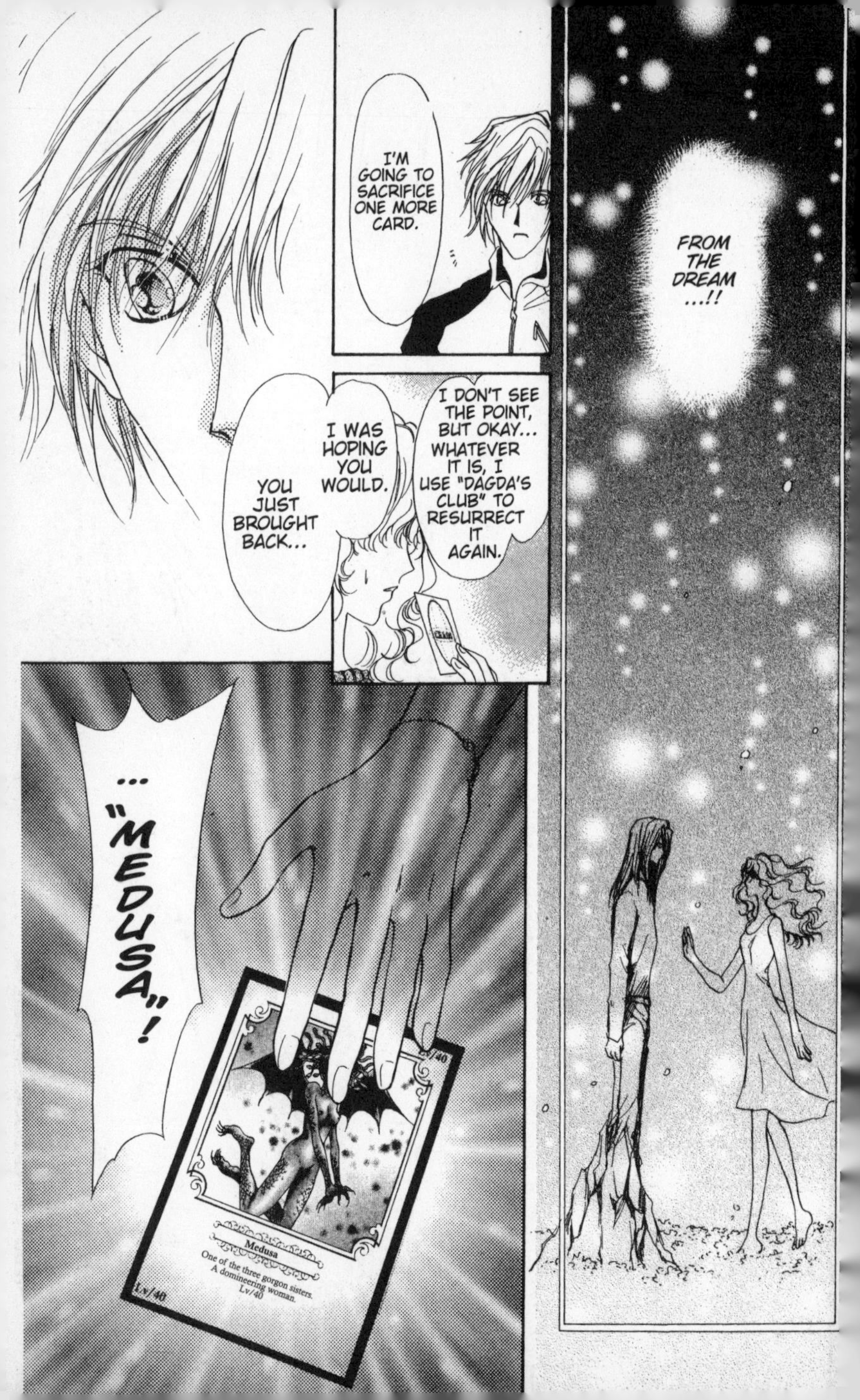
FROM THE DREAM ...!!
I'M GOING TO SACRIFICE ONE MORE CARD.
I DON'T SEE THE POINT, BUT OKAY... WHATEVER IT IS, I USE "DAGDA'S CLUB" TO RESURRECT IT AGAIN.
I WAS HOPING YOU WOULD.
YOU JUST BROUGHT BACK...
..."MEDUSA"!
Medusa
One of the three gorgon sisters. A domineering woman.
Lv/40

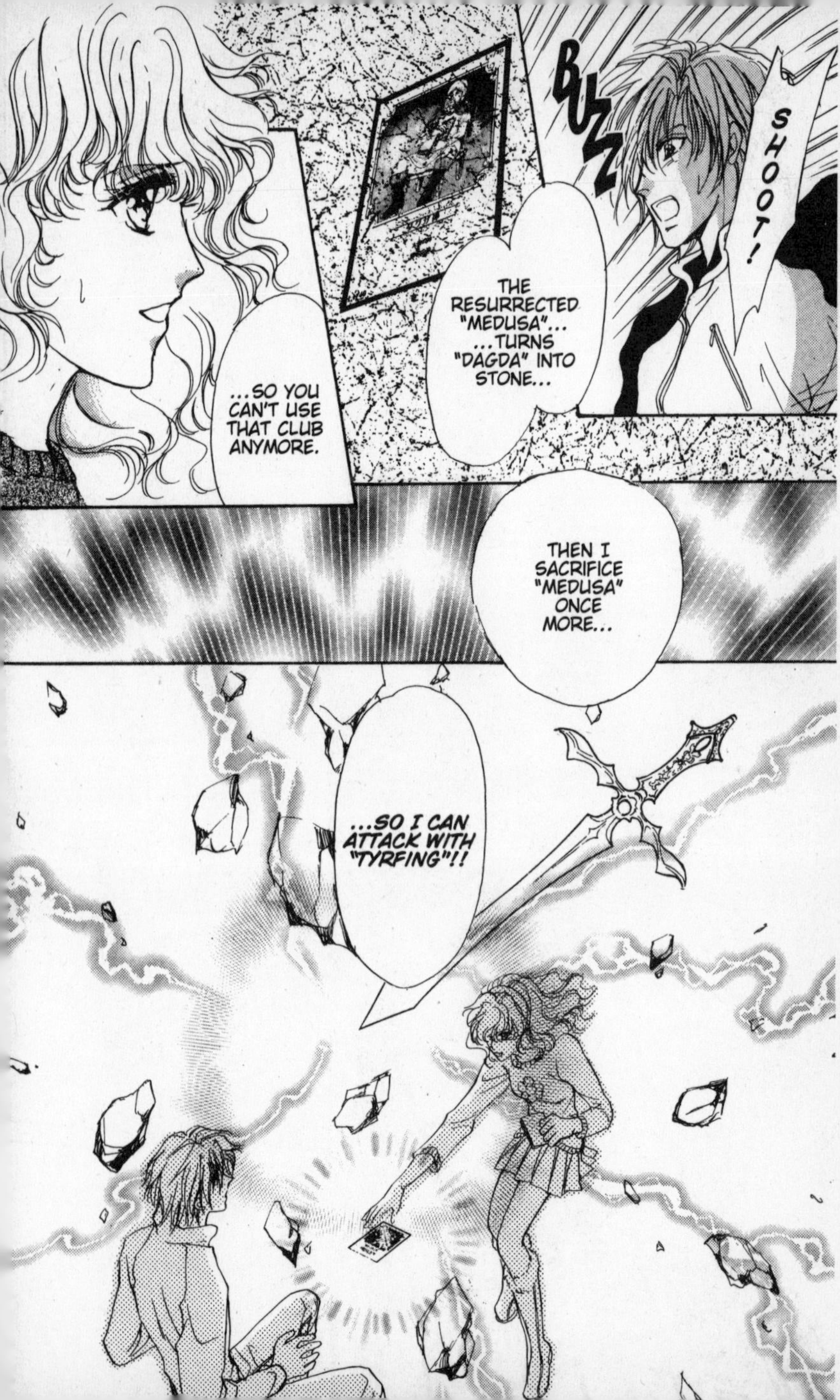
SHOOT!
BUZZ
THE RESURRECTED "MEDUSA"... ...TURNS "DAGDA" INTO STONE...
...SO YOU CAN'T USE THAT CLUB ANYMORE.
THEN I SACRIFICE "MEDUSA" ONCE MORE...
...SO I CAN ATTACK WITH "TYRFING"!!

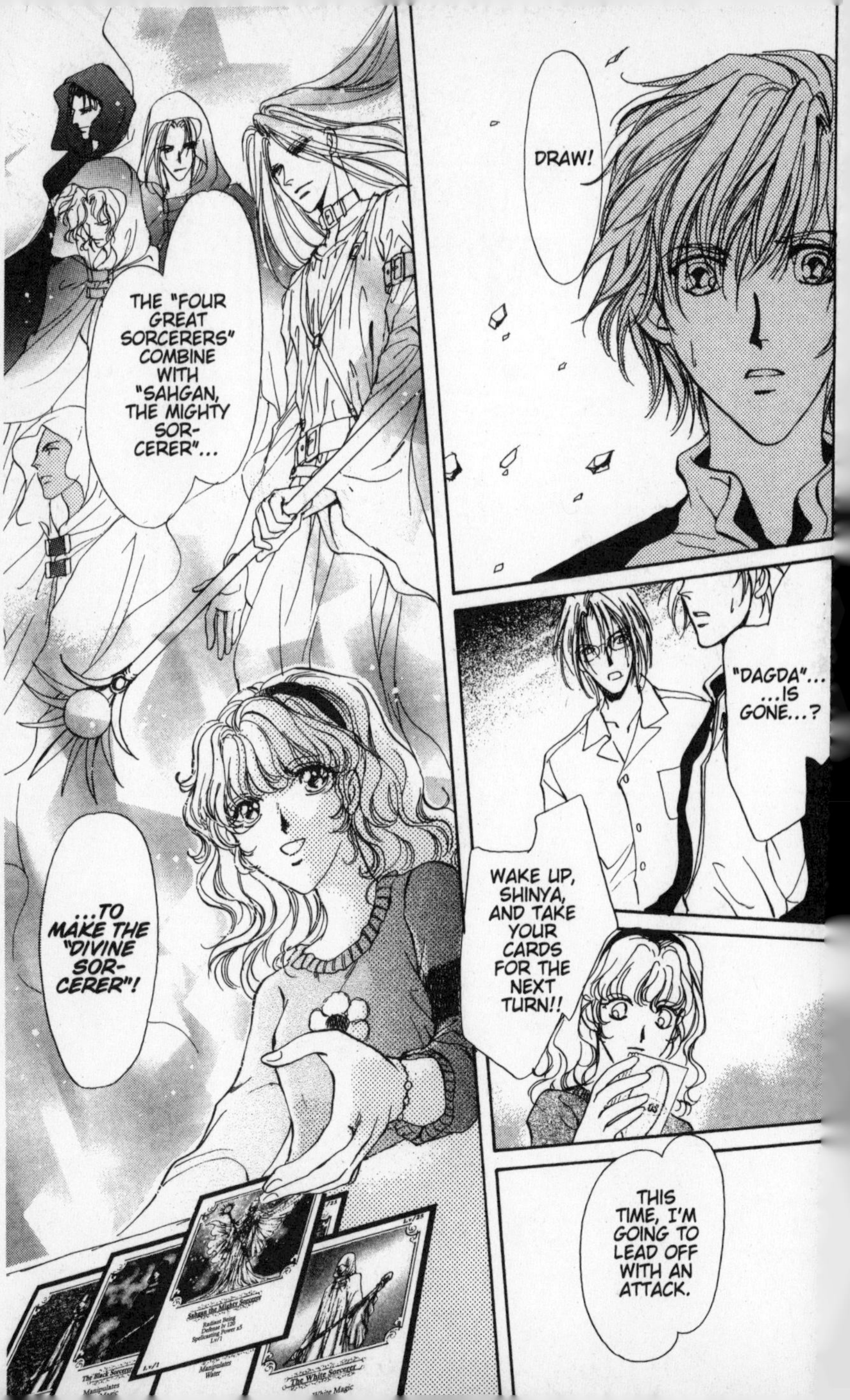
DRAW!
"DAGDA"... ...IS GONE...?
WAKE UP, SHINYA, AND TAKE YOUR CARDS FOR THE NEXT TURN!!
THIS TIME, I'M GOING TO LEAD OFF WITH AN ATTACK.
THE "FOUR GREAT SORCERERS" COMBINE WITH "SAHGAN, THE MIGHTY SOR-CERER"...
...TO MAKE THE "DIVINE SOR-CERER"!
Sahgan the Mighty Sorcerer
The Black Sorcerer
Manipulates Water
The White Sorcerer

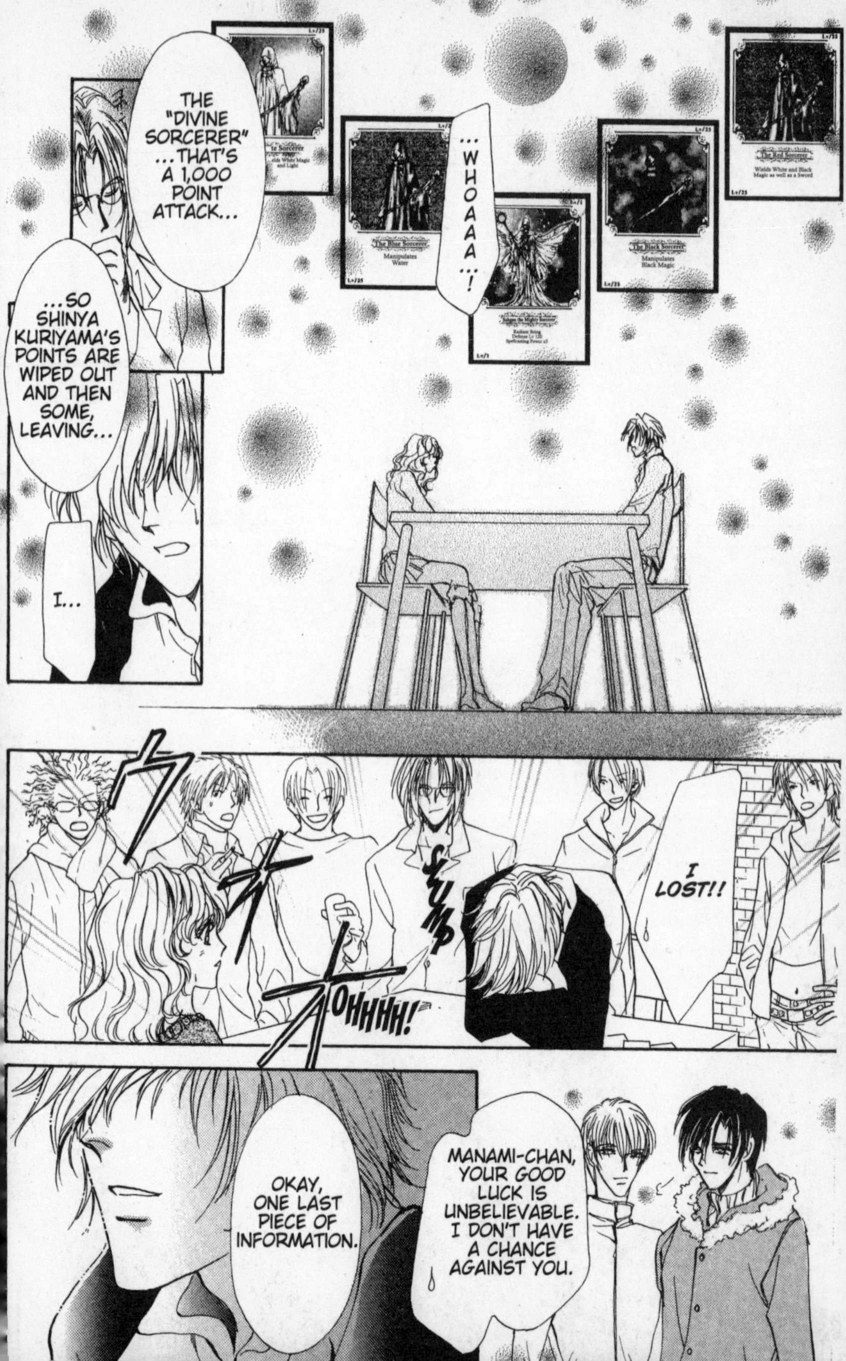

The Red Sorcerer
Wields White and Black Magic as well as a Sword
The Black Sorcerer
Manipulates Black Magic
Sahgan the Mighty Sorcerer
...WHOAAA...!
The Blue Sorcerer
Manipulates Water
THE "DIVINE SORCERER" ...THAT'S A 1,000 POINT ATTACK...
...SO SHINYA KURIYAMA'S POINTS ARE WIPED OUT AND THEN SOME, LEAVING...
I...
I LOST!!
SLUMP
OHHHH!
MANAMI-CHAN, YOUR GOOD LUCK IS UNBELIEVABLE. I DON'T HAVE A CHANCE AGAINST YOU.
OKAY, ONE LAST PIECE OF INFORMATION.

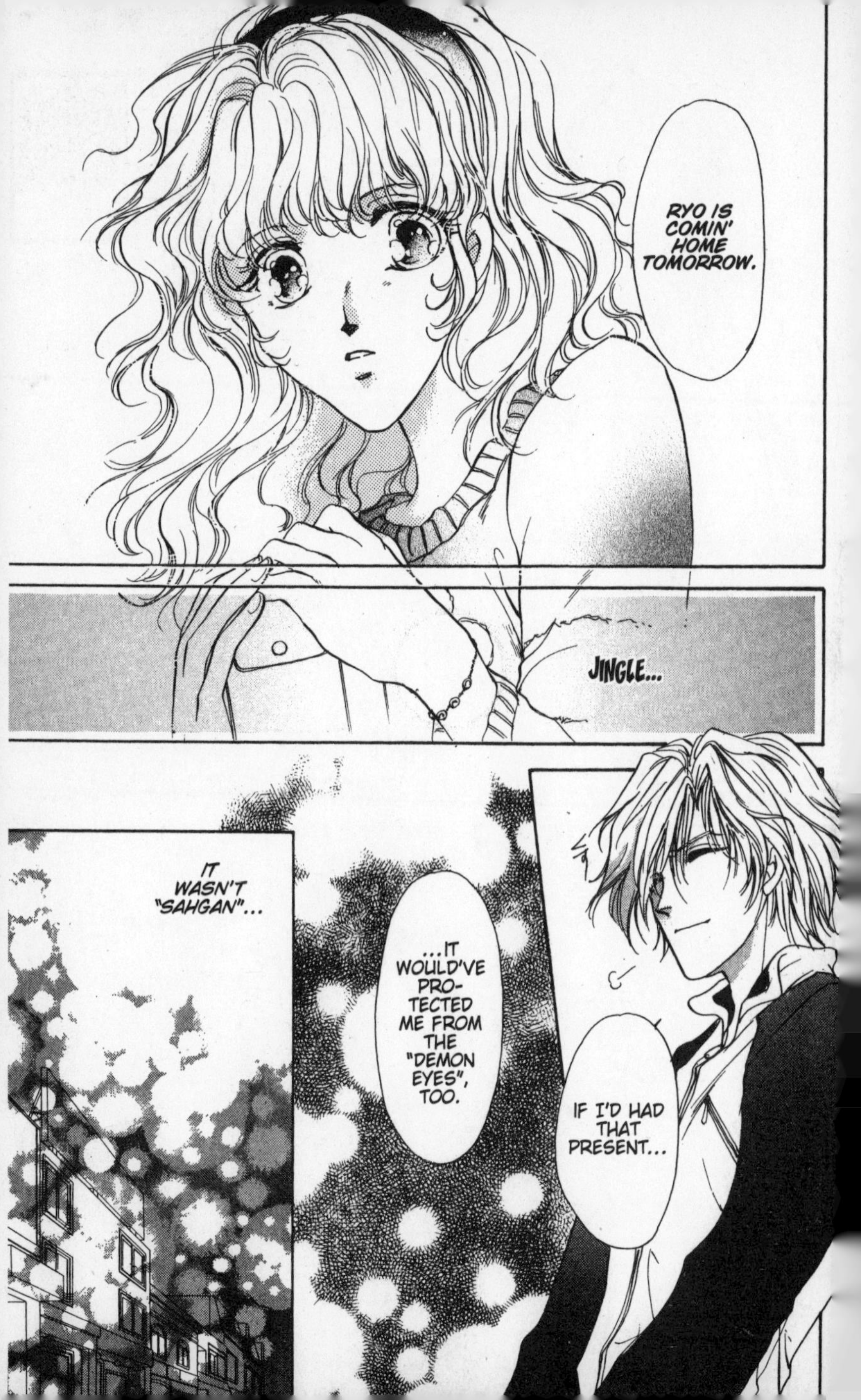
RYO IS COMIN' HOME TOMORROW.
JINGLE...
IF I'D HAD THAT PRESENT...
...IT WOULD'VE PRO-TECTED ME FROM THE "DEMON EYES", TOO.
IT WASN'T "SAHGAN"...

...WHO HELPED ME...

...IN THE DREAM.

UM...

...BOTH OF YOU, I'M SORRY.

I'M SORRY...

...FOR MAKING YOU WORRY.

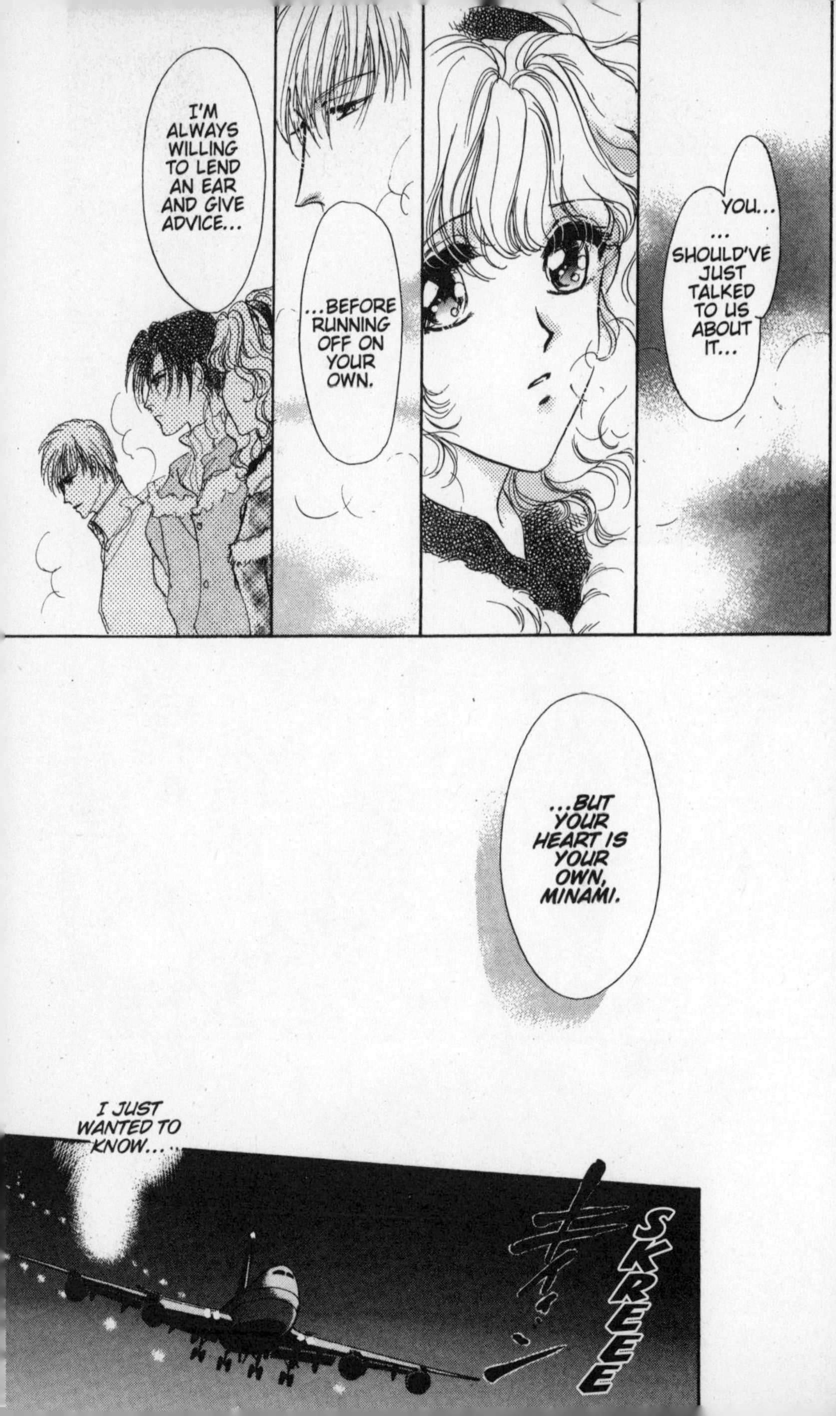
YOU... ...SHOULD'VE JUST TALKED TO US ABOUT IT...
...BEFORE RUNNING OFF ON YOUR OWN.
I'M ALWAYS WILLING TO LEND AN EAR AND GIVE ADVICE...
...BUT YOUR HEART IS YOUR OWN, MINAMI.
I JUST WANTED TO KNOW...
SKREEE

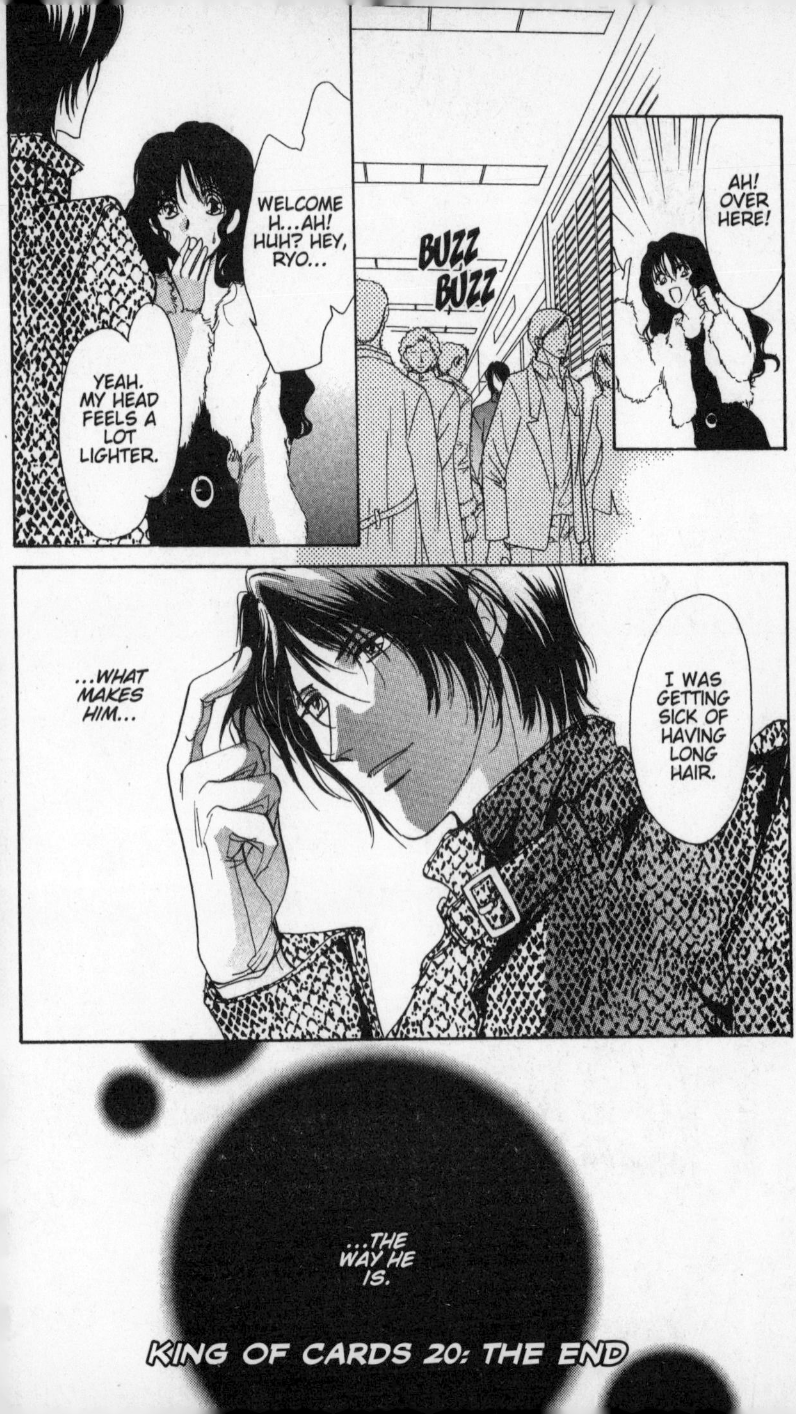
AH! OVER HERE!
BUZZ BUZZ
WELCOME H...AH! HUH? HEY, RYO...
YEAH. MY HEAD FEELS A LOT LIGHTER.
I WAS GETTING SICK OF HAVING LONG HAIR.
...WHAT MAKES HIM...
...THE WAY HE IS.

KING OF CARDS 20: THE END

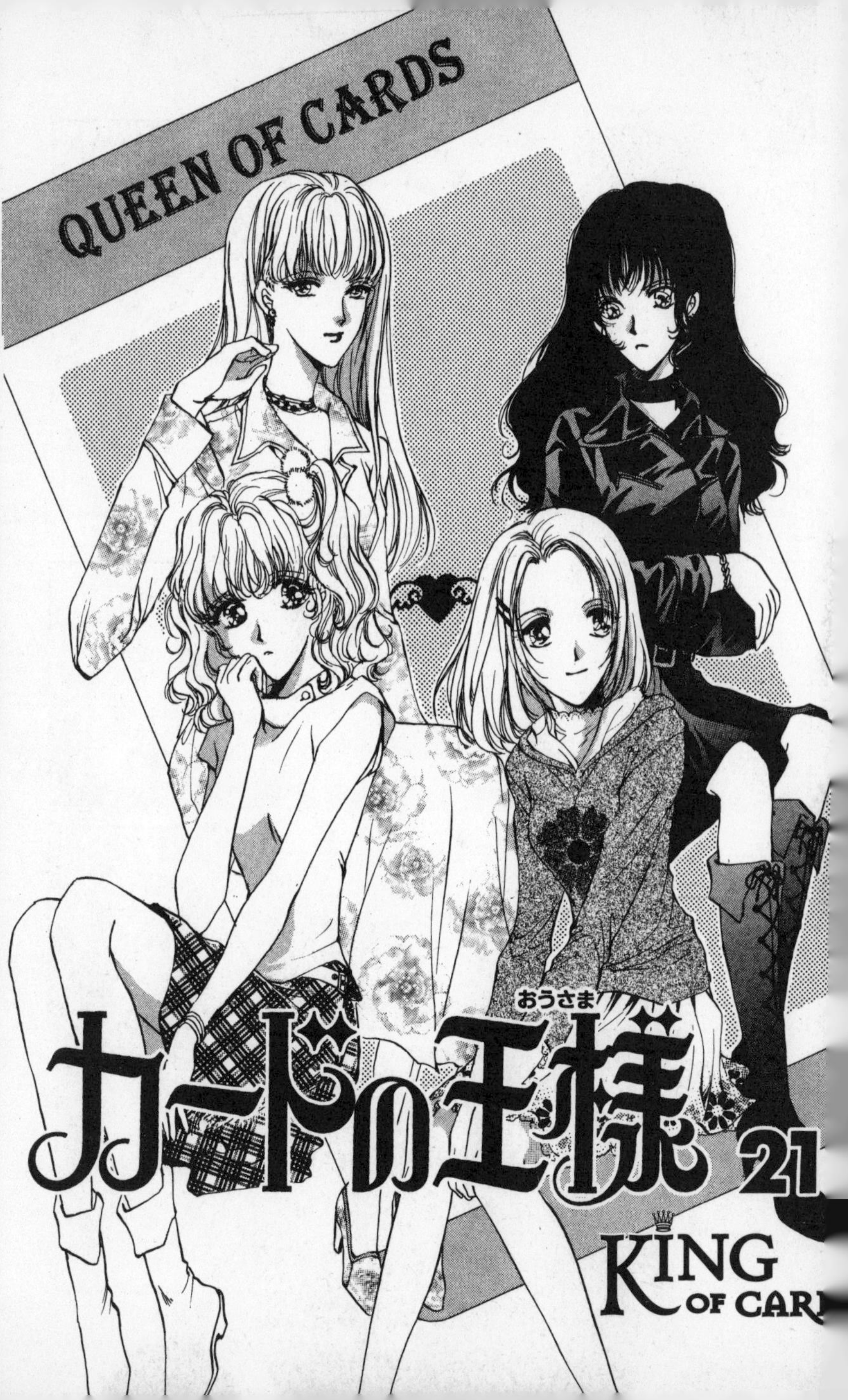
QUEEN OF CARDS
カードの王様(おうさま)
21
KING OF CAR

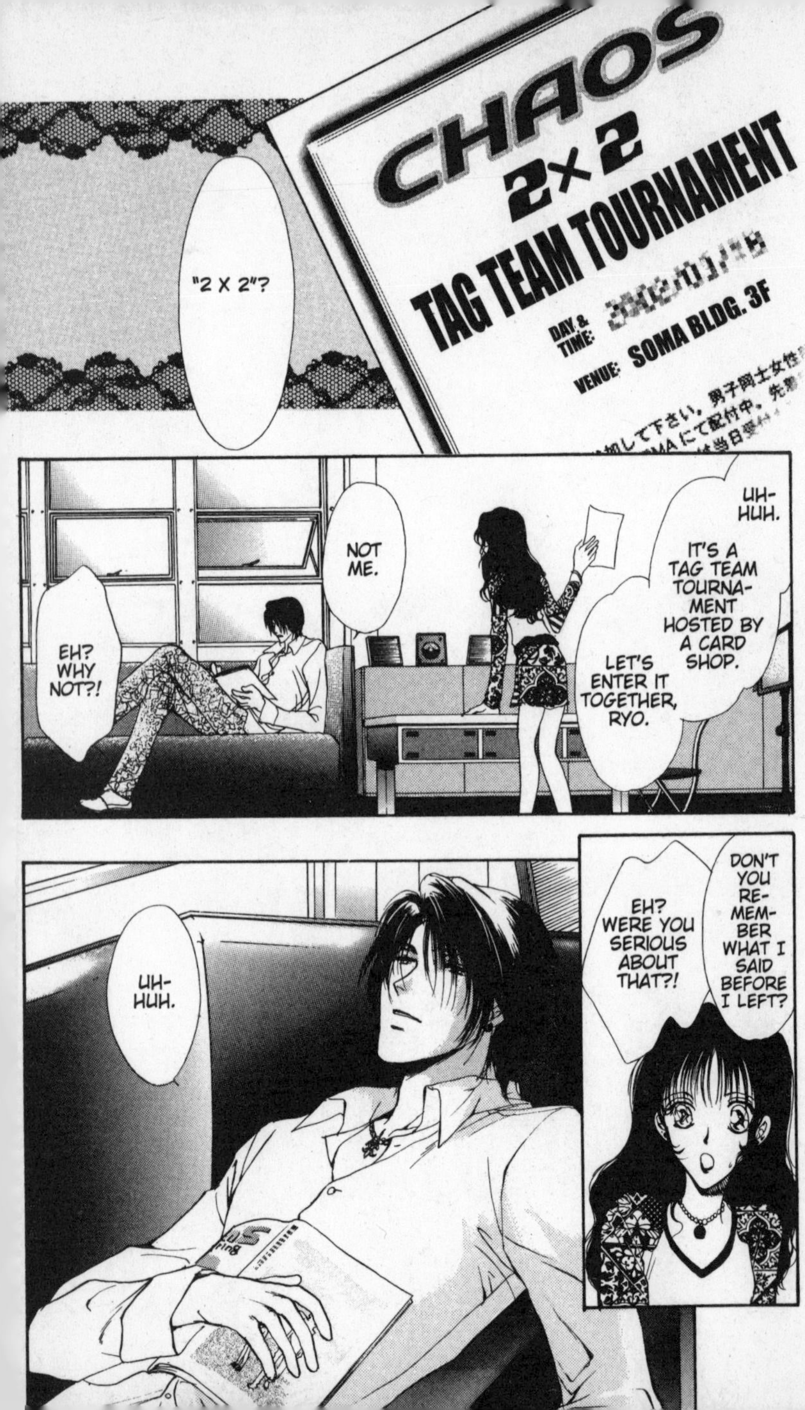
CHAOS
2x2
TAG TEAM TOURNAMENT
DAY & TIME:
VENUE: SOMA BLDG. 3F
"2 X 2"?
UH-HUH. IT'S A TAG TEAM TOURNAMENT HOSTED BY A CARD SHOP.
LET'S ENTER IT TOGETHER, RYO.
NOT ME.
EH? WHY NOT?!
DON'T YOU REMEMBER WHAT I SAID BEFORE I LEFT?
EH? WERE YOU SERIOUS ABOUT THAT?!
UH-HUH.

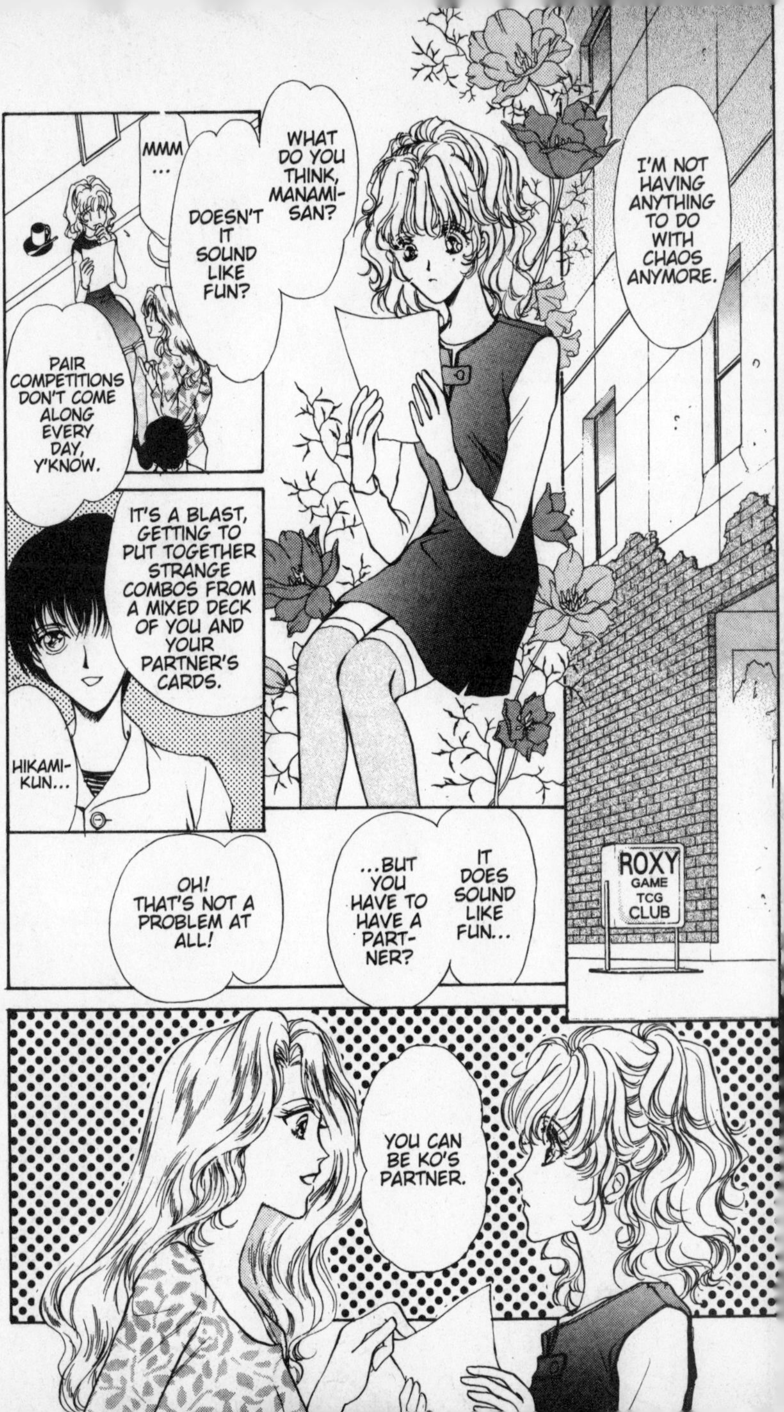
I'M NOT HAVING ANYTHING TO DO WITH CHAOS ANYMORE.
ROXY GAME TCG CLUB
WHAT DO YOU THINK, MANAMI-SAN?
DOESN'T IT SOUND LIKE FUN?
MMM ...
PAIR COMPETITIONS DON'T COME ALONG EVERY DAY, Y'KNOW.
IT'S A BLAST, GETTING TO PUT TOGETHER STRANGE COMBOS FROM A MIXED DECK OF YOU AND YOUR PARTNER'S CARDS.
HIKAMI-KUN...
IT DOES SOUND LIKE FUN...
...BUT YOU HAVE TO HAVE A PARTNER?
OH! THAT'S NOT A PROBLEM AT ALL!
YOU CAN BE KO'S PARTNER.

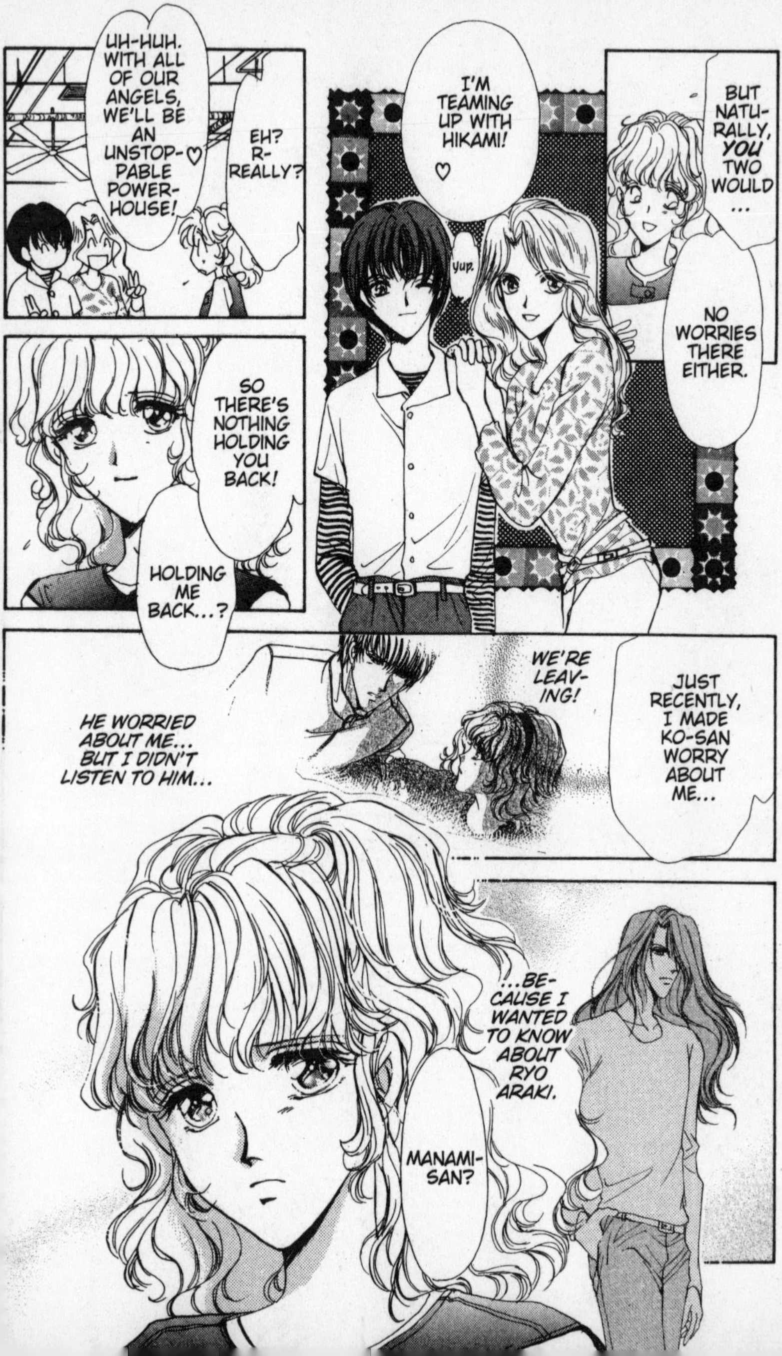
BUT NATURALLY, YOU TWO WOULD...
NO WORRIES THERE EITHER.
I'M TEAMING UP WITH HIKAMI! ♡
yup.
UH-HUH. WITH ALL OF OUR ANGELS, WE'LL BE AN UNSTOPPABLE POWERHOUSE! ♡
EH? R-REALLY?
SO THERE'S NOTHING HOLDING YOU BACK!
HOLDING ME BACK...?
JUST RECENTLY, I MADE KO-SAN WORRY ABOUT ME...
WE'RE LEAVING!
HE WORRIED ABOUT ME... BUT I DIDN'T LISTEN TO HIM...
...BECAUSE I WANTED TO KNOW ABOUT RYO ARAKI.
MANAMI-SAN?

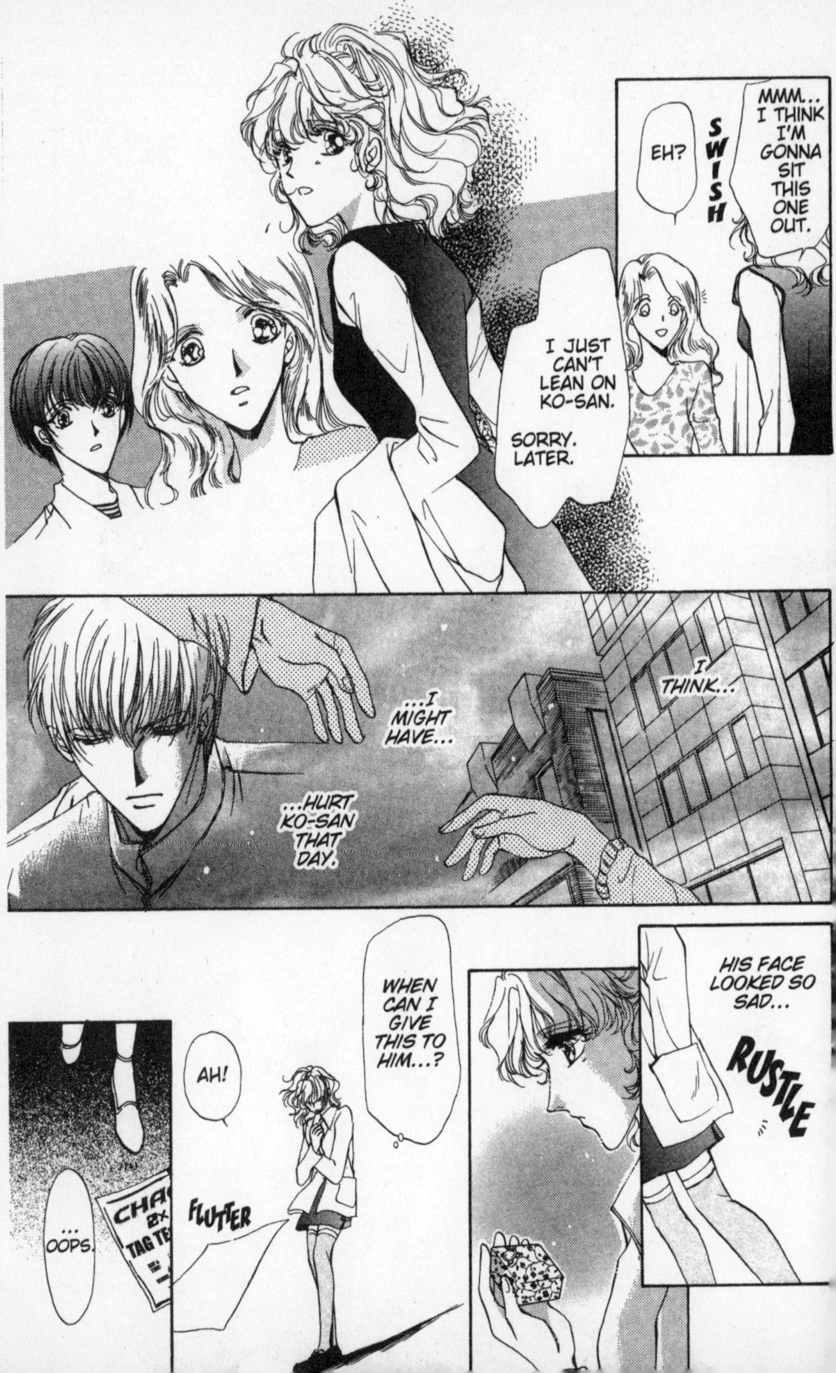
MMM... I THINK I'M GONNA SIT THIS ONE OUT.
SWISH
EH?
I JUST CAN'T LEAN ON KO-SAN.
SORRY. LATER.
I THINK...
...I MIGHT HAVE...
...HURT KO-SAN THAT DAY.
HIS FACE LOOKED SO SAD...
RUSTLE
WHEN CAN I GIVE THIS TO HIM...?
AH!
FLUTTER
... OOPS.

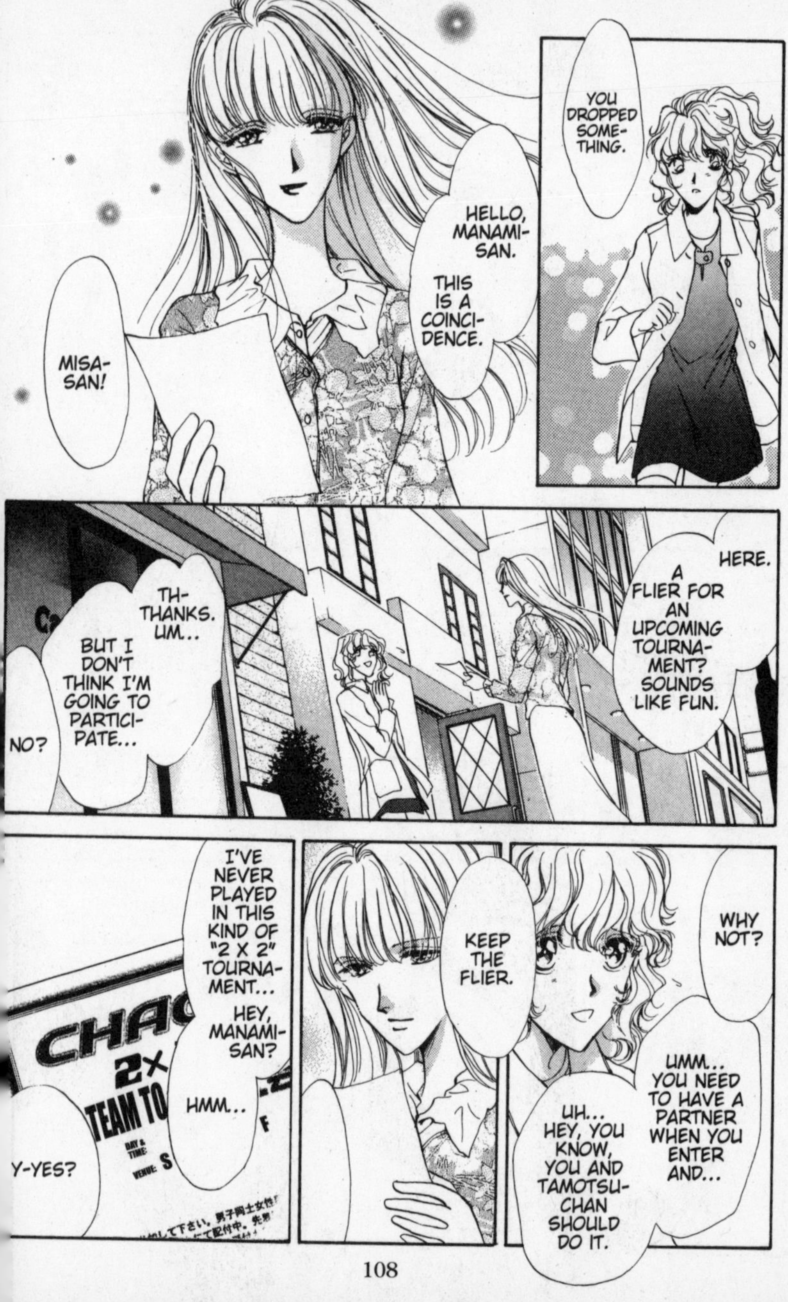
YOU DROPPED SOMETHING.
HELLO, MANAMI-SAN.
THIS IS A COINCIDENCE.
MISA-SAN!
HERE.
A FLIER FOR AN UPCOMING TOURNAMENT? SOUNDS LIKE FUN.
TH-THANKS. UM...
BUT I DON'T THINK I'M GOING TO PARTICIPATE...
NO?
WHY NOT?
UMM... YOU NEED TO HAVE A PARTNER WHEN YOU ENTER AND...
UH... HEY, YOU KNOW, YOU AND TAMOTSU-CHAN SHOULD DO IT.
KEEP THE FLIER.
I'VE NEVER PLAYED IN THIS KIND OF "2 X 2" TOURNAMENT...
HEY, MANAMI-SAN?
HMM...
Y-YES?

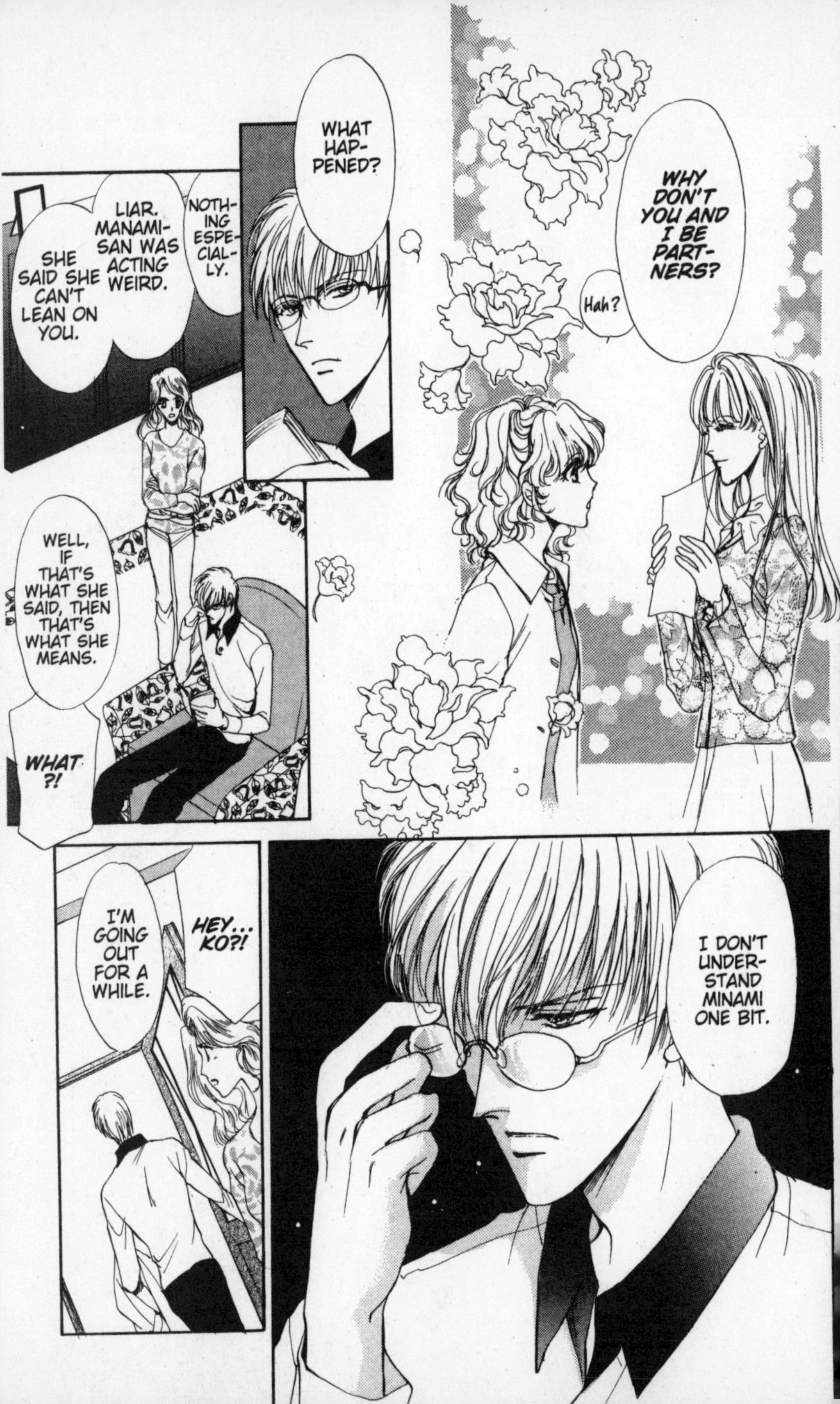
WHY DON'T YOU AND I BE PARTNERS?
Hah?
WHAT HAPPENED?
NOTHING ESPECIALLY.
LIAR. MANAMI-SAN WAS ACTING WEIRD.
SHE SAID SHE CAN'T LEAN ON YOU.
WELL, IF THAT'S WHAT SHE SAID, THEN THAT'S WHAT SHE MEANS.
WHAT?!
I DON'T UNDERSTAND MINAMI ONE BIT.
I'M GOING OUT FOR A WHILE.
HEY... KO?!

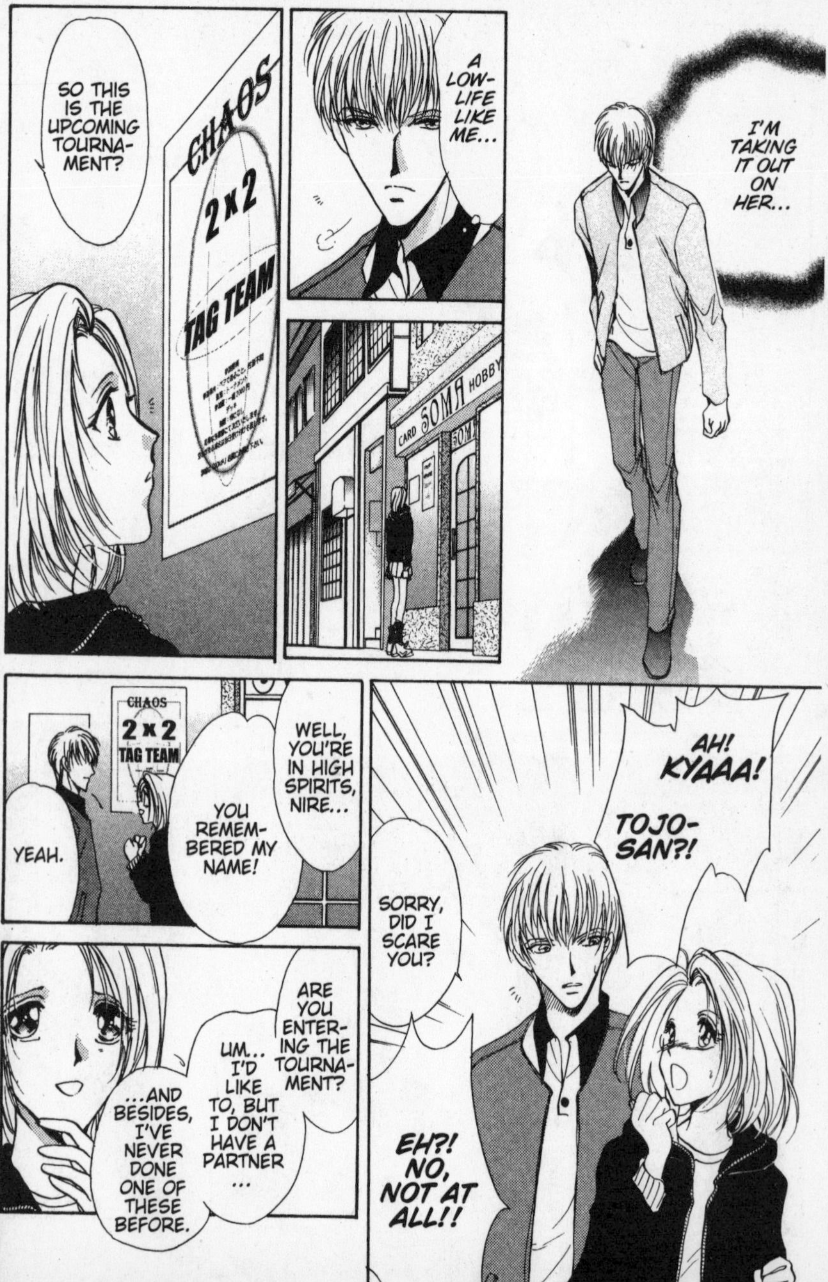
I'M TAKING IT OUT ON HER...
A LOW-LIFE LIKE ME...
CHAOS
2x2
TAG TEAM
HOBBY
CARD
SOMA
SO THIS IS THE UPCOMING TOURNAMENT?
AH! KYAAA!
TOJO-SAN?!
SORRY, DID I SCARE YOU?
EH?! NO, NOT AT ALL!!
WELL, YOU'RE IN HIGH SPIRITS, NIRE...
YOU REMEMBERED MY NAME!
YEAH.
ARE YOU ENTERING THE TOURNAMENT?
UM... I'D LIKE TO, BUT I DON'T HAVE A PARTNER...
...AND BESIDES, I'VE NEVER DONE ONE OF THESE BEFORE.

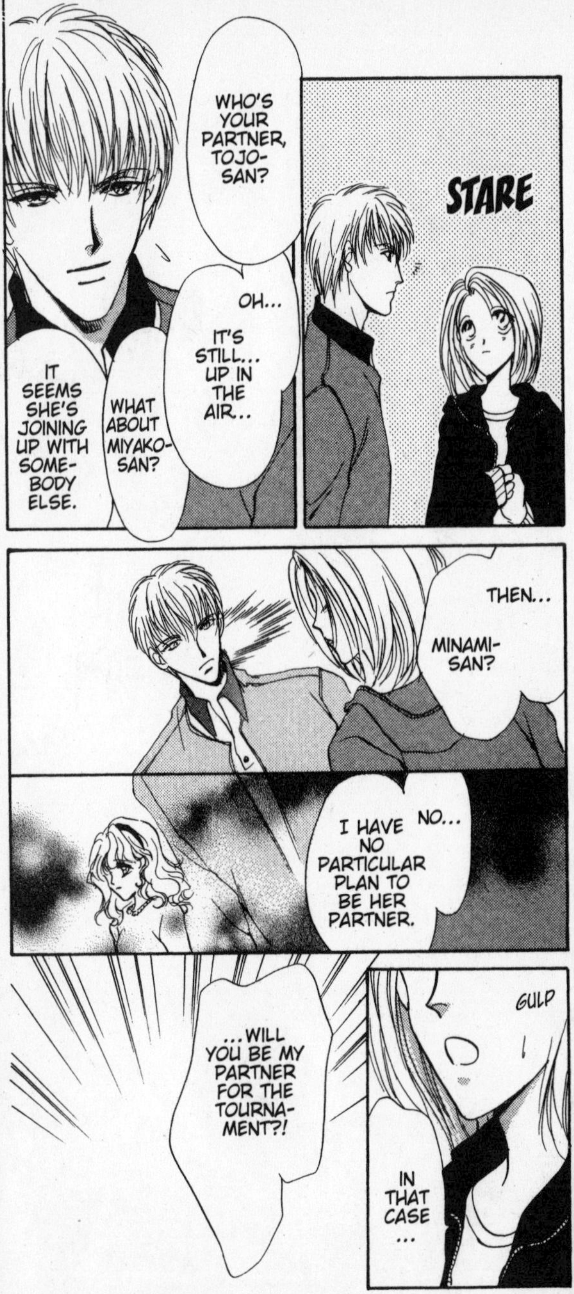
STARE
WHO'S YOUR PARTNER, TOJO-SAN?
OH...
IT'S STILL... UP IN THE AIR...
WHAT ABOUT MIYAKO-SAN?
IT SEEMS SHE'S JOINING UP WITH SOME-BODY ELSE.
THEN...
MINAMI-SAN?
NO...
I HAVE NO PARTICULAR PLAN TO BE HER PARTNER.
GULP
IN THAT CASE...
...WILL YOU BE MY PARTNER FOR THE TOURNA-MENT?!

I GET A LOT OF LETTERS SAYING THAT "THERE'S NOT ENOUGH TEXT ON THE CARDS", BUT TO TELL YOU THE TRUTH, I DO THAT ON PURPOSE, THE REASON BEING THAT IF I WRITE IN DETAIL ON THE CARDS, YOU SMART READERS WOULD FIGURE OUT THE OUTCOMES OF THE BATTLES ALL TOO SOON. ONE OF THE TECHNIQUES OF MANGA IS BEING VAGUE. I TRY TO WRITE AS LITTLE AS POSSIBLE ON THE CARDS, WHICH ALLOWS ME TO USE AND INTERPRET THEM IN THE STORIES IN DIFFERENT WAYS. IF "CHAOS" WAS AN ACTUAL GAME, MORE INFO WOULD HAVE TO BE WRITTEN ON THE EVENT CARDS, ETC. ACTUALLY, IN THE ACTUAL STORIES, THERE PROBABLY IS MORE INFO WRITTEN ON THE CARDS (THAT YOU, THE READERS, JUST DON'T GET TO SEE). AFTER ALL, THERE'S A LIMIT TO THE AMOUNT OF INFO MANAMI AND THE REST CAN MEMORIZE. MY LIMIT IS VERY LOW. I'M BAD AT POKER AND EVEN UNO...AH, AND BLACKJACK...

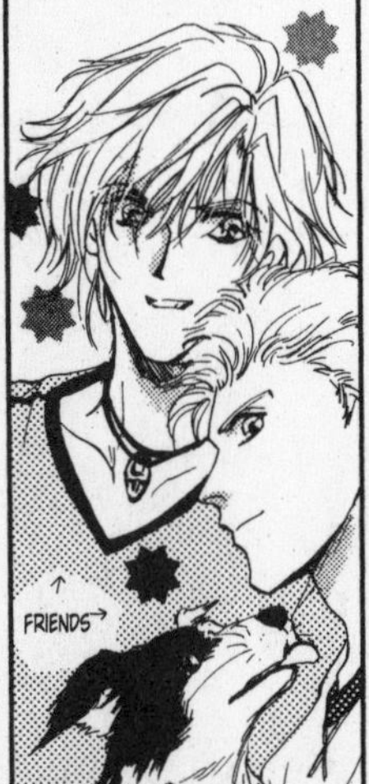
FRIENDS
SUZAKI

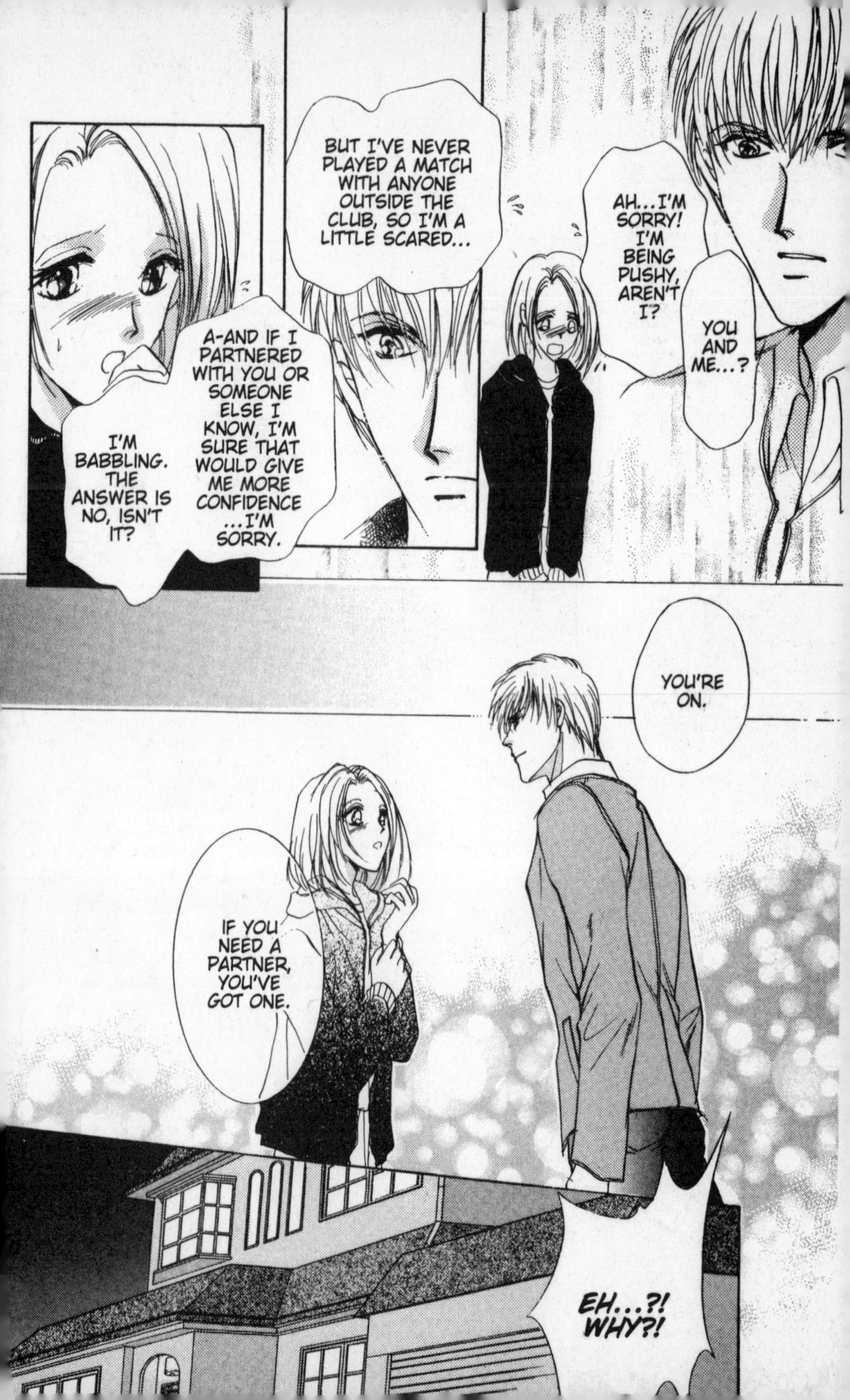
YOU AND ME...?
AH...I'M SORRY! I'M BEING PUSHY, AREN'T I?
BUT I'VE NEVER PLAYED A MATCH WITH ANYONE OUTSIDE THE CLUB, SO I'M A LITTLE SCARED...
A-AND IF I PARTNERED WITH YOU OR SOMEONE ELSE I KNOW, I'M SURE THAT WOULD GIVE ME MORE CONFIDENCE ...I'M SORRY.
I'M BABBLING. THE ANSWER IS NO, ISN'T IT?
YOU'RE ON.
IF YOU NEED A PARTNER, YOU'VE GOT ONE.
EH...?! WHY?!

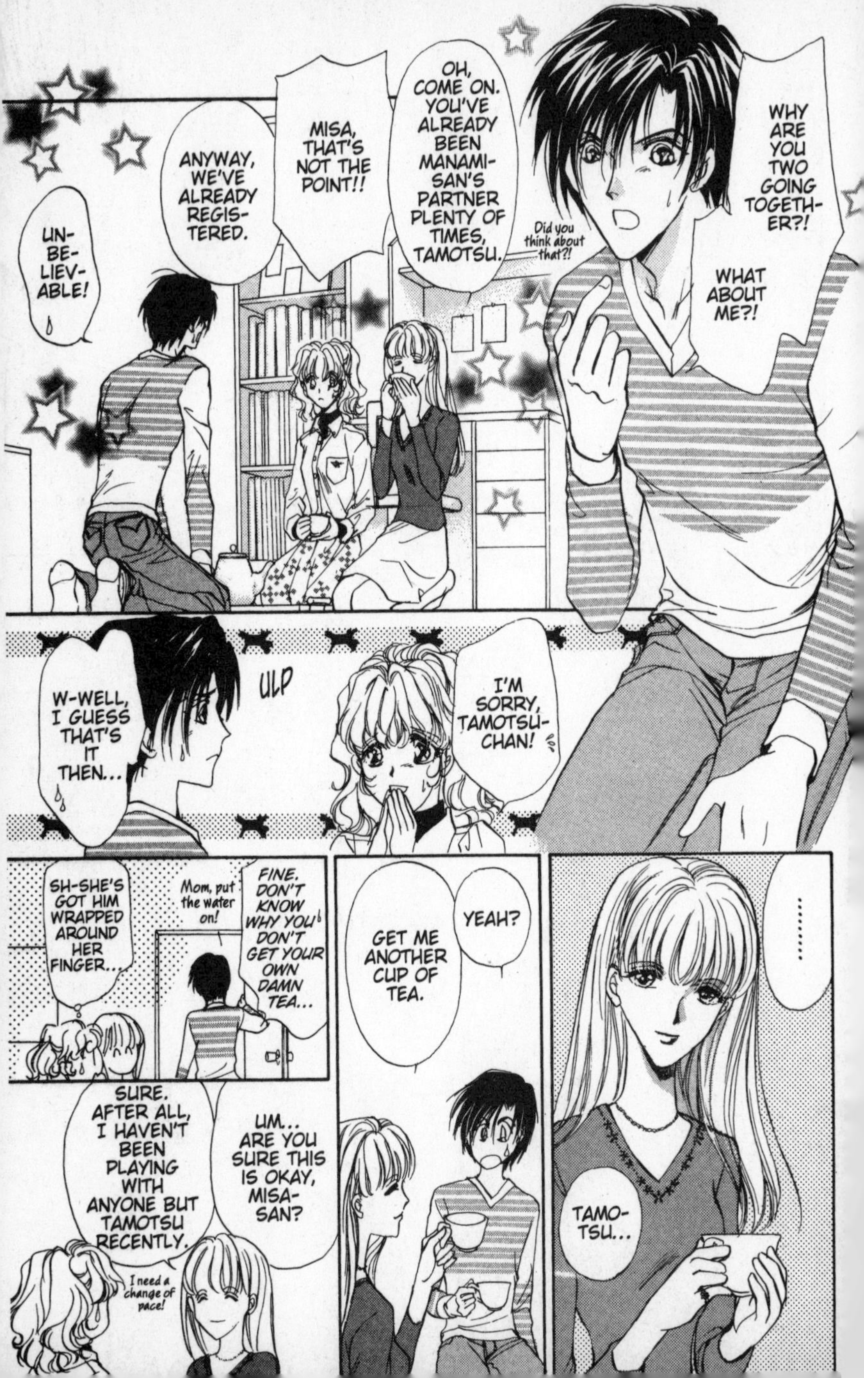
WHY ARE YOU TWO GOING TOGETHER?!
WHAT ABOUT ME?!
Did you think about that?!
OH, COME ON. YOU'VE ALREADY BEEN MANAMI-SAN'S PARTNER PLENTY OF TIMES, TAMOTSU.
MISA, THAT'S NOT THE POINT!!
ANYWAY, WE'VE ALREADY REGISTERED.
UNBELIEVABLE!
I'M SORRY, TAMOTSU-CHAN!
ULP
W-WELL, I GUESS THAT'S IT THEN...
......
TAMOTSU...
YEAH?
GET ME ANOTHER CUP OF TEA.
FINE. DON'T KNOW WHY YOU DON'T GET YOUR OWN DAMN TEA...
Mom, put the water on!
SH-SHE'S GOT HIM WRAPPED AROUND HER FINGER...
UM... ARE YOU SURE THIS IS OKAY, MISA-SAN?
SURE. AFTER ALL, I HAVEN'T BEEN PLAYING WITH ANYONE BUT TAMOTSU RECENTLY.
I need a change of pace!

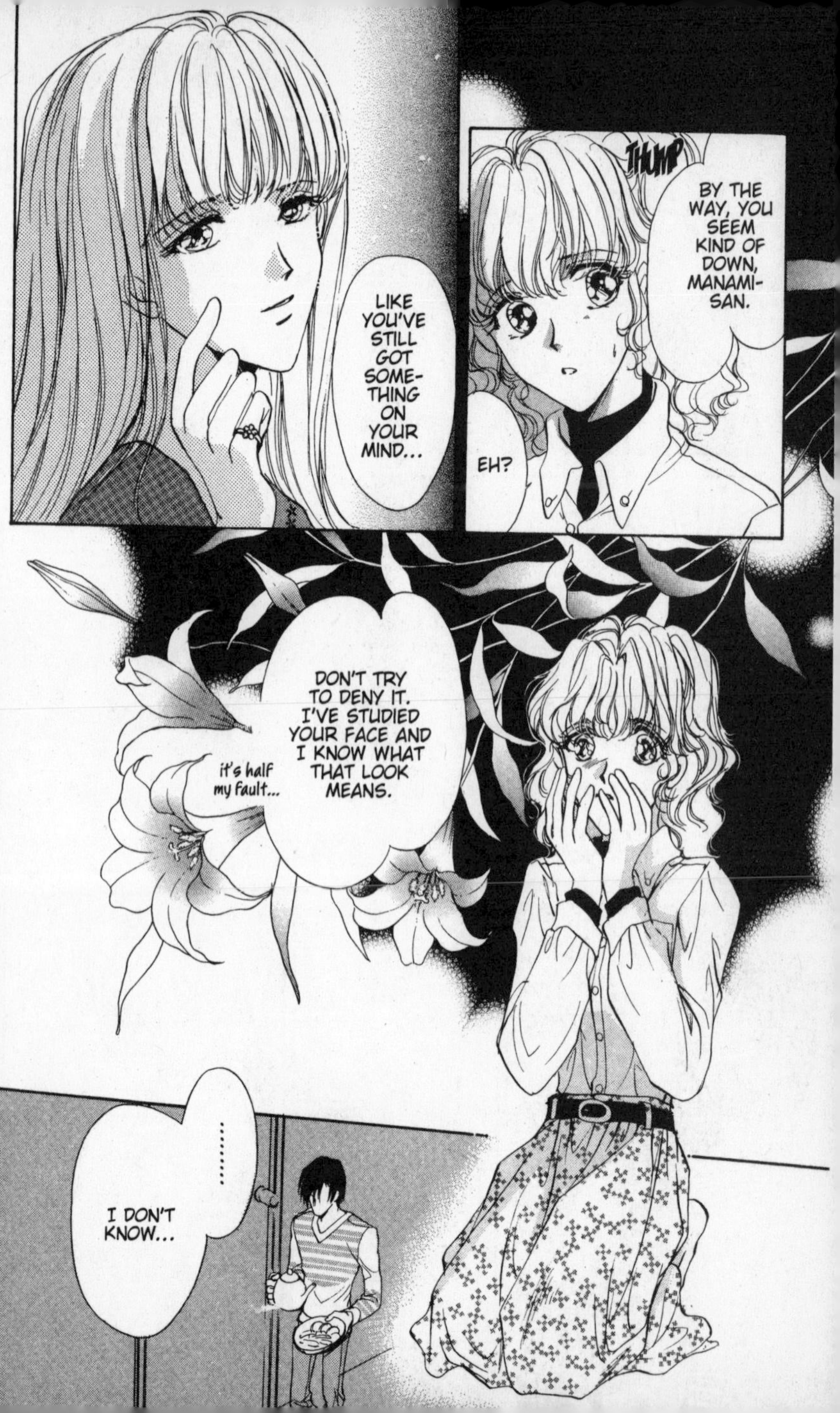
THUMP
BY THE WAY, YOU SEEM KIND OF DOWN, MANAMI-SAN.
EH?
LIKE YOU'VE STILL GOT SOMETHING ON YOUR MIND...
DON'T TRY TO DENY IT. I'VE STUDIED YOUR FACE AND I KNOW WHAT THAT LOOK MEANS.
it's half my fault...
......
I DON'T KNOW...

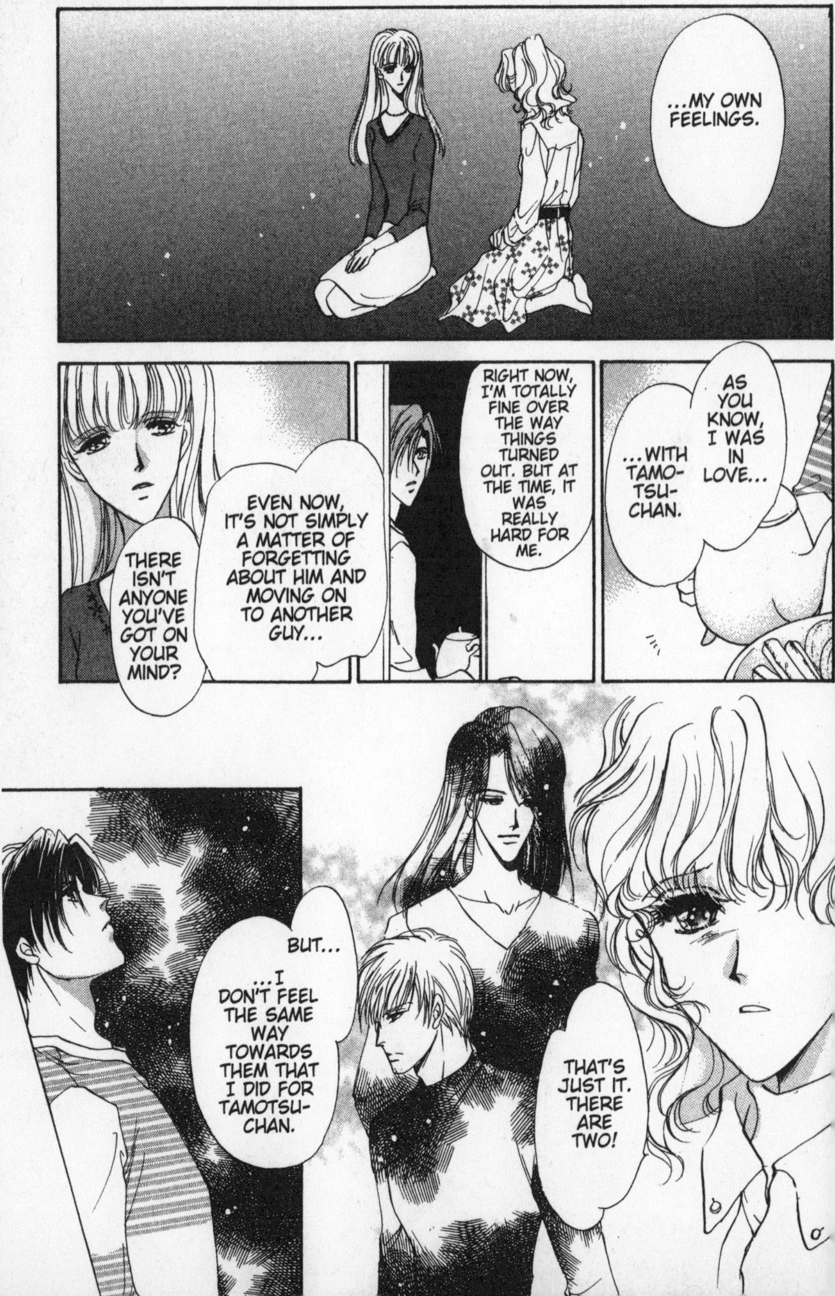
...MY OWN FEELINGS.
AS YOU KNOW, I WAS IN LOVE...
...WITH TAMOTSU-CHAN.
RIGHT NOW, I'M TOTALLY FINE OVER THE WAY THINGS TURNED OUT. BUT AT THE TIME, IT WAS REALLY HARD FOR ME.
EVEN NOW, IT'S NOT SIMPLY A MATTER OF FORGETTING ABOUT HIM AND MOVING ON TO ANOTHER GUY...
THERE ISN'T ANYONE YOU'VE GOT ON YOUR MIND?
THAT'S JUST IT. THERE ARE TWO!
BUT...
...I DON'T FEEL THE SAME WAY TOWARDS THEM THAT I DID FOR TAMOTSU-CHAN.

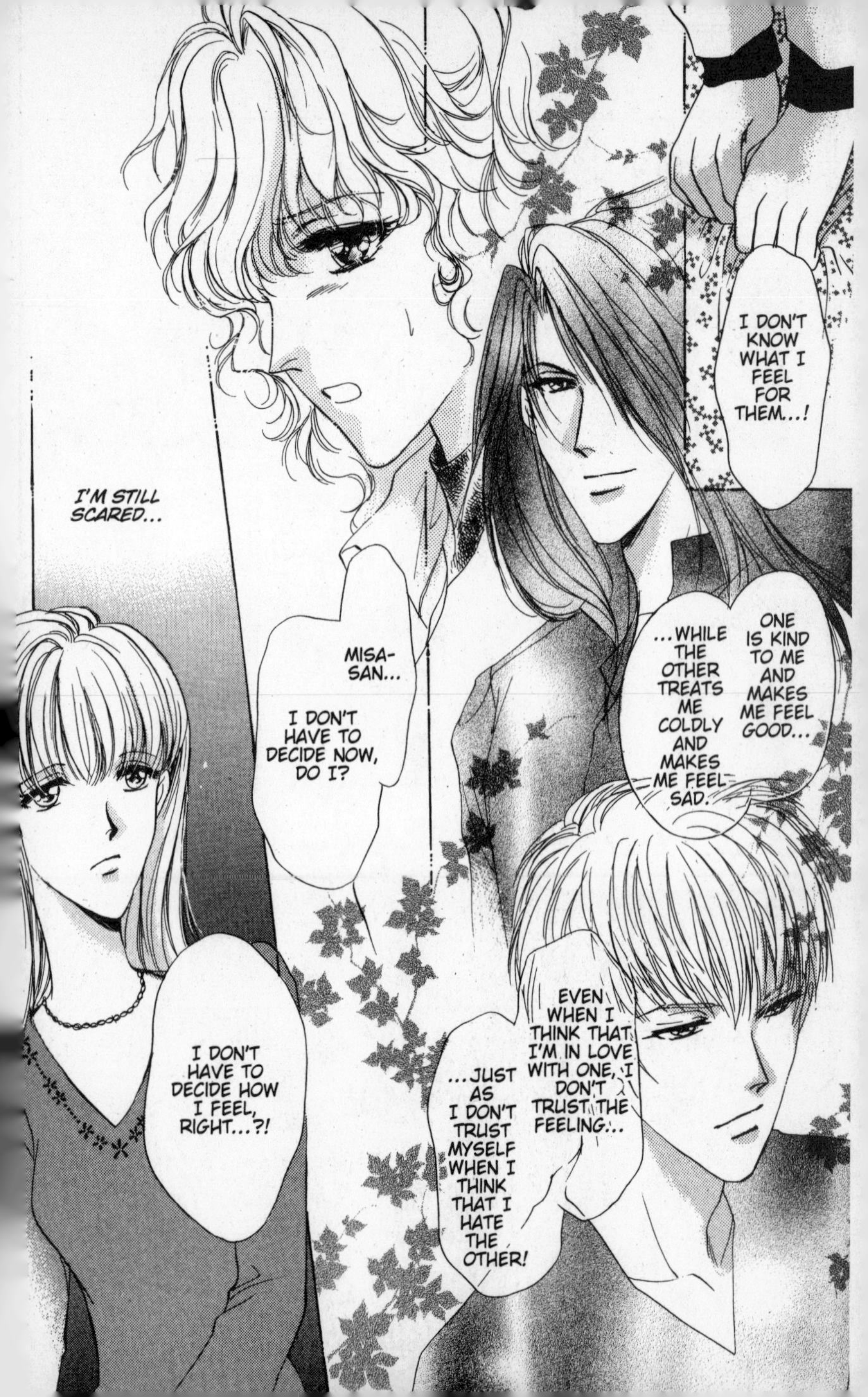
I DON'T KNOW WHAT I FEEL FOR THEM...!
ONE IS KIND TO ME AND MAKES ME FEEL GOOD...
...WHILE THE OTHER TREATS ME COLDLY AND MAKES ME FEEL SAD.
MISA-SAN...
I DON'T HAVE TO DECIDE NOW, DO I?
I'M STILL SCARED...
EVEN WHEN I THINK THAT I'M IN LOVE WITH ONE, I DON'T TRUST THE FEELING...
...JUST AS I DON'T TRUST MYSELF WHEN I THINK THAT I HATE THE OTHER!
I DON'T HAVE TO DECIDE HOW I FEEL, RIGHT...?!

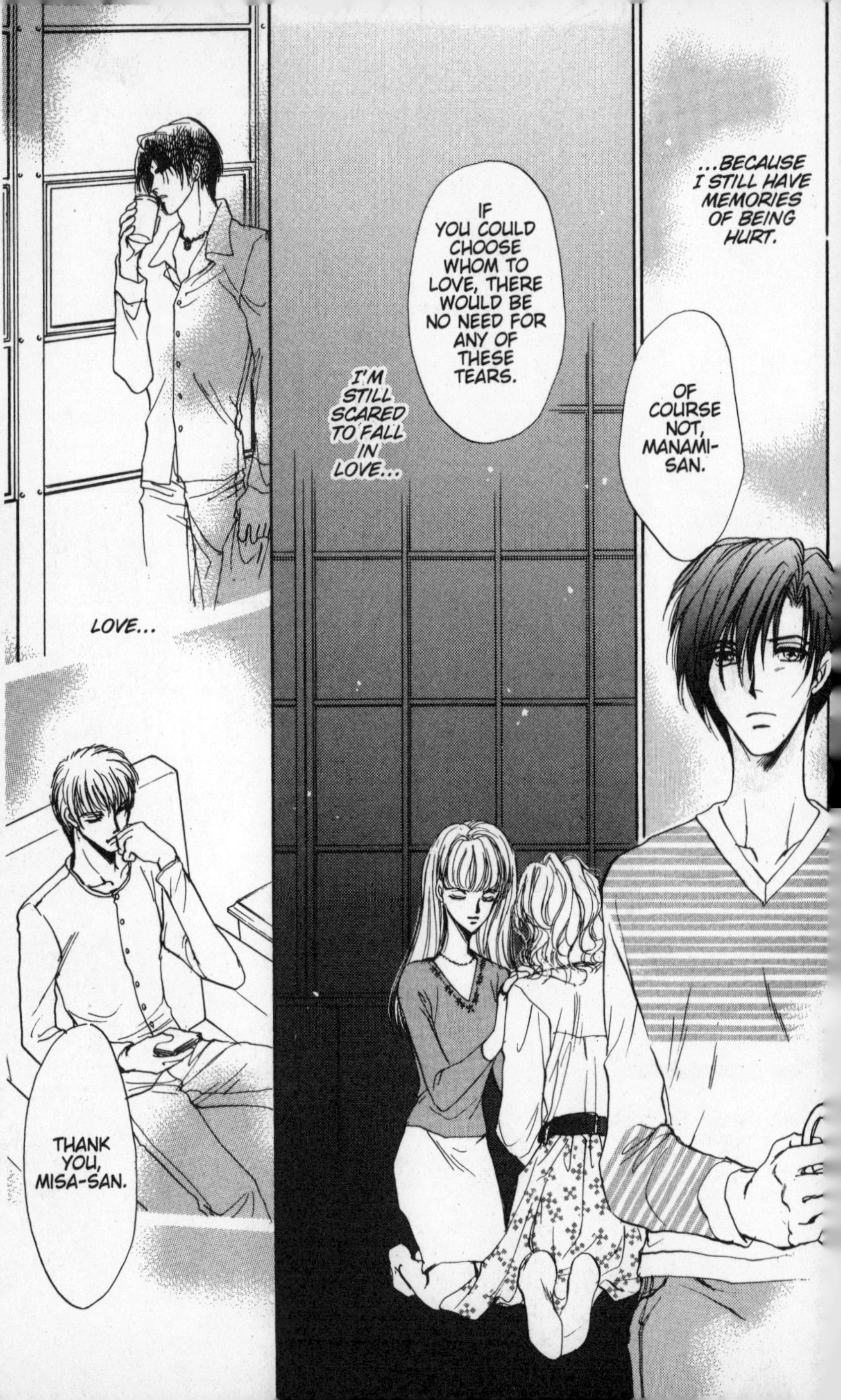
...BECAUSE I STILL HAVE MEMORIES OF BEING HURT.
OF COURSE NOT, MANAMI-SAN.
IF YOU COULD CHOOSE WHOM TO LOVE, THERE WOULD BE NO NEED FOR ANY OF THESE TEARS.
I'M STILL SCARED TO FALL IN LOVE...
LOVE...
THANK YOU, MISA-SAN.

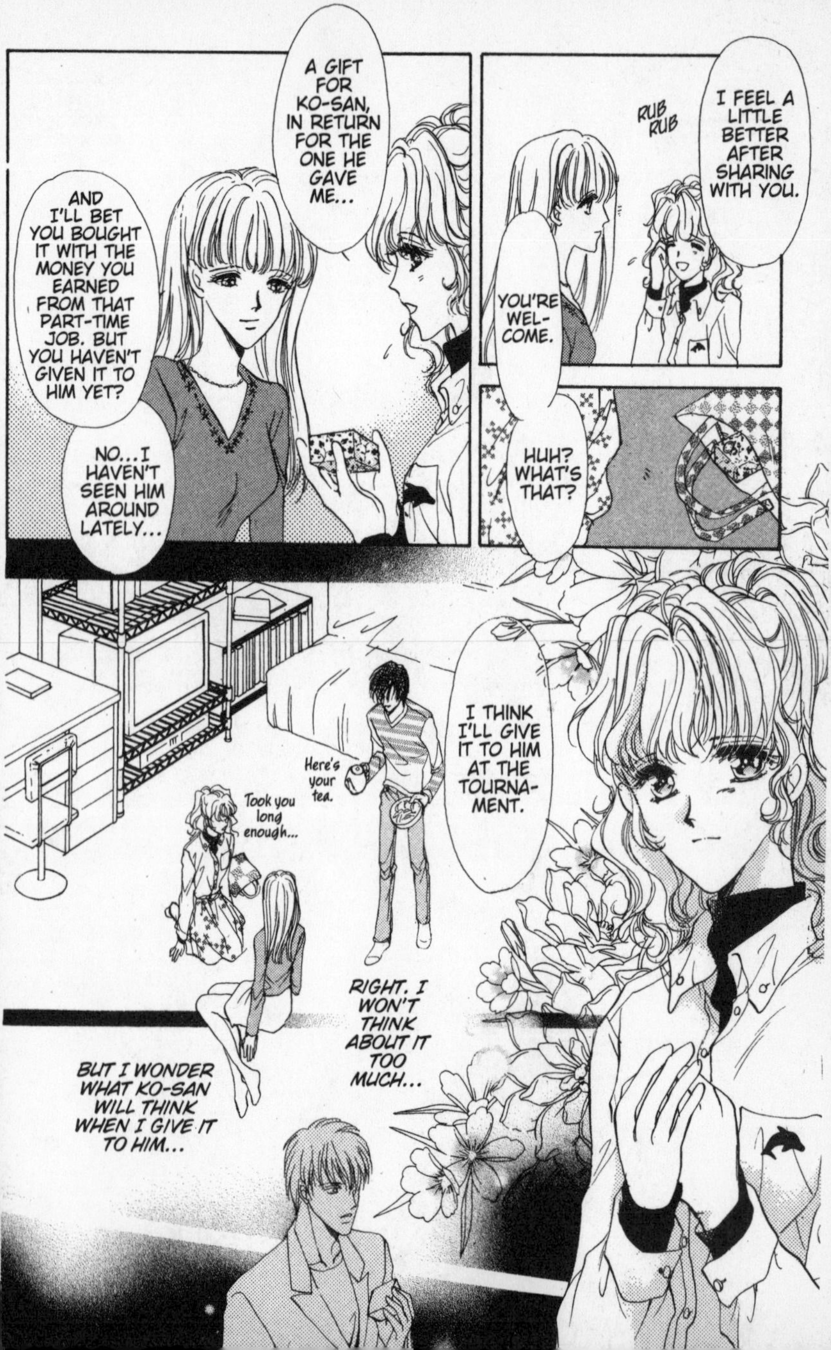
RUB RUB
I FEEL A LITTLE BETTER AFTER SHARING WITH YOU.
YOU'RE WEL-COME.
HUH? WHAT'S THAT?
A GIFT FOR KO-SAN, IN RETURN FOR THE ONE HE GAVE ME...
AND I'LL BET YOU BOUGHT IT WITH THE MONEY YOU EARNED FROM THAT PART-TIME JOB. BUT YOU HAVEN'T GIVEN IT TO HIM YET?
NO...I HAVEN'T SEEN HIM AROUND LATELY...
I THINK I'LL GIVE IT TO HIM AT THE TOURNA-MENT.
Here's your tea.
Took you long enough...
RIGHT. I WON'T THINK ABOUT IT TOO MUCH...
BUT I WONDER WHAT KO-SAN WILL THINK WHEN I GIVE IT TO HIM...

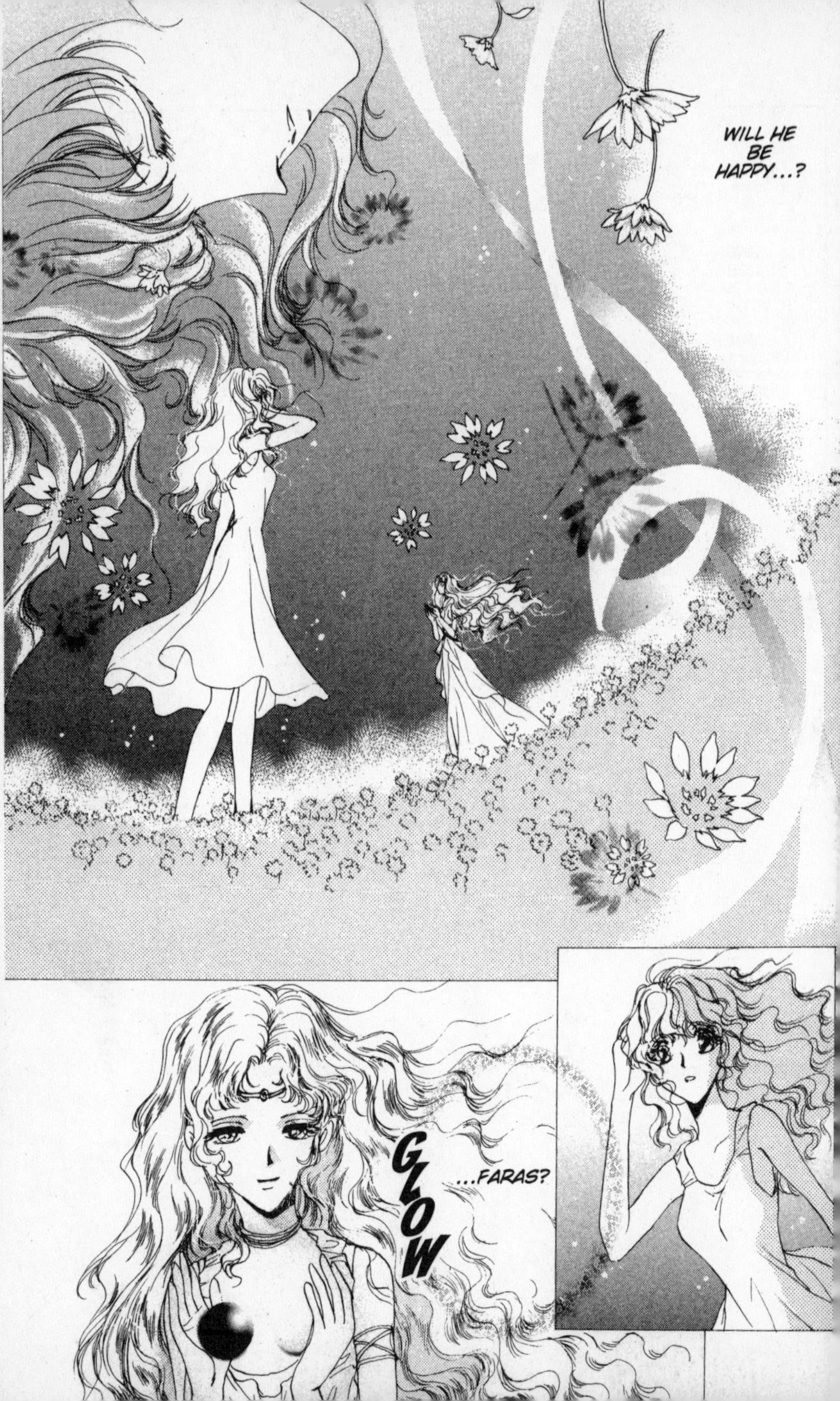
WILL HE BE HAPPY...?
GLOW
...FARAS?

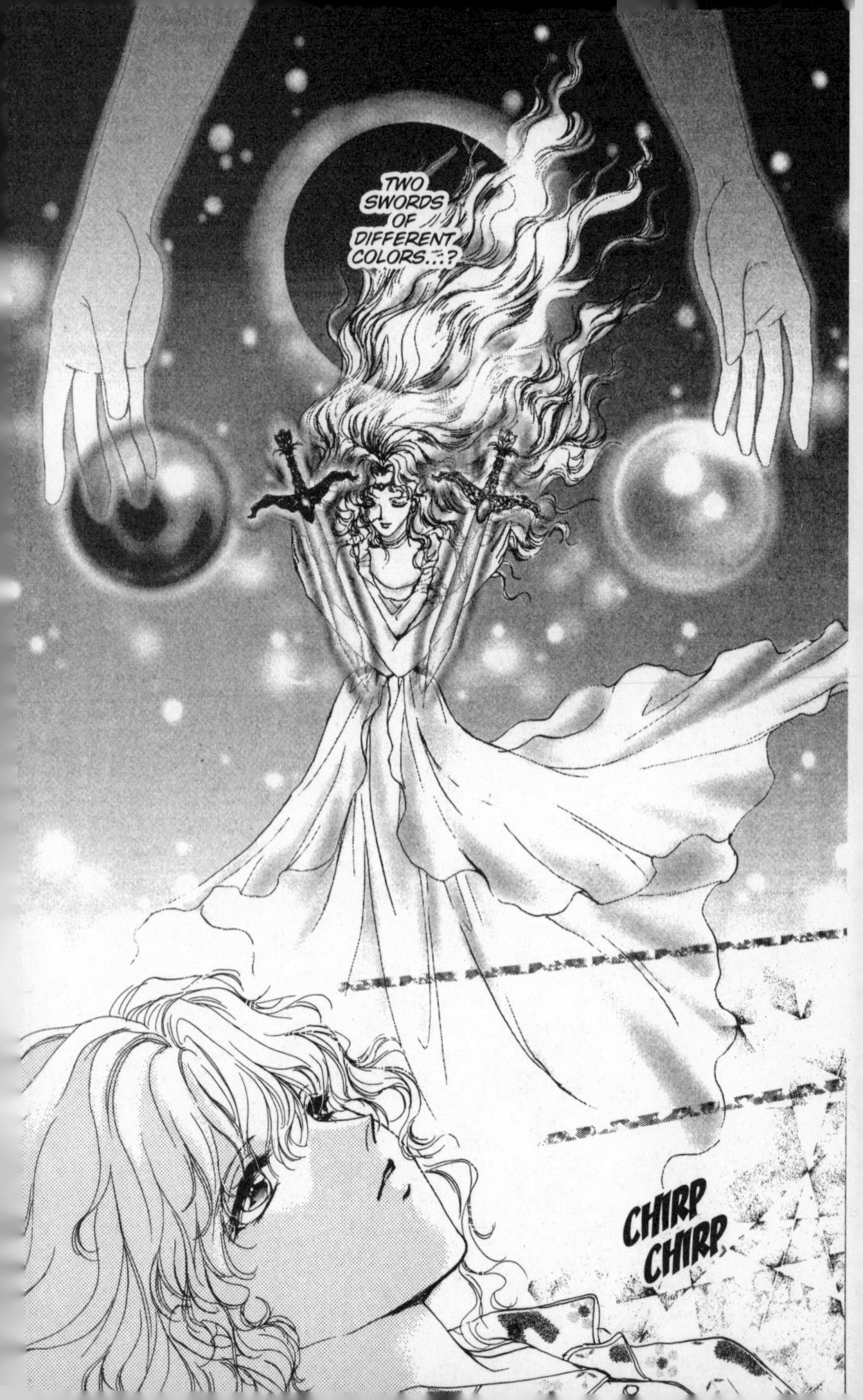

TWO SWORDS OF DIFFERENT COLORS...?
CHIRP CHIRP

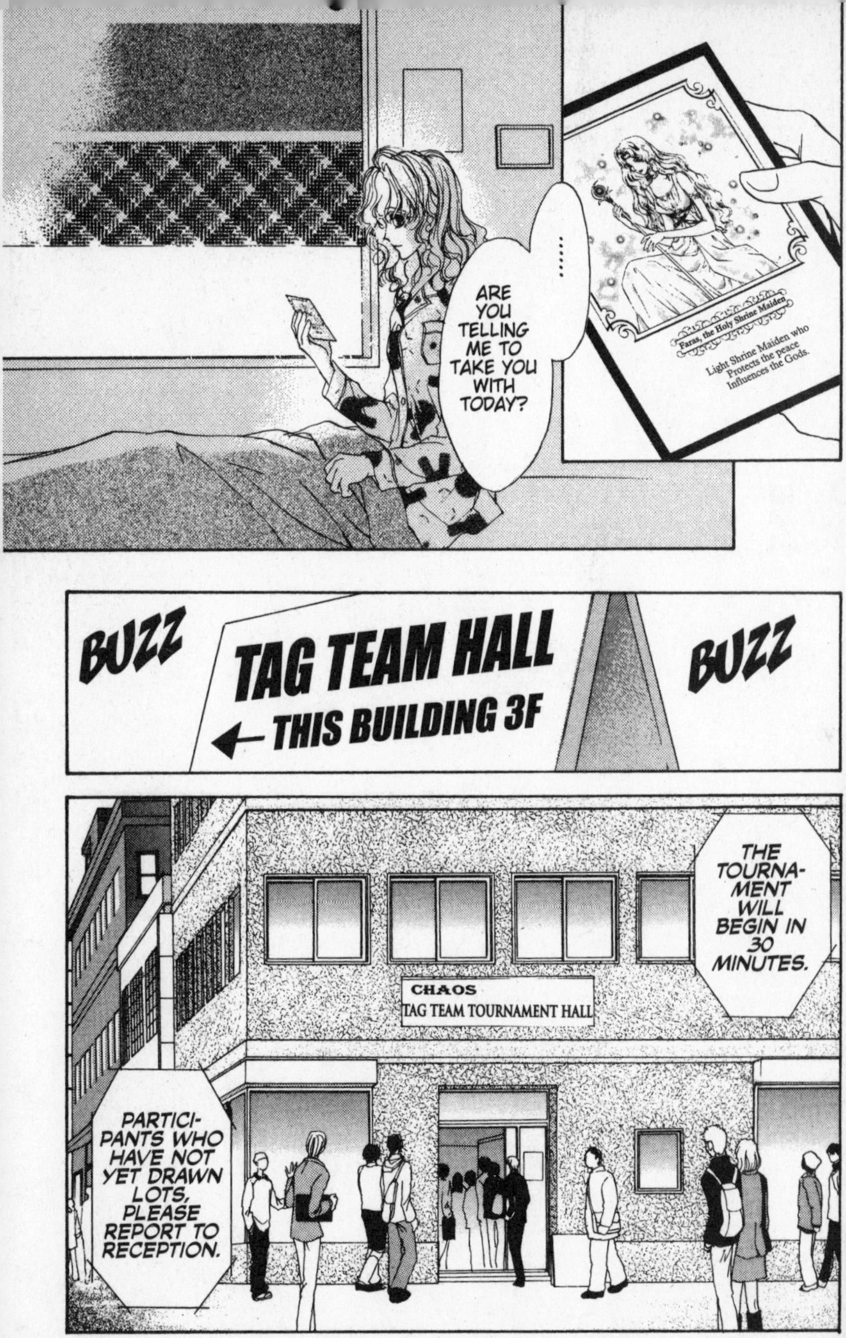
Paras, the Holy Shrine Maiden
Light Shrine Maiden who Protects the peace Influences the Gods.
......
ARE YOU TELLING ME TO TAKE YOU WITH TODAY?
BUZZ
TAG TEAM HALL
THIS BUILDING 3F
BUZZ
THE TOURNAMENT WILL BEGIN IN 30 MINUTES.
CHAOS
TAG TEAM TOURNAMENT HALL
PARTICIPANTS WHO HAVE NOT YET DRAWN LOTS, PLEASE REPORT TO RECEPTION.

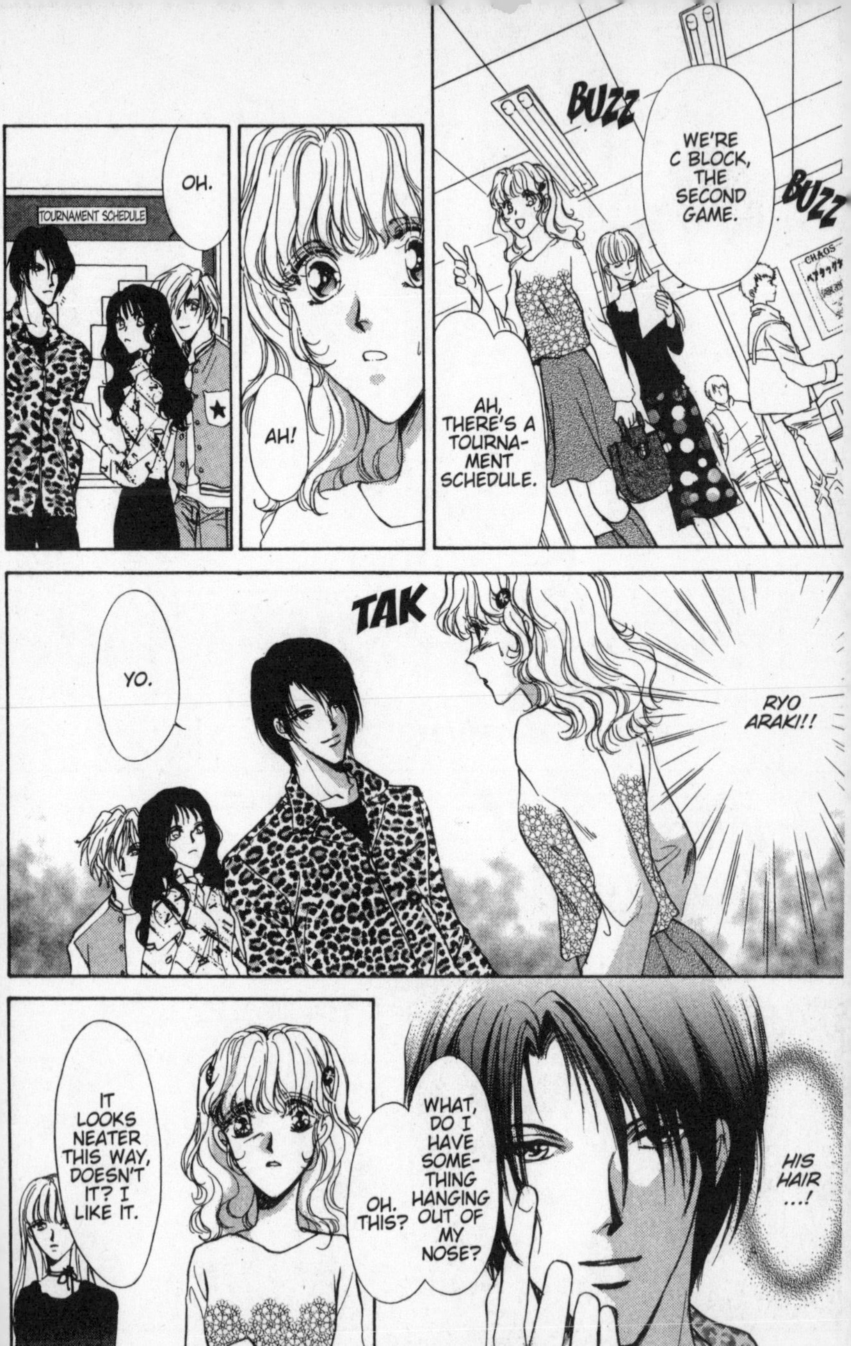
BUZZ
WE'RE C BLOCK, THE SECOND GAME.
BUZZ
CHAOS
AH, THERE'S A TOURNAMENT SCHEDULE.
AH!
TOURNAMENT SCHEDULE
OH.
TAK
RYO ARAKI!!
YO.
HIS HAIR ...!
WHAT, DO I HAVE SOMETHING HANGING OUT OF MY NOSE?
OH. THIS?
IT LOOKS NEATER THIS WAY, DOESN'T IT? I LIKE IT.

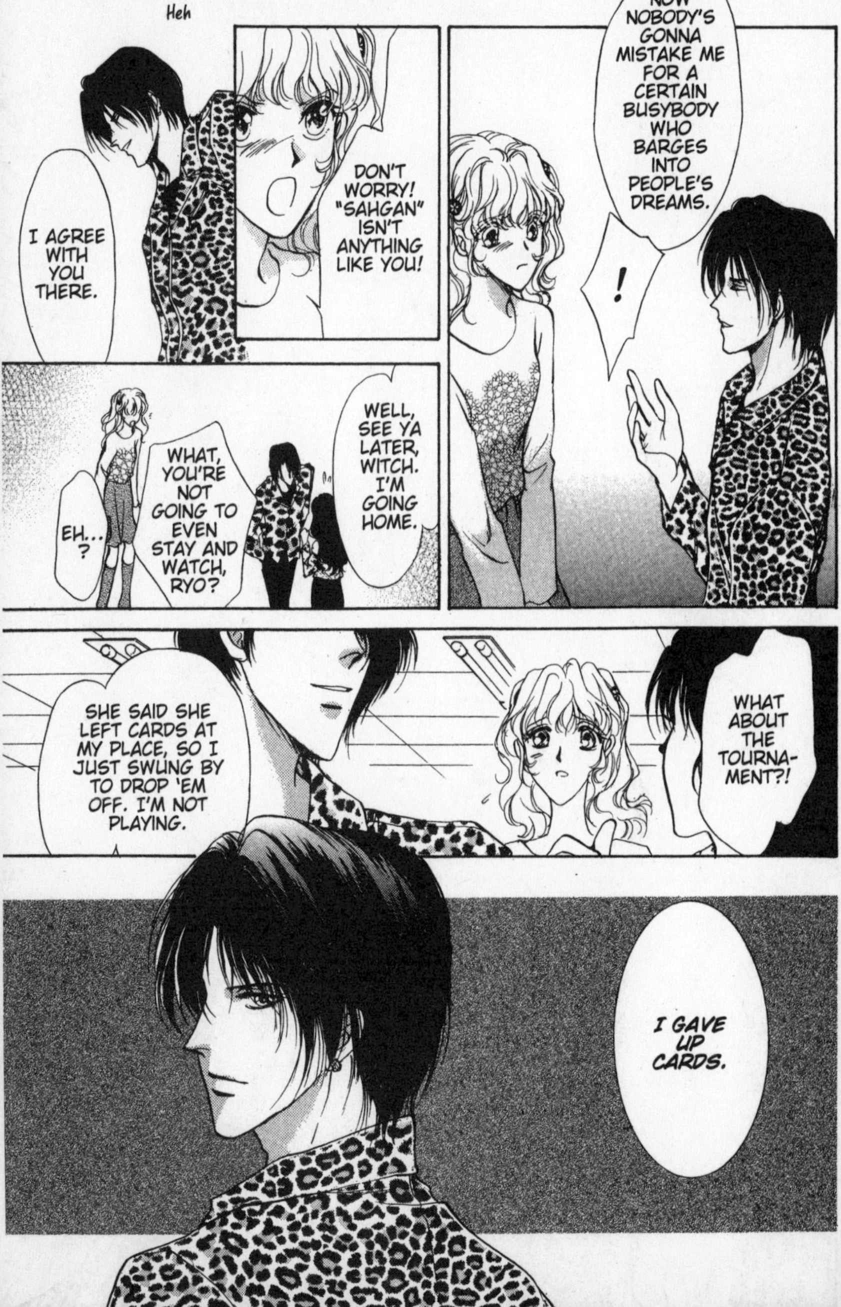
NOW NOBODY'S GONNA MISTAKE ME FOR A CERTAIN BUSYBODY WHO BARGES INTO PEOPLE'S DREAMS.
!
DON'T WORRY! "SAHGAN" ISN'T ANYTHING LIKE YOU!
Heh
I AGREE WITH YOU THERE.
WELL, SEE YA LATER, WITCH. I'M GOING HOME.
WHAT, YOU'RE NOT GOING TO EVEN STAY AND WATCH, RYO?
EH... ?
WHAT ABOUT THE TOURNAMENT?!
SHE SAID SHE LEFT CARDS AT MY PLACE, SO I JUST SWUNG BY TO DROP 'EM OFF. I'M NOT PLAYING.
I GAVE UP CARDS.

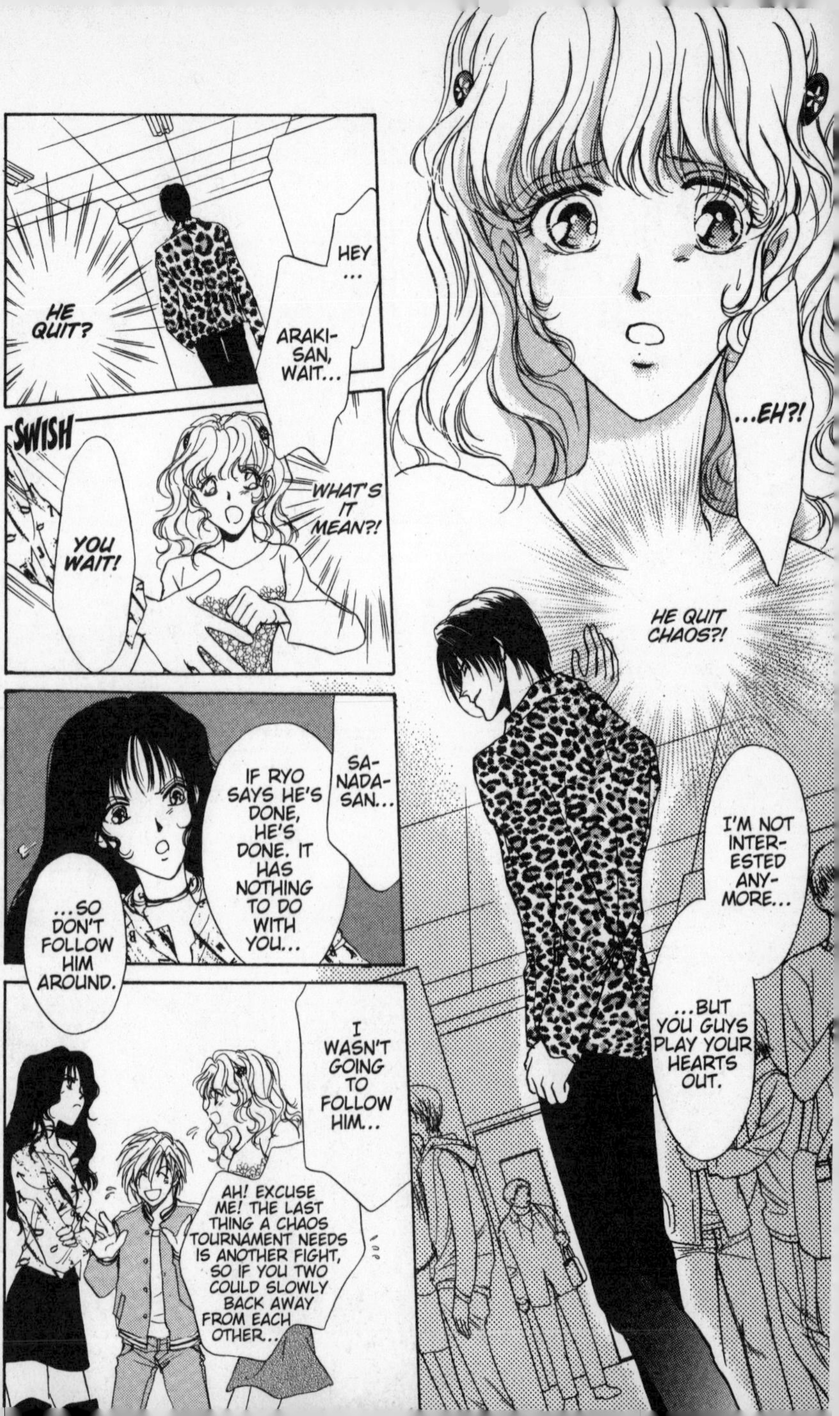
...EH?!
HE QUIT CHAOS?!
I'M NOT INTERESTED ANYMORE...
...BUT YOU GUYS PLAY YOUR HEARTS OUT.
HEY ...
ARAKI-SAN, WAIT...
HE QUIT?
SWISH
WHAT'S IT MEAN?!
YOU WAIT!
SANADA-SAN...
IF RYO SAYS HE'S DONE, HE'S DONE. IT HAS NOTHING TO DO WITH YOU...
...SO DON'T FOLLOW HIM AROUND.
I WASN'T GOING TO FOLLOW HIM...
AH! EXCUSE ME! THE LAST THING A CHAOS TOURNAMENT NEEDS IS ANOTHER FIGHT, SO IF YOU TWO COULD SLOWLY BACK AWAY FROM EACH OTHER...

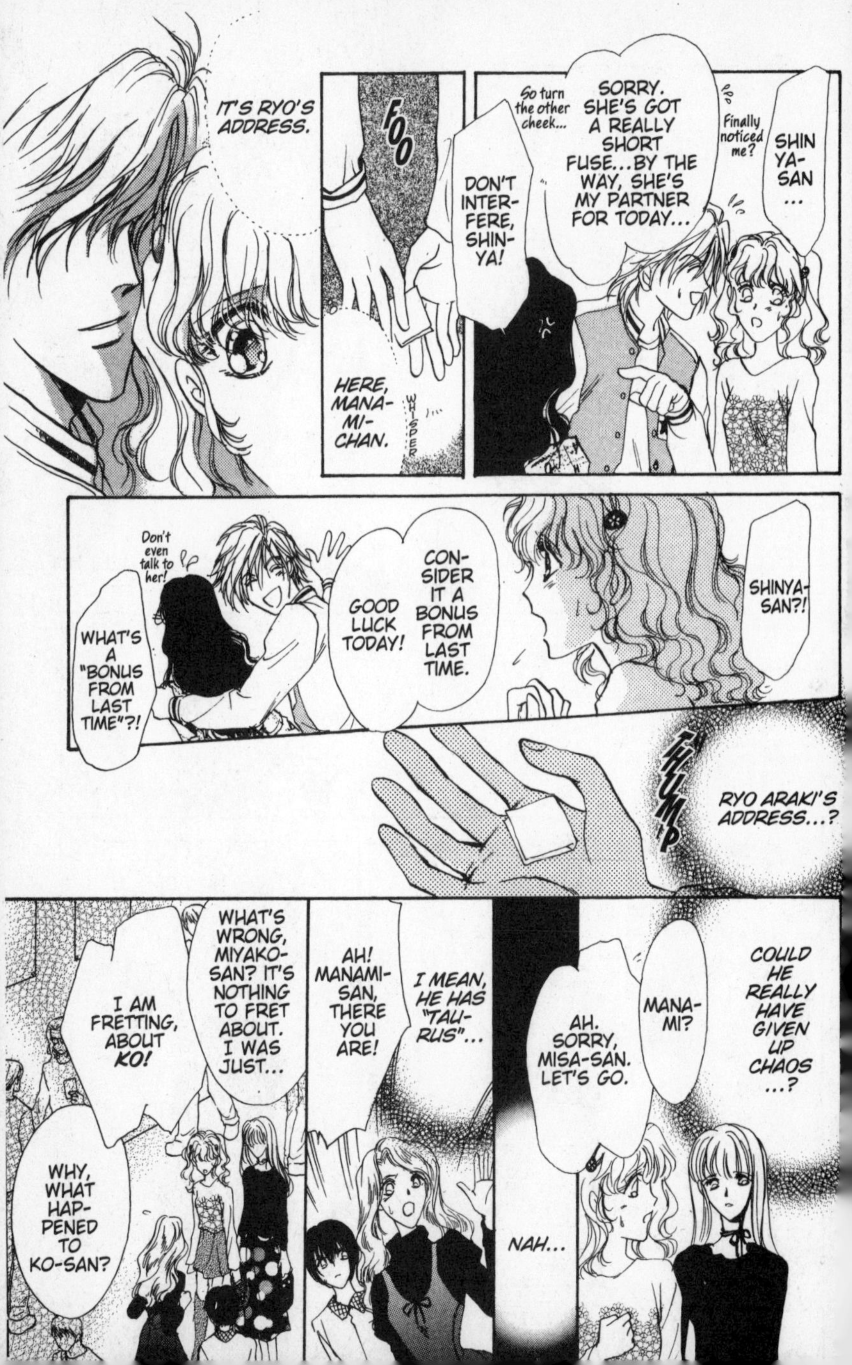
SHINYA-SAN...
Finally noticed me?
SORRY. SHE'S GOT A REALLY SHORT FUSE...BY THE WAY, SHE'S MY PARTNER FOR TODAY...
So turn the other cheek...
DON'T INTERFERE, SHINYA!
FOO
HERE, MANAMI-CHAN.
WHISPER
IT'S RYO'S ADDRESS.
SHINYA-SAN?!
CONSIDER IT A BONUS FROM LAST TIME.
GOOD LUCK TODAY!
Don't even talk to her!
WHAT'S A "BONUS FROM LAST TIME"?!
RYO ARAKI'S ADDRESS...?
THUMP
COULD HE REALLY HAVE GIVEN UP CHAOS...?
MANAMI?
AH. SORRY, MISA-SAN. LET'S GO.
NAH...
I MEAN, HE HAS "TAURUS"...
AH! MANAMI-SAN, THERE YOU ARE!
WHAT'S WRONG, MIYAKO-SAN? IT'S NOTHING TO FRET ABOUT. I WAS JUST...
I AM FRETTING, ABOUT KO!
WHY, WHAT HAPPENED TO KO-SAN?

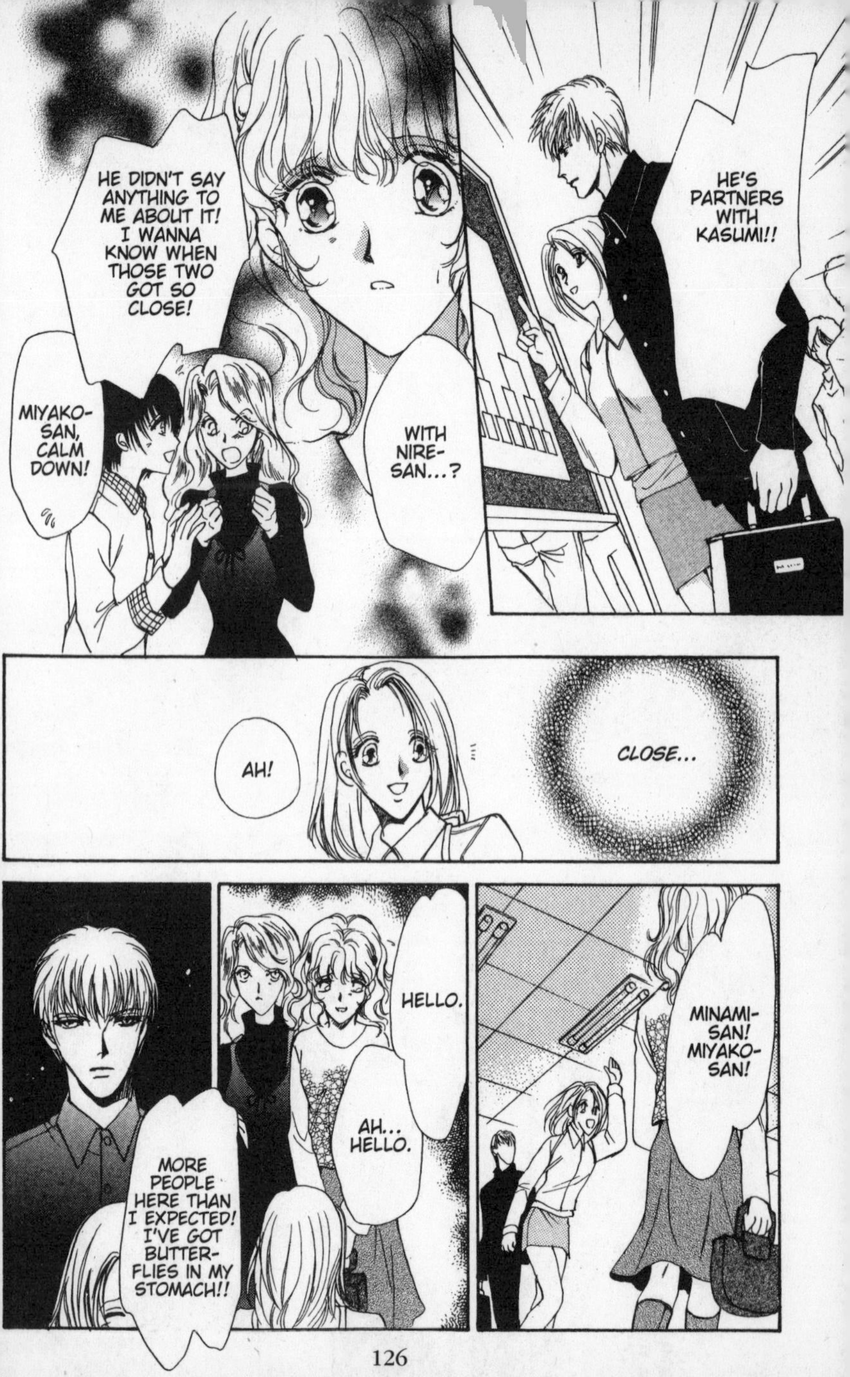
HE'S PARTNERS WITH KASUMI!!
WITH NIRE-SAN...?
HE DIDN'T SAY ANYTHING TO ME ABOUT IT! I WANNA KNOW WHEN THOSE TWO GOT SO CLOSE!
MIYAKO-SAN, CALM DOWN!
CLOSE...
AH!
MINAMI-SAN! MIYAKO-SAN!
HELLO.
AH... HELLO.
MORE PEOPLE HERE THAN I EXPECTED! I'VE GOT BUTTER-FLIES IN MY STOMACH!!

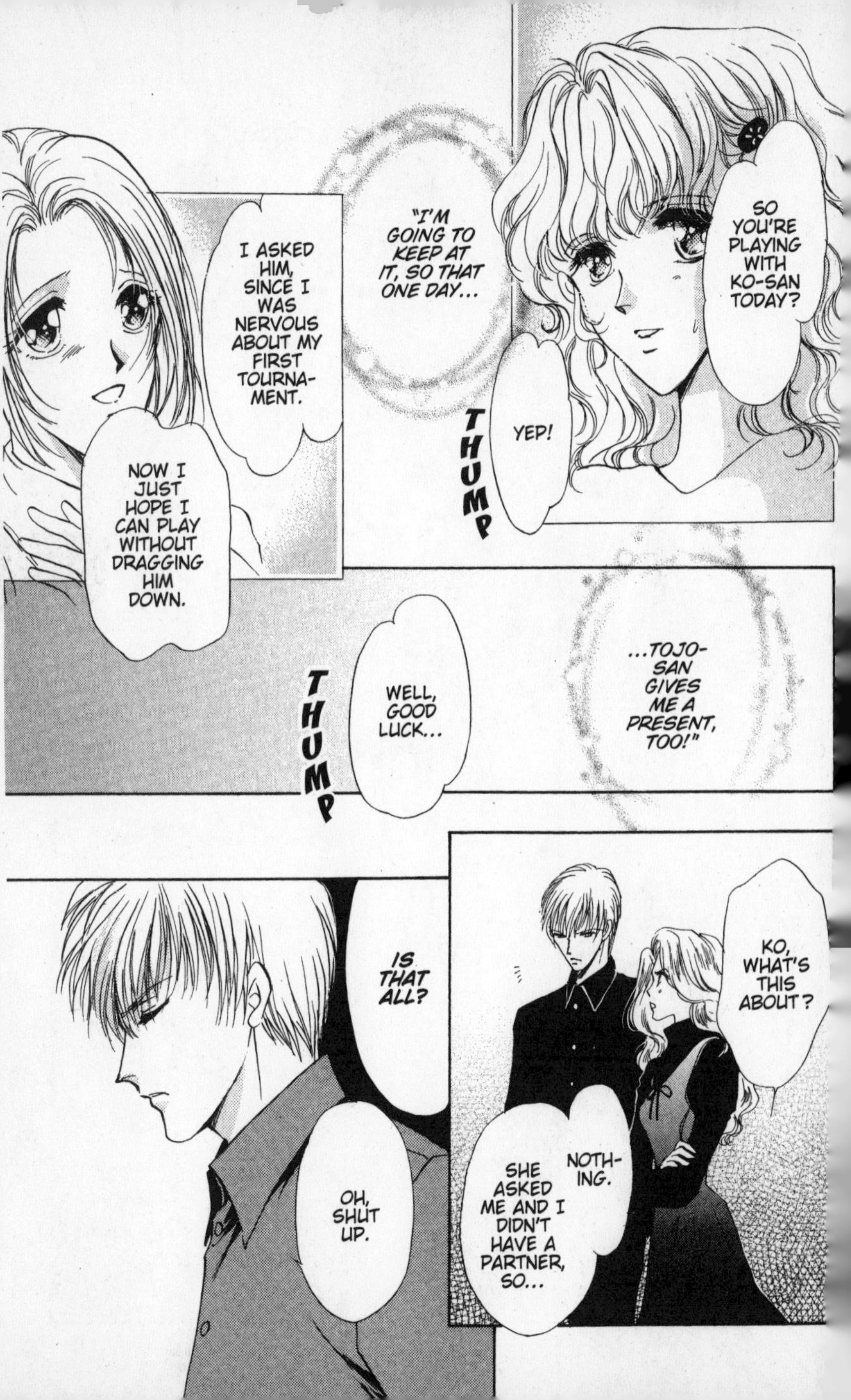
SO YOU'RE PLAYING WITH KO-SAN TODAY?
YEP!
THUMP
"I'M GOING TO KEEP AT IT, SO THAT ONE DAY...
I ASKED HIM, SINCE I WAS NERVOUS ABOUT MY FIRST TOURNAMENT.
NOW I JUST HOPE I CAN PLAY WITHOUT DRAGGING HIM DOWN.
...TOJO-SAN GIVES ME A PRESENT, TOO!"
WELL, GOOD LUCK...
THUMP
KO, WHAT'S THIS ABOUT?
NOTHING.
SHE ASKED ME AND I DIDN'T HAVE A PARTNER, SO...
IS THAT ALL?
OH, SHUT UP.

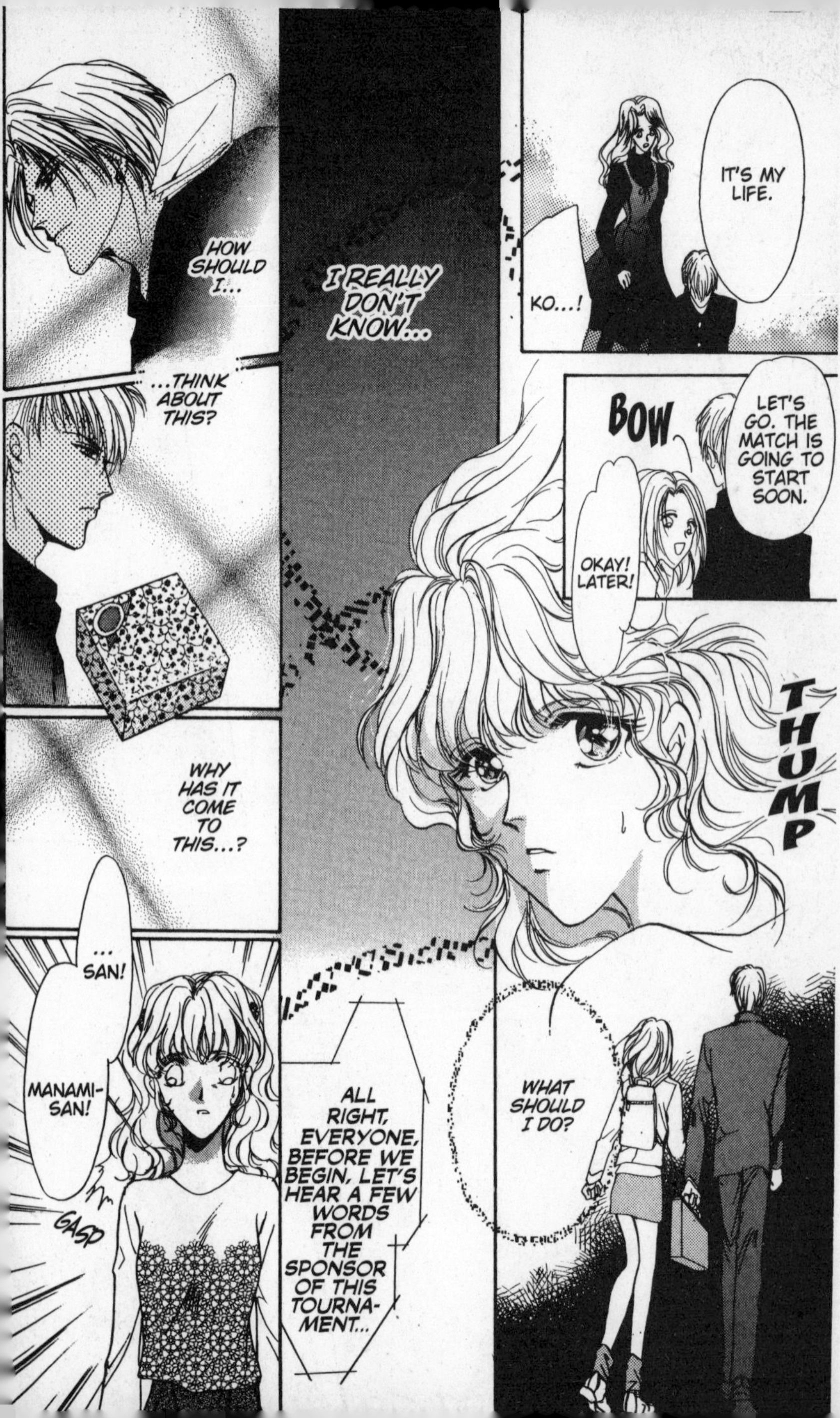
IT'S MY LIFE.
KO...!
LET'S GO. THE MATCH IS GOING TO START SOON.
BOW
OKAY! LATER!
THUMP
WHAT SHOULD I DO?
I REALLY DON'T KNOW...
ALL RIGHT, EVERYONE, BEFORE WE BEGIN, LET'S HEAR A FEW WORDS FROM THE SPONSOR OF THIS TOURNAMENT...
HOW SHOULD I...
...THINK ABOUT THIS?
WHY HAS IT COME TO THIS...?
...SAN!
MANAMI-SAN!
GASP

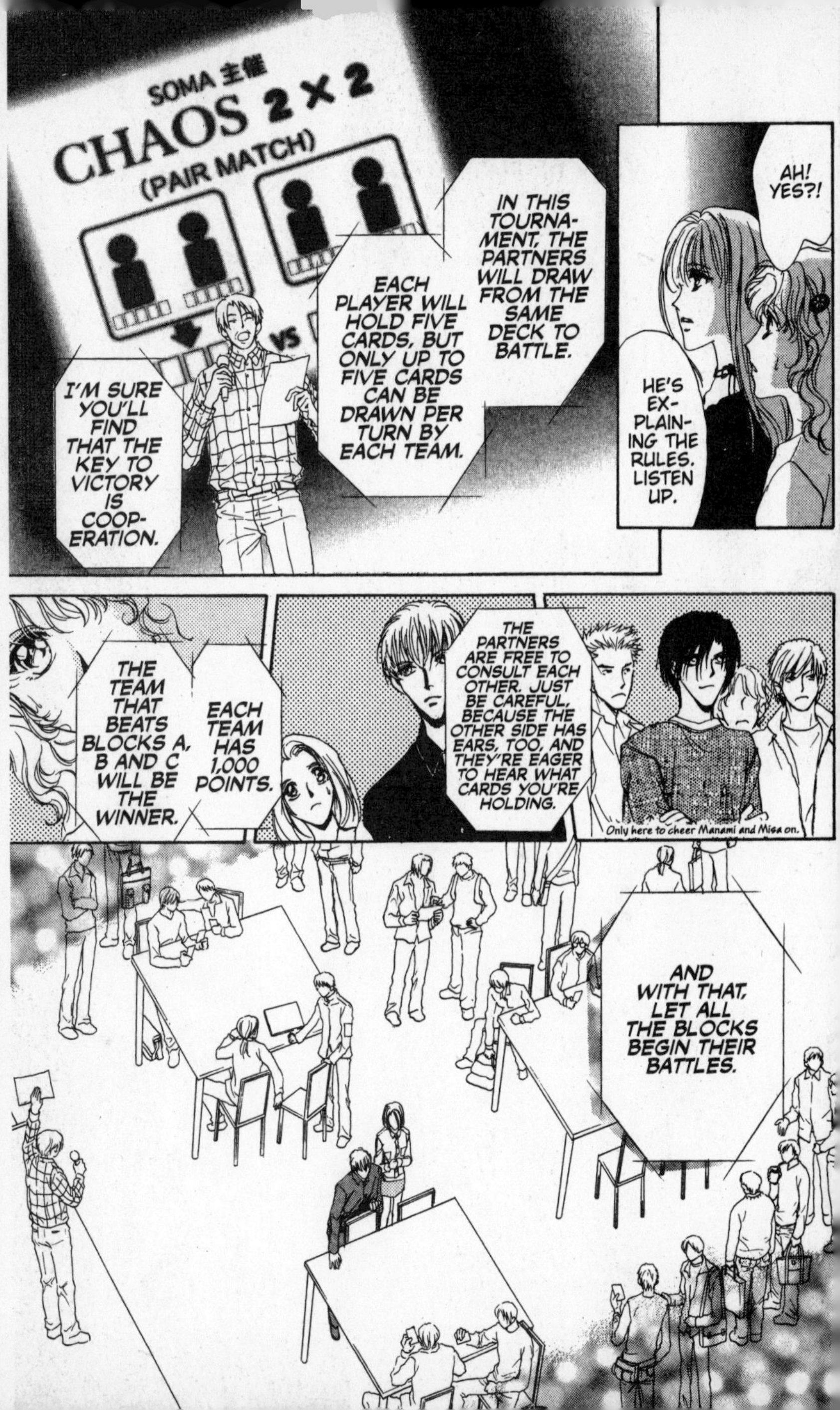
AH! YES?!
HE'S EXPLAINING THE RULES. LISTEN UP.
SOMA 主催
CHAOS 2×2
(PAIR MATCH)
VS
IN THIS TOURNAMENT, THE PARTNERS WILL DRAW FROM THE SAME DECK TO BATTLE.
EACH PLAYER WILL HOLD FIVE CARDS, BUT ONLY UP TO FIVE CARDS CAN BE DRAWN PER TURN BY EACH TEAM.
I'M SURE YOU'LL FIND THAT THE KEY TO VICTORY IS COOPERATION.
Only here to cheer Manami and Misa on.
THE PARTNERS ARE FREE TO CONSULT EACH OTHER. JUST BE CAREFUL, BECAUSE THE OTHER SIDE HAS EARS, TOO, AND THEY'RE EAGER TO HEAR WHAT CARDS YOU'RE HOLDING.
EACH TEAM HAS 1,000 POINTS.
THE TEAM THAT BEATS BLOCKS A, B AND C WILL BE THE WINNER.
AND WITH THAT, LET ALL THE BLOCKS BEGIN THEIR BATTLES.

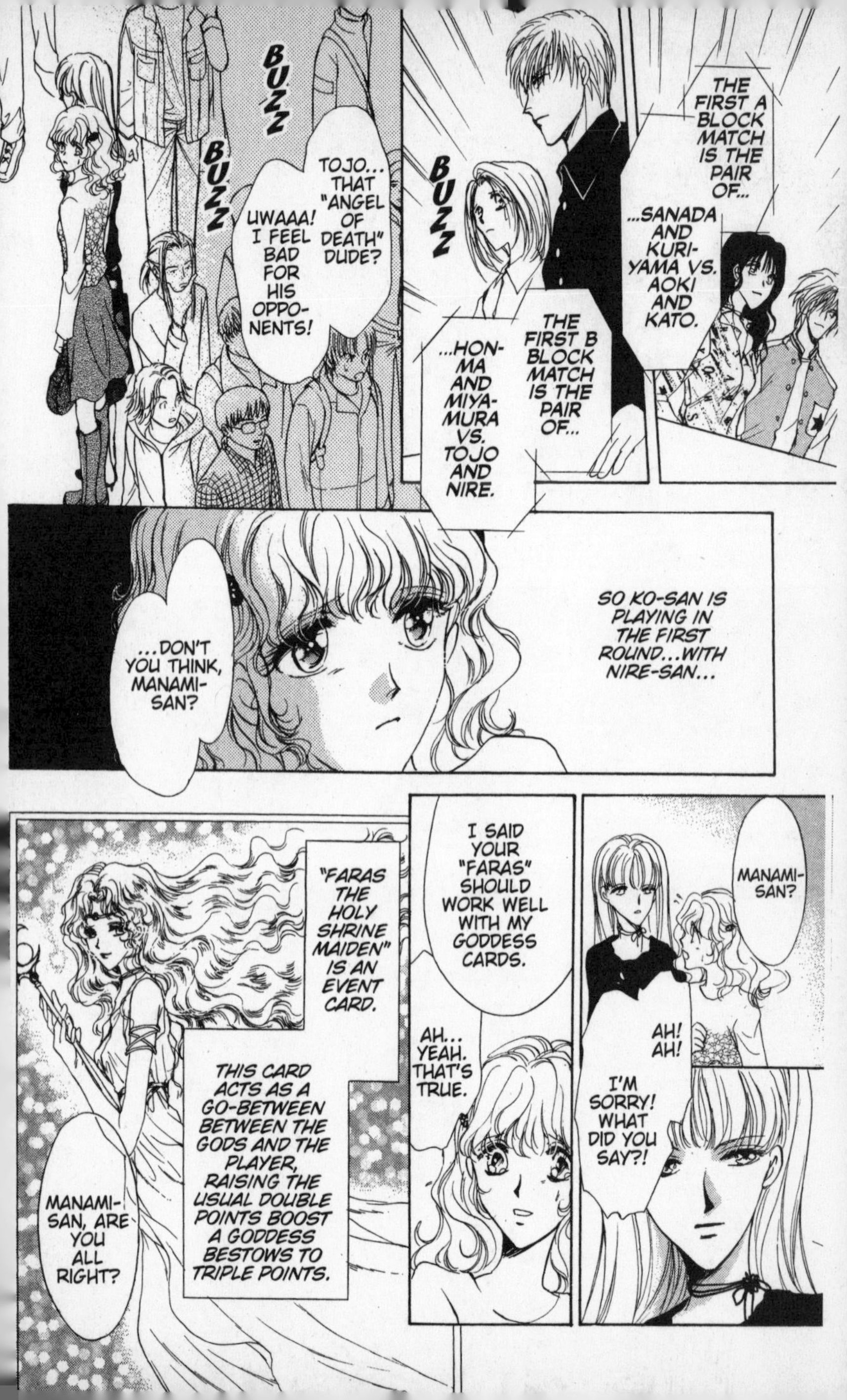
THE FIRST A BLOCK MATCH IS THE PAIR OF...
...SANADA AND KURI-YAMA VS. AOKI AND KATO.
BUZZ
THE FIRST B BLOCK MATCH IS THE PAIR OF...
...HON-MA AND MIYA-MURA VS. TOJO AND NIRE.
BUZZ
BUZZ
TOJO... THAT "ANGEL OF DEATH" DUDE?
UWAAA! I FEEL BAD FOR HIS OPPO-NENTS!
SO KO-SAN IS PLAYING IN THE FIRST ROUND...WITH NIRE-SAN...
...DON'T YOU THINK, MANAMI-SAN?
MANAMI-SAN?
AH! AH!
I'M SORRY! WHAT DID YOU SAY?!
I SAID YOUR "FARAS" SHOULD WORK WELL WITH MY GODDESS CARDS.
AH... YEAH. THAT'S TRUE.
"FARAS THE HOLY SHRINE MAIDEN" IS AN EVENT CARD.
THIS CARD ACTS AS A GO-BETWEEN BETWEEN THE GODS AND THE PLAYER, RAISING THE USUAL DOUBLE POINTS BOOST A GODDESS BESTOWS TO TRIPLE POINTS.
MANAMI-SAN, ARE YOU ALL RIGHT?

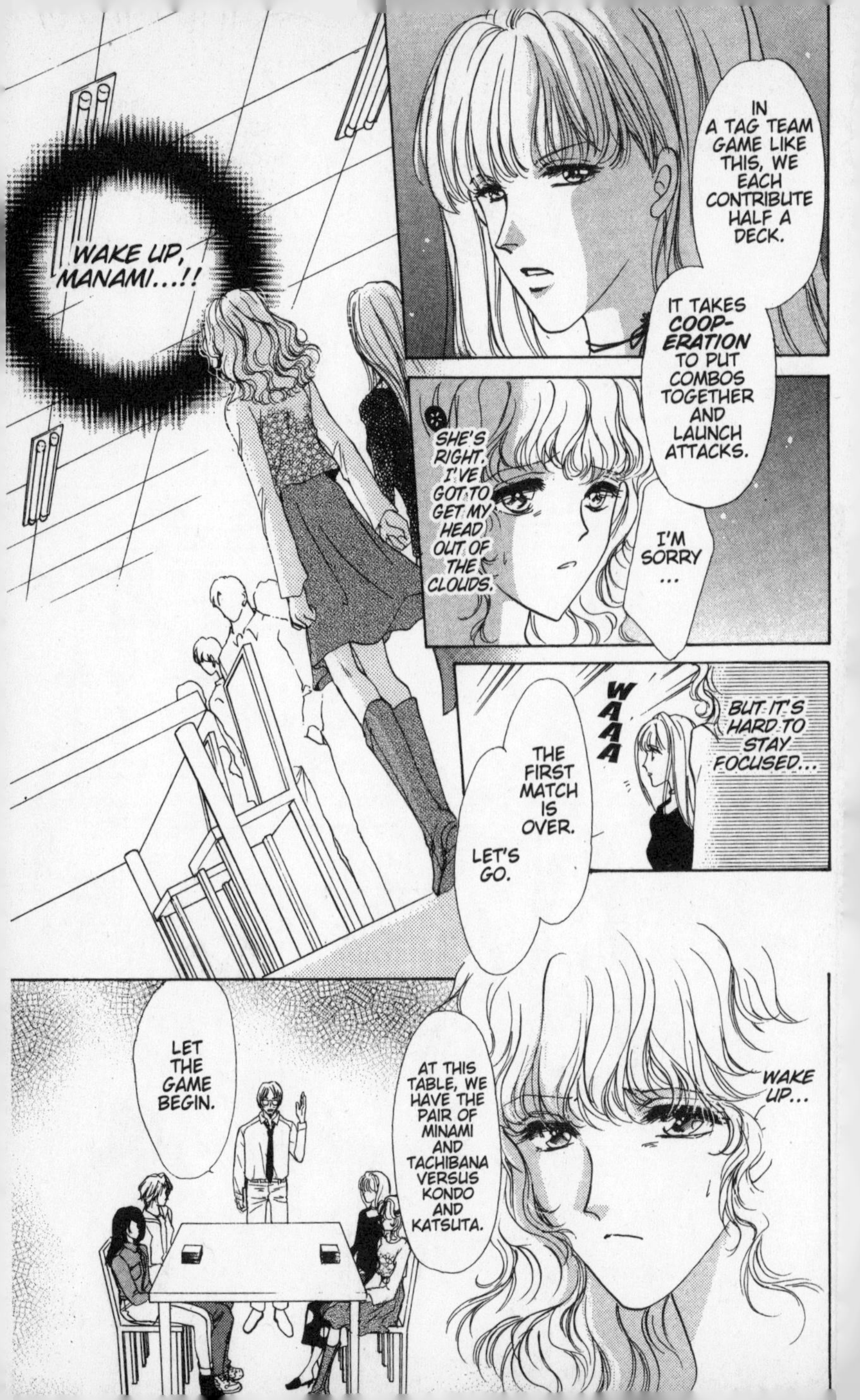
IN A TAG TEAM GAME LIKE THIS, WE EACH CONTRIBUTE HALF A DECK.
IT TAKES COOPERATION TO PUT COMBOS TOGETHER AND LAUNCH ATTACKS.
I'M SORRY...
SHE'S RIGHT. I'VE GOT TO GET MY HEAD OUT OF THE CLOUDS.
BUT IT'S HARD TO STAY FOCUSED...
WAAAA
THE FIRST MATCH IS OVER.
LET'S GO.
WAKE UP, MANAMI...!!
WAKE UP...
AT THIS TABLE, WE HAVE THE PAIR OF MINAMI AND TACHIBANA VERSUS KONDO AND KATSUTA.
LET THE GAME BEGIN.

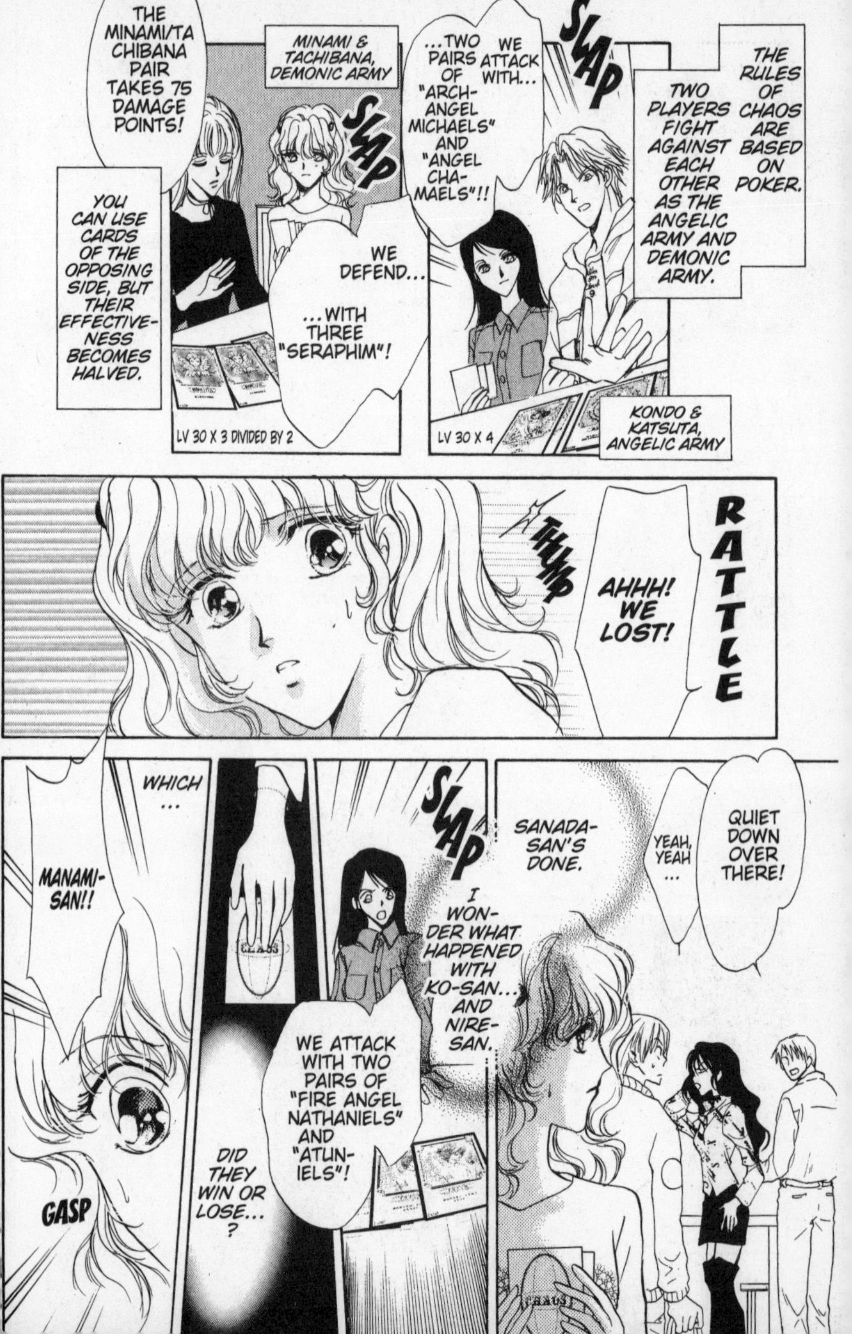
THE RULES OF CHAOS ARE BASED ON POKER.
TWO PLAYERS FIGHT AGAINST EACH OTHER AS THE ANGELIC ARMY AND DEMONIC ARMY.
SLAP
WE ATTACK WITH...
...TWO PAIRS OF "ARCH-ANGEL MICHAELS" AND "ANGEL CHA-MAELS"!!
KONDO & KATSUTA, ANGELIC ARMY
LV 30 X 4
MINAMI & TACHIBANA, DEMONIC ARMY
SLAP
WE DEFEND...
...WITH THREE "SERAPHIM"!
LV 30 X 3 DIVIDED BY 2
THE MINAMI/TA CHIBANA PAIR TAKES 75 DAMAGE POINTS!
YOU CAN USE CARDS OF THE OPPOSING SIDE, BUT THEIR EFFECTIVE-NESS BECOMES HALVED.
RATTLE
AHHH! WE LOST!
THUMP
QUIET DOWN OVER THERE!
YEAH, YEAH...
SANADA-SAN'S DONE.
I WON-DER WHAT HAPPENED WITH KO-SAN... AND NIRE-SAN.
SLAP
WE ATTACK WITH TWO PAIRS OF "FIRE ANGEL NATHANIELS" AND "ATUN-IELS"!
DID THEY WIN OR LOSE...?
WHICH...
MANAMI-SAN!!
GASP

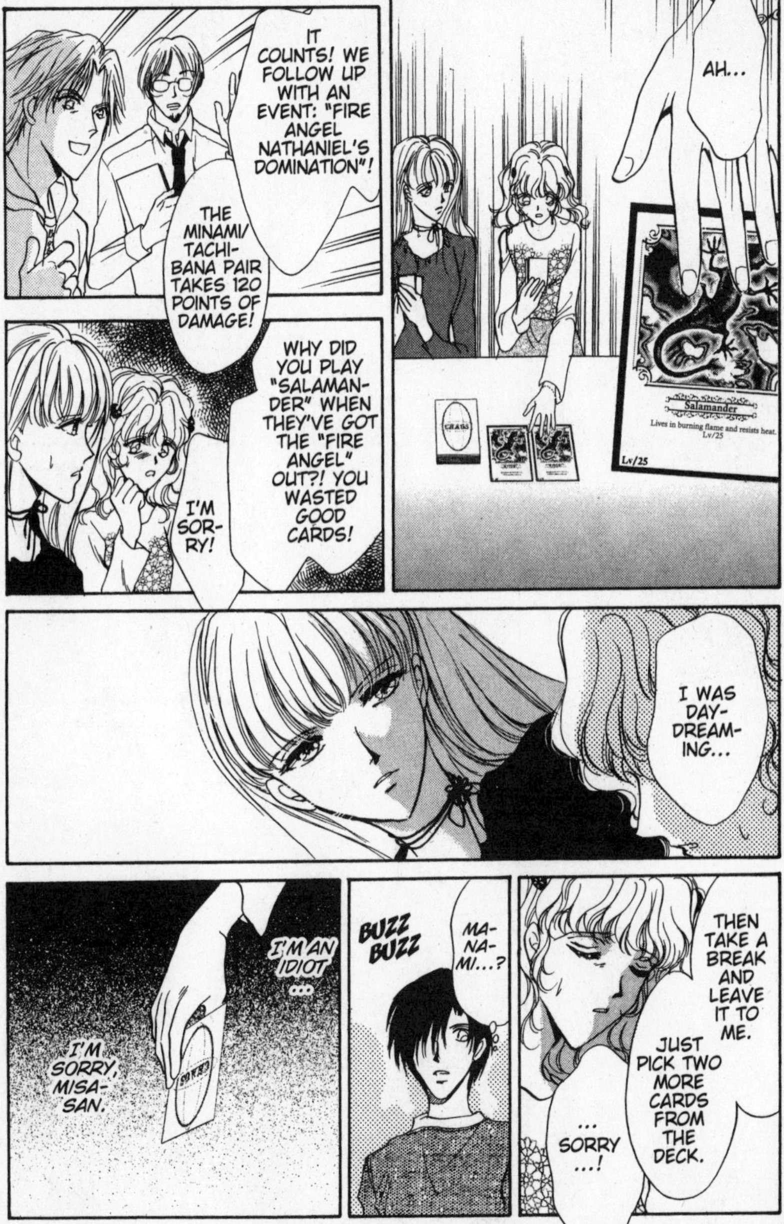
AH...
Salamander
Lives in burning flame and resists heat.
Lv/25
Lv/25
IT COUNTS! WE FOLLOW UP WITH AN EVENT: "FIRE ANGEL NATHANIEL'S DOMINATION"!
THE MINAMI/TACHIBANA PAIR TAKES 120 POINTS OF DAMAGE!
WHY DID YOU PLAY "SALAMANDER" WHEN THEY'VE GOT THE "FIRE ANGEL" OUT?! YOU WASTED GOOD CARDS!
I'M SORRY!
I WAS DAYDREAMING...
THEN TAKE A BREAK AND LEAVE IT TO ME.
JUST PICK TWO MORE CARDS FROM THE DECK.
...SORRY...!
BUZZ BUZZ
MANAMI...?
I'M AN IDIOT...
I'M SORRY, MISA-SAN.

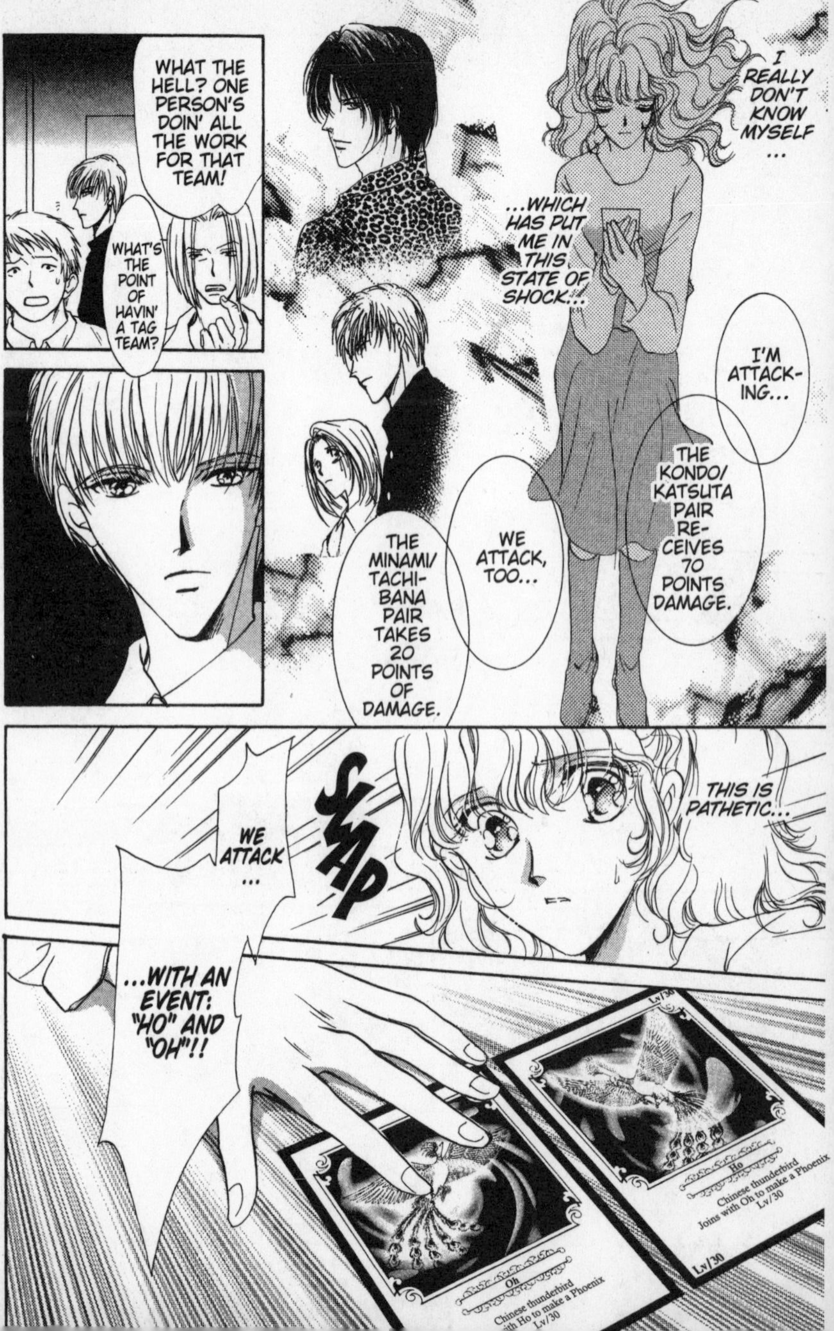

I REALLY DON'T KNOW MYSELF...
...WHICH HAS PUT ME IN THIS STATE OF SHOCK...
I'M ATTACKING...
THE KONDO/KATSUTA PAIR RECEIVES 70 POINTS DAMAGE.
WE ATTACK, TOO...
THE MINAMI/TACHIBANA PAIR TAKES 20 POINTS OF DAMAGE.
WHAT THE HELL? ONE PERSON'S DOIN' ALL THE WORK FOR THAT TEAM!
WHAT'S THE POINT OF HAVIN' A TAG TEAM?
THIS IS PATHETIC...
SWAP
WE ATTACK...
...WITH AN EVENT: "HO" AND "OH"!!
Lv/30
Ho
Chinese thunderbird
Joins with Oh to make a Phoenix
Lv/30
Lv/30
Oh
Chinese thunderbird
with Ho to make a Phoenix
Lv/30

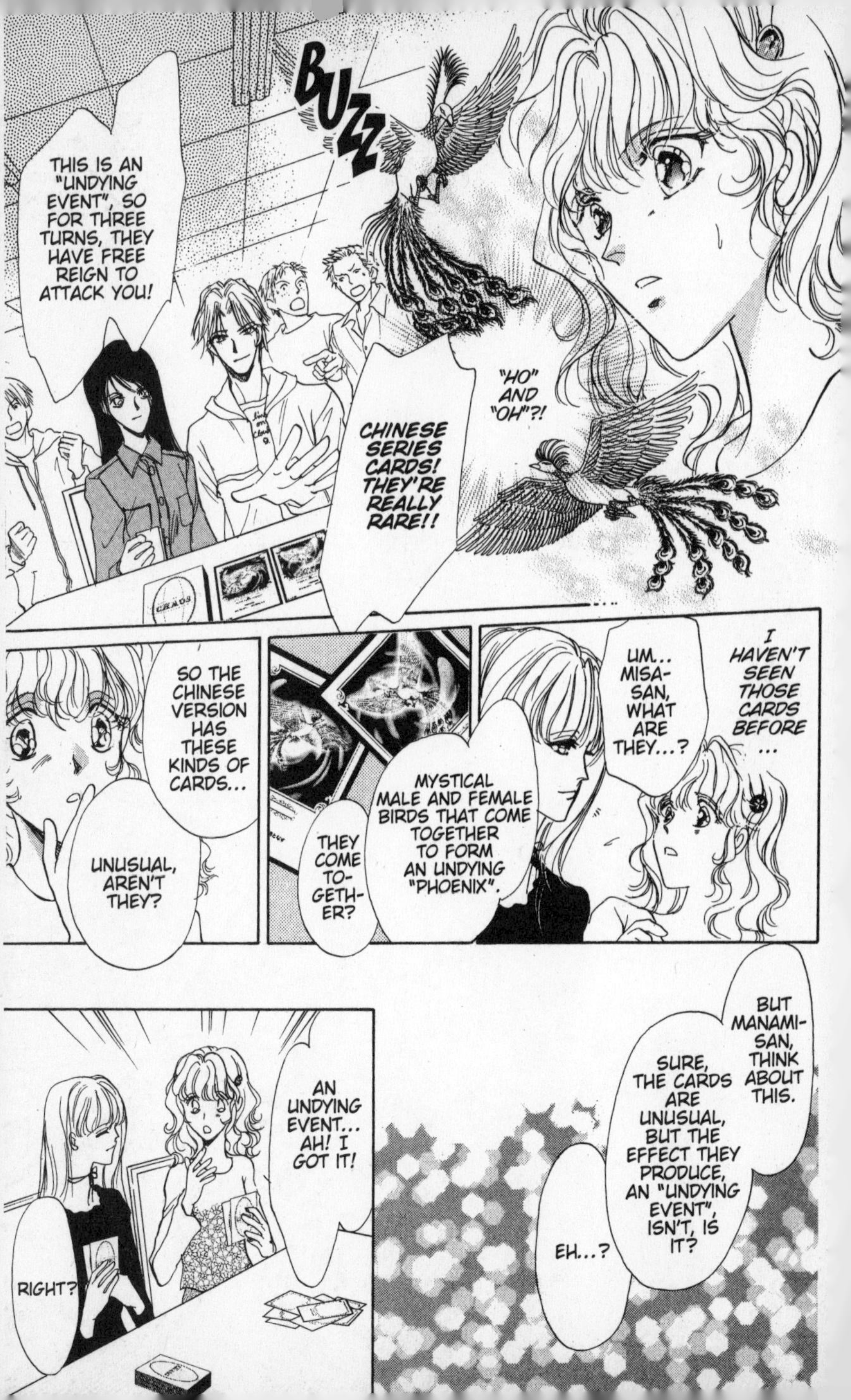
BUZZ
"HO" AND "OH"?!
CHINESE SERIES CARDS! THEY'RE REALLY RARE!!
THIS IS AN "UNDYING EVENT", SO FOR THREE TURNS, THEY HAVE FREE REIGN TO ATTACK YOU!
I HAVEN'T SEEN THOSE CARDS BEFORE...
UM... MISA-SAN, WHAT ARE THEY...?
MYSTICAL MALE AND FEMALE BIRDS THAT COME TOGETHER TO FORM AN UNDYING "PHOENIX".
THEY COME TO-GETH-ER?
SO THE CHINESE VERSION HAS THESE KINDS OF CARDS...
UNUSUAL, AREN'T THEY?
BUT MANAMI-SAN, THINK ABOUT THIS.
SURE, THE CARDS ARE UNUSUAL, BUT THE EFFECT THEY PRODUCE, AN "UNDYING EVENT", ISN'T, IS IT?
EH...?
AN UNDYING EVENT... AH! I GOT IT!
RIGHT?

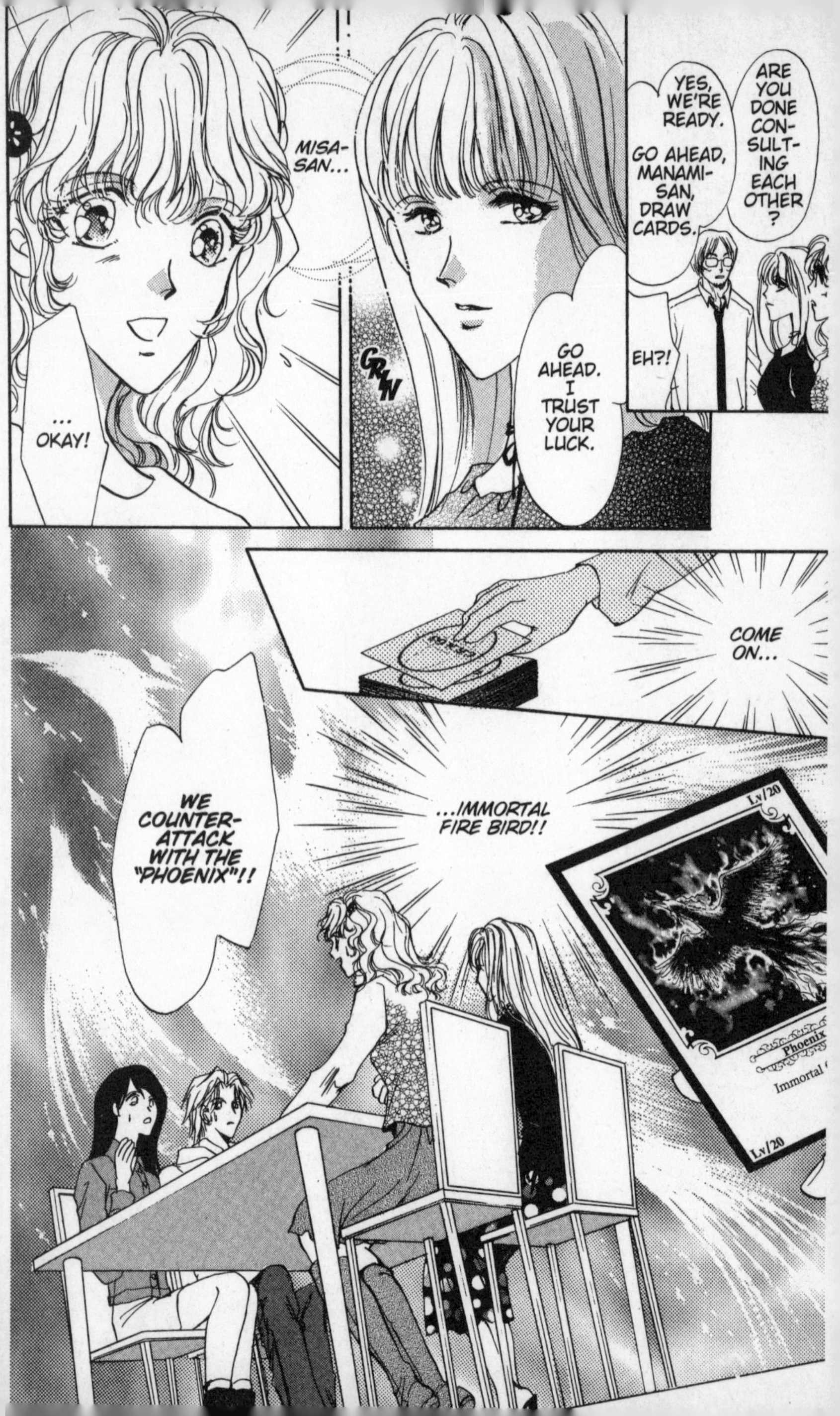
ARE YOU DONE CONSULTING EACH OTHER?
YES, WE'RE READY.
GO AHEAD, MANAMI-SAN, DRAW CARDS.
EH?!
GRIN
GO AHEAD. I TRUST YOUR LUCK.
MISA-SAN...
...OKAY!
COME ON...
...IMMORTAL FIRE BIRD!!
WE COUNTER-ATTACK WITH THE "PHOENIX"!!
Lv/20
Phoenix
Immortal
Lv/20

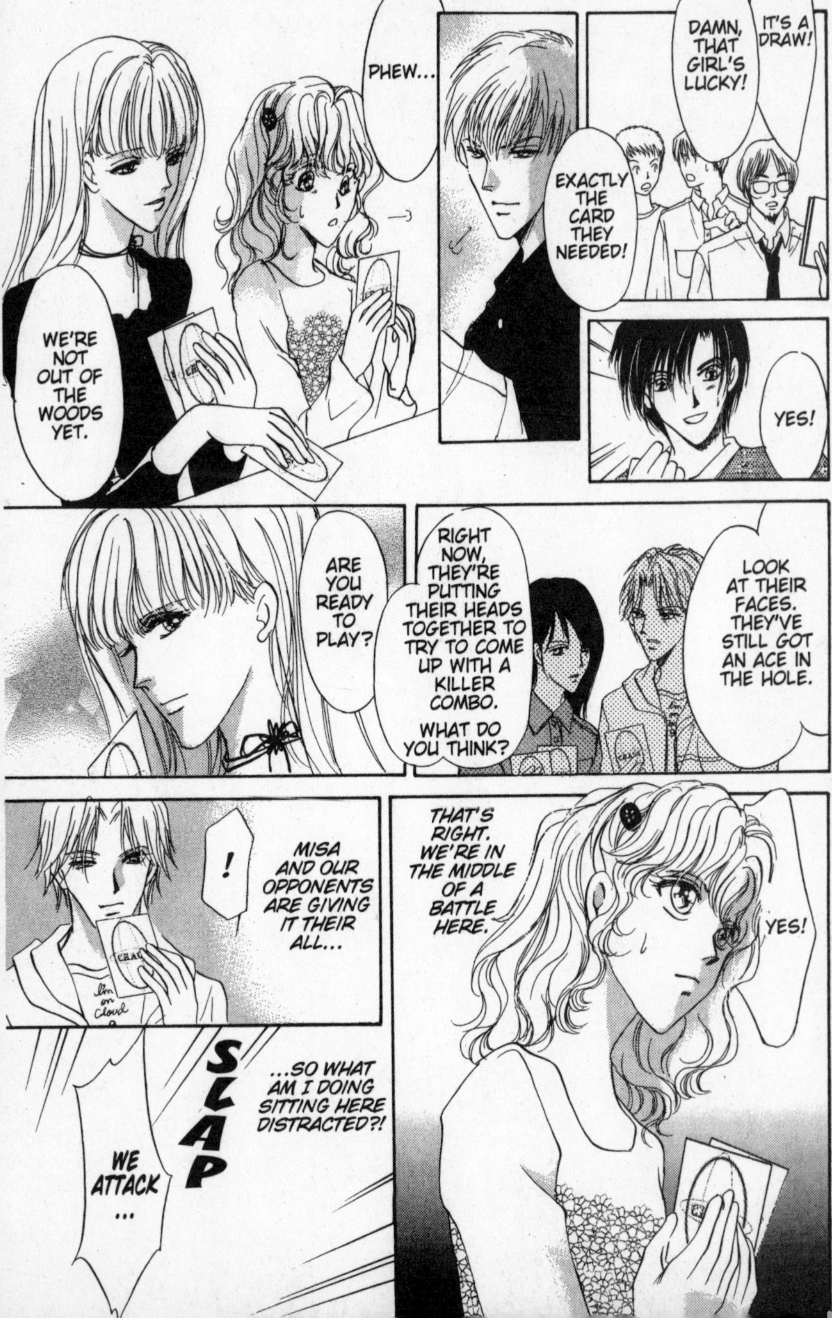
IT'S A DRAW!
DAMN, THAT GIRL'S LUCKY!
EXACTLY THE CARD THEY NEEDED!
YES!
PHEW...
WE'RE NOT OUT OF THE WOODS YET.
LOOK AT THEIR FACES. THEY'VE STILL GOT AN ACE IN THE HOLE.
RIGHT NOW, THEY'RE PUTTING THEIR HEADS TOGETHER TO TRY TO COME UP WITH A KILLER COMBO.
WHAT DO YOU THINK?
ARE YOU READY TO PLAY?
YES!
THAT'S RIGHT. WE'RE IN THE MIDDLE OF A BATTLE HERE.
!
MISA AND OUR OPPONENTS ARE GIVING IT THEIR ALL...
...SO WHAT AM I DOING SITTING HERE DISTRACTED?!
SLAP
WE ATTACK ...

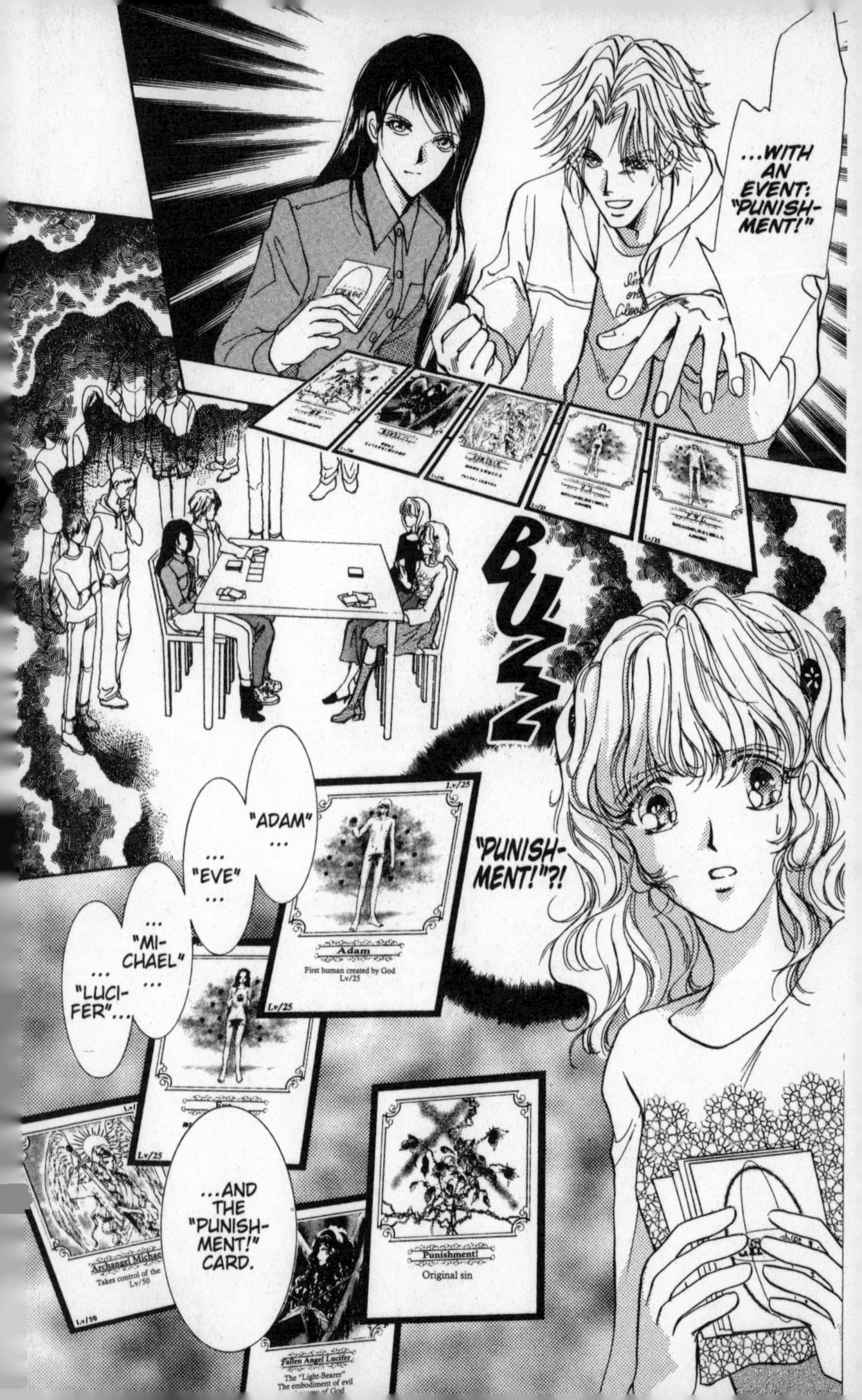
...WITH AN EVENT: "PUNISHMENT!"
BUZZ
"PUNISHMENT!"?!
"ADAM"...
..."EVE"...
..."MICHAEL"...
..."LUCIFER"...
Adam
First human created by God
Lv/25
...AND THE "PUNISHMENT!" CARD.
Punishment!
Original sin
Archangel Michael
Takes control of the
Lv/50
Fallen Angel Lucifer
The "Light-Bearer"
The embodiment of evil

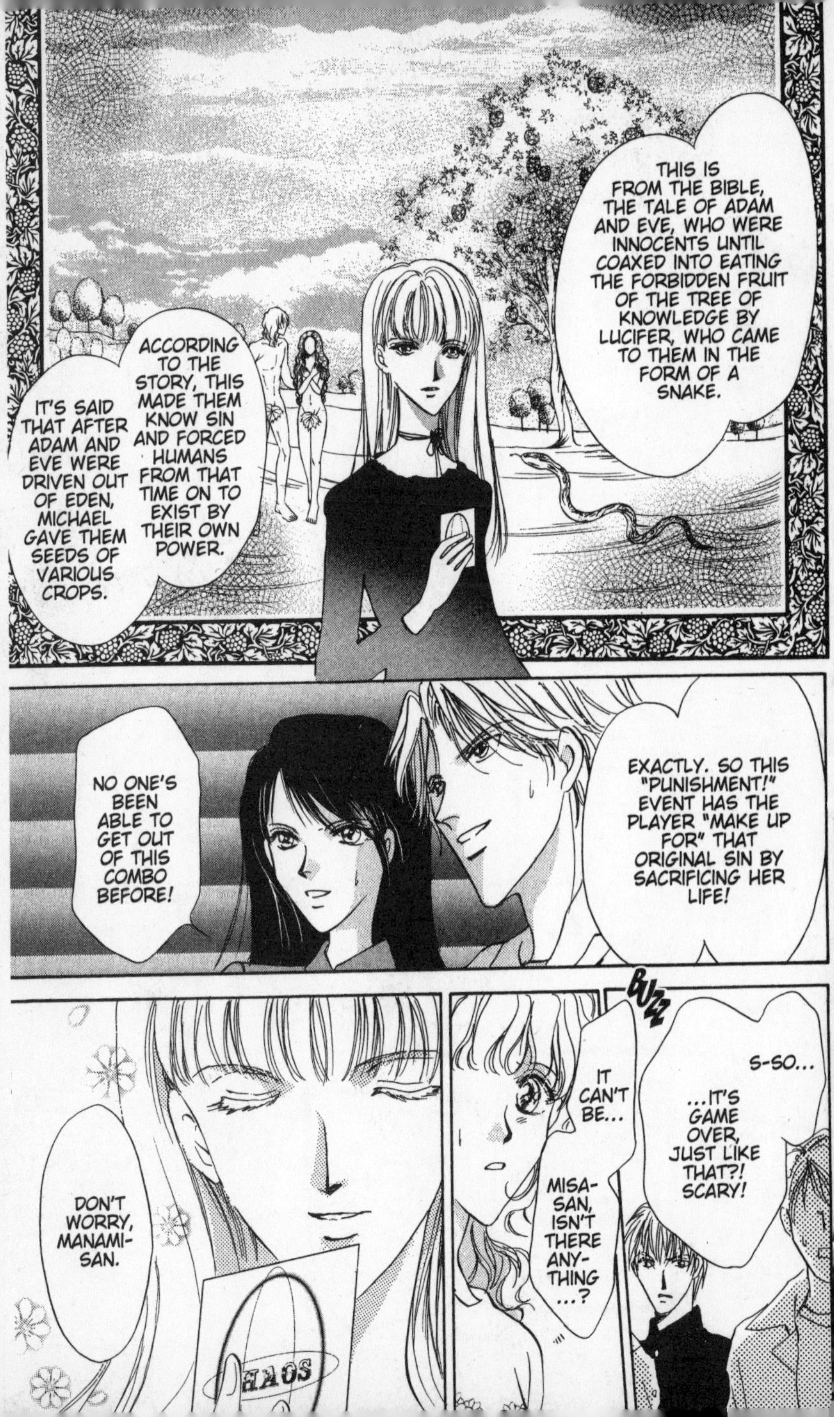
THIS IS FROM THE BIBLE, THE TALE OF ADAM AND EVE, WHO WERE INNOCENTS UNTIL COAXED INTO EATING THE FORBIDDEN FRUIT OF THE TREE OF KNOWLEDGE BY LUCIFER, WHO CAME TO THEM IN THE FORM OF A SNAKE.
ACCORDING TO THE STORY, THIS MADE THEM KNOW SIN AND FORCED HUMANS FROM THAT TIME ON TO EXIST BY THEIR OWN POWER.
IT'S SAID THAT AFTER ADAM AND EVE WERE DRIVEN OUT OF EDEN, MICHAEL GAVE THEM SEEDS OF VARIOUS CROPS.
EXACTLY. SO THIS "PUNISHMENT!" EVENT HAS THE PLAYER "MAKE UP FOR" THAT ORIGINAL SIN BY SACRIFICING HER LIFE!
NO ONE'S BEEN ABLE TO GET OUT OF THIS COMBO BEFORE!
S-SO...
...IT'S GAME OVER, JUST LIKE THAT?! SCARY!
BUZZ
IT CAN'T BE...
MISA-SAN, ISN'T THERE ANYTHING...?
DON'T WORRY, MANAMI-SAN.
HAOS

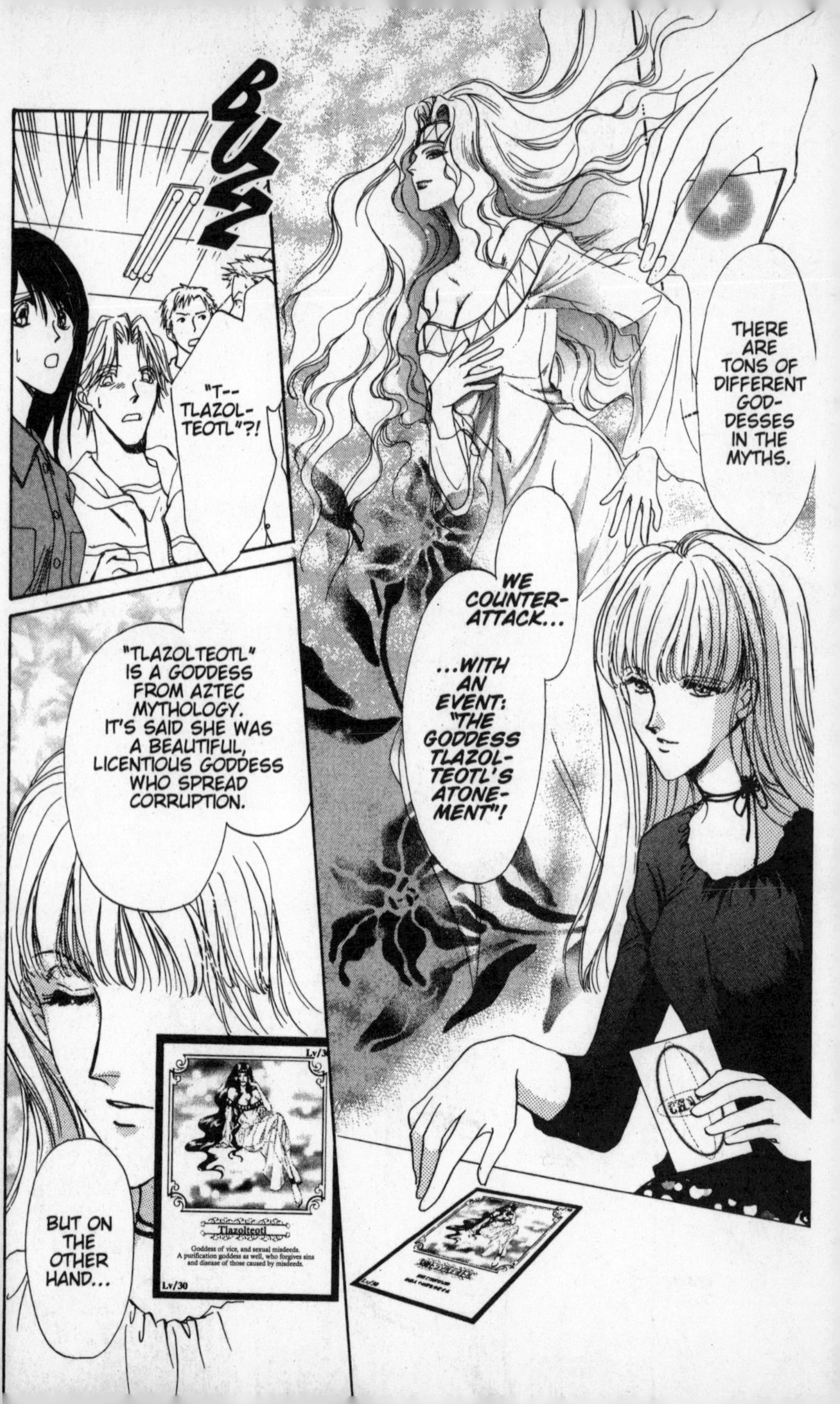

THERE ARE TONS OF DIFFERENT GOD-DESSES IN THE MYTHS.
WE COUNTER-ATTACK...
...WITH AN EVENT: "THE GODDESS TLAZOL-TEOTL'S ATONE-MENT"!
BUZZ
"T-- TLAZOL-TEOTL"?!
"TLAZOLTEOTL" IS A GODDESS FROM AZTEC MYTHOLOGY. IT'S SAID SHE WAS A BEAUTIFUL, LICENTIOUS GODDESS WHO SPREAD CORRUPTION.
Tlazolteotl
Goddess of vice, and sexual misdeeds. A purification goddess as well, who forgives sins and disease of those caused by misdeeds.
Lv/30
BUT ON THE OTHER HAND...

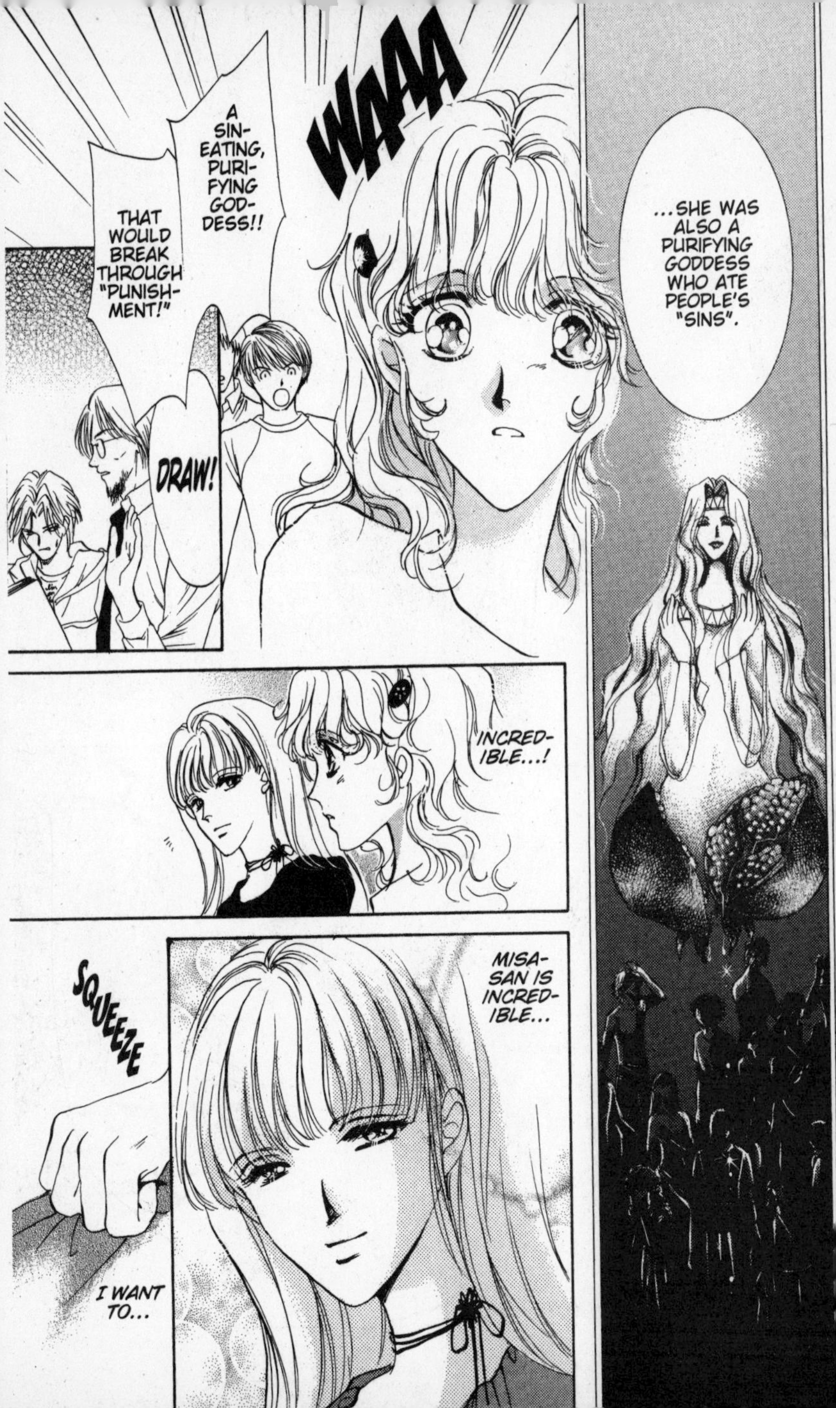
...SHE WAS ALSO A PURIFYING GODDESS WHO ATE PEOPLE'S "SINS".
WAAA
A SIN-EATING, PURIFYING GODDESS!!
THAT WOULD BREAK THROUGH "PUNISHMENT!"
DRAW!
INCREDIBLE...!
MISA-SAN IS INCREDIBLE...
SQUEEZE
I WANT TO...

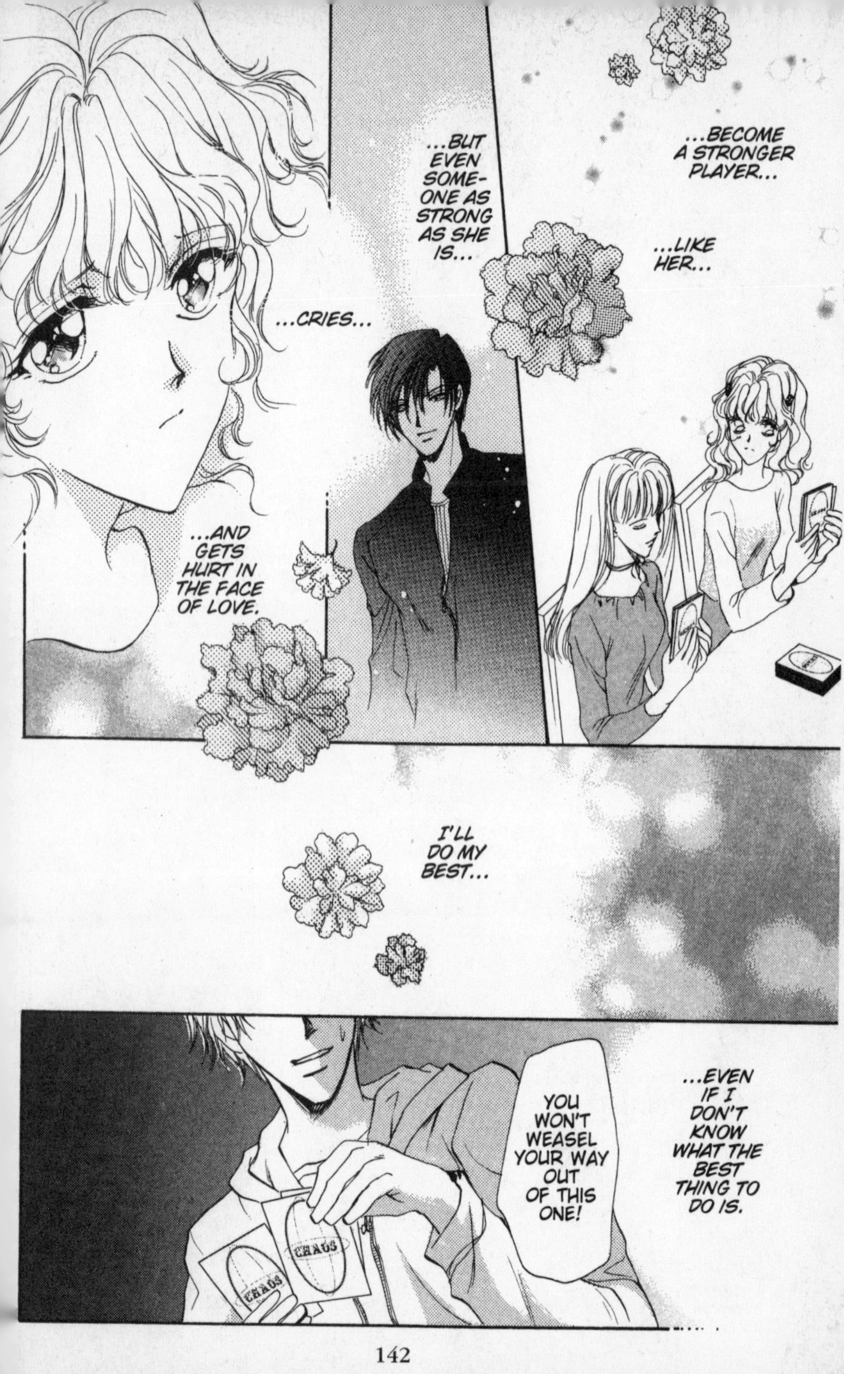
...BECOME A STRONGER PLAYER...
...LIKE HER...
...BUT EVEN SOMEONE AS STRONG AS SHE IS...
...CRIES...
...AND GETS HURT IN THE FACE OF LOVE.
I'LL DO MY BEST...
...EVEN IF I DON'T KNOW WHAT THE BEST THING TO DO IS.
YOU WON'T WEASEL YOUR WAY OUT OF THIS ONE!
CHAOS
CHAOS

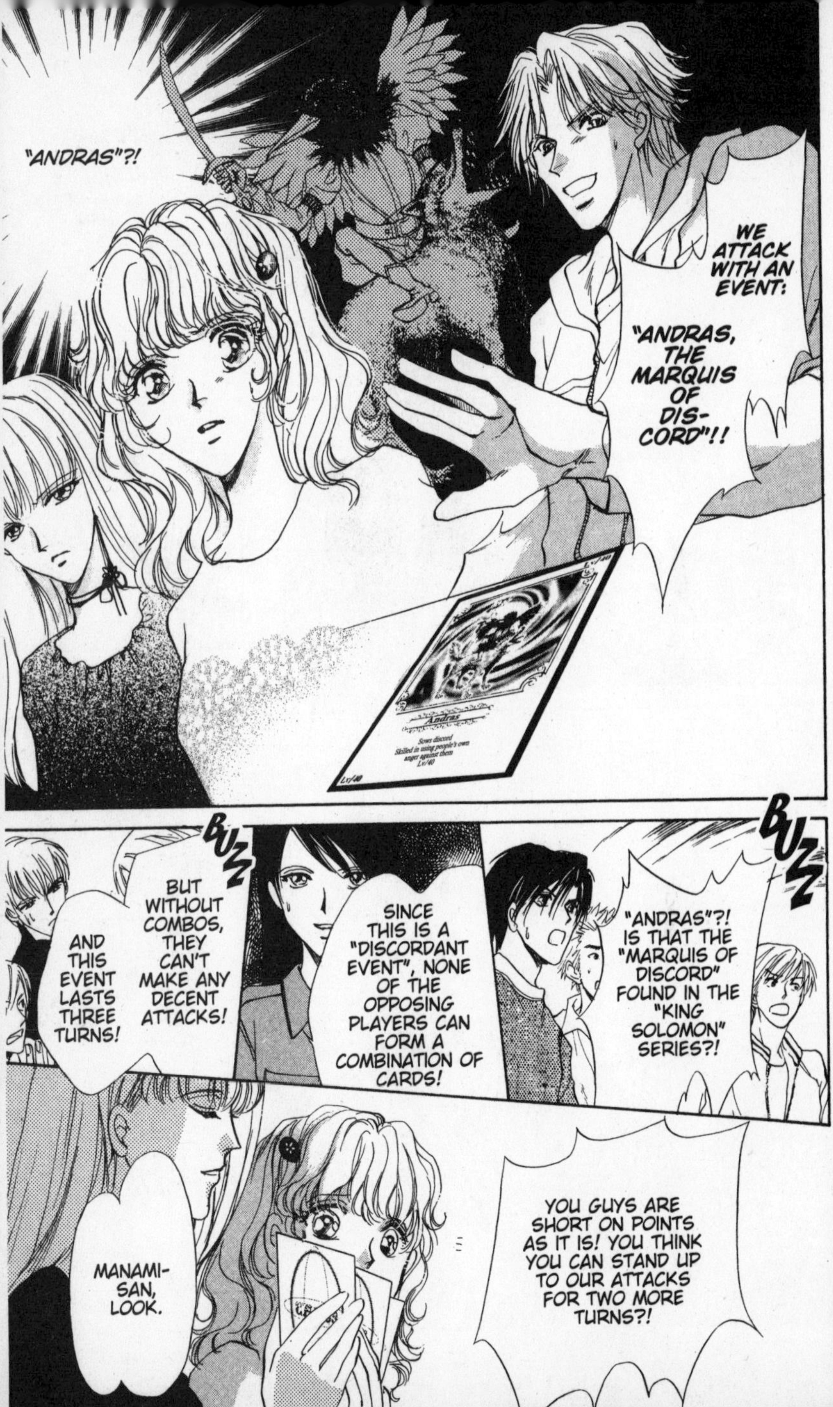
WE ATTACK WITH AN EVENT:
"ANDRAS, THE MARQUIS OF DISCORD"!!
"ANDRAS"?!
Andras
Sows discord
Skilled in using people's own anger against them
Lv/40
BUZZ
"ANDRAS"?! IS THAT THE "MARQUIS OF DISCORD" FOUND IN THE "KING SOLOMON" SERIES?!
SINCE THIS IS A "DISCORDANT EVENT", NONE OF THE OPPOSING PLAYERS CAN FORM A COMBINATION OF CARDS!
BUZZ
BUT WITHOUT COMBOS, THEY CAN'T MAKE ANY DECENT ATTACKS!
AND THIS EVENT LASTS THREE TURNS!
YOU GUYS ARE SHORT ON POINTS AS IT IS! YOU THINK YOU CAN STAND UP TO OUR ATTACKS FOR TWO MORE TURNS?!
MANAMI-SAN, LOOK.

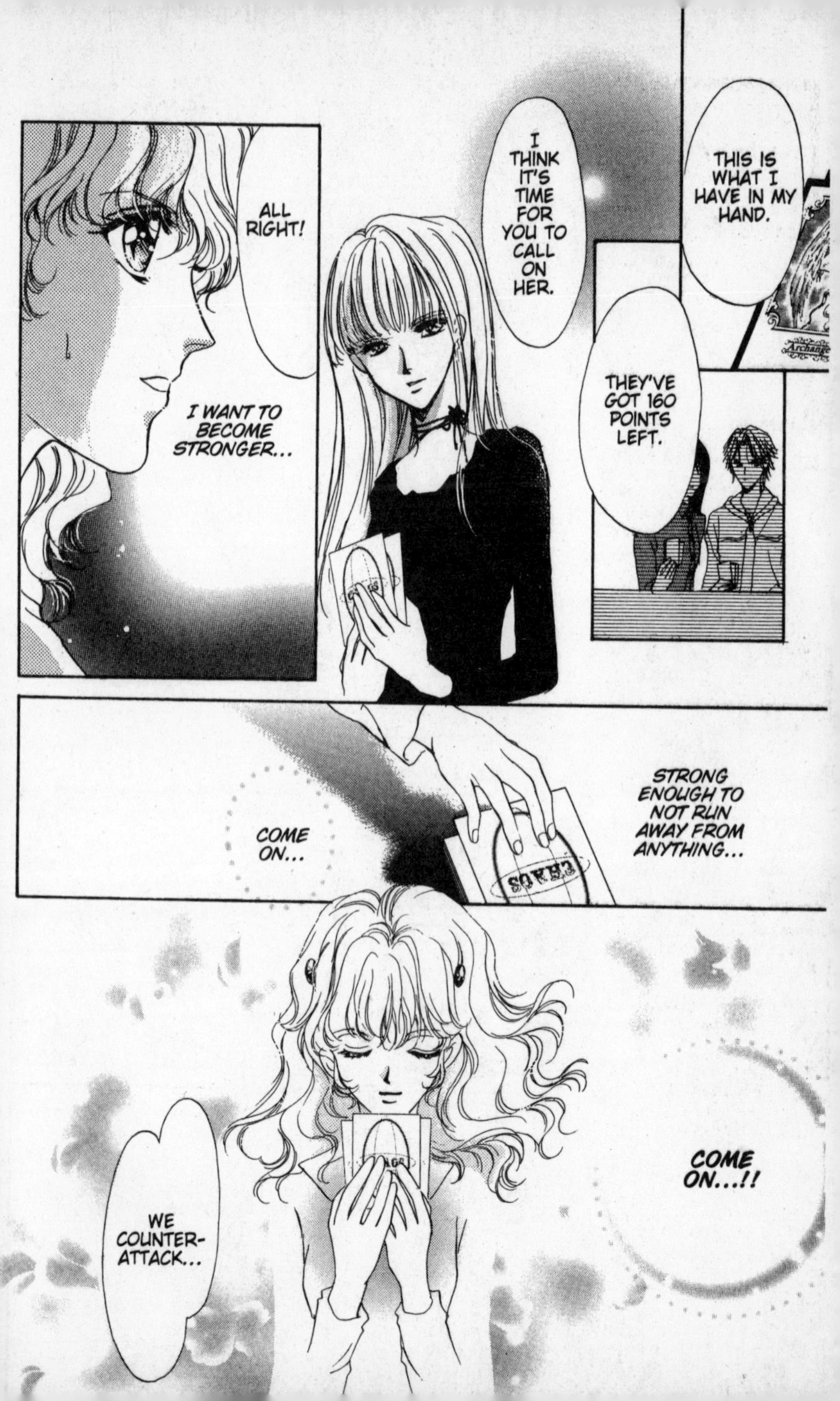
THIS IS WHAT I HAVE IN MY HAND.
THEY'VE GOT 160 POINTS LEFT.
I THINK IT'S TIME FOR YOU TO CALL ON HER.
ALL RIGHT!
I WANT TO BECOME STRONGER...
STRONG ENOUGH TO NOT RUN AWAY FROM ANYTHING...
COME ON...
COME ON...!!
WE COUNTER-ATTACK...

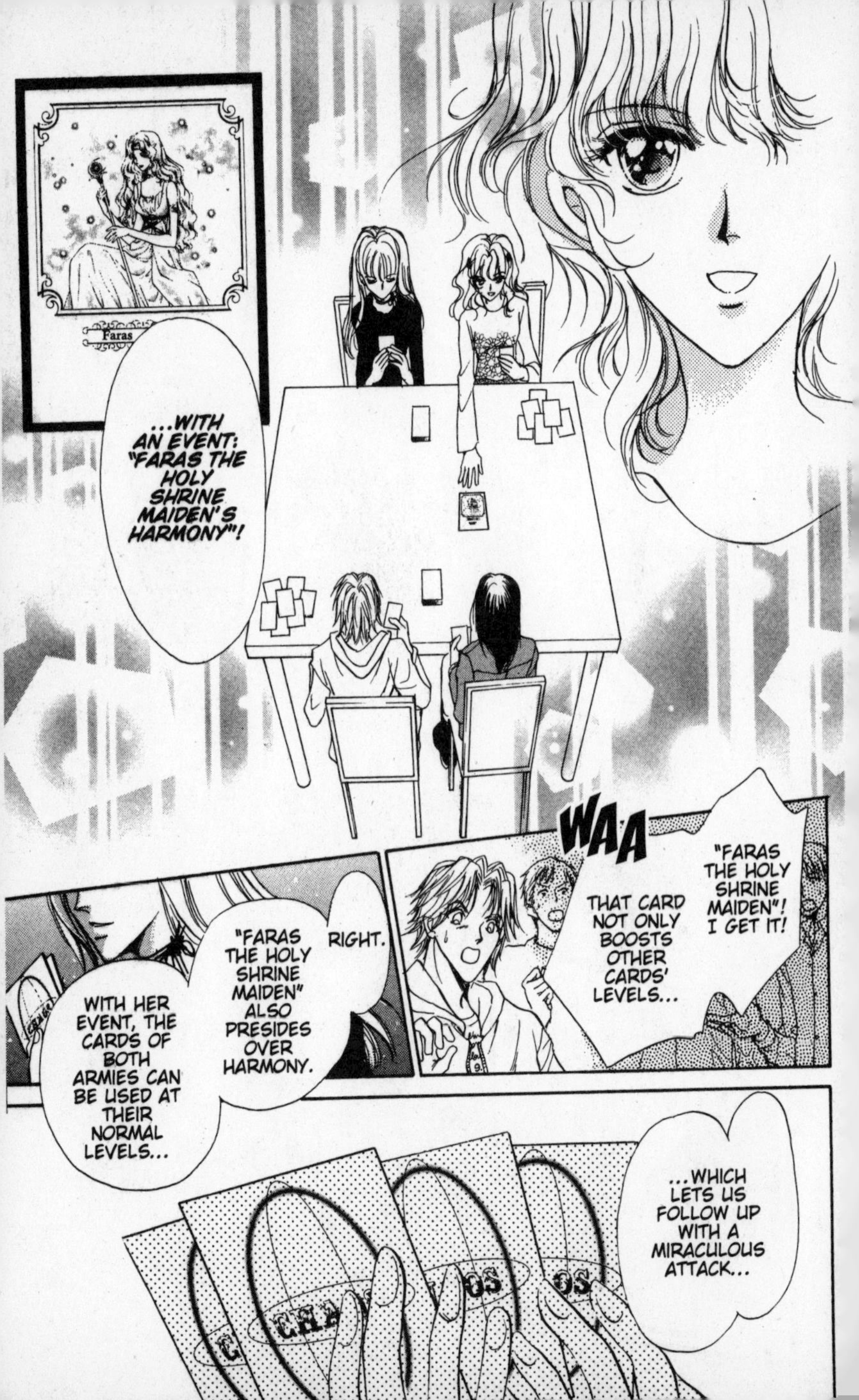
Faras
...WITH AN EVENT: "FARAS THE HOLY SHRINE MAIDEN'S HARMONY"!
WAA
"FARAS THE HOLY SHRINE MAIDEN"! I GET IT!
THAT CARD NOT ONLY BOOSTS OTHER CARDS' LEVELS...
RIGHT.
"FARAS THE HOLY SHRINE MAIDEN" ALSO PRESIDES OVER HARMONY.
WITH HER EVENT, THE CARDS OF BOTH ARMIES CAN BE USED AT THEIR NORMAL LEVELS...
...WHICH LETS US FOLLOW UP WITH A MIRACULOUS ATTACK...

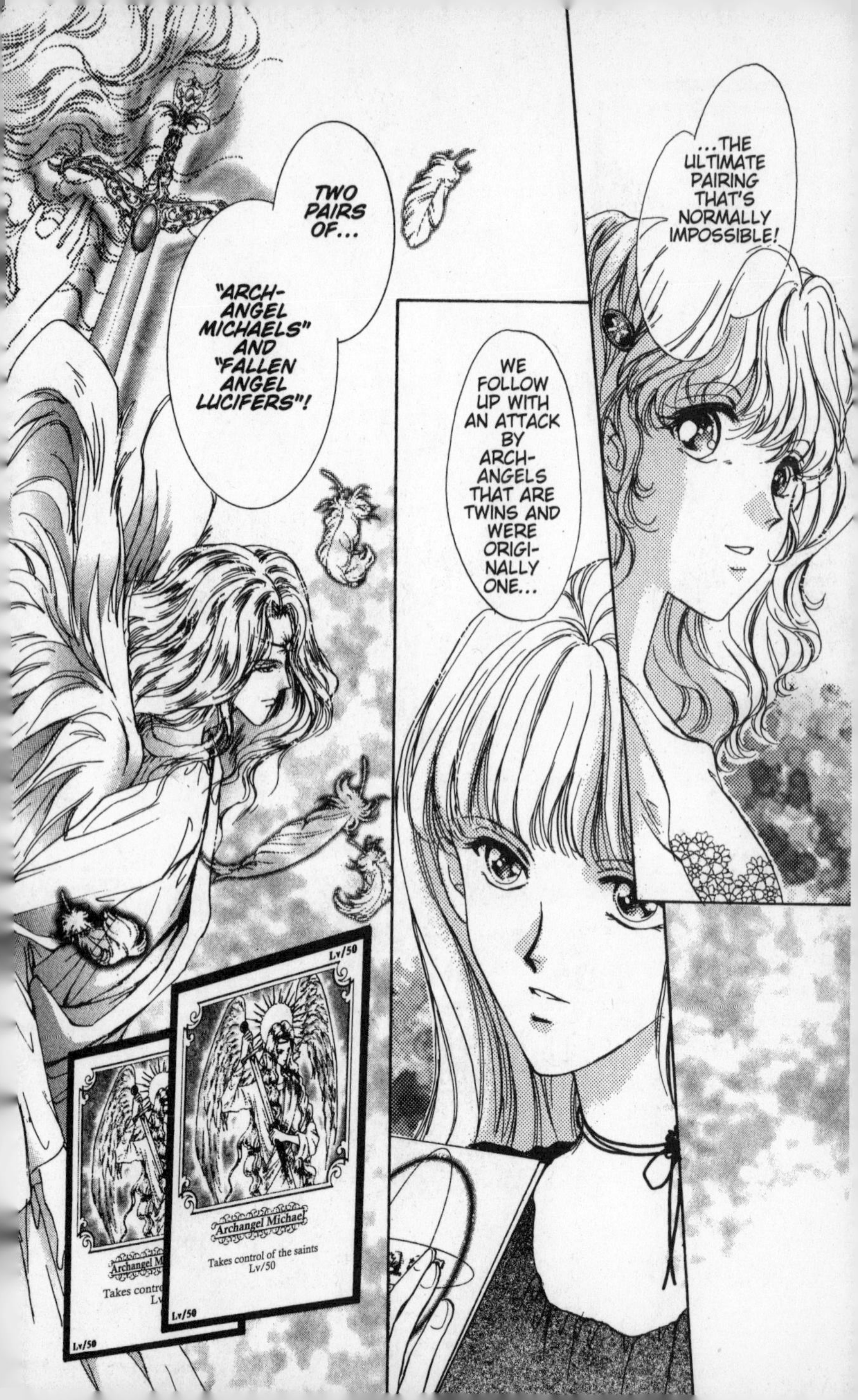
...THE ULTIMATE PAIRING THAT'S NORMALLY IMPOSSIBLE!
WE FOLLOW UP WITH AN ATTACK BY ARCH-ANGELS THAT ARE TWINS AND WERE ORIGI-NALLY ONE...
TWO PAIRS OF...
"ARCH-ANGEL MICHAELS" AND "FALLEN ANGEL LUCIFERS"!
Lv/50
Archangel Michael
Takes control of the saints
Lv/50
Lv/50
Lv/50

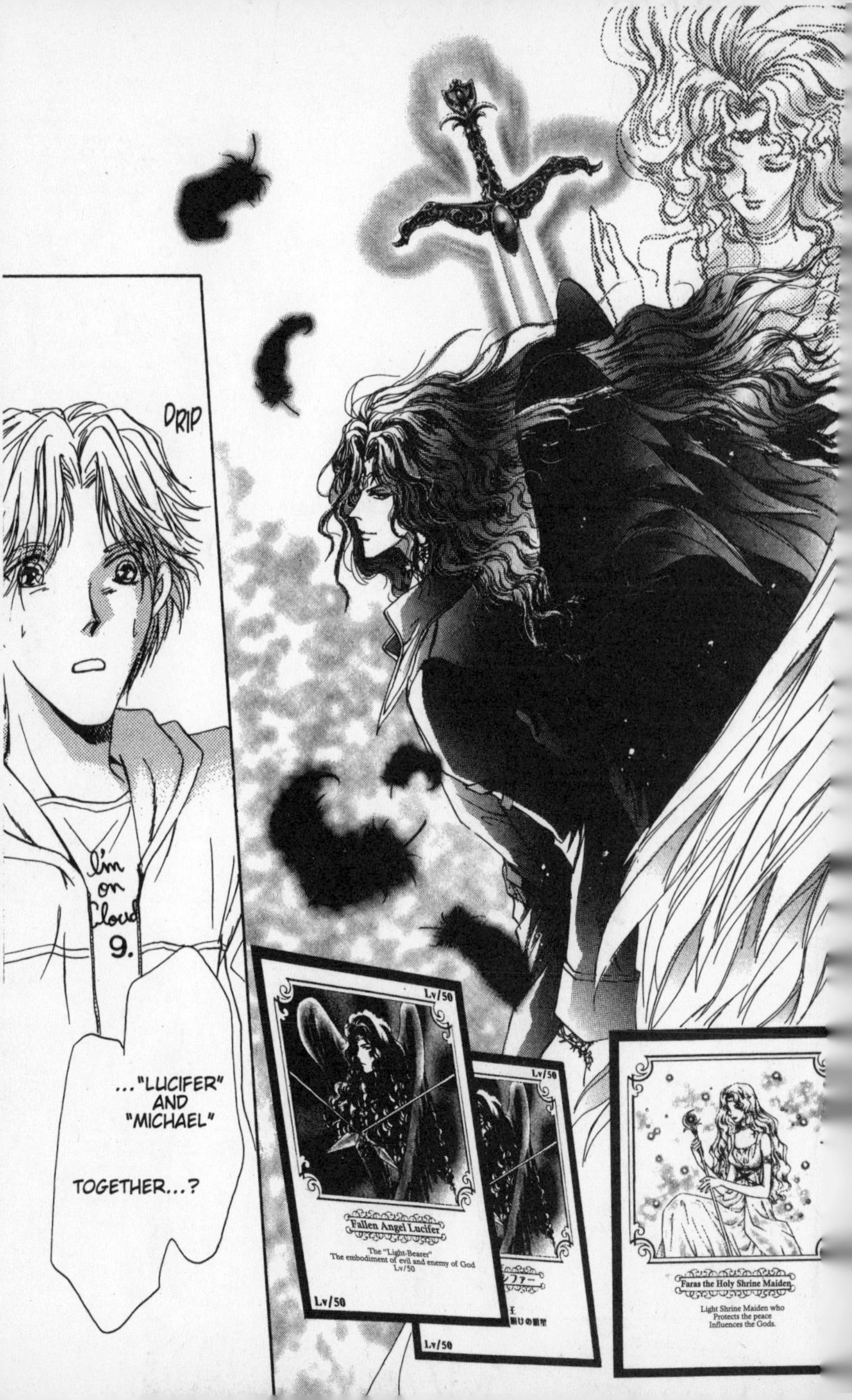
Faras the Holy Shrine Maiden
Light Shrine Maiden who
Protects the peace
Influences the Gods.
Lv/50
Lv/50
Lv/50
Fallen Angel Lucifer
The "Light-Bearer"
The embodiment of evil and enemy of God
Lv/50
Lv/50
DRIP
I'm on Cloud 9.
..."LUCIFER" AND "MICHAEL"
TOGETHER...?

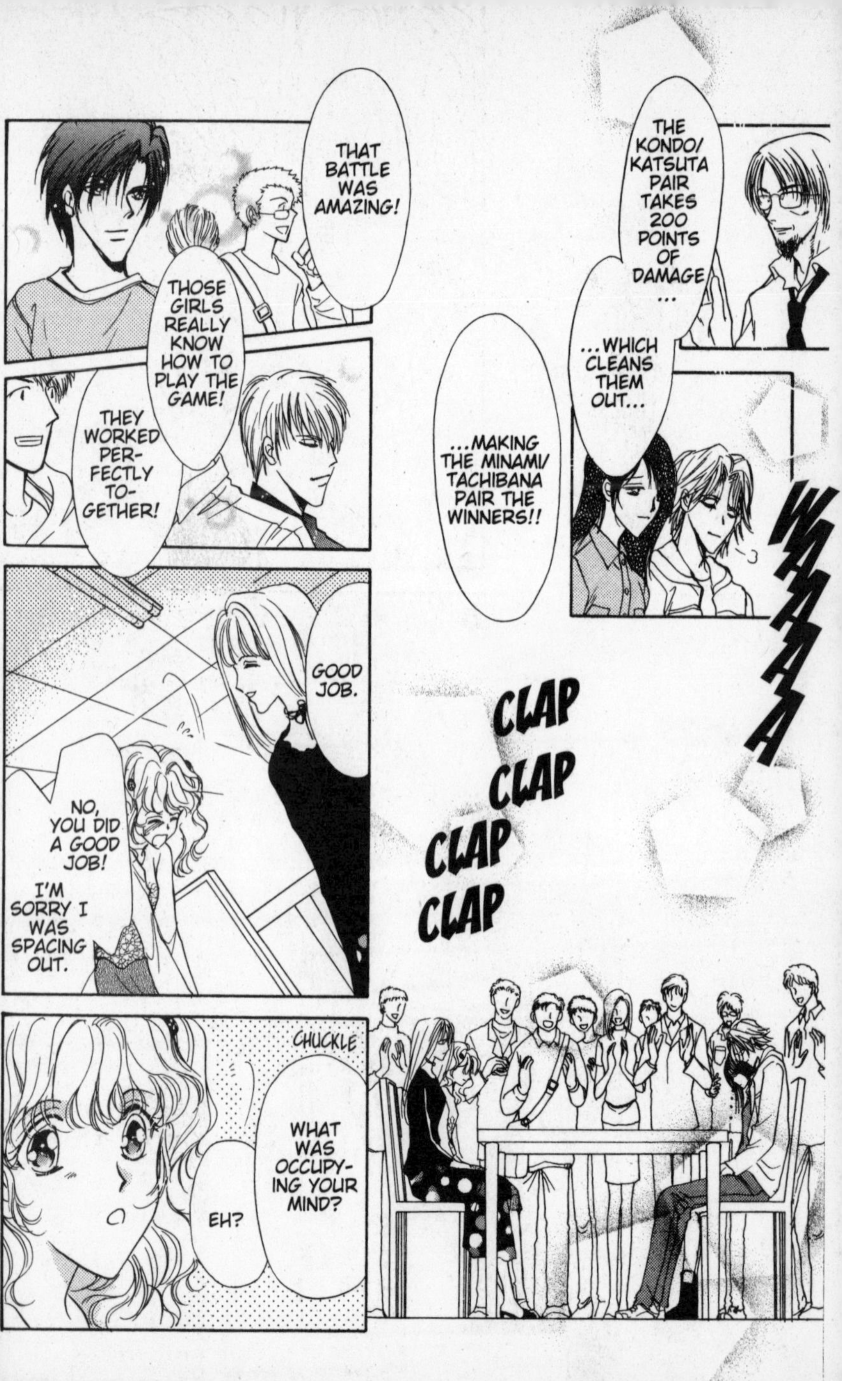

THE KONDO/ KATSUTA PAIR TAKES 200 POINTS OF DAMAGE...
...WHICH CLEANS THEM OUT...
...MAKING THE MINAMI/ TACHIBANA PAIR THE WINNERS!!
WAAAAA
CLAP CLAP CLAP CLAP
THAT BATTLE WAS AMAZING!
THOSE GIRLS REALLY KNOW HOW TO PLAY THE GAME!
THEY WORKED PER-FECTLY TO-GETHER!
GOOD JOB.
NO, YOU DID A GOOD JOB!
I'M SORRY I WAS SPACING OUT.
CHUCKLE
WHAT WAS OCCUPY-ING YOUR MIND?
EH?

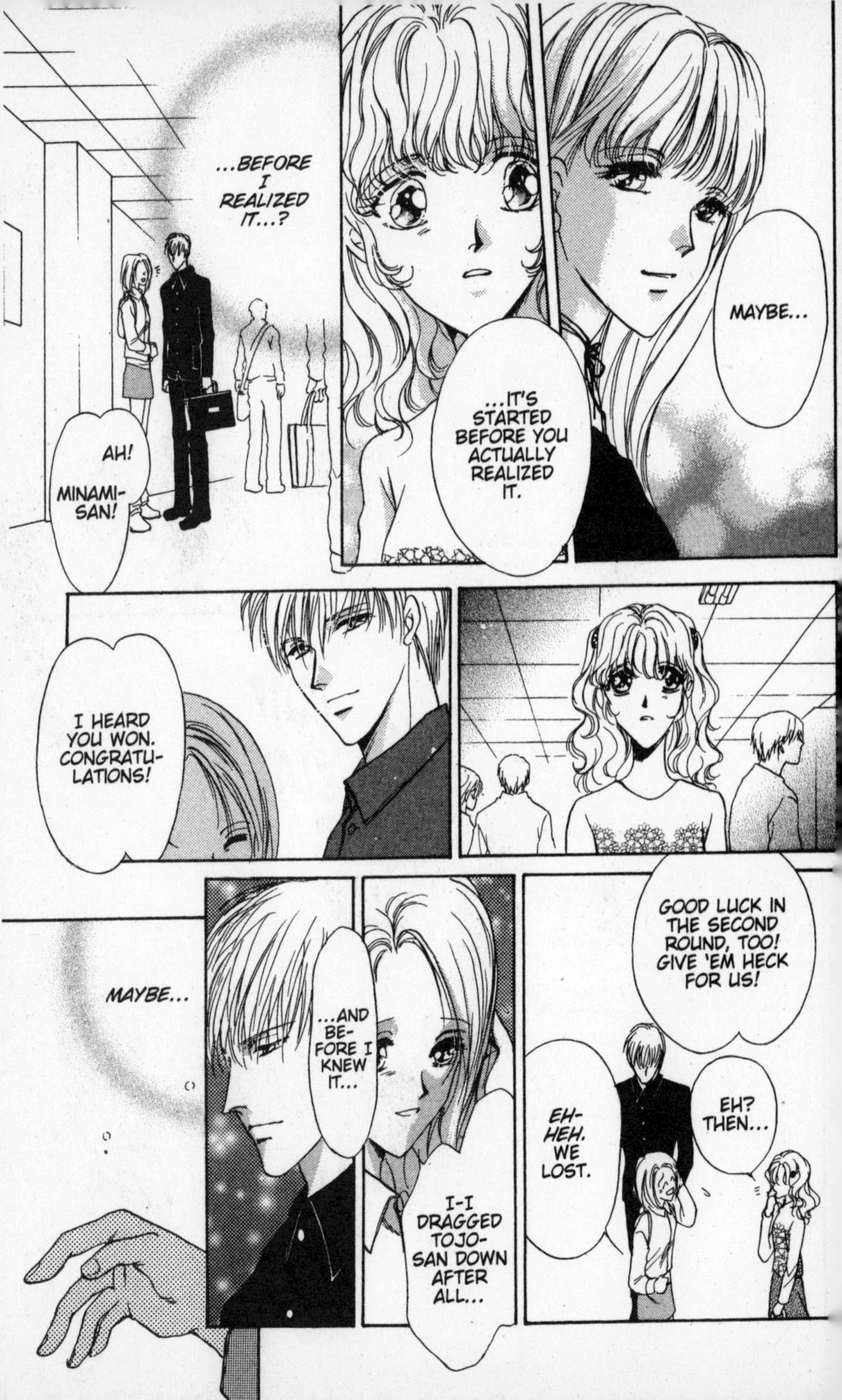
MAYBE...
...IT'S STARTED BEFORE YOU ACTUALLY REALIZED IT.
...BEFORE I REALIZED IT...?
AH! MINAMI-SAN!
I HEARD YOU WON. CONGRATULATIONS!
GOOD LUCK IN THE SECOND ROUND, TOO! GIVE 'EM HECK FOR US!
EH? THEN...
EH-HEH. WE LOST.
...AND BEFORE I KNEW IT...
I-I DRAGGED TOJO-SAN DOWN AFTER ALL...
MAYBE...

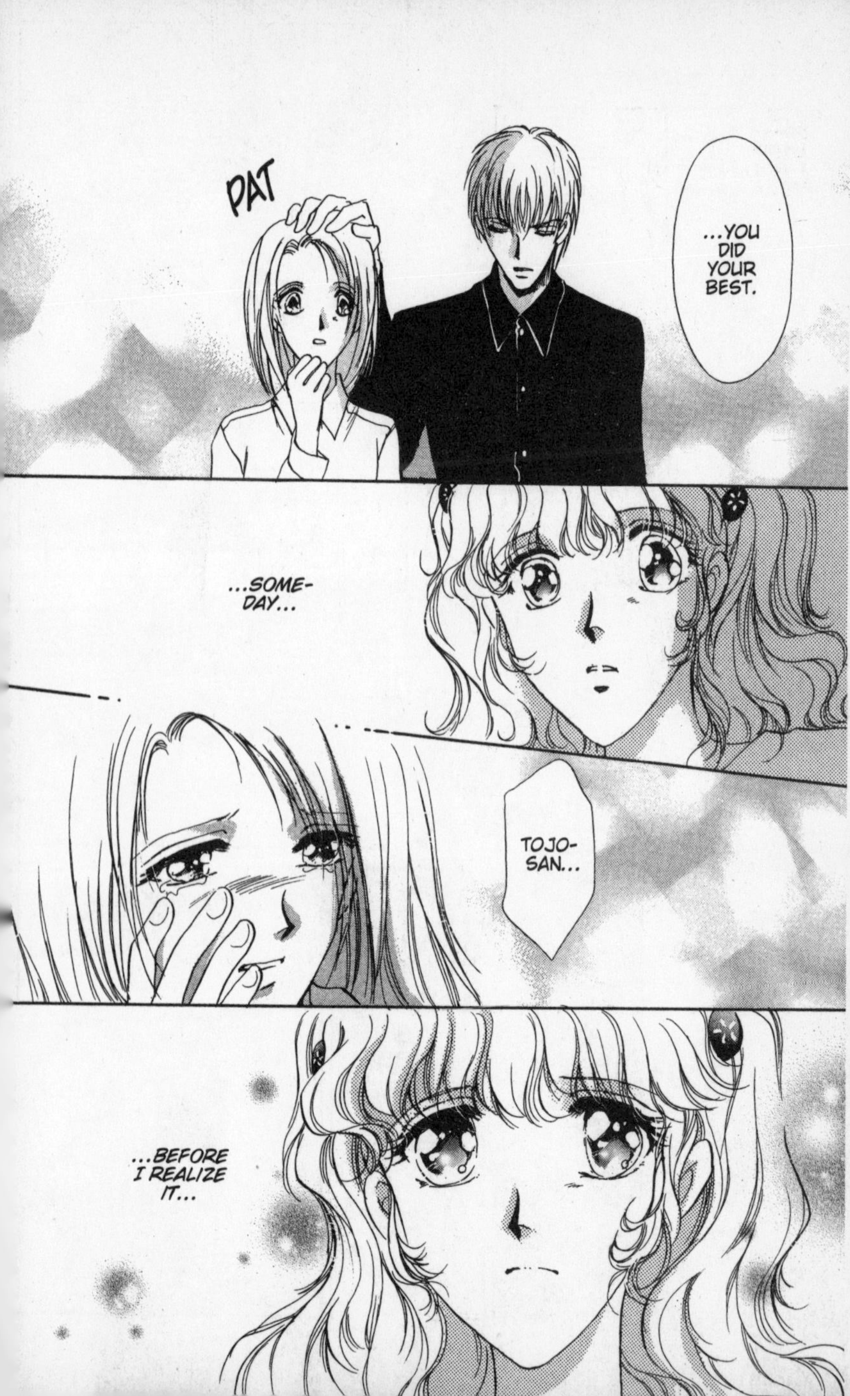
...YOU DID YOUR BEST.
PAT
...SOME-DAY...
TOJO-SAN...
...BEFORE I REALIZE IT...

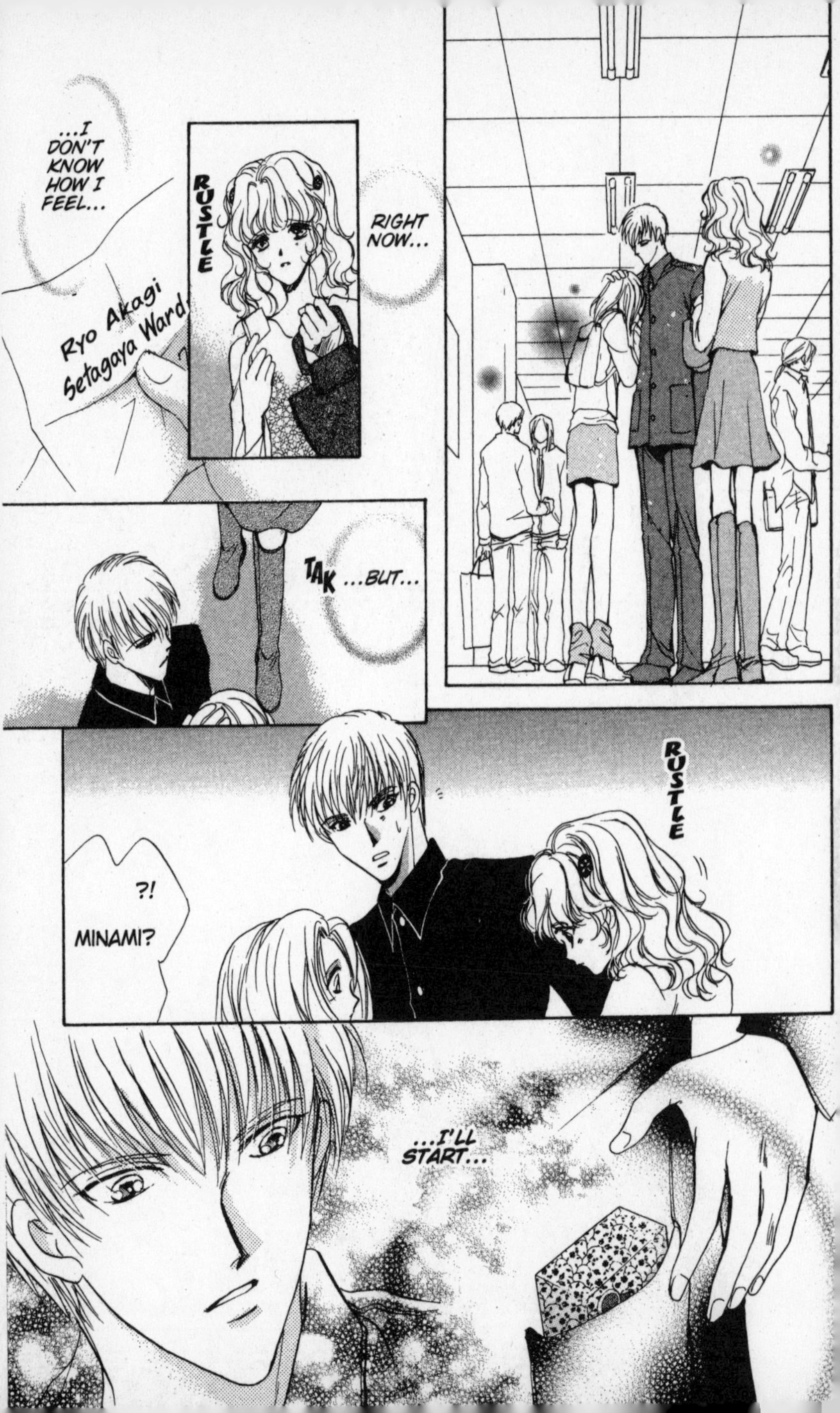
...I DON'T KNOW HOW I FEEL...
RUSTLE
RIGHT NOW...
Ryo Akagi
Setagaya Ward
TAK
...BUT...
RUSTLE
?!
MINAMI?
...I'LL START...

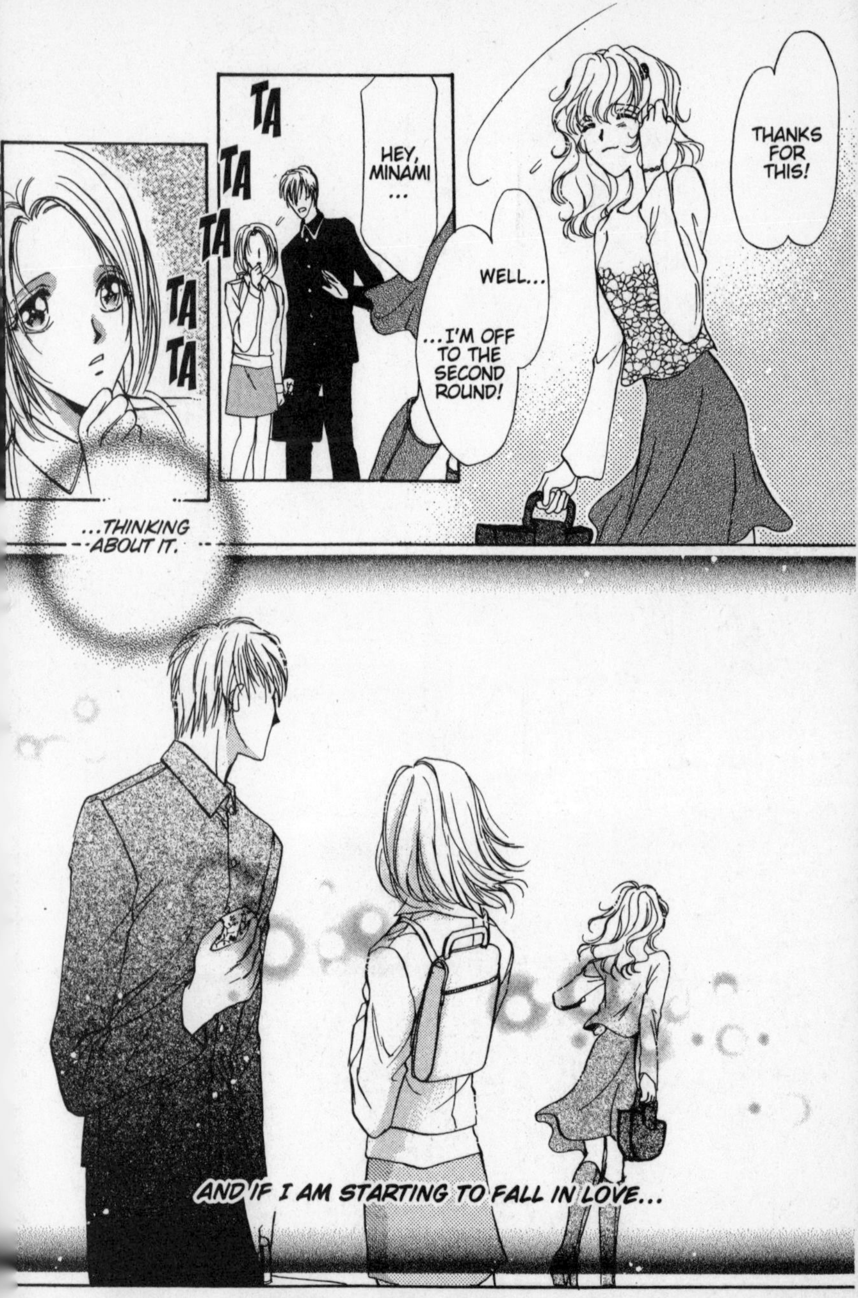
THANKS FOR THIS!
WELL...
...I'M OFF TO THE SECOND ROUND!
HEY, MINAMI ...
TA TA TA TA TA
...THINKING ABOUT IT.
AND IF I AM STARTING TO FALL IN LOVE...

KING OF CARDS 21: THE END

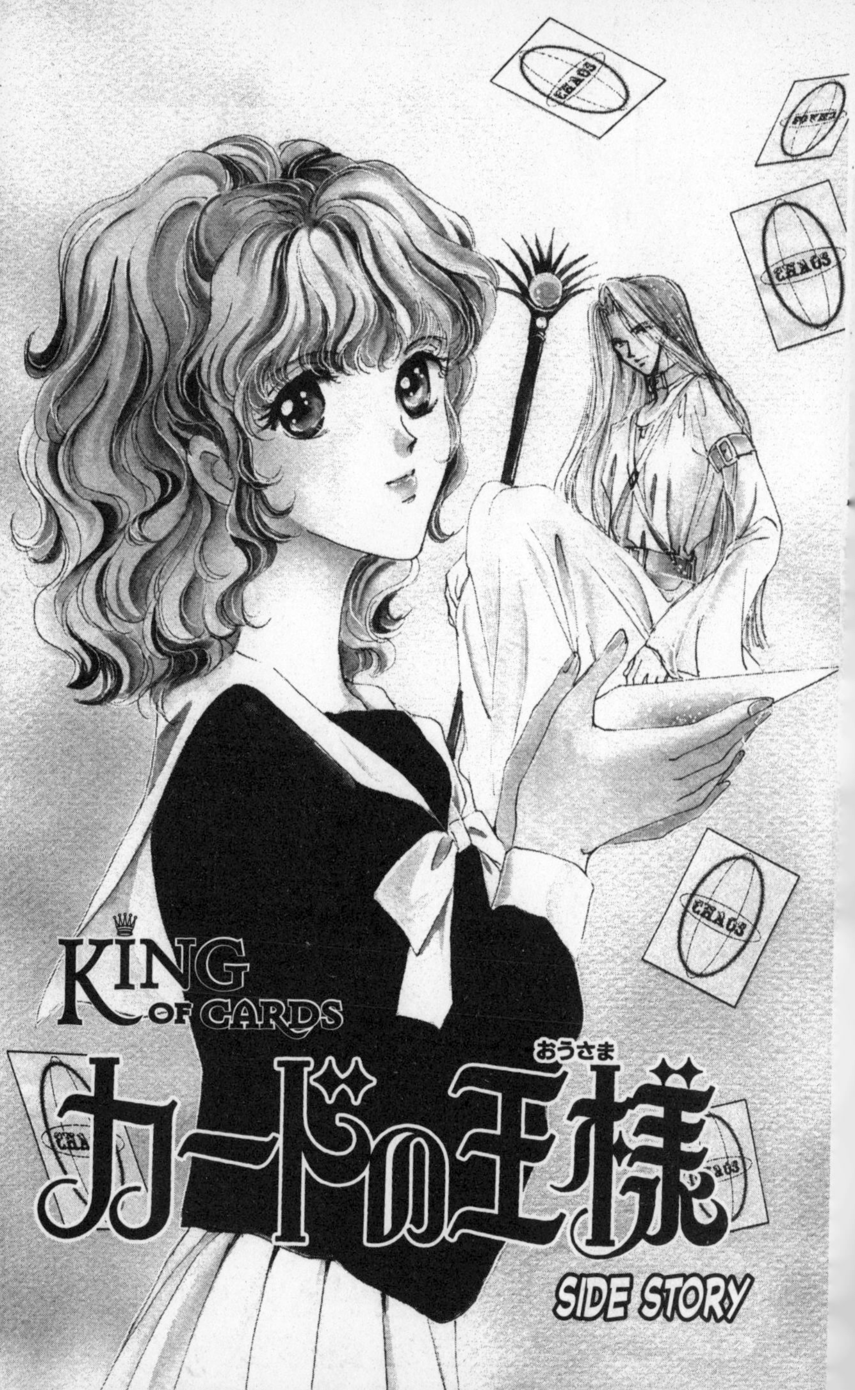
CHAOS
KING OF CARDS
カードの王様(おうさま)
SIDE STORY

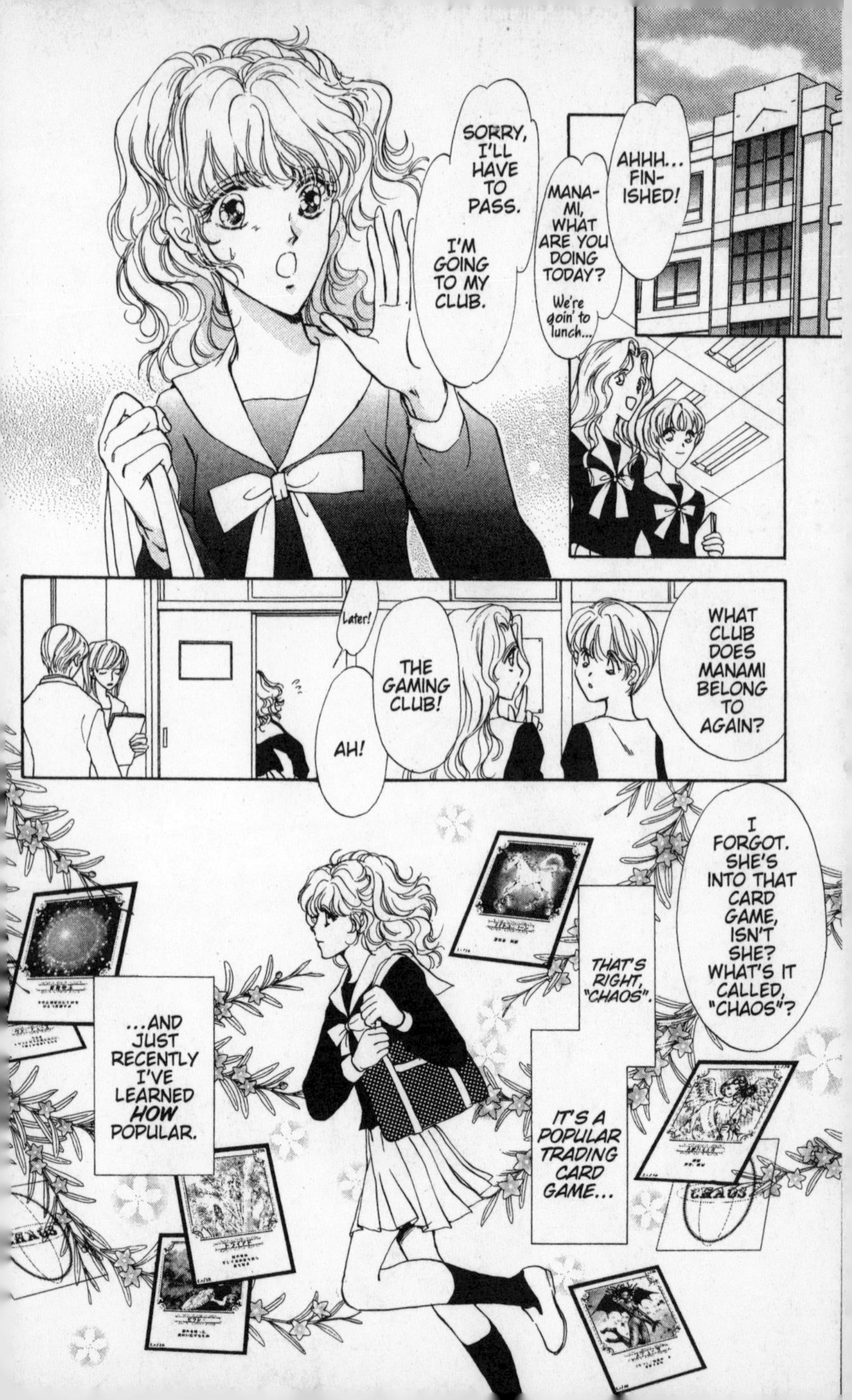
AHHH... FIN-ISHED!
MANA-MI, WHAT ARE YOU DOING TODAY?
We're goin' to lunch...
SORRY, I'LL HAVE TO PASS.
I'M GOING TO MY CLUB.
WHAT CLUB DOES MANAMI BELONG TO AGAIN?
THE GAMING CLUB!
Later!
AH!
I FORGOT. SHE'S INTO THAT CARD GAME, ISN'T SHE? WHAT'S IT CALLED, "CHAOS"?
THAT'S RIGHT, "CHAOS".
IT'S A POPULAR TRADING CARD GAME...
...AND JUST RECENTLY I'VE LEARNED *HOW* POPULAR.

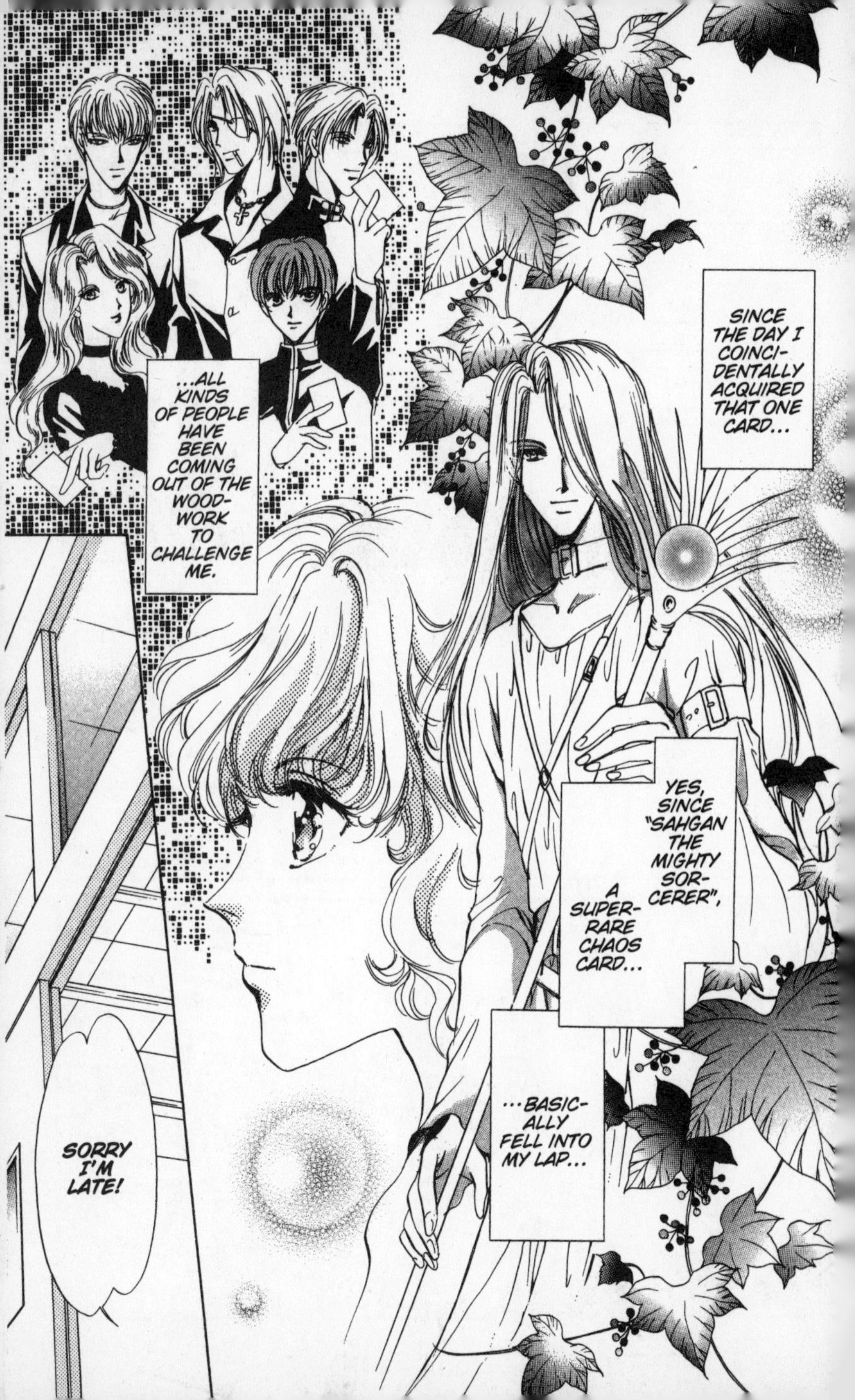
SINCE THE DAY I COINCIDENTALLY ACQUIRED THAT ONE CARD...
...ALL KINDS OF PEOPLE HAVE BEEN COMING OUT OF THE WOODWORK TO CHALLENGE ME.
YES, SINCE "SAHGAN THE MIGHTY SORCERER",
A SUPER-RARE CHAOS CARD...
...BASICALLY FELL INTO MY LAP...
SORRY I'M LATE!

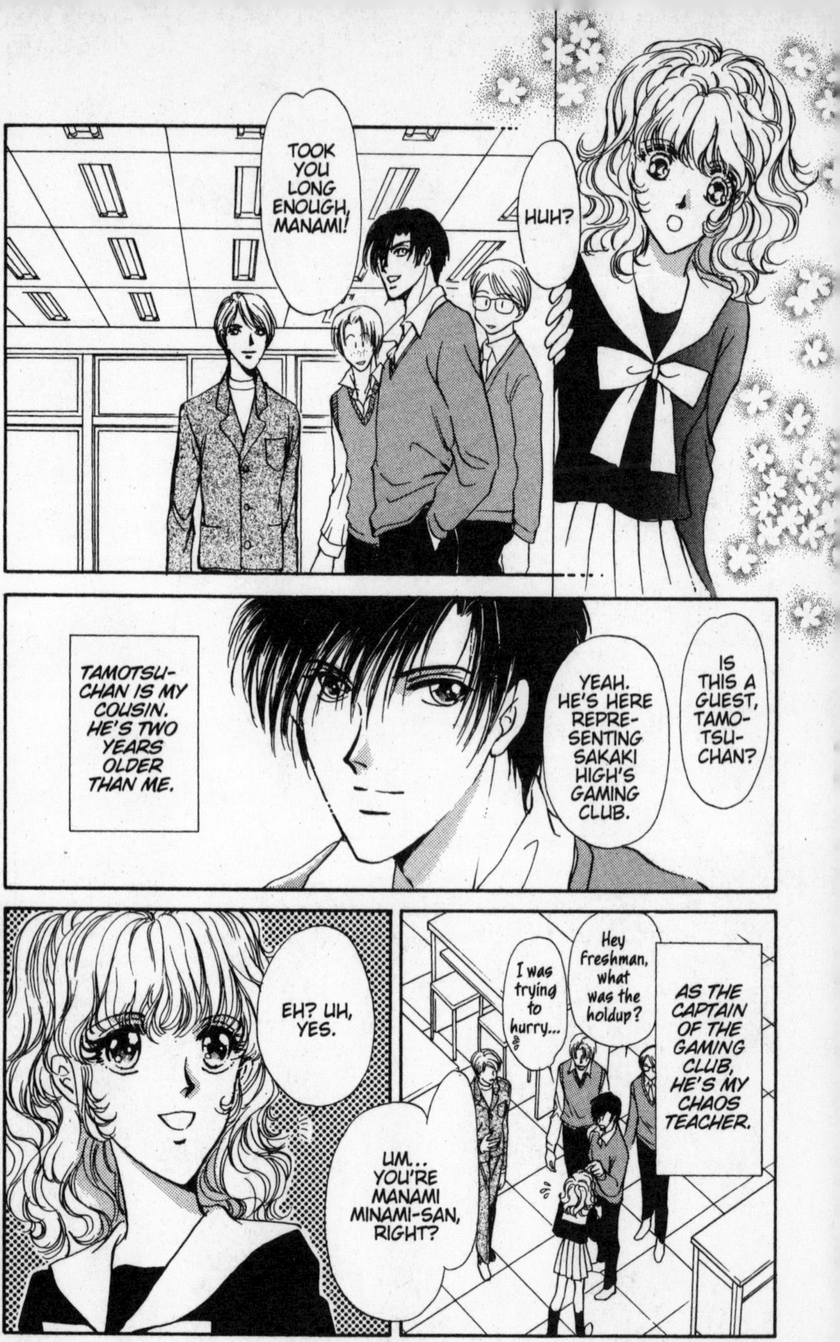
HUH?
TOOK YOU LONG ENOUGH, MANAMI!
IS THIS A GUEST, TAMOTSU-CHAN?
YEAH. HE'S HERE REPRESENTING SAKAKI HIGH'S GAMING CLUB.
TAMOTSU-CHAN IS MY COUSIN. HE'S TWO YEARS OLDER THAN ME.
AS THE CAPTAIN OF THE GAMING CLUB, HE'S MY CHAOS TEACHER.
Hey freshman, what was the holdup?
I was trying to hurry...
UM... YOU'RE MANAMI MINAMI-SAN, RIGHT?
EH? UH, YES.

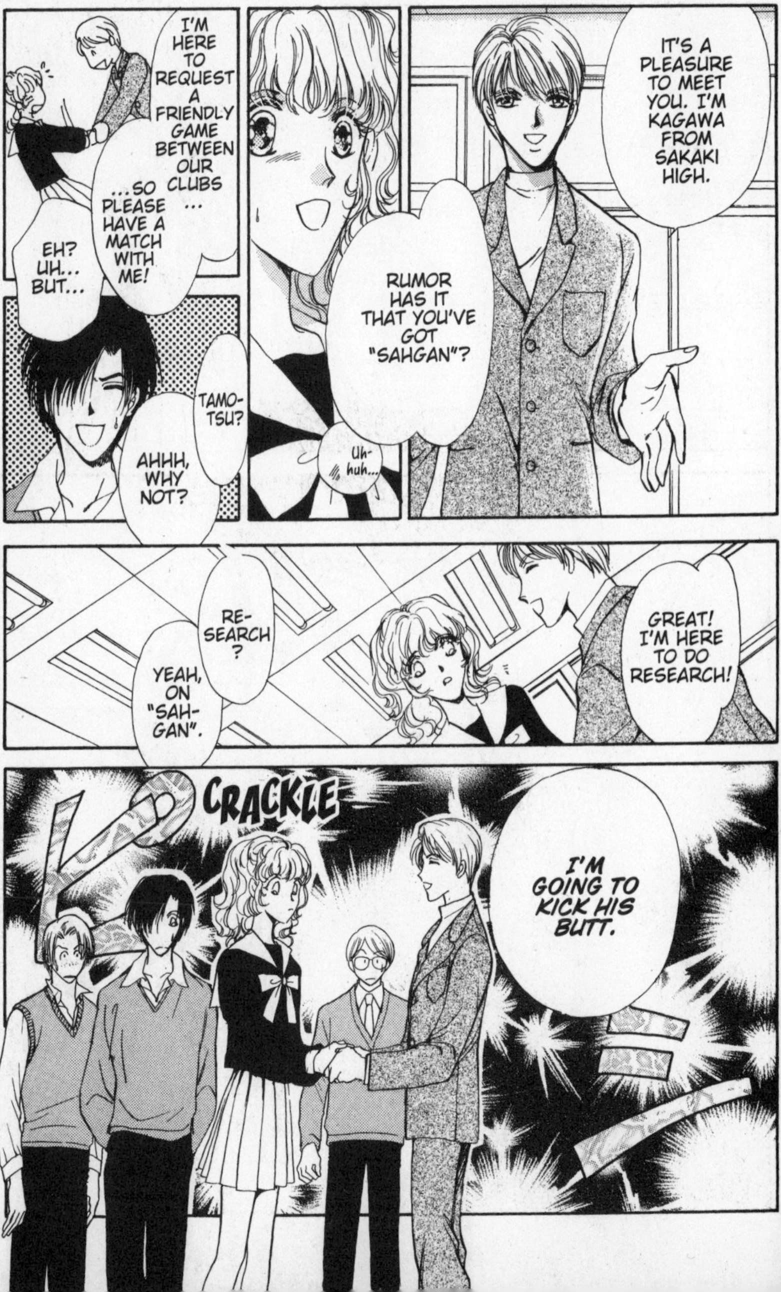
IT'S A PLEASURE TO MEET YOU. I'M KAGAWA FROM SAKAKI HIGH.
RUMOR HAS IT THAT YOU'VE GOT "SAHGAN"?
Uh-huh...
I'M HERE TO REQUEST A FRIENDLY GAME BETWEEN OUR CLUBS ...
...SO PLEASE HAVE A MATCH WITH ME!
EH? UH... BUT...
TAMO-TSU?
AHHH, WHY NOT?
GREAT! I'M HERE TO DO RESEARCH!
RE-SEARCH?
YEAH, ON "SAH-GAN".
CRACKLE
I'M GOING TO KICK HIS BUTT.

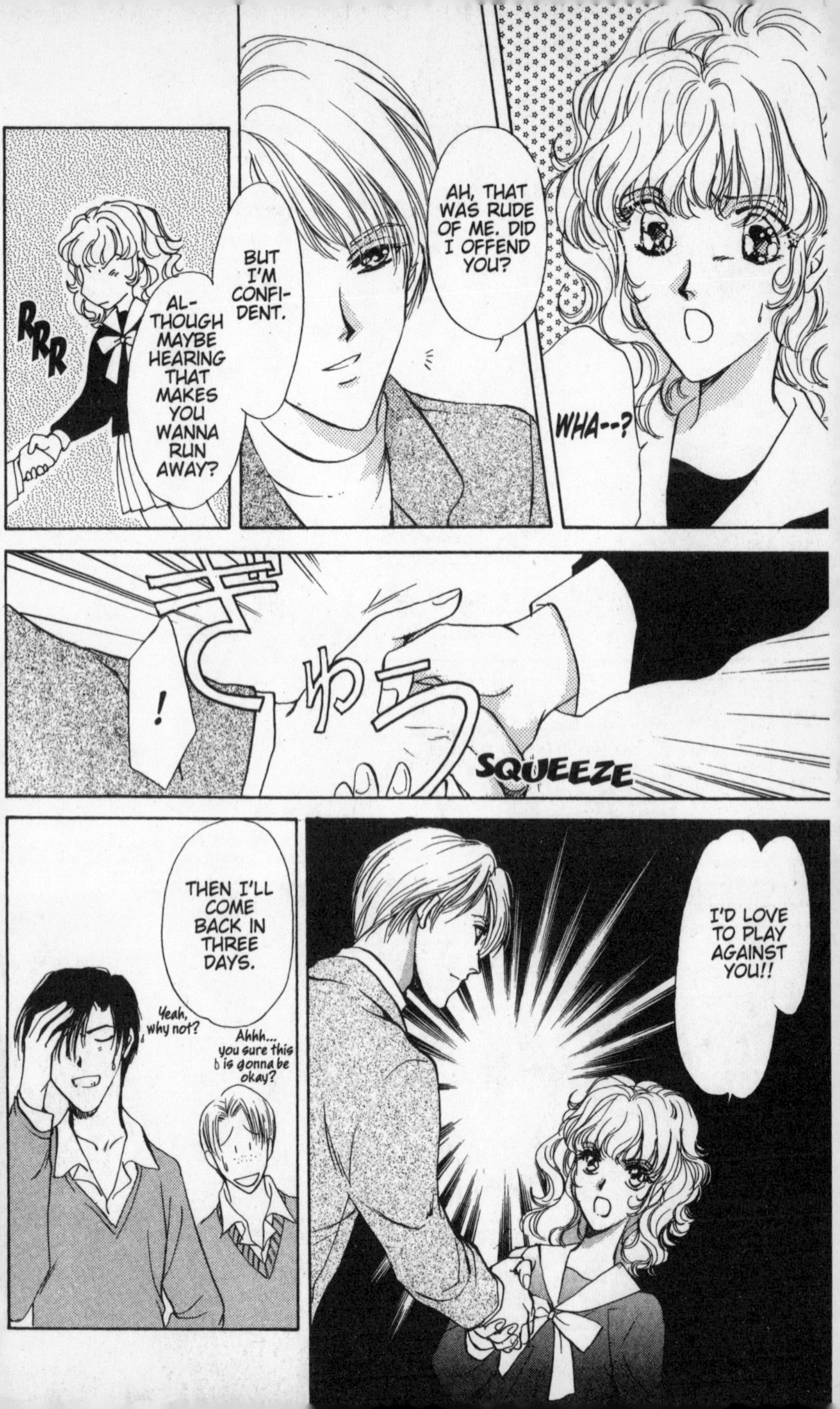
WHA--?
AH, THAT WAS RUDE OF ME. DID I OFFEND YOU?
BUT I'M CONFIDENT.
AL-THOUGH MAYBE HEARING THAT MAKES YOU WANNA RUN AWAY?
RRR
ぎゅう
!
SQUEEZE
I'D LOVE TO PLAY AGAINST YOU!!
THEN I'LL COME BACK IN THREE DAYS.
Ahhh... you sure this is gonna be okay?
Yeah, why not?

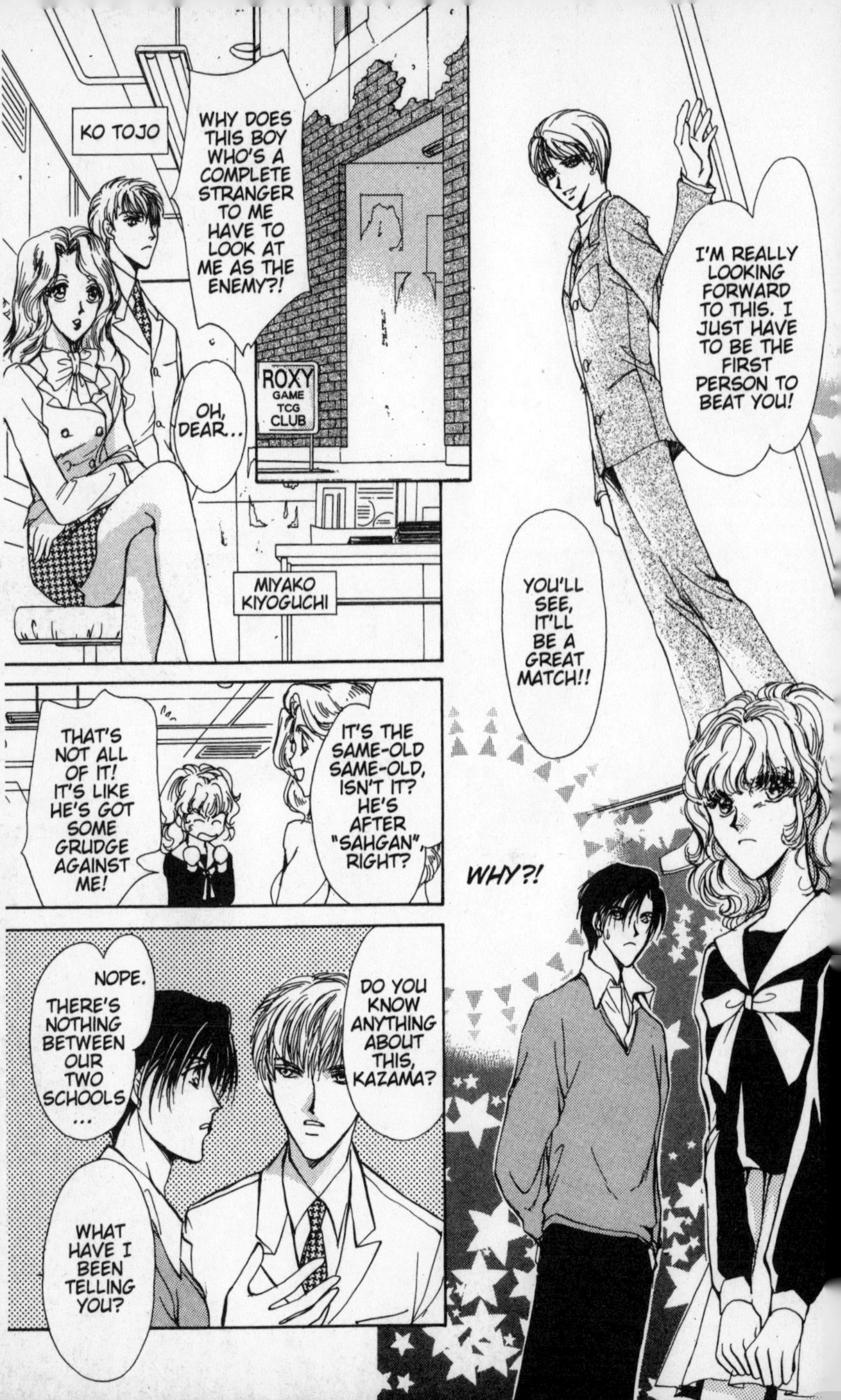
I'M REALLY LOOKING FORWARD TO THIS. I JUST HAVE TO BE THE FIRST PERSON TO BEAT YOU!
YOU'LL SEE, IT'LL BE A GREAT MATCH!!
WHY?!
WHY DOES THIS BOY WHO'S A COMPLETE STRANGER TO ME HAVE TO LOOK AT ME AS THE ENEMY?!
KO TOJO
ROXY GAME TCG CLUB
OH, DEAR...
MIYAKO KIYOGUCHI
IT'S THE SAME-OLD SAME-OLD, ISN'T IT? HE'S AFTER "SAHGAN", RIGHT?
THAT'S NOT ALL OF IT! IT'S LIKE HE'S GOT SOME GRUDGE AGAINST ME!
DO YOU KNOW ANYTHING ABOUT THIS, KAZAMA?
NOPE. THERE'S NOTHING BETWEEN OUR TWO SCHOOLS ...
WHAT HAVE I BEEN TELLING YOU?

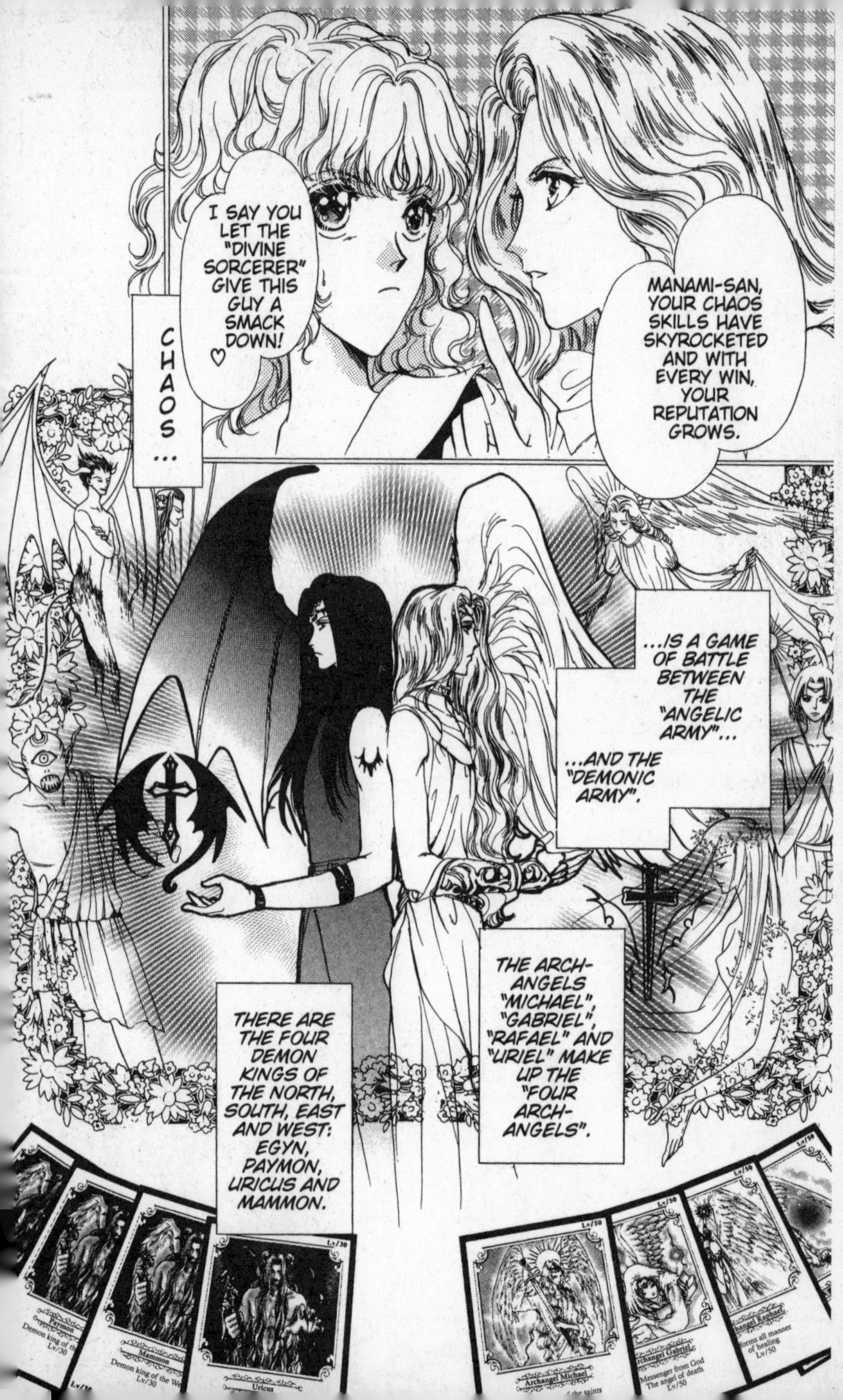
MANAMI-SAN, YOUR CHAOS SKILLS HAVE SKYROCKETED AND WITH EVERY WIN, YOUR REPUTATION GROWS.
I SAY YOU LET THE "DIVINE SORCERER" GIVE THIS GUY A SMACK DOWN! ♡
CHAOS...
...IS A GAME OF BATTLE BETWEEN THE "ANGELIC ARMY"...
...AND THE "DEMONIC ARMY".
THE ARCH-ANGELS "MICHAEL", "GABRIEL", "RAFAEL" AND "URIEL" MAKE UP THE "FOUR ARCH-ANGELS".
THERE ARE THE FOUR DEMON KINGS OF THE NORTH, SOUTH, EAST AND WEST: EGYN, PAYMON, URICUS AND MAMMON.
Paymon
Mammon
Lv/30
Uricus
Archangel Michael
Archangel Gabriel
Messenger from God
The angel of death
Lv/50
of healing

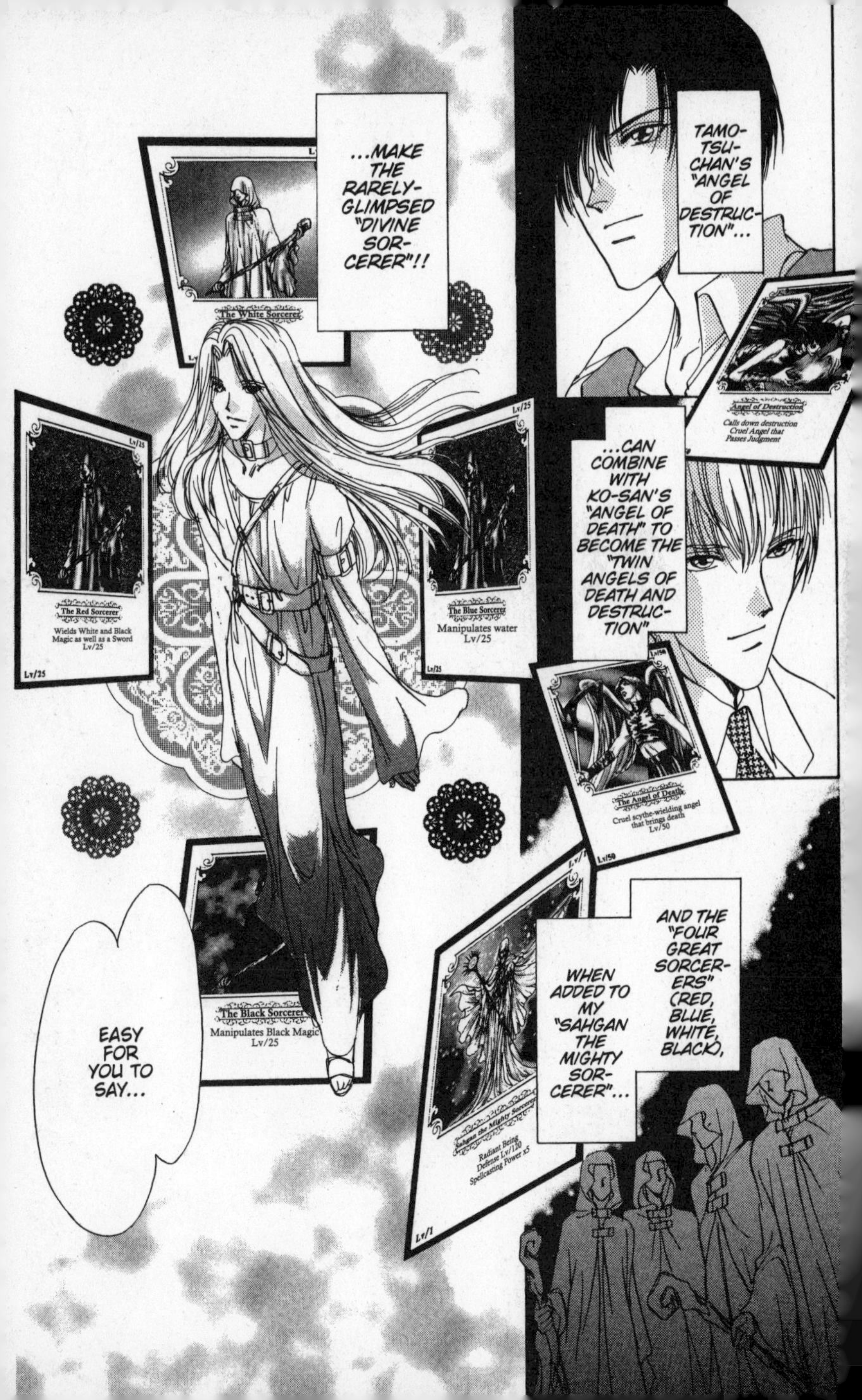
TAMOTSU-CHAN'S "ANGEL OF DESTRUCTION"...
Angel of Destruction
Calls down destruction
Cruel Angel that Passes Judgment
...CAN COMBINE WITH KO-SAN'S "ANGEL OF DEATH" TO BECOME THE "TWIN ANGELS OF DEATH AND DESTRUCTION"
The Angel of Death
Cruel scythe-wielding angel that brings death
Lv/50
AND THE "FOUR GREAT SORCERERS" (RED, BLUE, WHITE, BLACK),
WHEN ADDED TO MY "SAHGAN THE MIGHTY SORCERER"...
Sahgan the Mighty Sorcerer
Radiant Being
Defense Lv/120
Spellcasting Power x5
Lv/1
...MAKE THE RARELY-GLIMPSED "DIVINE SORCERER"!!
The White Sorcerer
The Red Sorcerer
Wields White and Black Magic as well as a Sword
Lv/25
The Blue Sorcerer
Manipulates water
Lv/25
The Black Sorcerer
Manipulates Black Magic
Lv/25
EASY FOR YOU TO SAY...

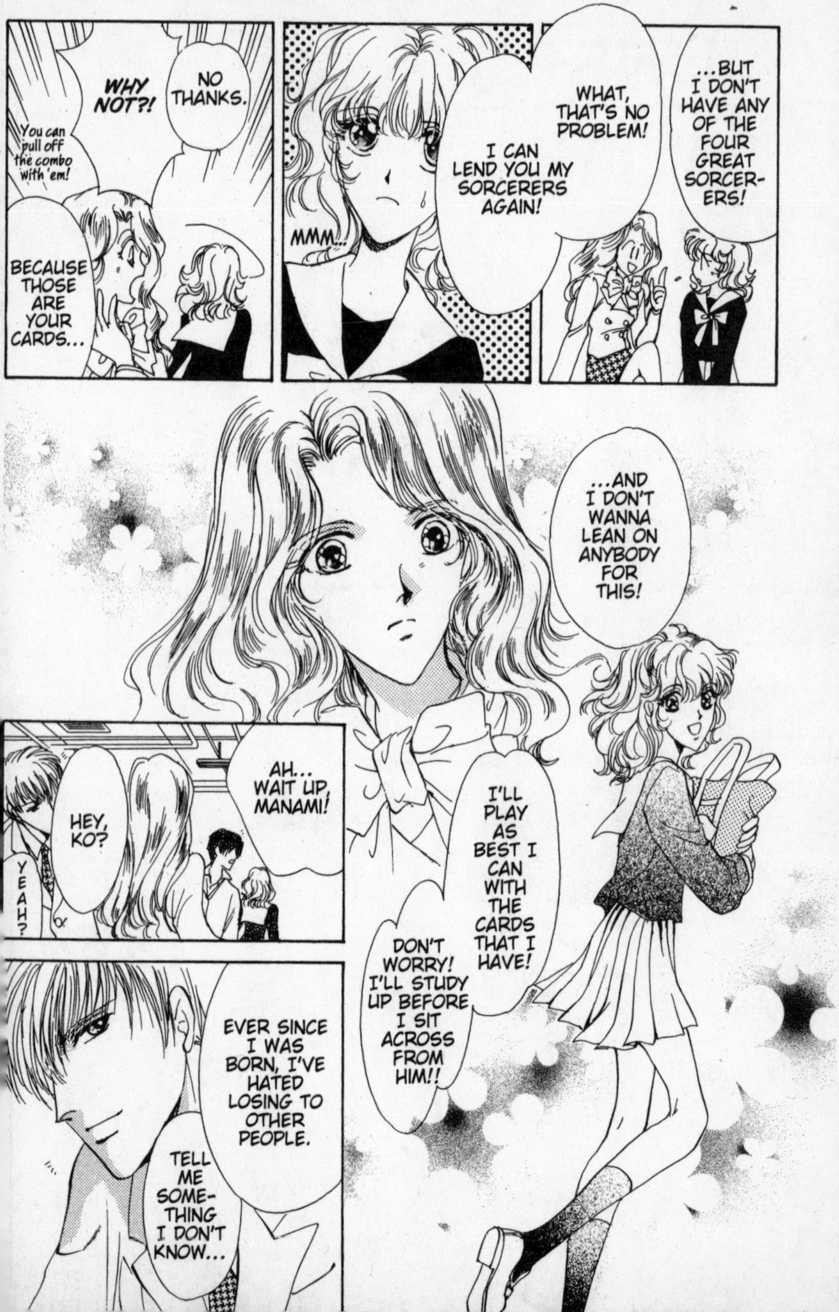
...BUT I DON'T HAVE ANY OF THE FOUR GREAT SORCERERS!
WHAT, THAT'S NO PROBLEM!
I CAN LEND YOU MY SORCERERS AGAIN!
MMM...
NO THANKS.
WHY NOT?!
You can pull off the combo with 'em!
BECAUSE THOSE ARE YOUR CARDS...
...AND I DON'T WANNA LEAN ON ANYBODY FOR THIS!
I'LL PLAY AS BEST I CAN WITH THE CARDS THAT I HAVE!
DON'T WORRY! I'LL STUDY UP BEFORE I SIT ACROSS FROM HIM!!
AH... WAIT UP, MANAMI!
HEY, KO?
YEAH?
EVER SINCE I WAS BORN, I'VE HATED LOSING TO OTHER PEOPLE.
TELL ME SOMETHING I DON'T KNOW...

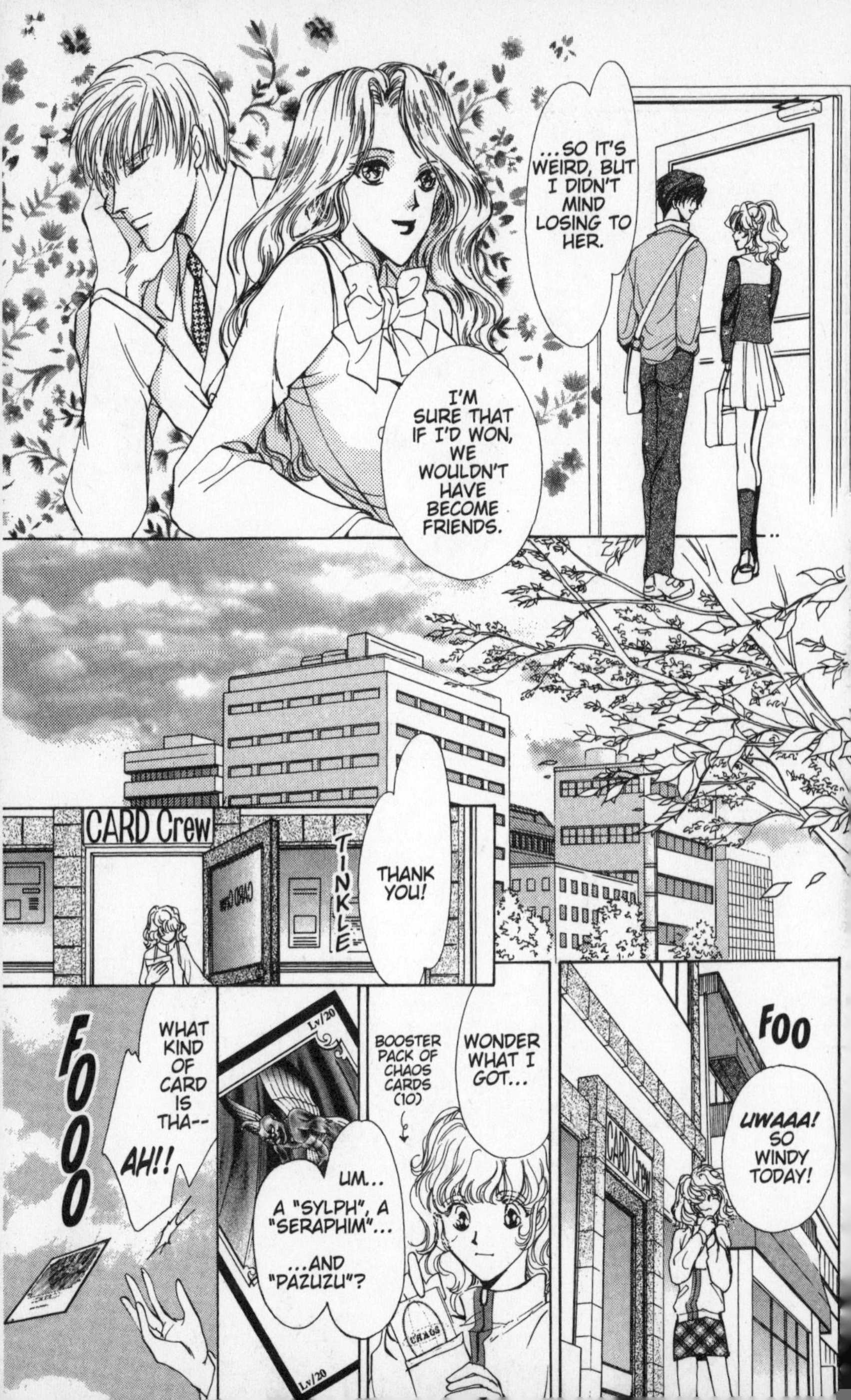
...SO IT'S WEIRD, BUT I DIDN'T MIND LOSING TO HER.
I'M SURE THAT IF I'D WON, WE WOULDN'T HAVE BECOME FRIENDS.
CARD Crew
TINKLE
THANK YOU!
FOO
UWAAA! SO WINDY TODAY!
CARD Crew
WONDER WHAT I GOT...
BOOSTER PACK OF CHAOS CARDS (10)
UM... A "SYLPH", A "SERAPHIM"... ...AND "PAZUZU"?
CHAOS
WHAT KIND OF CARD IS THA--
AH!!
FOOO

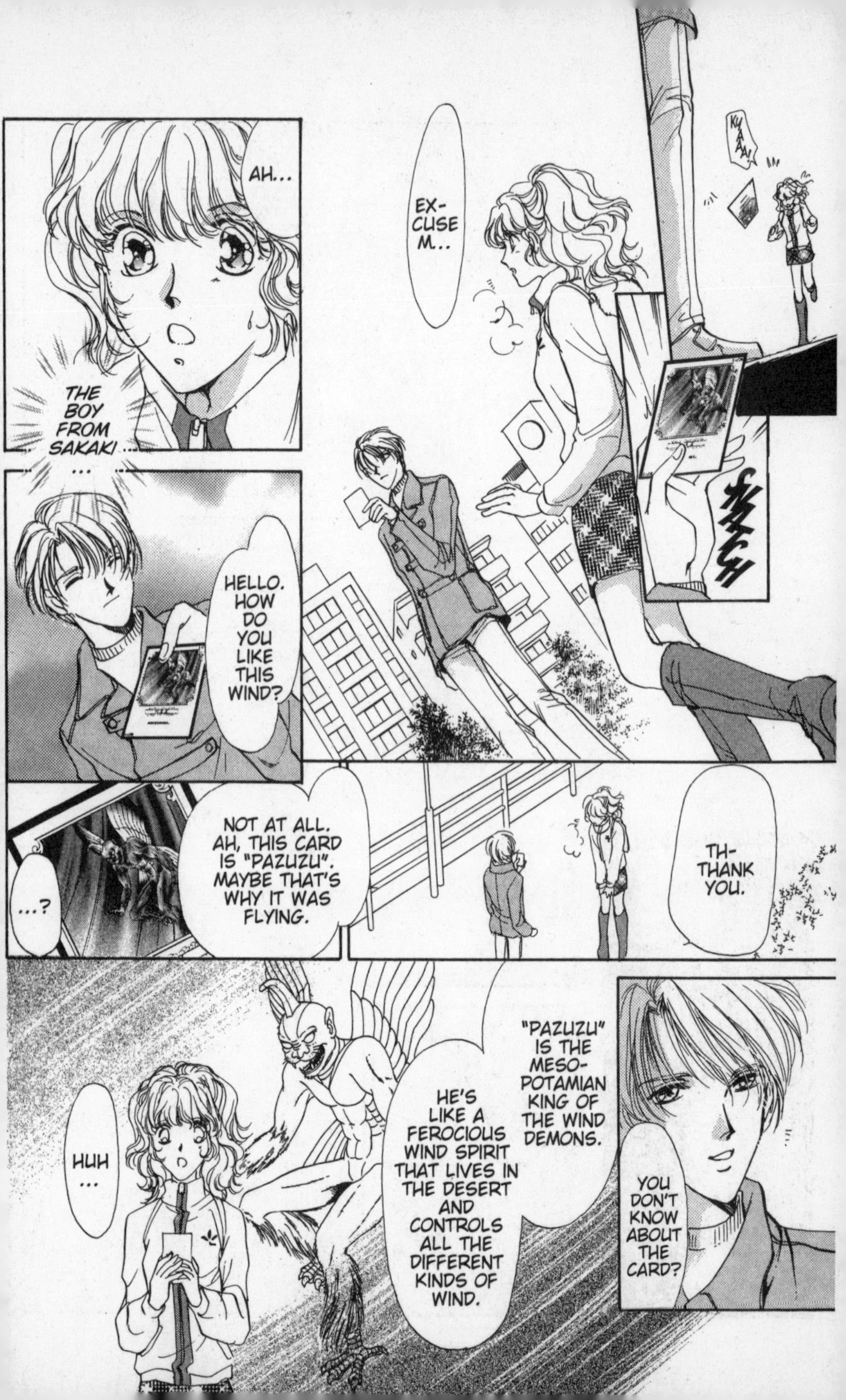
KYAAA!
EX-CUSE M...
AH...
THE BOY FROM SAKAKI...
...
HELLO. HOW DO YOU LIKE THIS WIND?
TH-THANK YOU.
NOT AT ALL. AH, THIS CARD IS "PAZUZU". MAYBE THAT'S WHY IT WAS FLYING.
...?
YOU DON'T KNOW ABOUT THE CARD?
"PAZUZU" IS THE MESO-POTAMIAN KING OF THE WIND DEMONS.
HE'S LIKE A FEROCIOUS WIND SPIRIT THAT LIVES IN THE DESERT AND CONTROLS ALL THE DIFFERENT KINDS OF WIND.
HUH ...

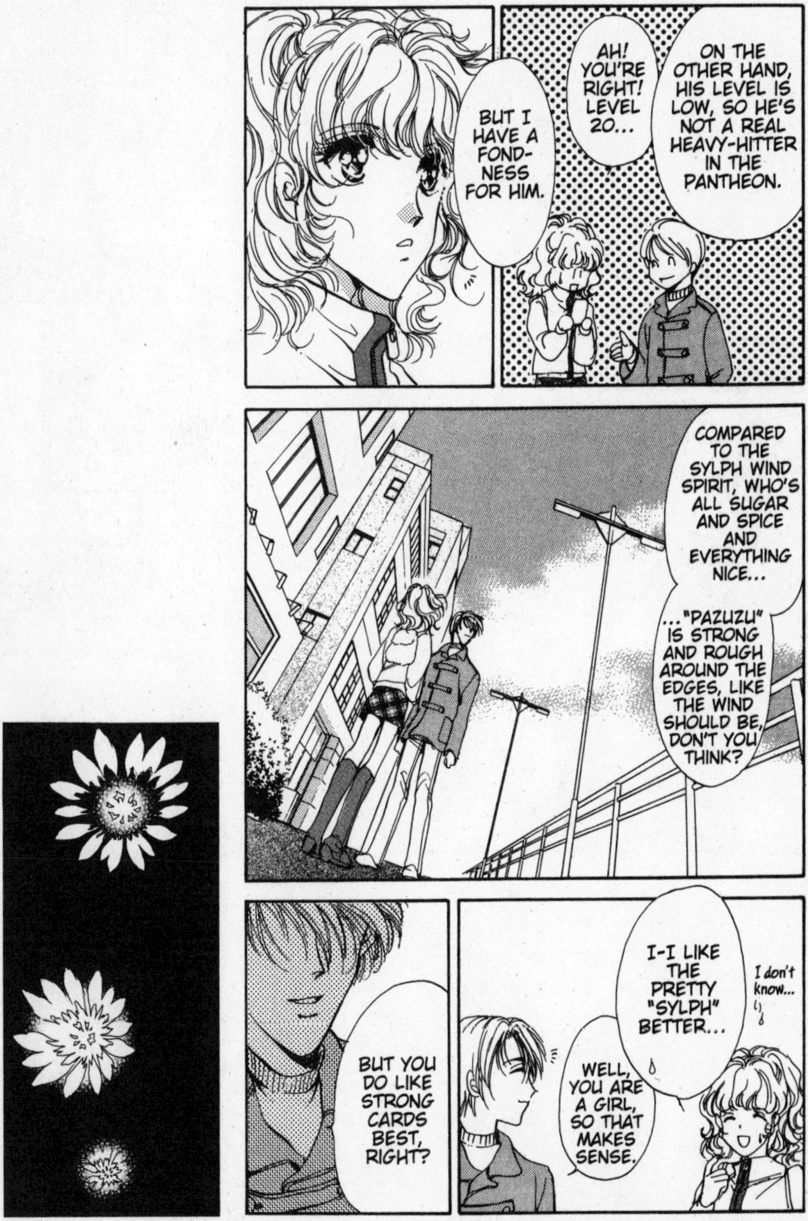
ON THE OTHER HAND, HIS LEVEL IS LOW, SO HE'S NOT A REAL HEAVY-HITTER IN THE PANTHEON.
AH! YOU'RE RIGHT! LEVEL 20...
BUT I HAVE A FOND-NESS FOR HIM.
COMPARED TO THE SYLPH WIND SPIRIT, WHO'S ALL SUGAR AND SPICE AND EVERYTHING NICE...
..."PAZUZU" IS STRONG AND ROUGH AROUND THE EDGES, LIKE THE WIND SHOULD BE, DON'T YOU THINK?
I don't know...
I-I LIKE THE PRETTY "SYLPH" BETTER...
WELL, YOU ARE A GIRL, SO THAT MAKES SENSE.
BUT YOU DO LIKE STRONG CARDS BEST, RIGHT?

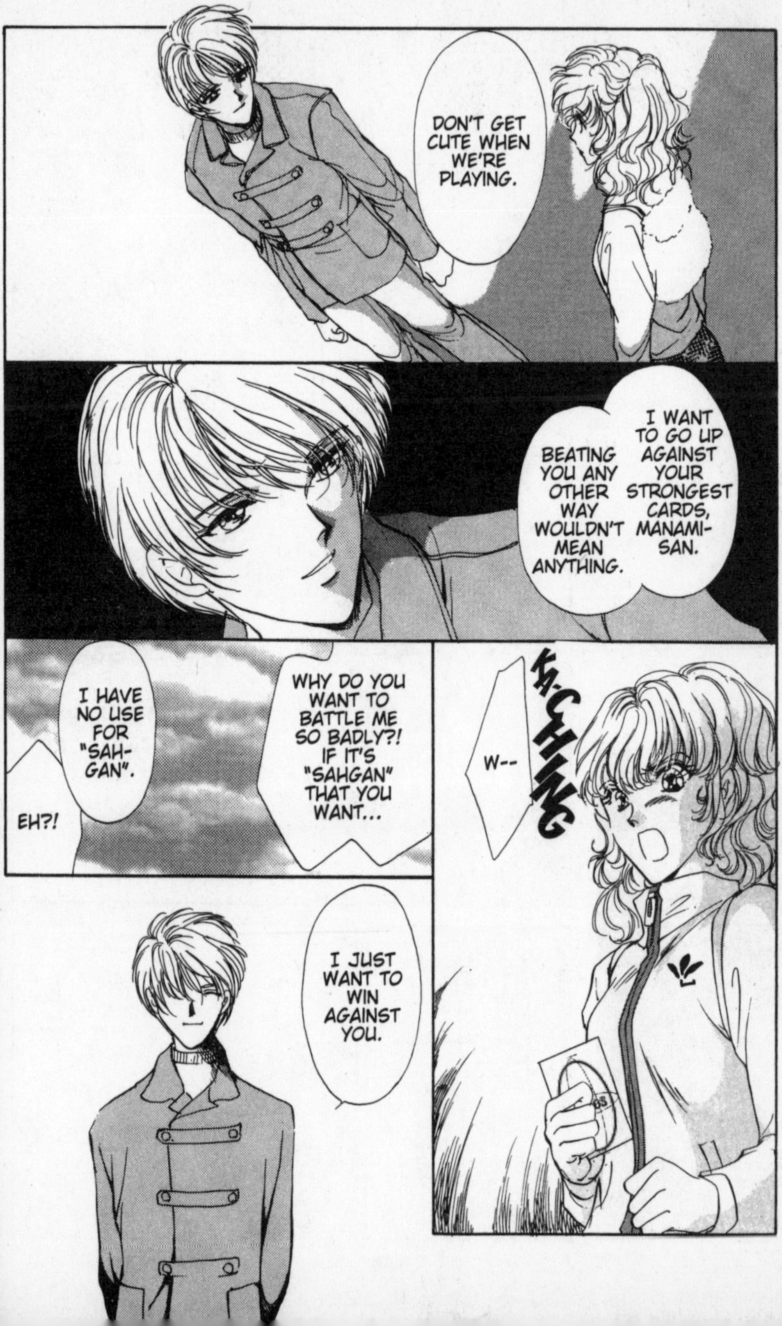

DON'T GET CUTE WHEN WE'RE PLAYING.
I WANT TO GO UP AGAINST YOUR STRONGEST CARDS, MANAMI-SAN.
BEATING YOU ANY OTHER WAY WOULDN'T MEAN ANYTHING.
KA-CHING
W--
WHY DO YOU WANT TO BATTLE ME SO BADLY?! IF IT'S "SAHGAN" THAT YOU WANT...
I HAVE NO USE FOR "SAHGAN".
EH?!
I JUST WANT TO WIN AGAINST YOU.

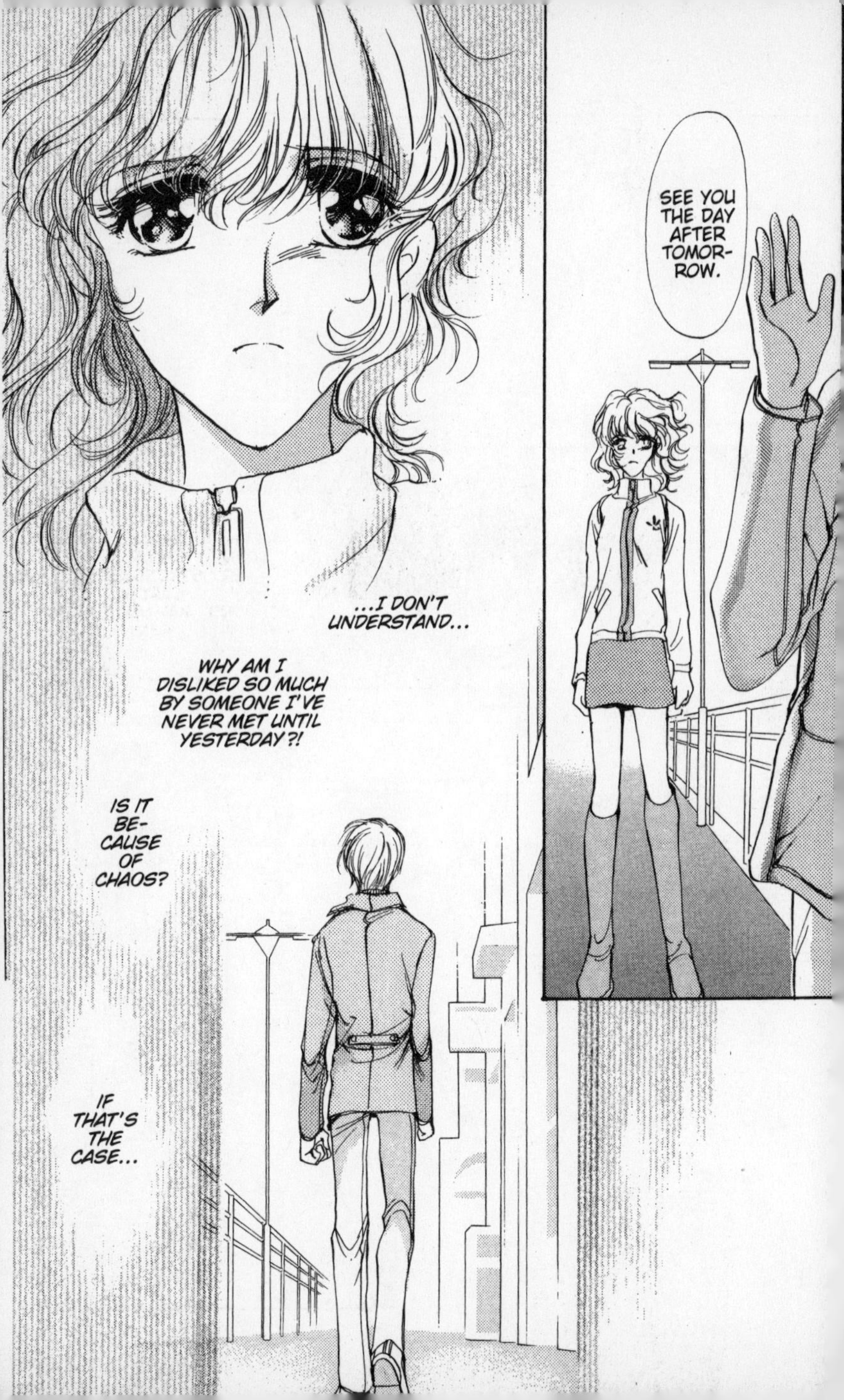
SEE YOU THE DAY AFTER TOMOR-ROW.
...I DON'T UNDERSTAND...
WHY AM I DISLIKED SO MUCH BY SOMEONE I'VE NEVER MET UNTIL YESTERDAY?!
IS IT BE-CAUSE OF CHAOS?
IF THAT'S THE CASE...

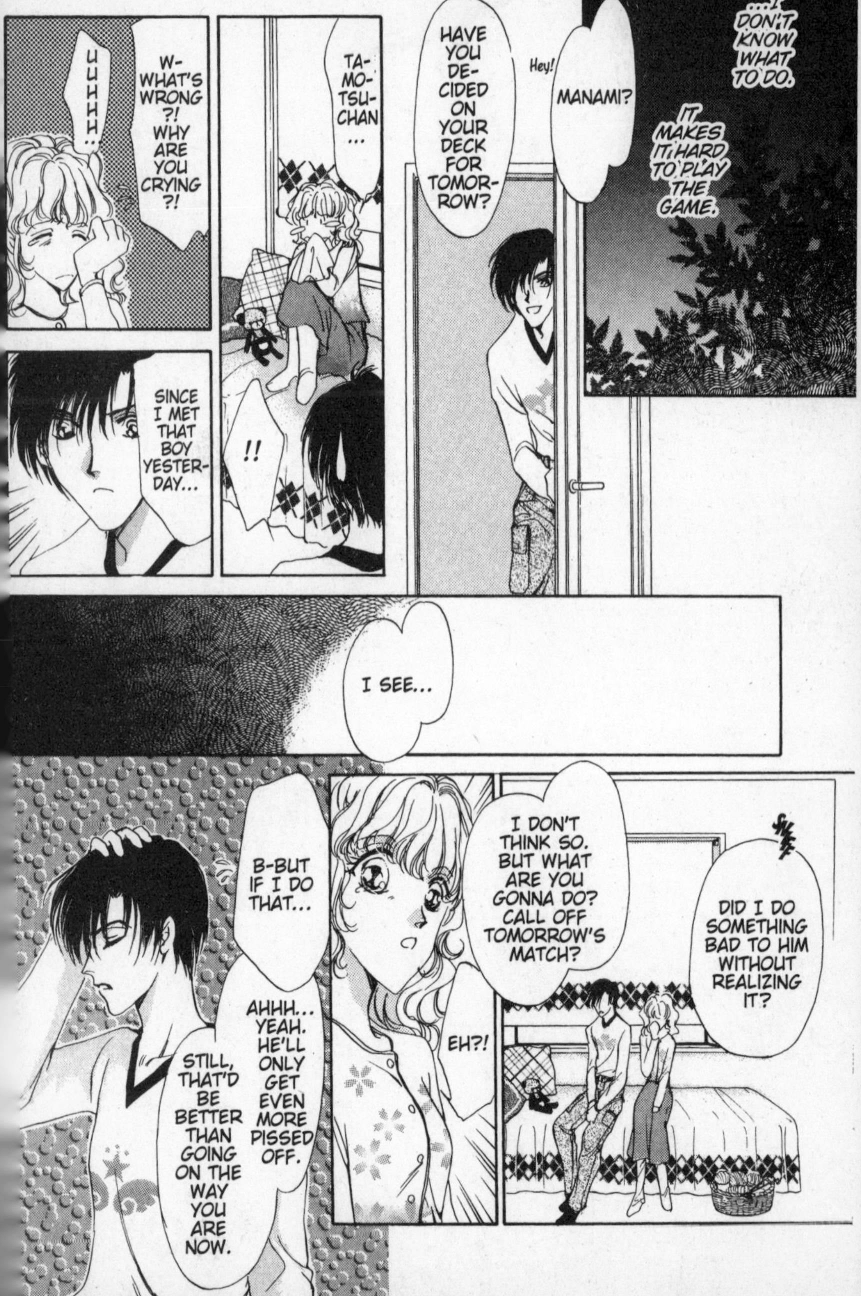
...I DON'T KNOW WHAT TO DO.
IT MAKES IT HARD TO PLAY THE GAME.
MANAMI?
Hey!
HAVE YOU DE-CIDED ON YOUR DECK FOR TOMOR-ROW?
TA-MO-TSU-CHAN...
!!
W-WHAT'S WRONG?! WHY ARE YOU CRYING?!
UHHHH...
SINCE I MET THAT BOY YESTER-DAY...
I SEE...
DID I DO SOMETHING BAD TO HIM WITHOUT REALIZING IT?
I DON'T THINK SO. BUT WHAT ARE YOU GONNA DO? CALL OFF TOMORROW'S MATCH?
EH?!
B-BUT IF I DO THAT...
AHHH... YEAH. HE'LL ONLY GET EVEN MORE PISSED OFF.
STILL, THAT'D BE BETTER THAN GOING ON THE WAY YOU ARE NOW.

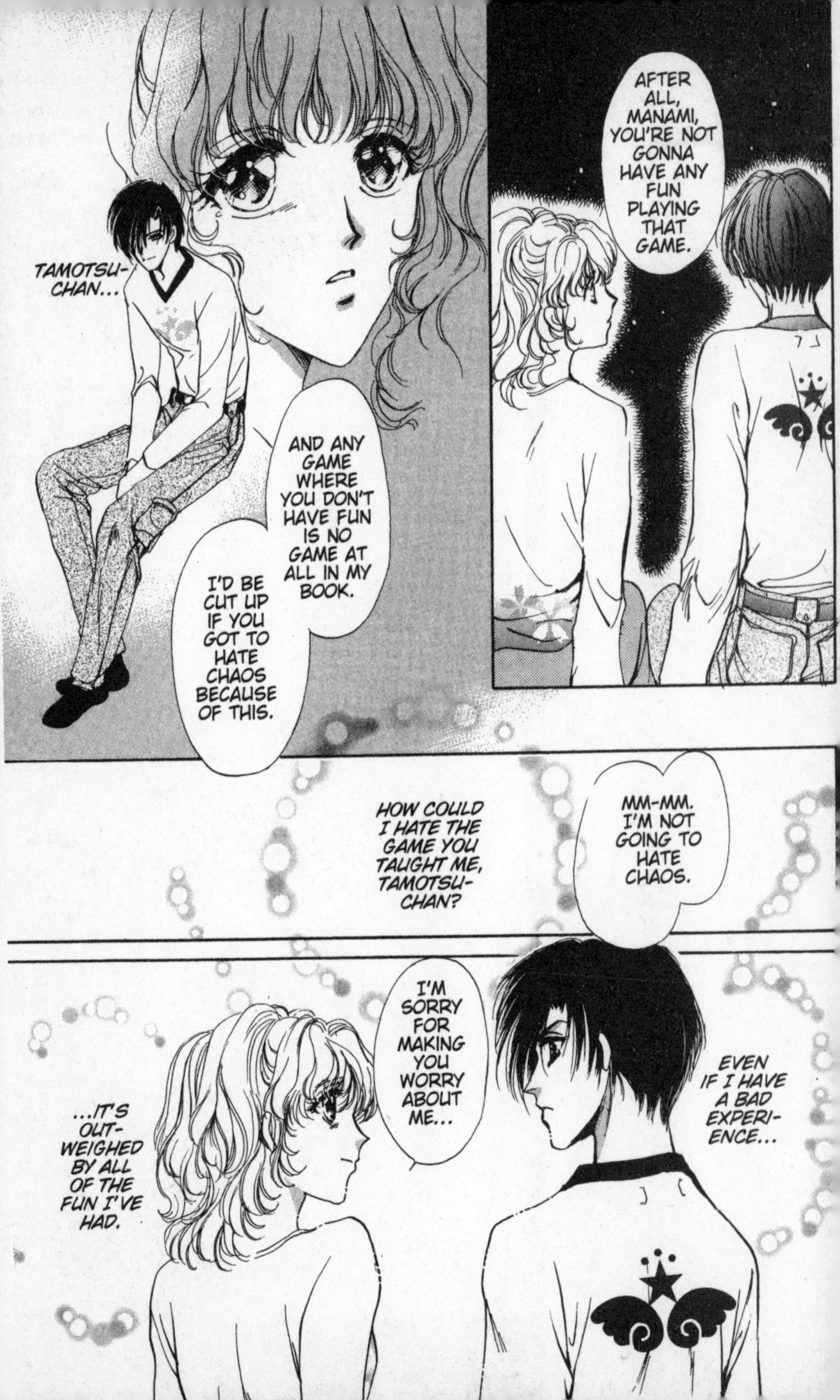
AFTER ALL, MANAMI, YOU'RE NOT GONNA HAVE ANY FUN PLAYING THAT GAME.
TAMOTSU-CHAN...
AND ANY GAME WHERE YOU DON'T HAVE FUN IS NO GAME AT ALL IN MY BOOK.
I'D BE CUT UP IF YOU GOT TO HATE CHAOS BECAUSE OF THIS.
MM-MM. I'M NOT GOING TO HATE CHAOS.
HOW COULD I HATE THE GAME YOU TAUGHT ME, TAMOTSU-CHAN?
I'M SORRY FOR MAKING YOU WORRY ABOUT ME...
EVEN IF I HAVE A BAD EXPERIENCE...
...IT'S OUTWEIGHED BY ALL OF THE FUN I'VE HAD.

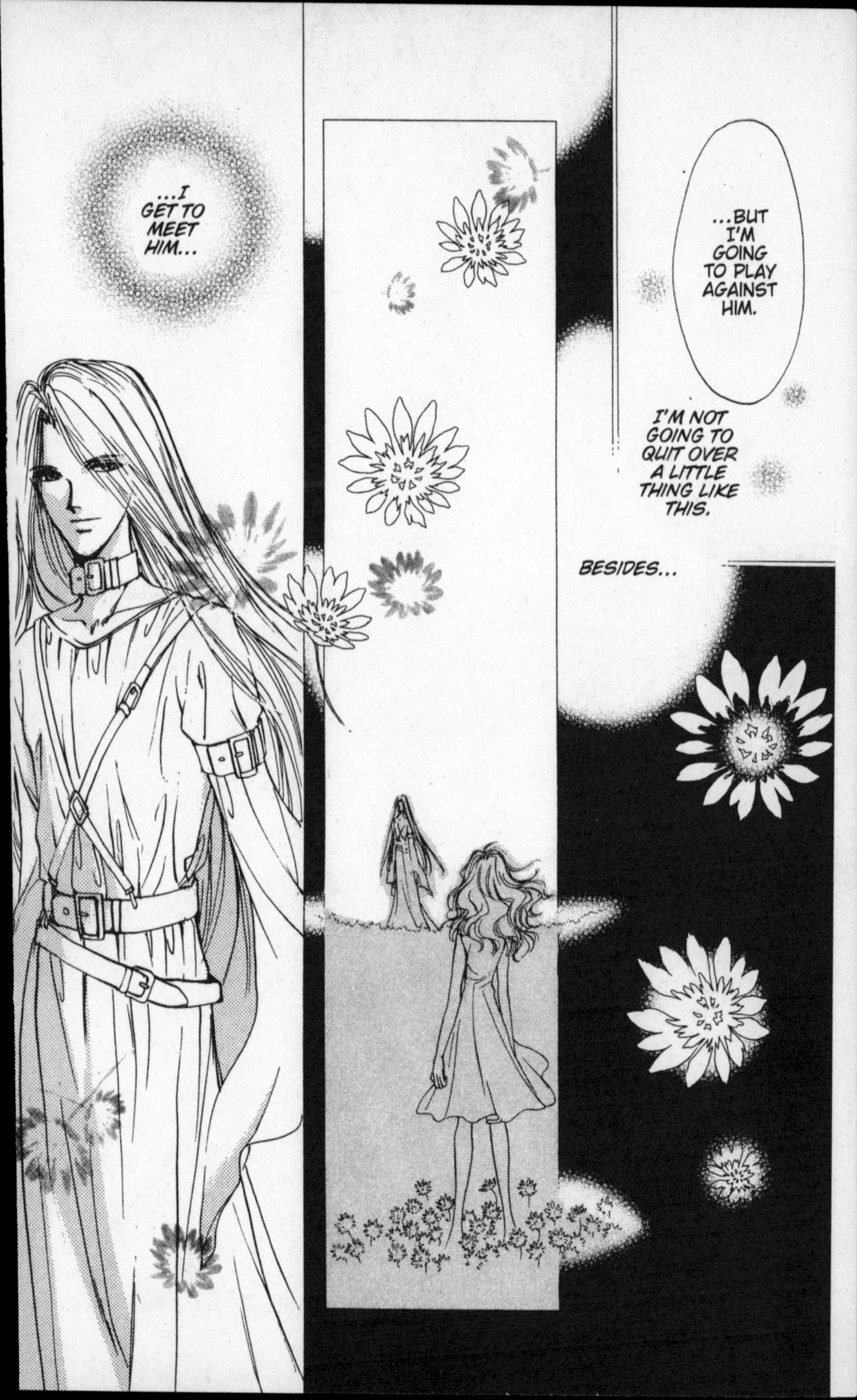
...BUT I'M GOING TO PLAY AGAINST HIM.
I'M NOT GOING TO QUIT OVER A LITTLE THING LIKE THIS.
BESIDES...
...I GET TO MEET HIM...

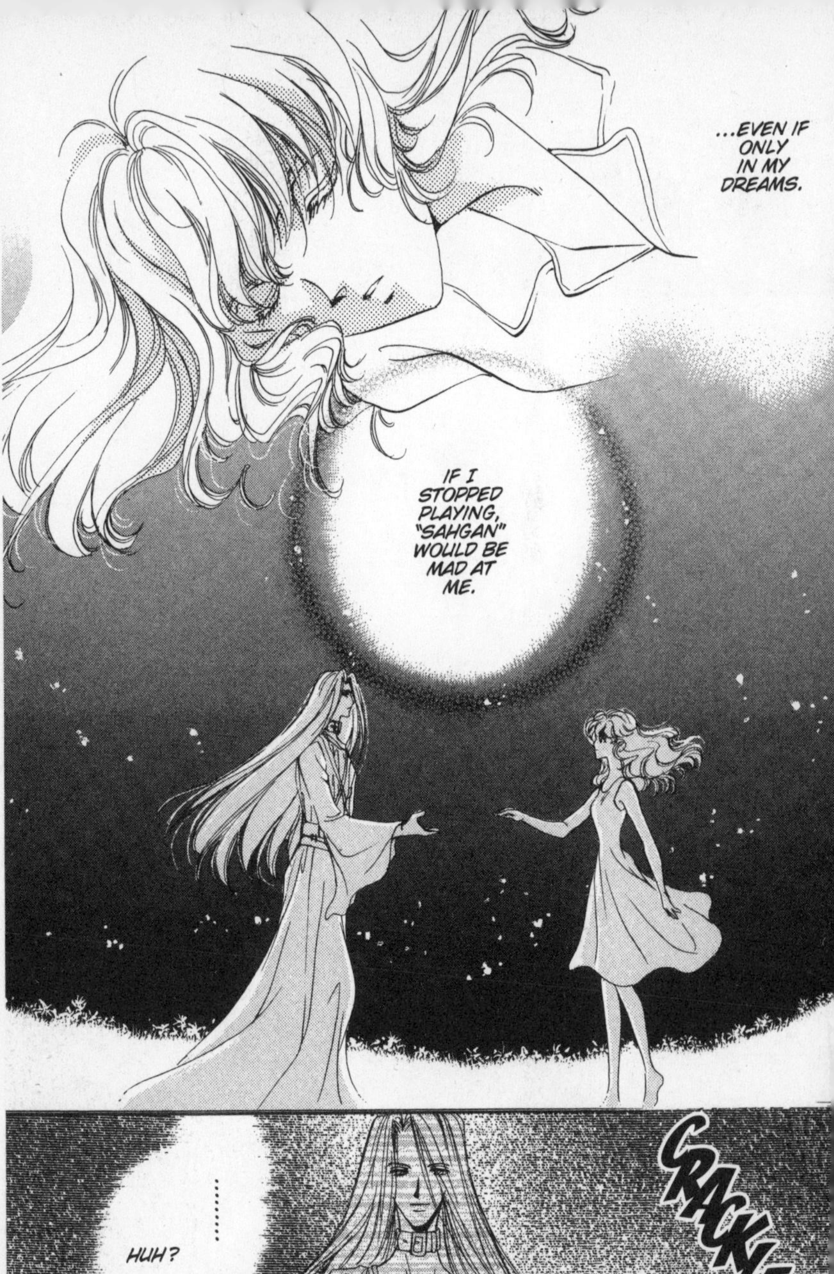
...EVEN IF ONLY IN MY DREAMS.
IF I STOPPED PLAYING, "SAHGAN" WOULD BE MAD AT ME.
CRACKLE
......
HUH?

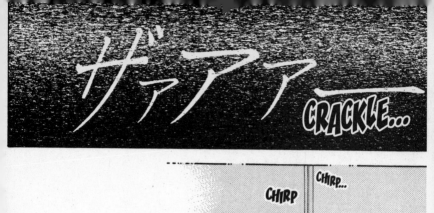

ザァァァ——

CRACKLE...

CHIRP...

CHIRP

THE
...

BUT...

THE
IMAGES
GOT ALL
STATICY...

Even though it
was a dream...

...SAHGAN
ALWAYS
GIVES ME A
PLAYING
HINT IN THE
DREAM...

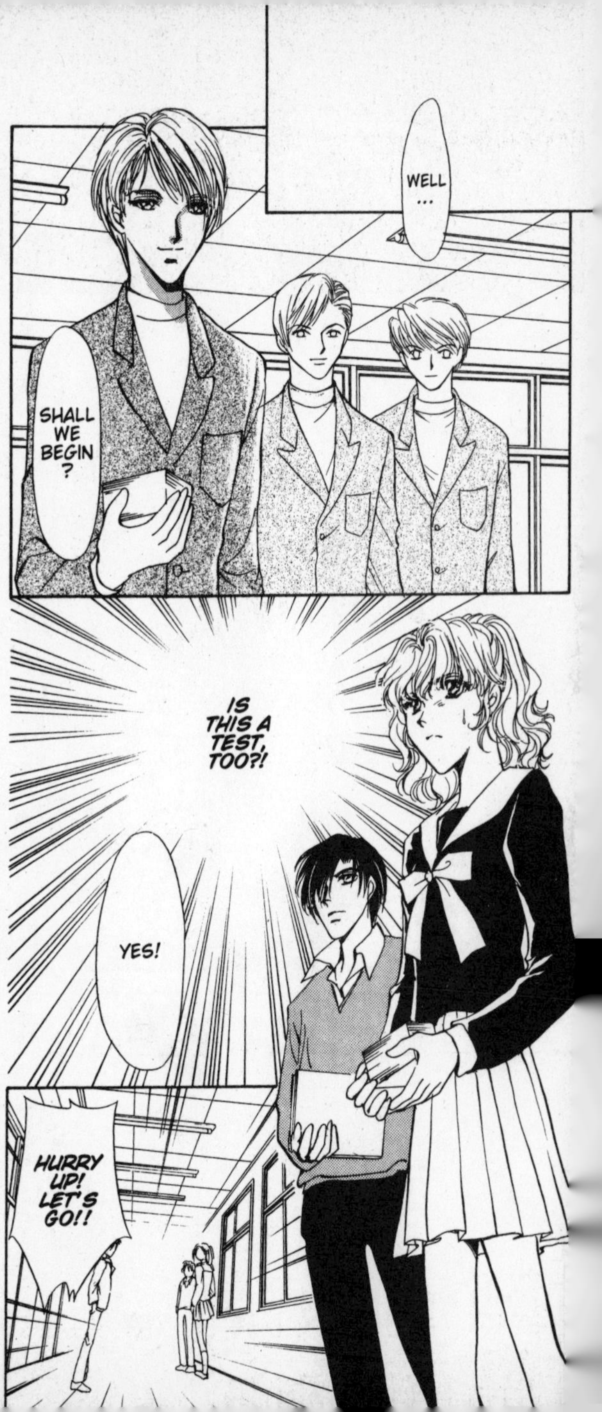
WELL ...
SHALL WE BEGIN?
IS THIS A TEST, TOO?!
YES!
HURRY UP! LET'S GO!!

WELL, HERE WE ARE. I DID THIS SIDE STORY FOR HANA TO YUME* AND SHOVED IT INTO THIS VOLUME! IT TAKES PLACE BEFORE THE RELATIONSHIPS GET ALL MIXED UP, SO I KEPT THE MATCH SCENE, ETC. SIMPLE AND IT WAS EASY TO DRAW. I THOUGHT GOING WITH THIS UNKNOWN FOR AN OPPONENT INSTEAD OF THE "EARLY DAYS" GHOUL BROTHERS OR HIKAMI-KUN PROVIDED FOR A FUN, SLIGHTLY DIFFERENT FLAVOR TO THE STORY. BY THE WAY, THIS EPISODE TAKES PLACE BETWEEN VOLUME ONE AND TWO. AFTER THIS, THE CHRISTMAS TOURNAMENT TAKES PLACE.

COME TO THINK OF IT, I HADN'T ORIGINALLY ENVISIONED THE SIDE STORY AS BEING THIS LONG...ANYWAY, IN OUR NEXT VOLUME, SOME LIGHT IS SHED ON ARAKI'S SECRETS. I'M TRYING TO CREATE SOME NEW DEVELOPMENTS FOR THE STORY.

I HOPE YOU KEEP READING! THANK YOU TO ALL OF THOSE READERS WHO'VE WRITTEN IN WITH THEIR THOUGHTS! ENERGY FOR TOMORROW!

THIS HAS BEEN TATENO, HOPING TO SEE YOU AGAIN IN VOLUME 7!

* ***HANA TO YUME:*** JAPANESE PUBLICATION WHERE KING OF CARDS WAS ORIGINALLY SERIALIZED.

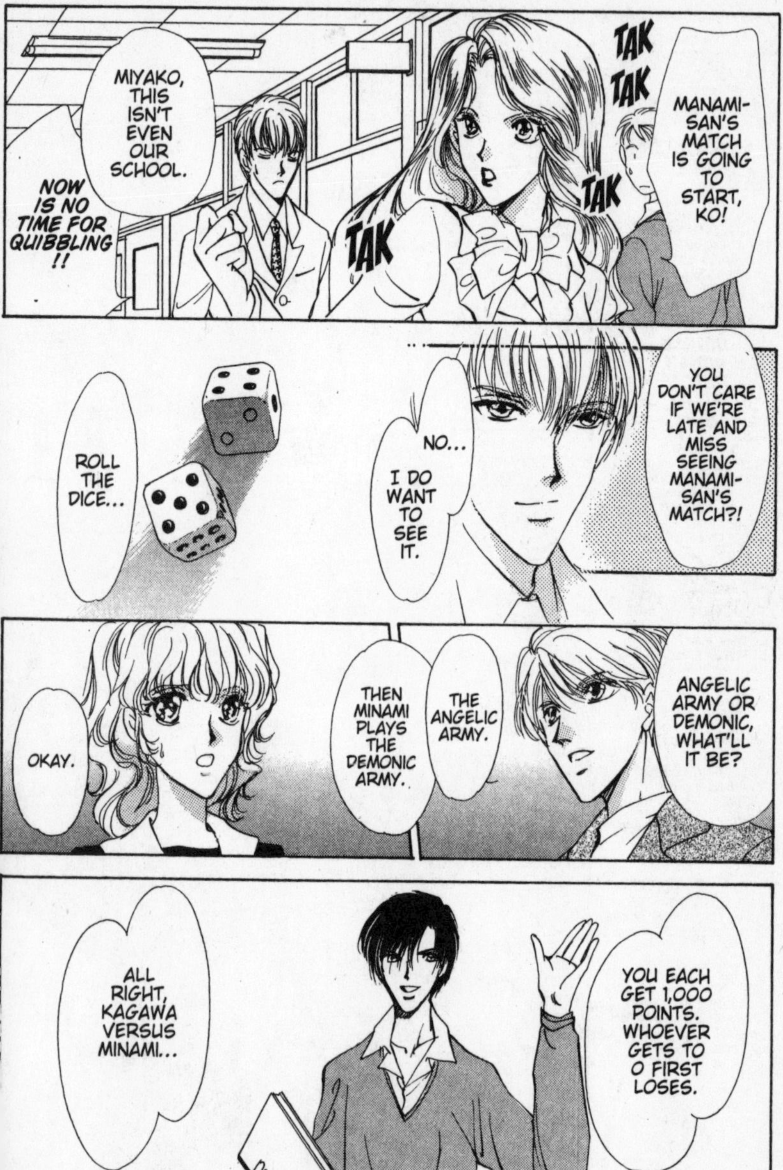
MANAMI-SAN'S MATCH IS GOING TO START, KO!
TAK TAK
TAK
TAK
MIYAKO, THIS ISN'T EVEN OUR SCHOOL.
NOW IS NO TIME FOR QUIBBLING !!
YOU DON'T CARE IF WE'RE LATE AND MISS SEEING MANAMI-SAN'S MATCH?!
...
NO... I DO WANT TO SEE IT.
ROLL THE DICE...
ANGELIC ARMY OR DEMONIC, WHAT'LL IT BE?
THE ANGELIC ARMY.
THEN MINAMI PLAYS THE DEMONIC ARMY.
OKAY.
YOU EACH GET 1,000 POINTS. WHOEVER GETS TO 0 FIRST LOSES.
ALL RIGHT, KAGAWA VERSUS MINAMI...

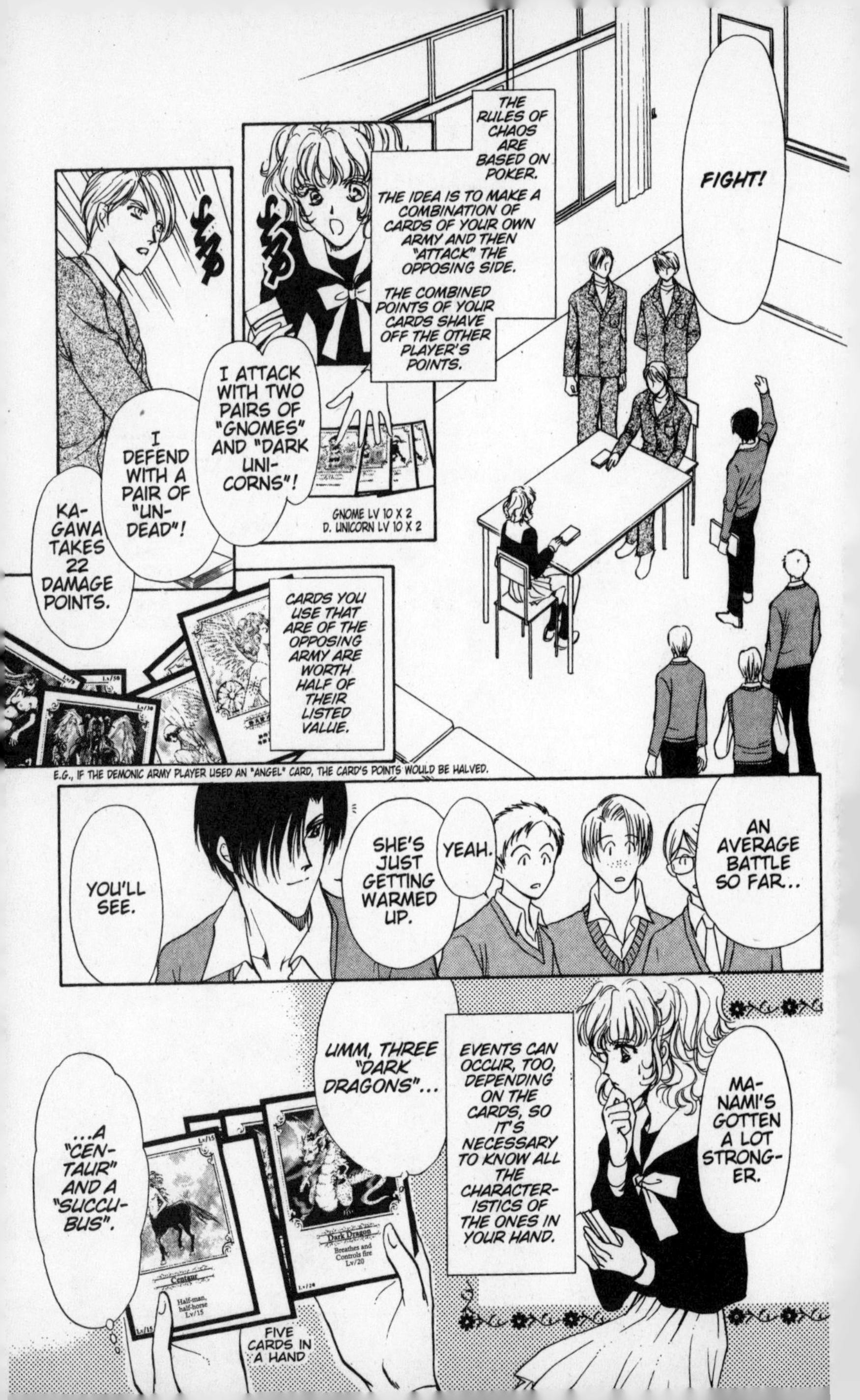
FIGHT!
THE RULES OF CHAOS ARE BASED ON POKER.
THE IDEA IS TO MAKE A COMBINATION OF CARDS OF YOUR OWN ARMY AND THEN "ATTACK" THE OPPOSING SIDE.
THE COMBINED POINTS OF YOUR CARDS SHAVE OFF THE OTHER PLAYER'S POINTS.
I ATTACK WITH TWO PAIRS OF "GNOMES" AND "DARK UNI-CORNS"!
GNOME LV 10 X 2
D. UNICORN LV 10 X 2
I DEFEND WITH A PAIR OF "UN-DEAD"!
KA-GAWA TAKES 22 DAMAGE POINTS.
CARDS YOU USE THAT ARE OF THE OPPOSING ARMY ARE WORTH HALF OF THEIR LISTED VALUE.
E.G., IF THE DEMONIC ARMY PLAYER USED AN "ANGEL" CARD, THE CARD'S POINTS WOULD BE HALVED.
AN AVERAGE BATTLE SO FAR...
YEAH.
SHE'S JUST GETTING WARMED UP.
YOU'LL SEE.
MA-NAMI'S GOTTEN A LOT STRONG-ER.
EVENTS CAN OCCUR, TOO, DEPENDING ON THE CARDS, SO IT'S NECESSARY TO KNOW ALL THE CHARACTER-ISTICS OF THE ONES IN YOUR HAND.
UMM, THREE "DARK DRAGONS"...
...A "CEN-TAUR" AND A "SUCCU-BUS".
Dark Dragon
Breathes and Controls fire
Lv/20
Centaur
Half-man, half-horse
Lv/15
FIVE CARDS IN A HAND

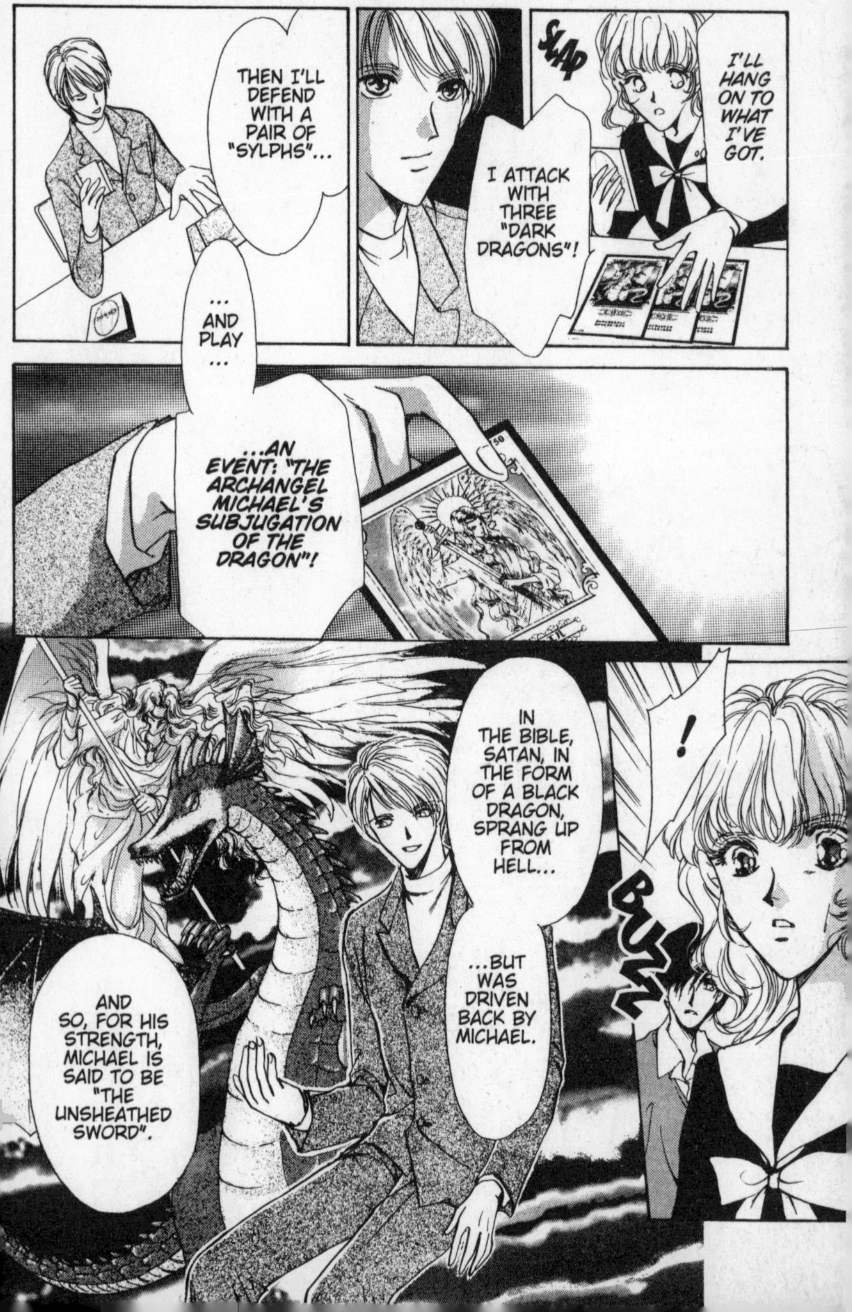
SLAP
I'LL HANG ON TO WHAT I'VE GOT.
I ATTACK WITH THREE "DARK DRAGONS"!
THEN I'LL DEFEND WITH A PAIR OF "SYLPHS"...
... AND PLAY ...
...AN EVENT: "THE ARCHANGEL MICHAEL'S SUBJUGATION OF THE DRAGON"!
!
BUZZ
IN THE BIBLE, SATAN, IN THE FORM OF A BLACK DRAGON, SPRANG UP FROM HELL...
...BUT WAS DRIVEN BACK BY MICHAEL.
AND SO, FOR HIS STRENGTH, MICHAEL IS SAID TO BE "THE UNSHEATHED SWORD".

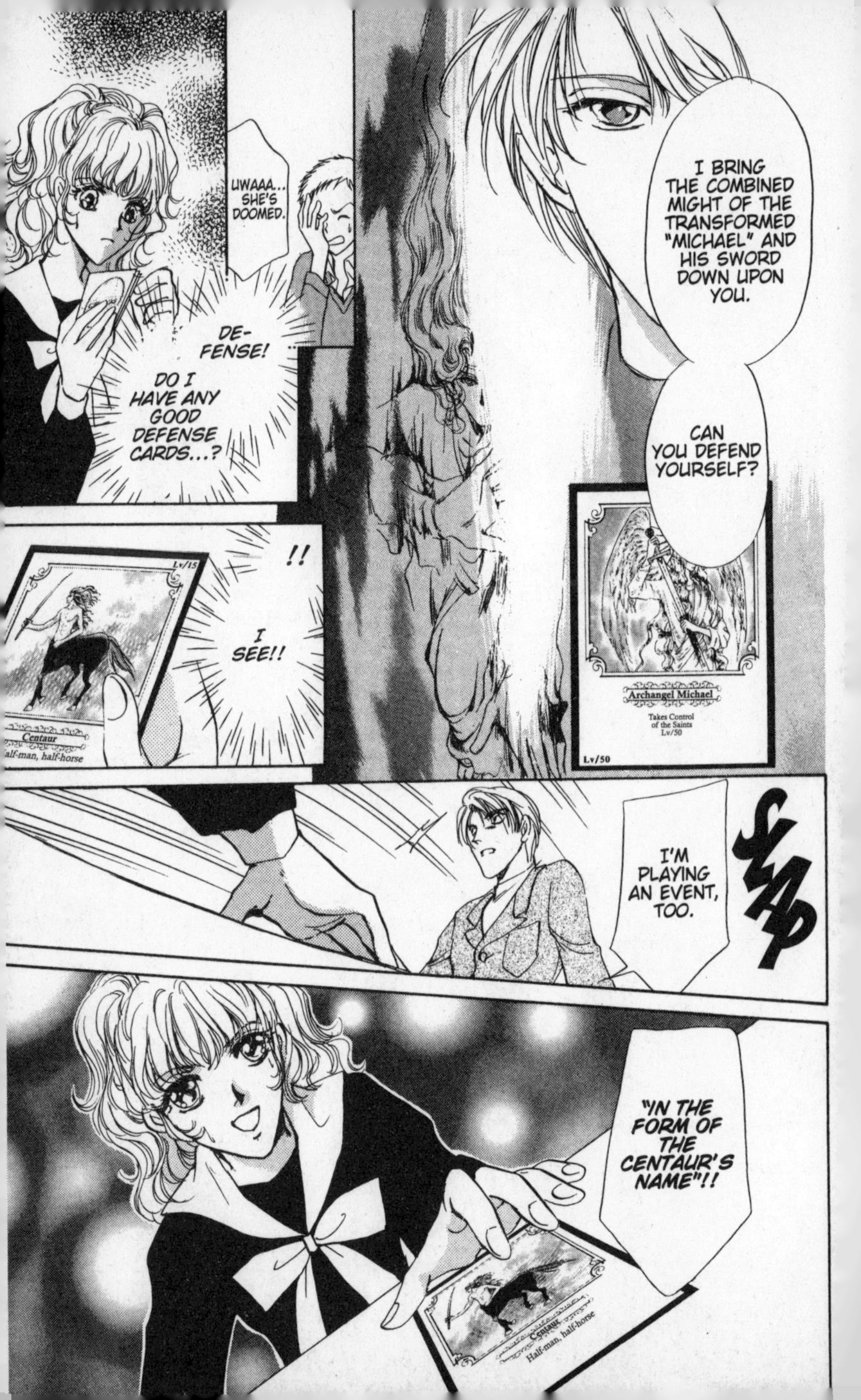
I BRING THE COMBINED MIGHT OF THE TRANSFORMED "MICHAEL" AND HIS SWORD DOWN UPON YOU.
CAN YOU DEFEND YOURSELF?
Archangel Michael
Takes Control of the Saints Lv/50
Lv/50
UWAAA... SHE'S DOOMED.
DE-FENSE!
DO I HAVE ANY GOOD DEFENSE CARDS...?
!!
I SEE!!
Lv/15
Centaur
Half-man, half-horse
SLAP
I'M PLAYING AN EVENT, TOO.
"IN THE FORM OF THE CENTAUR'S NAME"!!
Centaur
Half-man, half-horse

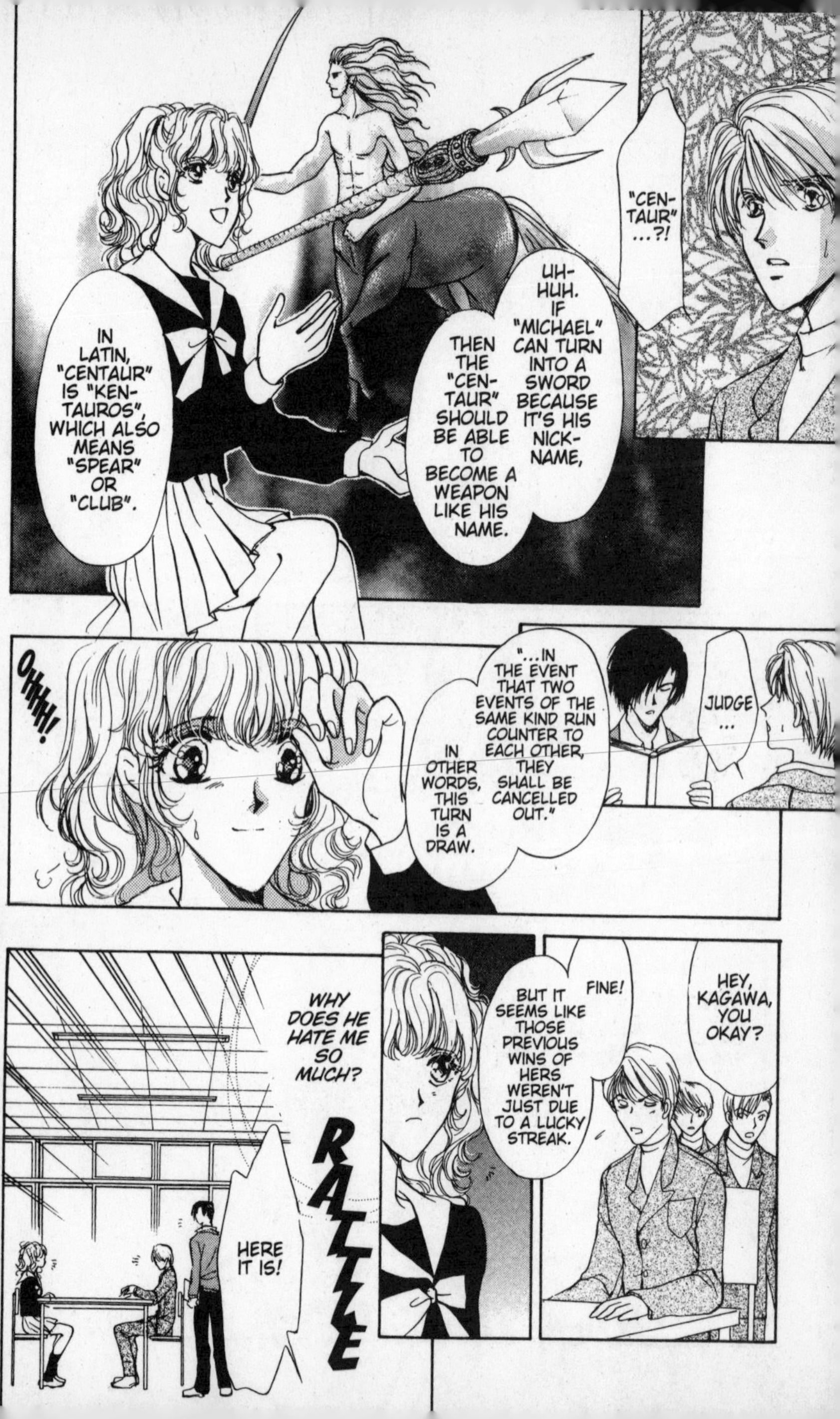
"CENTAUR"...?!
UH-HUH. IF "MICHAEL" CAN TURN INTO A SWORD BECAUSE IT'S HIS NICKNAME,
THEN THE "CENTAUR" SHOULD BE ABLE TO BECOME A WEAPON LIKE HIS NAME.
IN LATIN, "CENTAUR" IS "KENTAUROS", WHICH ALSO MEANS "SPEAR" OR "CLUB".
JUDGE...
"...IN THE EVENT THAT TWO EVENTS OF THE SAME KIND RUN COUNTER TO EACH OTHER, THEY SHALL BE CANCELLED OUT."
IN OTHER WORDS, THIS TURN IS A DRAW.
OHHHH!
HEY, KAGAWA, YOU OKAY?
FINE!
BUT IT SEEMS LIKE THOSE PREVIOUS WINS OF HERS WEREN'T JUST DUE TO A LUCKY STREAK.
WHY DOES HE HATE ME SO MUCH?
RATTLE
HERE IT IS!

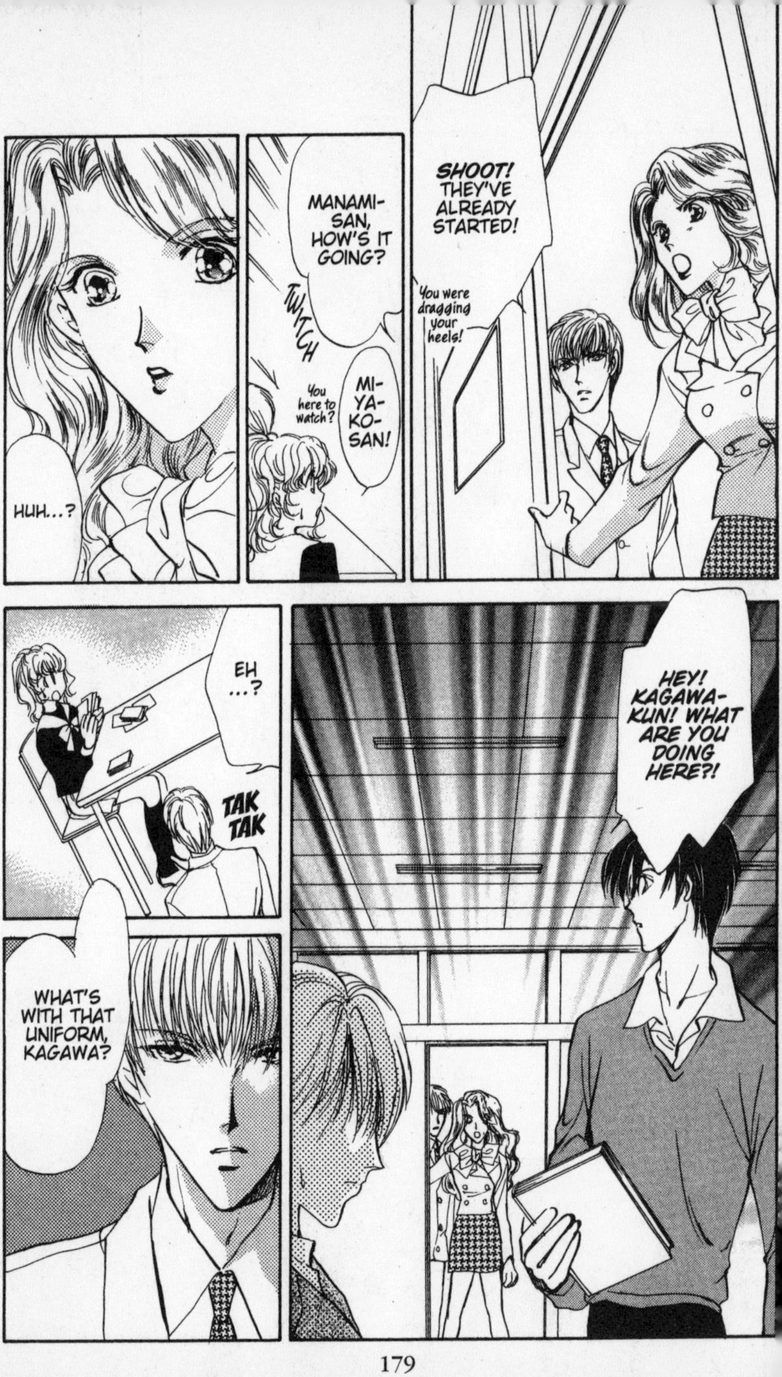
SHOOT! THEY'VE ALREADY STARTED!
You were dragging your heels!
MANAMI-SAN, HOW'S IT GOING?
TWITCH
MI-YA-KO-SAN!
You here to watch?
HUH...?
HEY! KAGAWA-KUN! WHAT ARE YOU DOING HERE?!
EH ...?
TAK TAK
WHAT'S WITH THAT UNIFORM, KAGAWA?

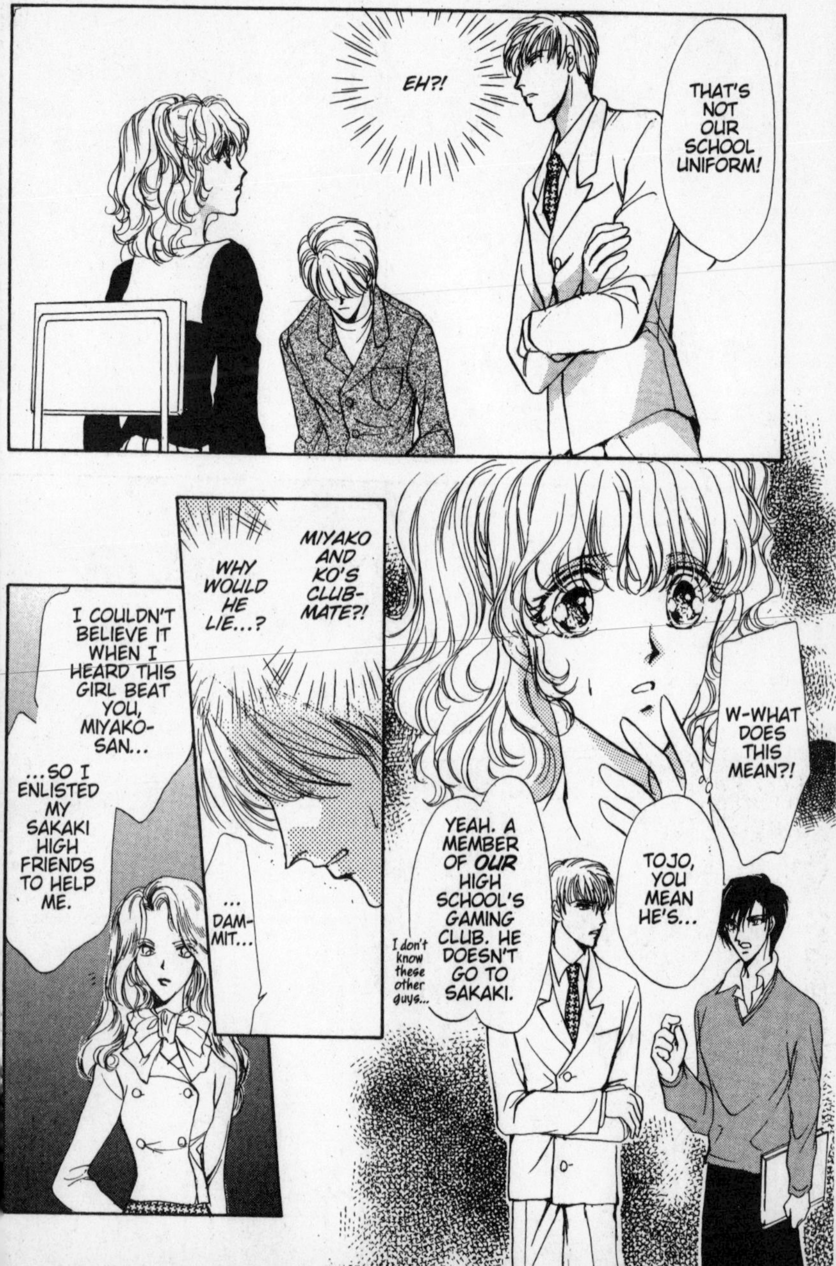

THAT'S NOT OUR SCHOOL UNIFORM!
EH?!
W-WHAT DOES THIS MEAN?!
TOJO, YOU MEAN HE'S...
YEAH. A MEMBER OF **OUR** HIGH SCHOOL'S GAMING CLUB. HE DOESN'T GO TO SAKAKI.
I don't know these other guys...
MIYAKO AND KO'S CLUB-MATE?!
WHY WOULD HE LIE...?
... DAMMIT...
I COULDN'T BELIEVE IT WHEN I HEARD THIS GIRL BEAT YOU, MIYAKO-SAN...
...SO I ENLISTED MY SAKAKI HIGH FRIENDS TO HELP ME.

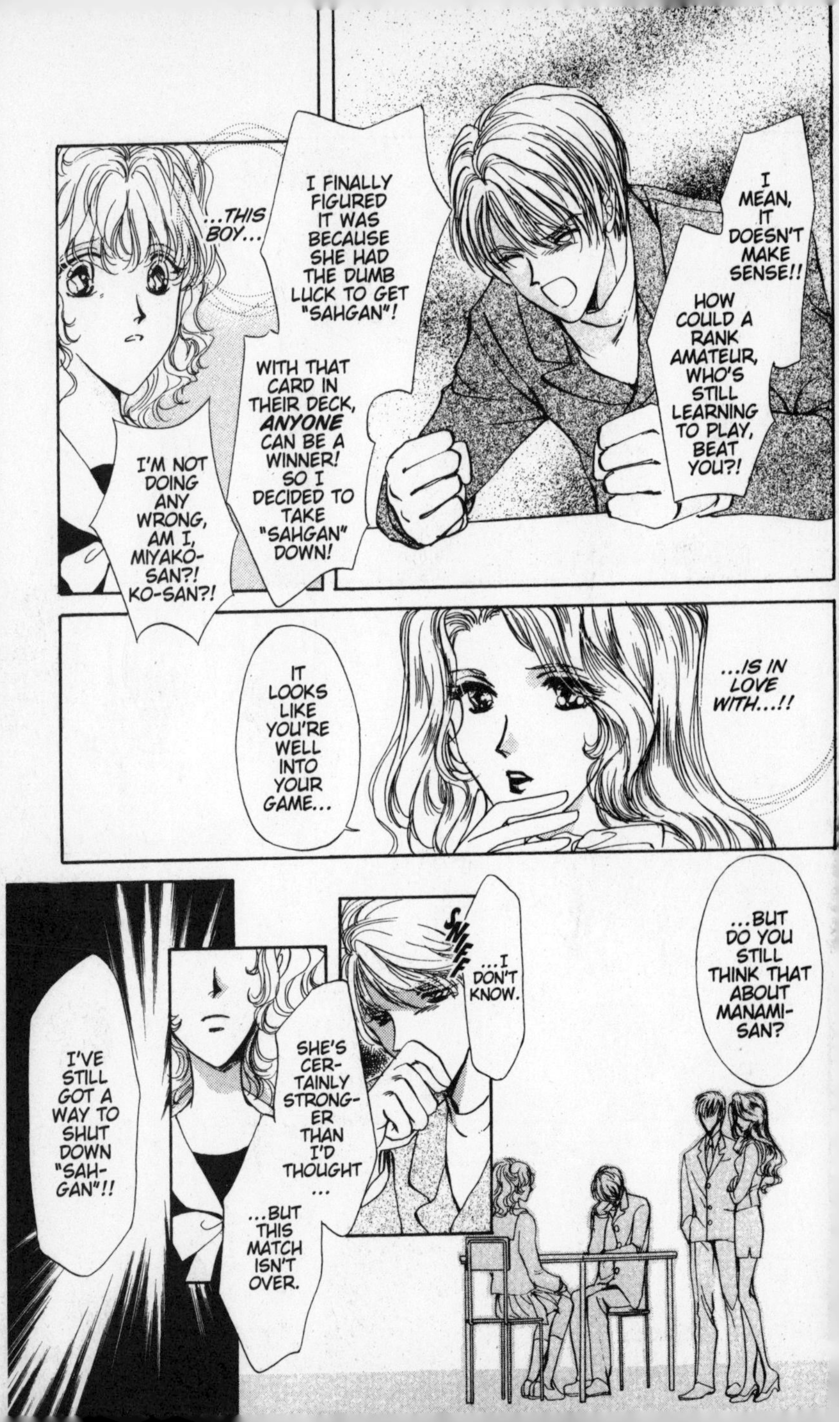
I MEAN, IT DOESN'T MAKE SENSE!!
HOW COULD A RANK AMATEUR, WHO'S STILL LEARNING TO PLAY, BEAT YOU?!
I FINALLY FIGURED IT WAS BECAUSE SHE HAD THE DUMB LUCK TO GET "SAHGAN"!
WITH THAT CARD IN THEIR DECK, ***ANYONE*** CAN BE A WINNER! SO I DECIDED TO TAKE "SAHGAN" DOWN!
...THIS BOY...
I'M NOT DOING ANY WRONG, AM I, MIYAKO-SAN?! KO-SAN?!
...IS IN LOVE WITH...!!
IT LOOKS LIKE YOU'RE WELL INTO YOUR GAME...
...BUT DO YOU STILL THINK THAT ABOUT MANAMI-SAN?
SNIFF
...I DON'T KNOW.
SHE'S CER-TAINLY STRONG-ER THAN I'D THOUGHT...
...BUT THIS MATCH ISN'T OVER.
I'VE STILL GOT A WAY TO SHUT DOWN "SAH-GAN"!!

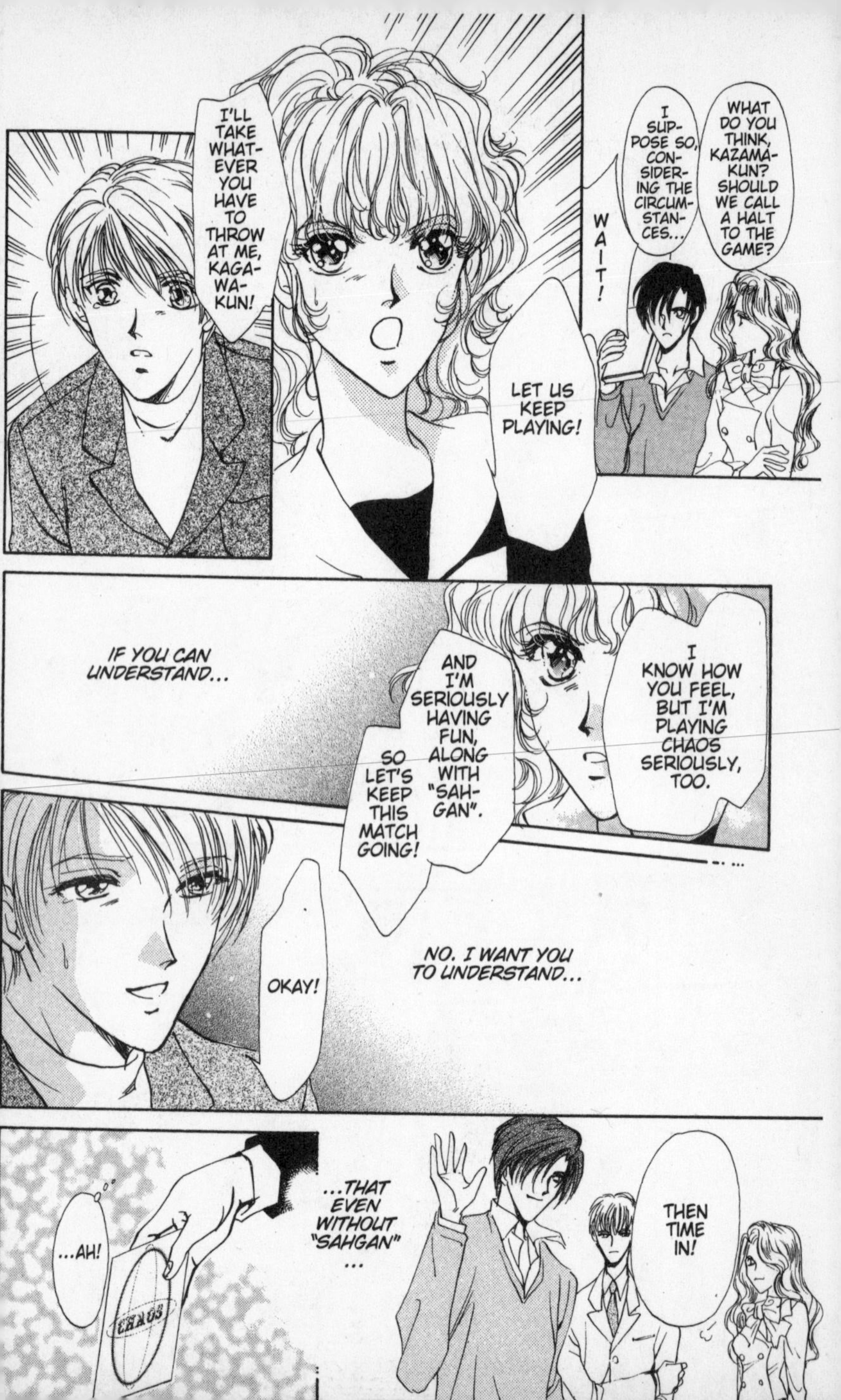
WHAT DO YOU THINK, KAZAMA-KUN? SHOULD WE CALL A HALT TO THE GAME?
I SUPPOSE SO, CONSIDERING THE CIRCUMSTANCES...
WAIT!
LET US KEEP PLAYING!
I'LL TAKE WHATEVER YOU HAVE TO THROW AT ME, KAGAWA-KUN!
I KNOW HOW YOU FEEL, BUT I'M PLAYING CHAOS SERIOUSLY, TOO.
AND I'M SERIOUSLY HAVING FUN, ALONG WITH "SAHGAN".
SO LET'S KEEP THIS MATCH GOING!
IF YOU CAN UNDERSTAND...
--...
NO. I WANT YOU TO UNDERSTAND...
OKAY!
THEN TIME IN!
...THAT EVEN WITHOUT "SAHGAN"...
...AH!

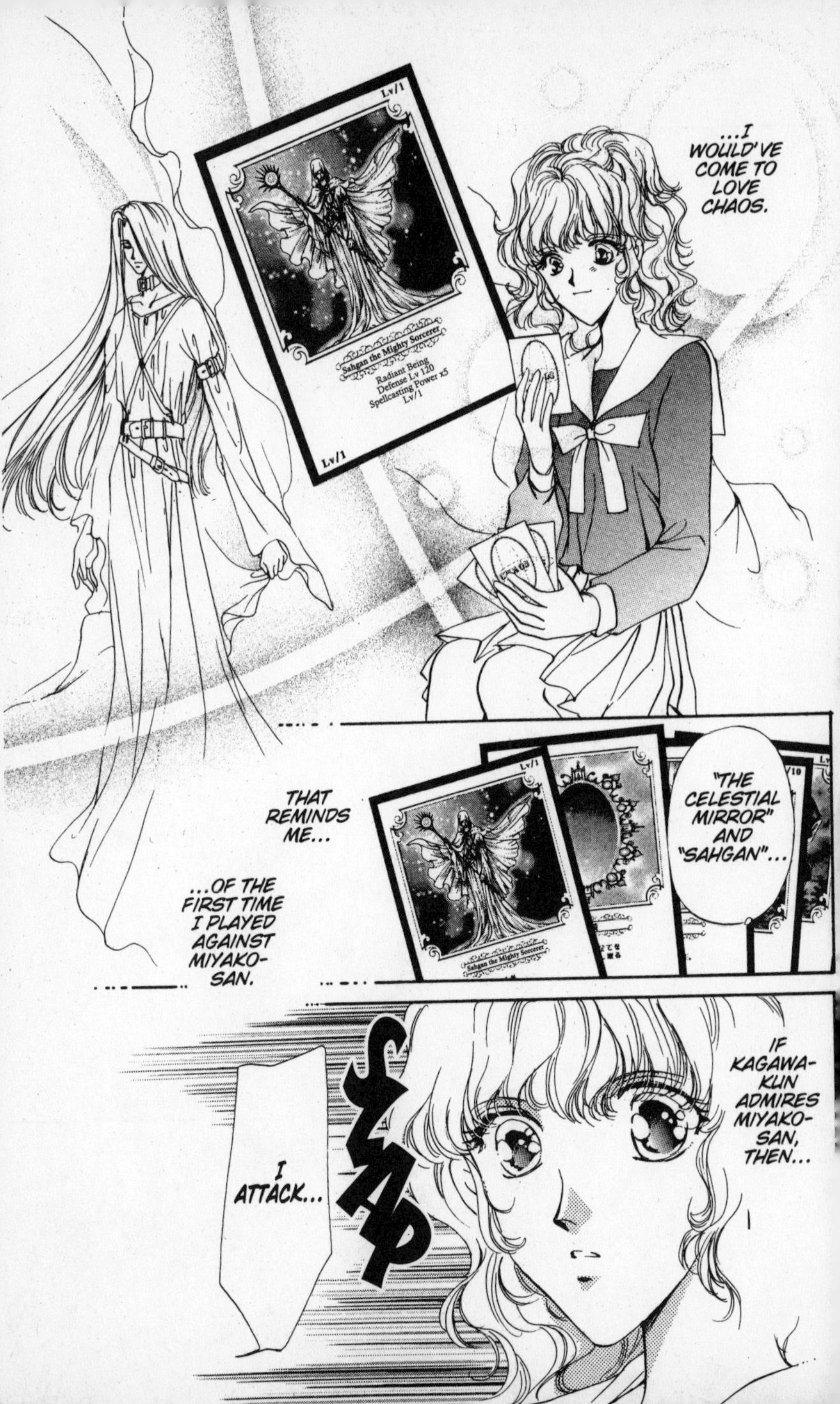
...I WOULD'VE COME TO LOVE CHAOS.
Lv/1
Sahgan the Mighty Sorcerer
Radiant Being
Defense Lv 120
Spellcasting Power x5
Lv/1
Lv/1
"THE CELESTIAL MIRROR" AND "SAHGAN"...
Sahgan the Mighty Sorcerer
THAT REMINDS ME...
...OF THE FIRST TIME I PLAYED AGAINST MIYAKO-SAN.
IF KAGAWA-KUN ADMIRES MIYAKO-SAN, THEN...
SLAP
I ATTACK...

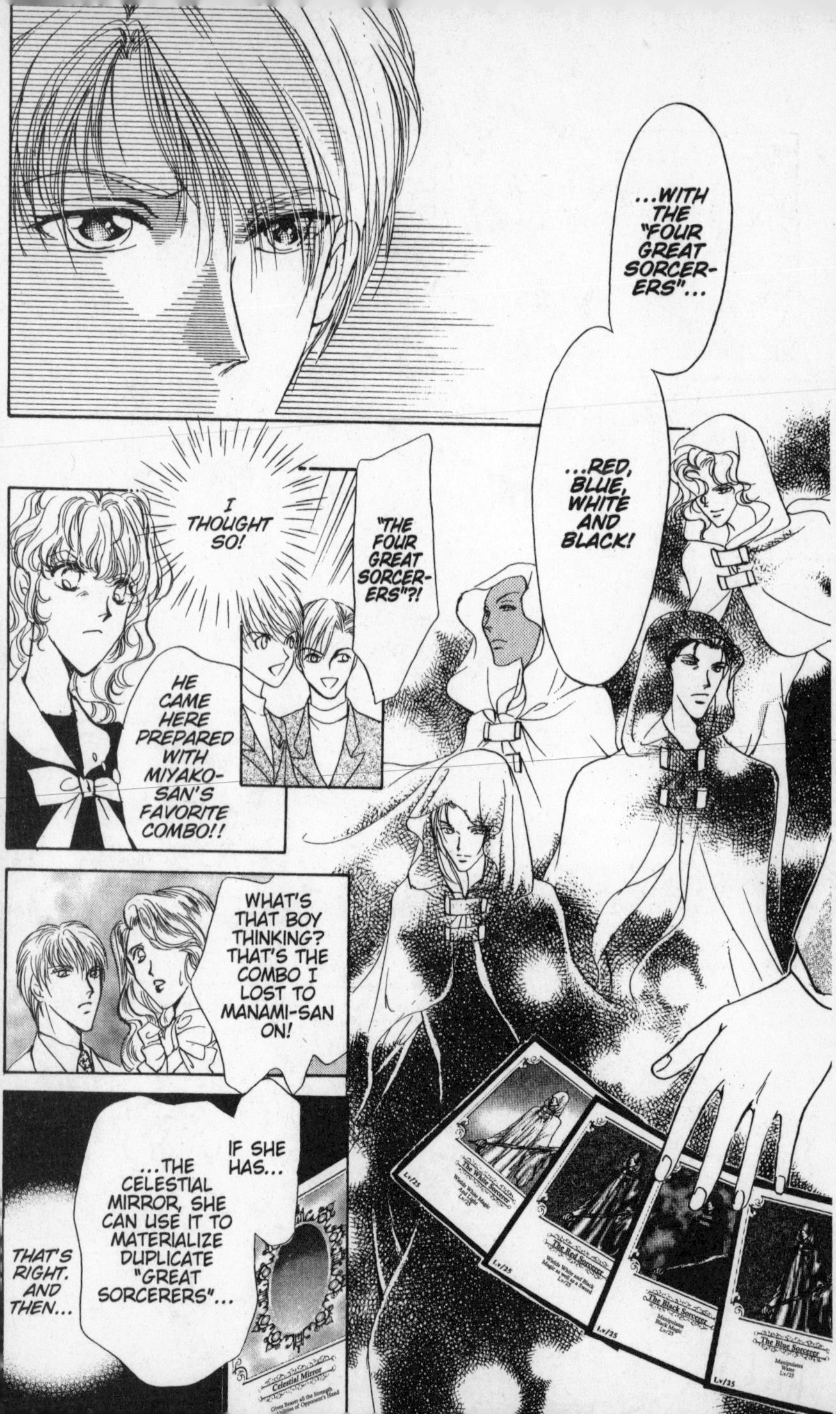
...WITH THE "FOUR GREAT SORCERERS"...
...RED, BLUE, WHITE AND BLACK!
"THE FOUR GREAT SORCERERS"?!
I THOUGHT SO!
HE CAME HERE PREPARED WITH MIYAKO-SAN'S FAVORITE COMBO!!
WHAT'S THAT BOY THINKING? THAT'S THE COMBO I LOST TO MANAMI-SAN ON!
The White Sorcerer
The Red Sorcerer
The Black Sorcerer
The Blue Sorcerer
IF SHE HAS...
...THE CELESTIAL MIRROR, SHE CAN USE IT TO MATERIALIZE DUPLICATE "GREAT SORCERERS"...
THAT'S RIGHT. AND THEN...
Celestial Mirror

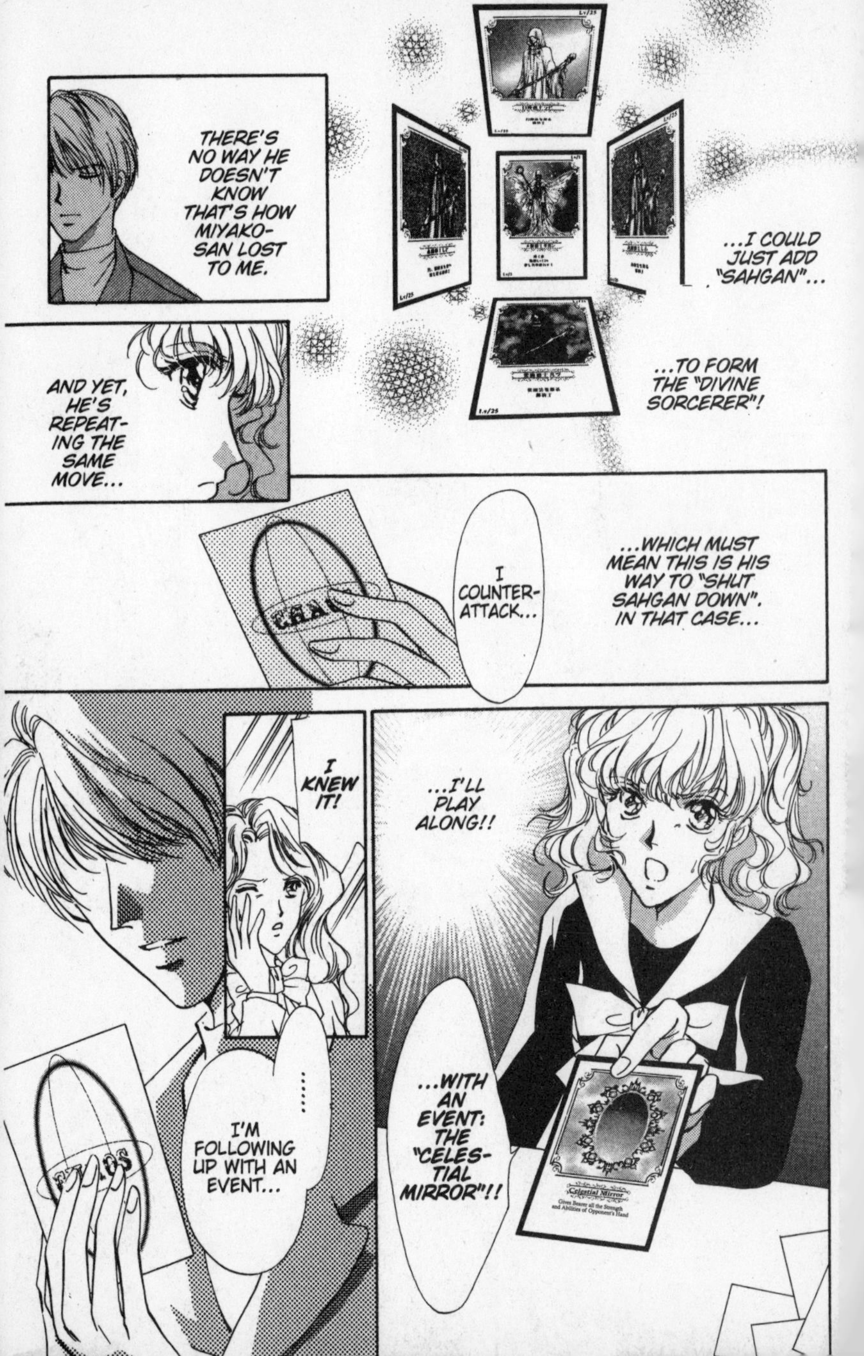
...I COULD JUST ADD "SAHGAN"...
...TO FORM THE "DIVINE SORCERER"!
THERE'S NO WAY HE DOESN'T KNOW THAT'S HOW MIYAKO-SAN LOST TO ME.
AND YET, HE'S REPEAT-ING THE SAME MOVE...
...WHICH MUST MEAN THIS IS HIS WAY TO "SHUT SAHGAN DOWN". IN THAT CASE...
I COUNTER-ATTACK...
...I'LL PLAY ALONG!!
...WITH AN EVENT: THE "CELES-TIAL MIRROR"!!
Celestial Mirror
Gives Bearer all the Strength and Abilities of Opponent's Hand
I KNEW IT!
......
I'M FOLLOWING UP WITH AN EVENT...

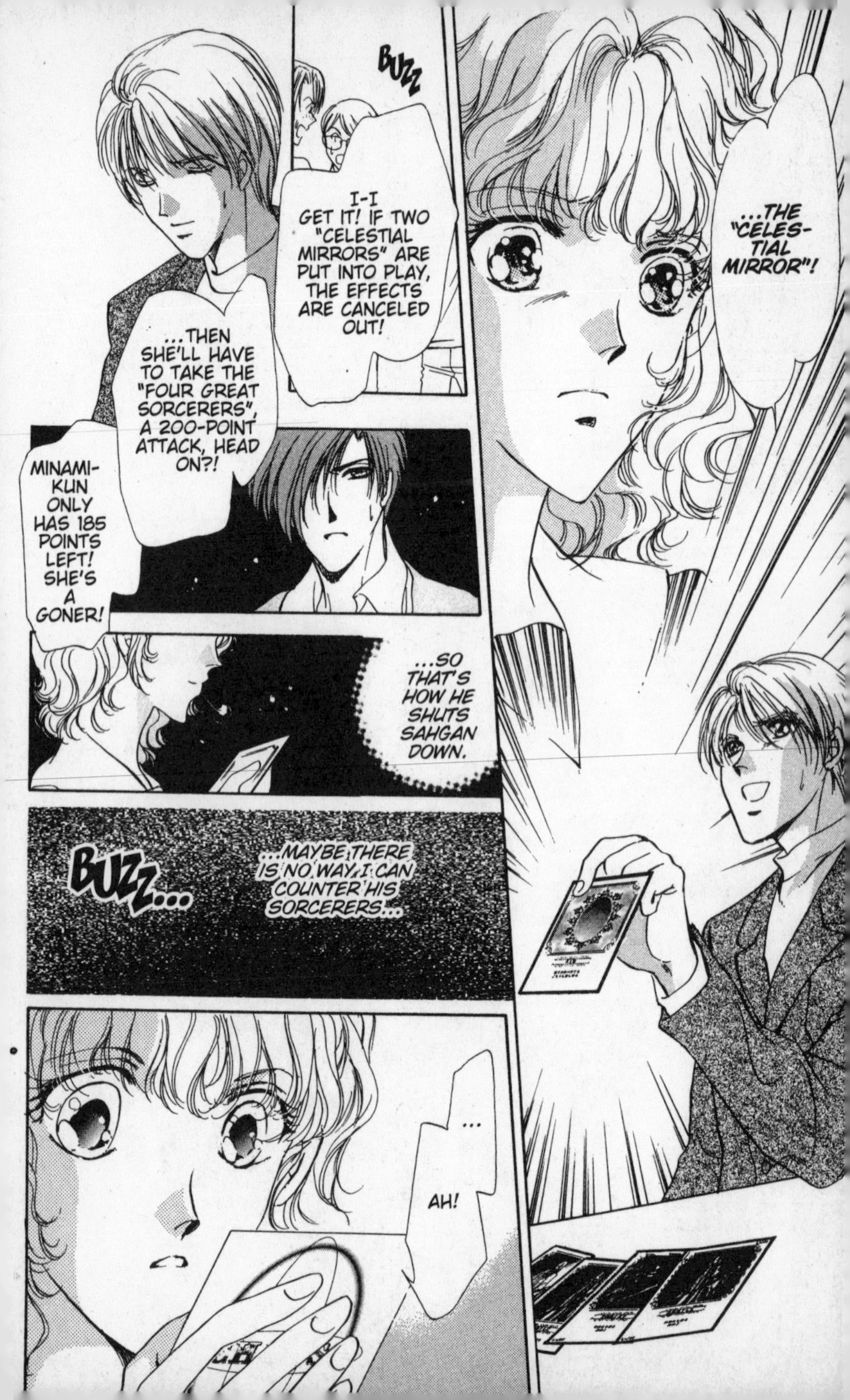

..."THE "CELESTIAL MIRROR"!
BUZZ
I-I GET IT! IF TWO "CELESTIAL MIRRORS" ARE PUT INTO PLAY, THE EFFECTS ARE CANCELED OUT!
...THEN SHE'LL HAVE TO TAKE THE "FOUR GREAT SORCERERS", A 200-POINT ATTACK, HEAD ON?!
MINAMI-KUN ONLY HAS 185 POINTS LEFT! SHE'S A GONER!
...SO THAT'S HOW HE SHUTS SAHGAN DOWN.
BUZZ...
...MAYBE THERE IS NO WAY I CAN COUNTER HIS SORCERERS...
...
AH!

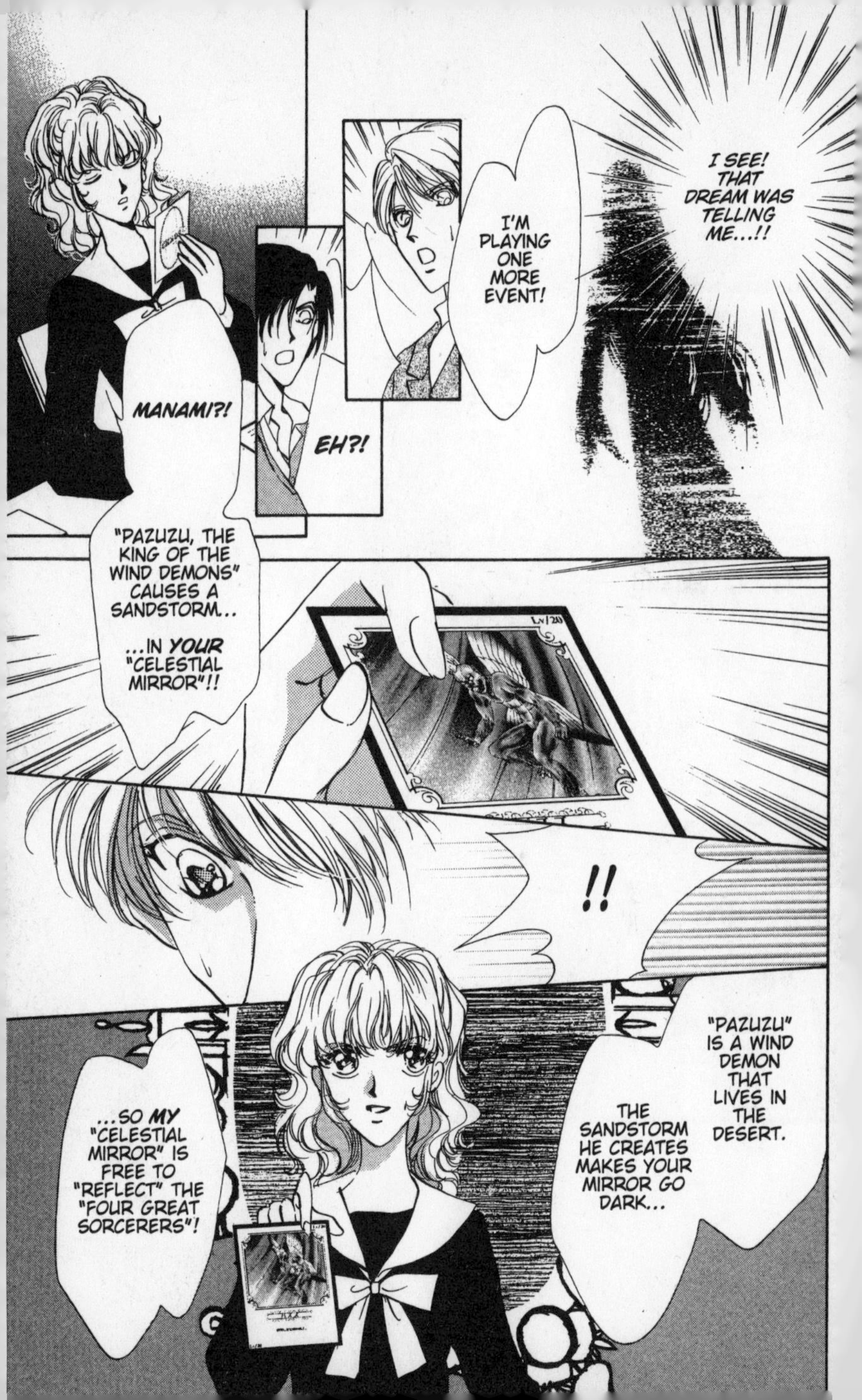
I SEE! THAT DREAM WAS TELLING ME...!!
I'M PLAYING ONE MORE EVENT!
EH?!
MANAMI?!
"PAZUZU, THE KING OF THE WIND DEMONS" CAUSES A SANDSTORM...
...IN *YOUR* "CELESTIAL MIRROR"!!
!!
"PAZUZU" IS A WIND DEMON THAT LIVES IN THE DESERT.
THE SANDSTORM HE CREATES MAKES YOUR MIRROR GO DARK...
...SO *MY* "CELESTIAL MIRROR" IS FREE TO "REFLECT" THE "FOUR GREAT SORCERERS"!

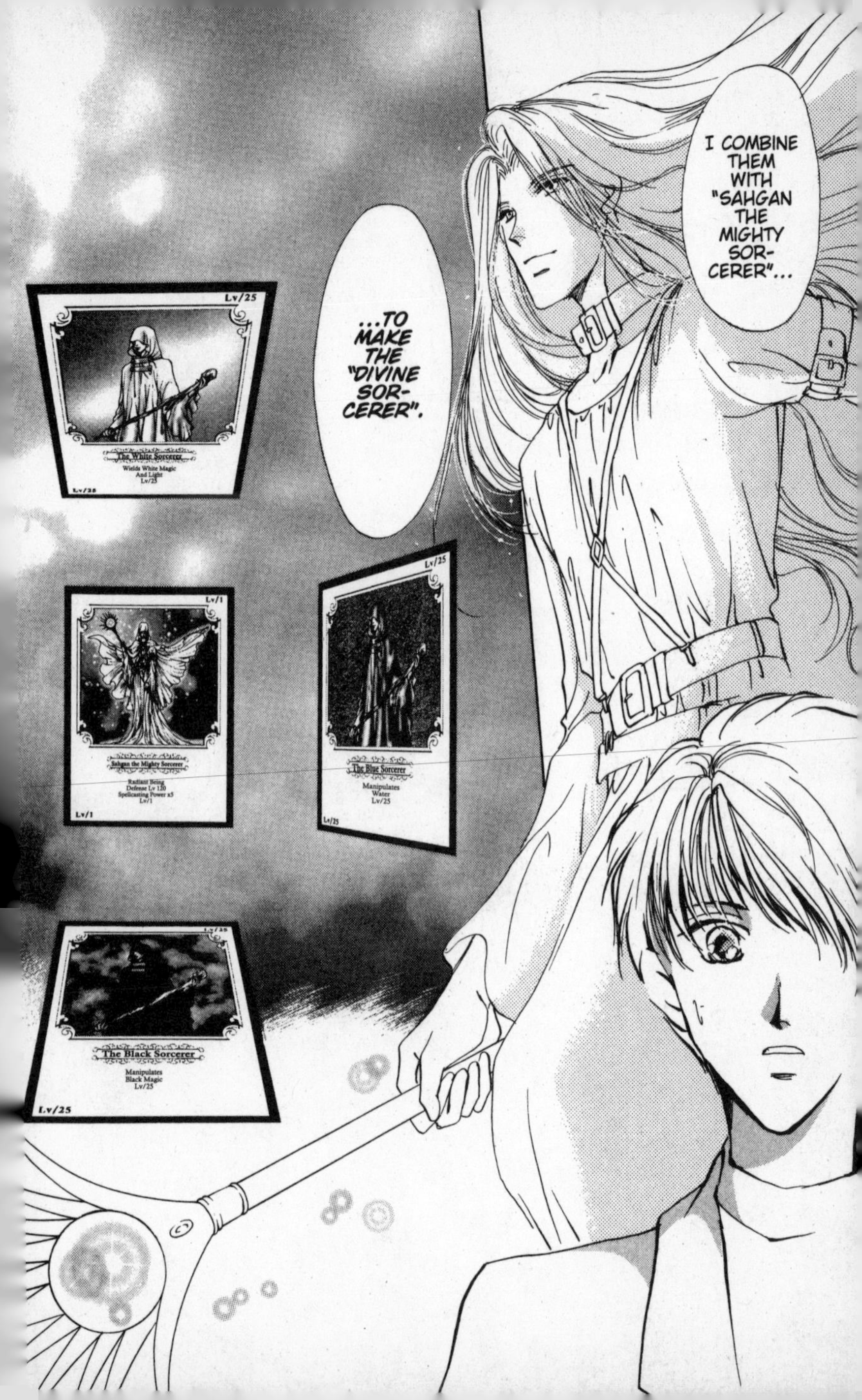
I COMBINE THEM WITH "SAHGAN THE MIGHTY SOR-CERER"...
...TO MAKE THE "DIVINE SOR-CERER".
Lv/25
The White Sorcerer
Wields White Magic And Light Lv/25
Lv/25
Lv/25
The Blue Sorcerer
Manipulates Water Lv/25
Lv/25
Lv/1
Sahgan the Mighty Sorcerer
Radiant Being Defense Lv 120 Spellcasting Power x5 Lv/1
Lv/1
Lv/25
The Black Sorcerer
Manipulates Black Magic Lv/25
Lv/25

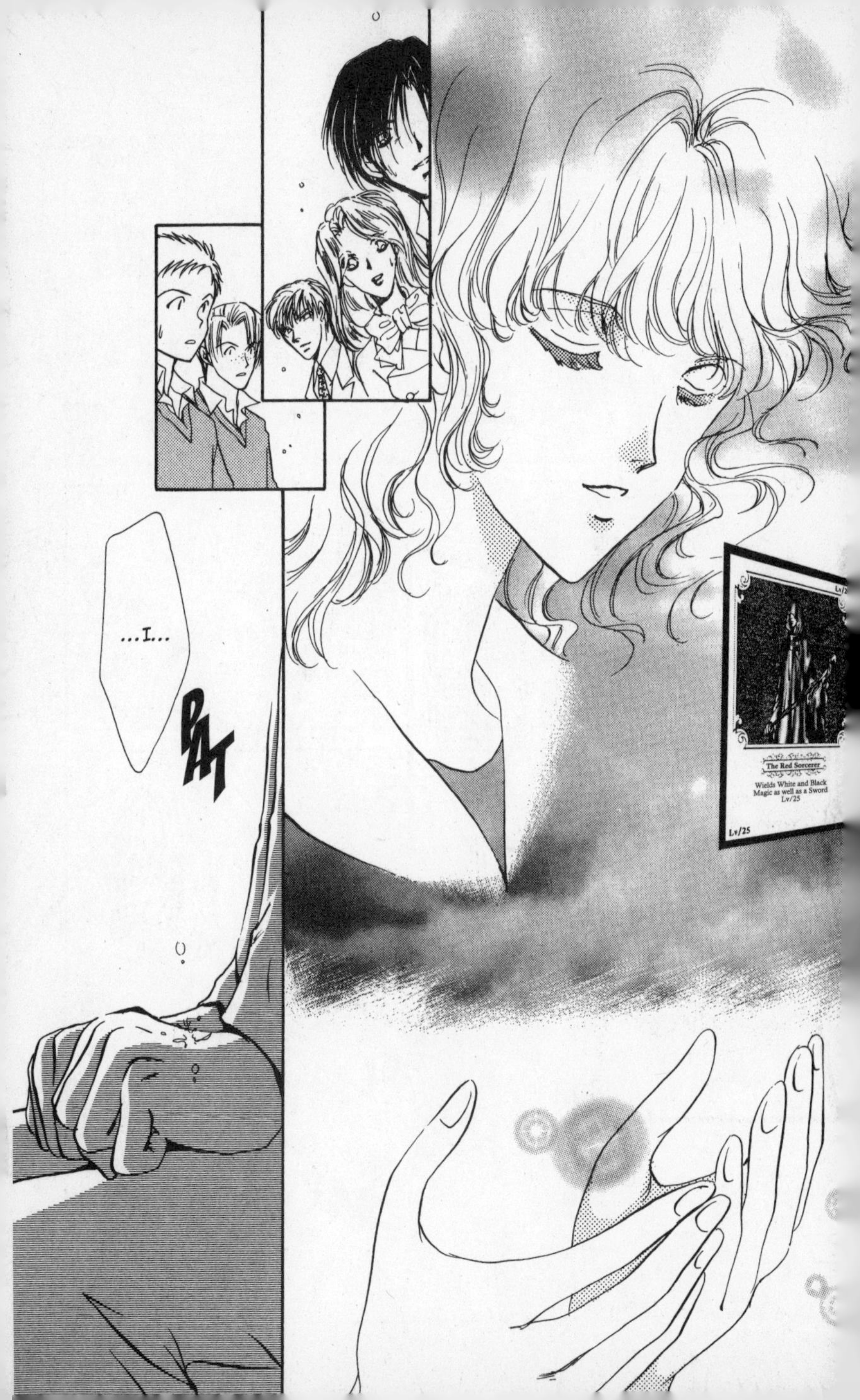
The Red Sorcerer
Wields White and Black Magic as well as a Sword Lv/25
Lv/25
...I...
PAT

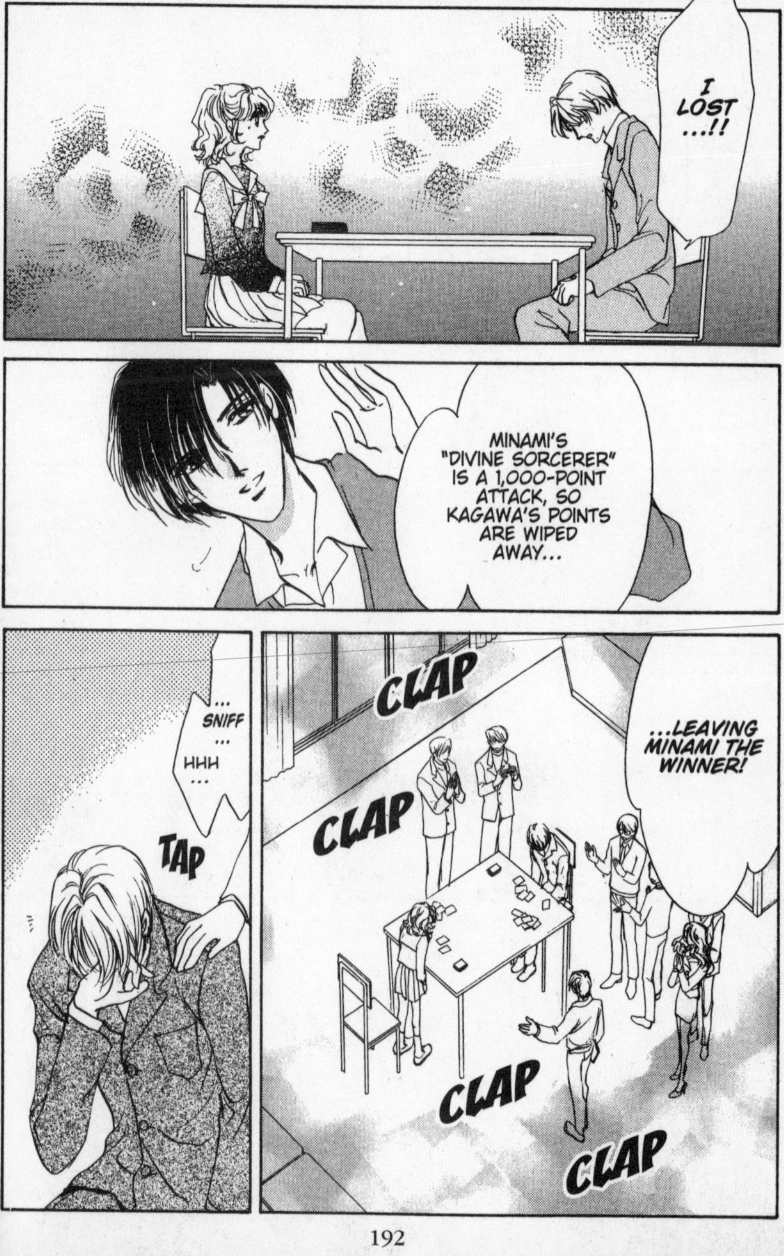
I LOST ...!!
MINAMI'S "DIVINE SORCERER" IS A 1,000-POINT ATTACK, SO KAGAWA'S POINTS ARE WIPED AWAY...
...LEAVING MINAMI THE WINNER!
CLAP
CLAP
CLAP
CLAP
... SNIFF ... HHH ...
TAP

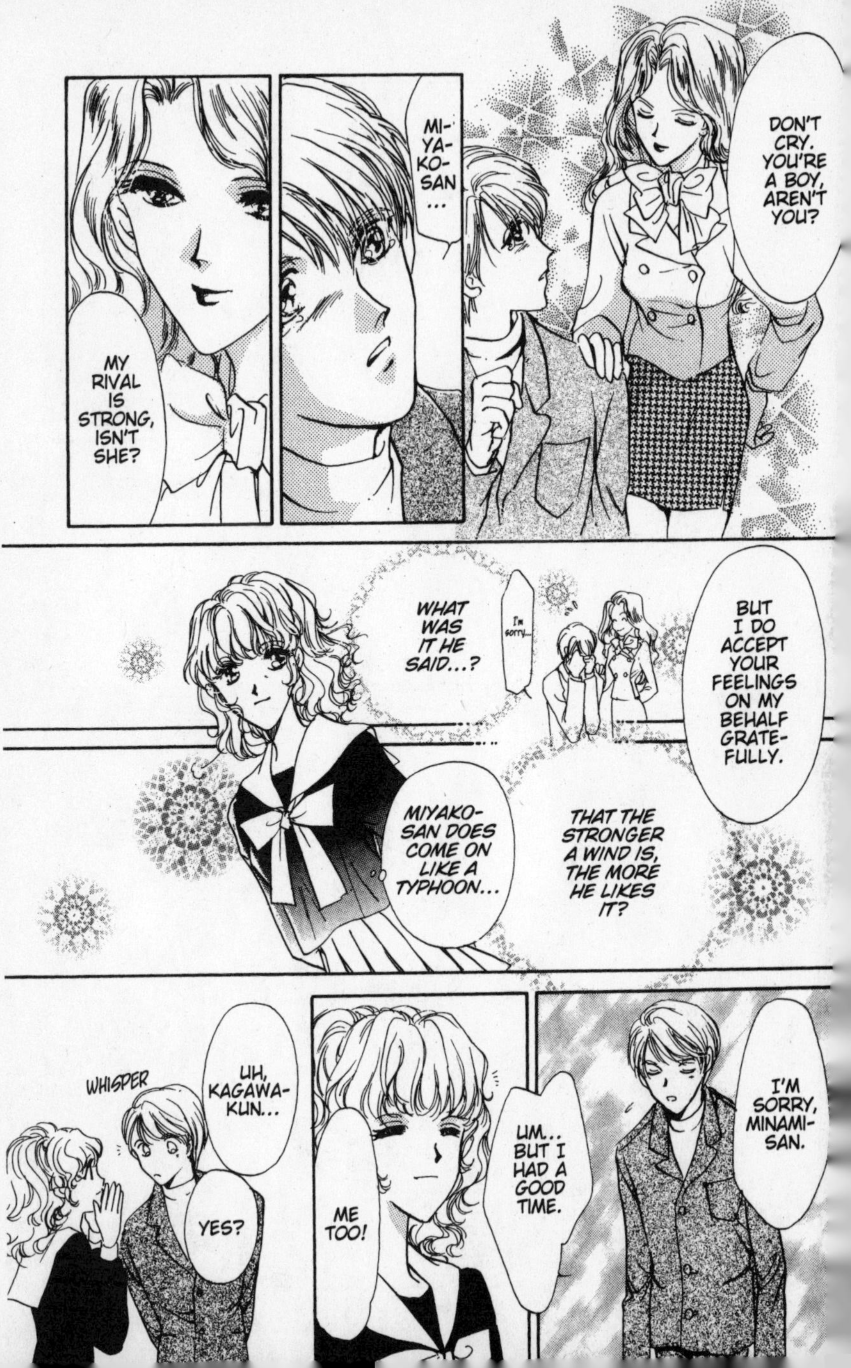
DON'T CRY. YOU'RE A BOY, AREN'T YOU?
MI-YA-KO-SAN...
MY RIVAL IS STRONG, ISN'T SHE?
BUT I DO ACCEPT YOUR FEELINGS ON MY BEHALF GRATEFULLY.
I'm sorry...
WHAT WAS IT HE SAID...?
THAT THE STRONGER A WIND IS, THE MORE HE LIKES IT?
MIYAKO-SAN DOES COME ON LIKE A TYPHOON...
I'M SORRY, MINAMI-SAN.
UM.. BUT I HAD A GOOD TIME.
ME TOO!
UH, KAGAWA-KUN...
WHISPER
YES?

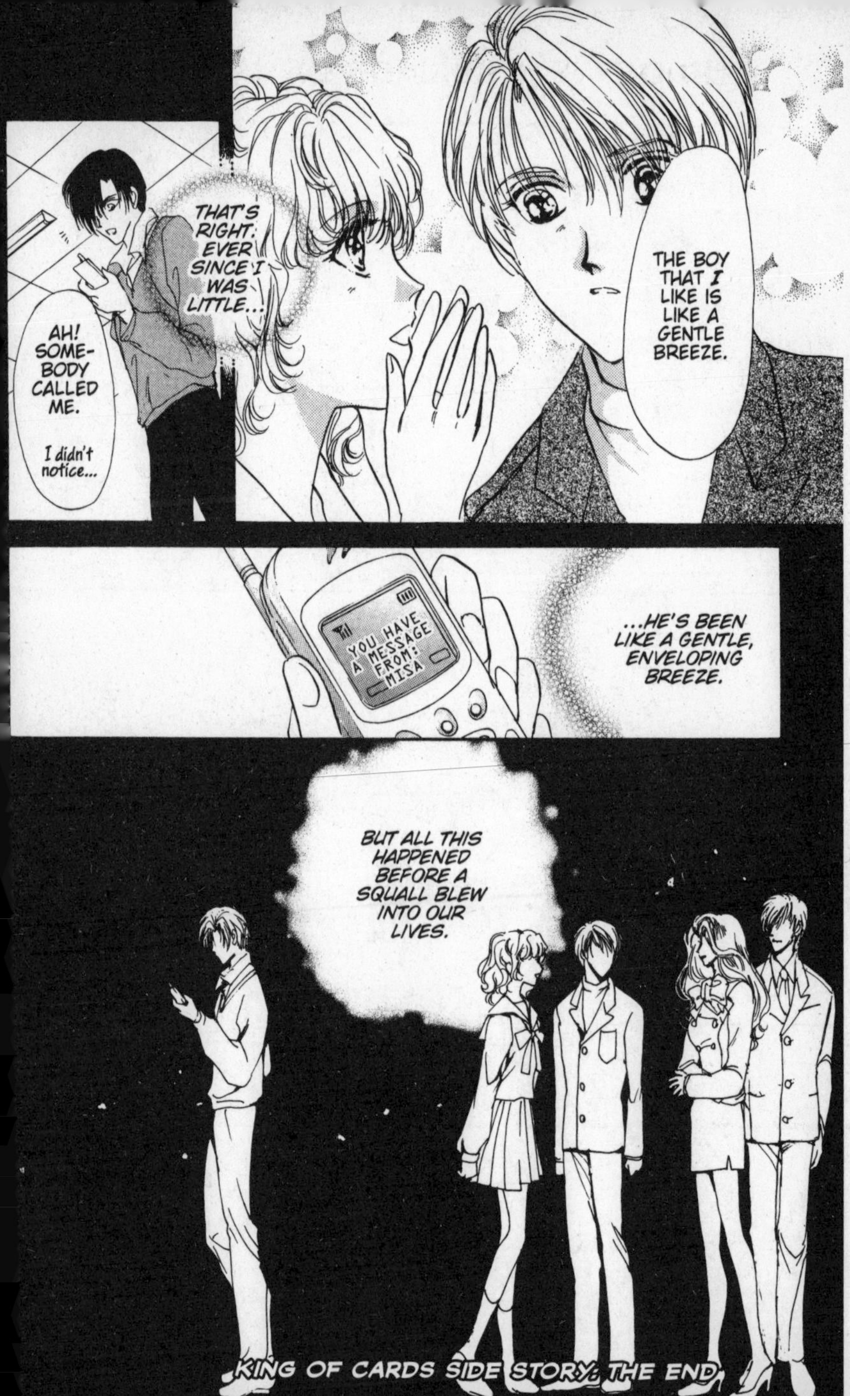
THE BOY THAT I LIKE IS LIKE A GENTLE BREEZE.
THAT'S RIGHT. EVER SINCE I WAS LITTLE...
AH! SOME-BODY CALLED ME.
I didn't notice...
...HE'S BEEN LIKE A GENTLE, ENVELOPING BREEZE.
YOU HAVE A MESSAGE FROM: MISA
BUT ALL THIS HAPPENED BEFORE A SQUALL BLEW INTO OUR LIVES.
KING OF CARDS SIDE STORY: THE END

FIND OUT IF IT'S HEADS OR TAILS IN MAY!

KING OF CARDS
Volume 7

By Makoto Tateno. Manami receives a letter from a mysterious
who also owns a Sahgan card. They meet up to compare t
ultra-rare cards, and Manami discovers hers might be a fake! Man
faces some tough competitors—including a famous Chaos lad
league player and a guy simply called the "Baron"—but even th
matches can't compare to the competition going on in her he
When a suggestion from Tamotsu coincides with a Sahgan dream,
Manami really flip a coin to choose between Ko and Araki?

ARE SHINOBU AND SAIZO MORE THAN JUST FRIENDS? FIND OUT NOW!

TERU TERU X SHONEN

Volume 4

By Shigeru Takao. The school festival has finally ended, and thankfully, Chiyo didn't completely destroy it. In fact, her desperate attempts to earn Saizo's affections have only driven Shinobu and Saizo closer together. Saizo's adoptive brother Sasuke gets some important news from back home, forcing a return to his village. What's the big secret that he can't reveal?

A TRAUMATIZED TEEN AND AN ECCENTRIC WRITER FORM A BOND. ON SALE NOW!

The Name of the Flower
Volume 1

By Ken Saito. Devastated by the loss of both parents, 18-year-old Chouko Mizushima loses her will to live. After living in several different homes, she settles in with a handsome young writer named Kei Mizushima. Kei's need for privacy and unease with emotion make these two a very unlikely pair. But when Chouko starts tending to Kei's flower garden, he sees her in a completely new light.

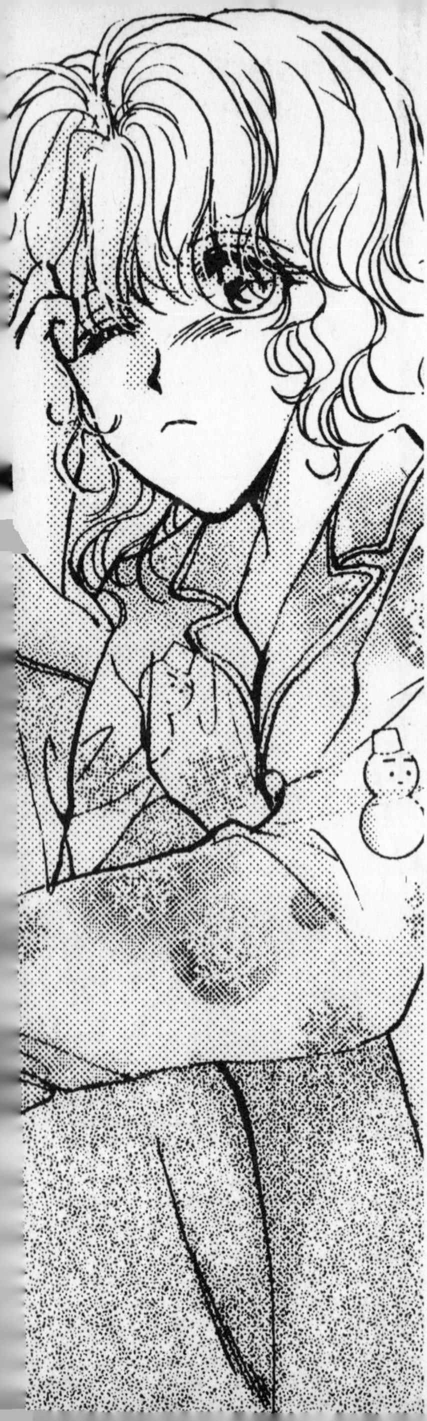

KNOW WHAT'S INSIDE

With the wide variety of manga available, CMX understands it can be confusing to determine age-appropriate material. We rate our books in four categories: EVERYONE, TEEN, TEEN + and MATURE. For the TEEN, TEEN + and MATURE categories, we include additional, specific descriptions to assist consumers in determining if the book is age appropriate. (Our MATURE books are shipped shrink-wrapped with a Parental Advisory sticker affixed to the wrapper.)

E

EVERYONE

Titles with this rating are appropriate for all age readers. They contain no offensive material. They may contain mild violence and/or some comic mischief.

T

TEEN

Titles with this rating are appropriate for a teen audience and older. They may contain some violent content, language, and/or suggestive themes.

T+

TEEN PLUS

Titles with this rating are appropriate for an audience of 16 and older. They may contain partial nudity, mild profanity and more intense violence.

M

MATURE

Titles with this rating are appropriate only for mature readers. They may contain graphic violence, nudity, sex and content suitable only for older readers.

cmx

CARD NO OUSAMA by Makoto Tateno © 2000 Makoto
Tateno. All rights reserved. First published in Japan in 2002
by HAKUSENSHA, INC., Tokyo.

KING OF CARDS Volume 6, published by WildStorm
Productions, an imprint of DC Comics, 888 Prospect St.
#240, La Jolla, CA 92037. English Translation © 2009. All
Rights Reserved. English translation rights in U.S.A. and
Canada arranged with HAKUSENSHA, INC., through
Tuttle-Mori Agency, Inc., Tokyo. CMX is a trademark of DC
Comics. The stories, characters, and incidents mentioned in
this magazine are entirely fictional. Printed on recyclable
paper. WildStorm does not read or accept unsolicited
submissions of ideas, stories or artwork. Printed in Canada.

DC Comics, a Warner Bros. Entertainment Company.

Sheldon Drzka – Translation and Adaptation
Troy Peteri – Lettering
Larry Berry – Design
Jim Chadwick – Editor

ISBN: 978-1-4012-1416-6

All the pages in this book were created—and are printed here—in Japanese RIGHT-to-LEFT format. No artwork has been reversed or altered, so you can read the stories the way the creators meant for them to be read.

FLIP IT!

RIGHT TO LEFT?!

Traditional Japanese manga starts at the upper right-hand corner, and moves right-to-left as it goes down the page. Follow this guide for an easy understanding.

For more information and sneak previews, visit cmxmanga.com. Call 1-888-COMIC BOOK for the nearest comics shop or head to your local book store.

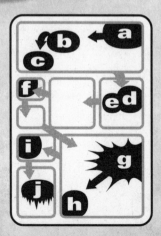

cmx